NORTHERN BRITISH COLUMBIA CANOE TRIPS:

VOLUME TWO

NORTHERN BRITISH COLUMBIA CANOE TRIPS:

VOLUME TWO

By Laurel Archer

RMB

Victoria Vancouver Calgary

Rocky Mountain Books
www.rmbooks.com

Library and Archives Canada Cataloguing in Publication

Archer, Laurel, 1964-

Northern British Columbia canoe trips / by Laurel Archer.

Includes bibliographical references and indexes.

ISBN 978-1-897522-13-4 (v. 1).—ISBN 978-1-926855-04-2 (v. 2)

    1. Canoes and canoeing—British Columbia, Northern—Guidebooks.
2. Wild and scenic rivers—British Columbia, Northern—Guidebooks.
3. British Columbia, Northern—Guidebooks. I. Title.

Volume 1 also issued as an electronic monograph in HTML format: ISBN 978-1-897522-91-2 (v. 1)
Volume 2 also issued as an electronic monograph in HTML format: ISBN 978-1-926855-12-7 (v. 2)

GV776.15.B7A73   2010 797.12209711'8   C2010-902814-7

Printed in Canada

Rocky Mountain Books acknowledges the financial support for its publishing program from the Government of Canada through the Canada Book Fund (CBF), Canada Council for the Arts, and the province of British Columbia through the British Columbia Arts Council and the Book Publishing Tax Credit.

This book has been printed with FSC-certified, acid-free papers, processed chlorine free and printed with vegetable-based inks.

Mixed Sources
Cert no. SW-COC-001271
© 1996 FSC
FSC

Disclaimer

The actions described in this book may be considered inherently dangerous activities. Individuals undertake these activities at their own risk. The information put forth in this guide has been collected from a variety of sources and is not guaranteed to be completely accurate or reliable. Many conditions and some information may change owing to weather and numerous other factors beyond the control of the authors and publishers. Individual canoeists and/or hikers must determine the risks, use their own judgment, and take full responsibility for their actions. Do not depend on any information found in this book for your own personal safety. Your safety depends on your own good judgment based on your skills, education, and experience. It is up to the users of this guidebook to acquire the necessary skills for safe experiences and to exercise caution in potentially hazardous areas. The authors and publishers of this guide accept no responsibility for your actions or the results that occur from another's actions, choices, or judgments. If you have any doubt as to your safety or your ability to attempt anything described in this guidebook, do not attempt it.

CONTENTS

ACKNOWLEDGEMENTS

I wouldn't have written the two volumes of this guidebook or my previous guidebook to canoeing in northern Saskatchewan if it hadn't been for the many people over the years whose teaching, mentoring and confidence in me made my paddling and writing endeavours possible. I couldn't list everyone, even if I could remember all their names! But they will know who are they are. I thank these individuals for countless things: a tip on reading maps; a kind word about my writing; sharing their history and travel stories; forgiving me my mistakes while I was learning to be an outdoor leader; and all the other forms of support and empowerment I have been so fortunate to receive. Particularly, I thank those people who encouraged me to live a different sort of life, one of exploration and putting into practice skills as old as the cultures of the first people of the North Country.

In that regard, my first formal acknowledgement is of my father and mother's greatest gifts to me. They instilled in me a love for the outdoors and the belief I could do anything I wanted. Charles Hinckley Archer (1912–1995) happily encouraged me to explore the physical world since I was a child. When I fell into the deep end of a swimming pool at about age three, he was there to pull me out. But he let me come up on my own, and when I was spluttering and safely hanging onto the side, he looked down at me with a big smile and a laugh. Why would I ever be afraid of water after that? I instantly believed I could swim! He'd boost me up in a tree to see some cool bugs, taking the chance I would fall, but ensuring I would not, simply by allowing me to find out what it was like to be on the edge. He encouraged me to follow my instincts and passions, and stood patiently by as his youngest daughter took her own sometimes rocky and definitely watery path to personal fulfillment. I wish he were alive today to see the results of the freedom and self-confidence he gave me.

My mother, May Partridge, listened to me prattle over books for hours pretending I could read, long before I actually could. She constantly made up stories for me and encouraged me to do the same, and I came to believe in the magic of words through her. She was the prime instigator in getting the family out to enjoy the natural world by hiking, camping and fishing, and she is also the reason I started paddling a canoe. She bought one so we could tour Crooked Lake in southern Saskatchewan, where we had a cottage for several years. Now I steer the canoe, and Ma has come with me on many trips, including four routes in the two volumes of this paddling guide alone. She's trusted me to take her down river after river and on routes I knew very little about. Beyond helping me research and paddle the rivers, she helped me finish this book on time by getting my references in proper format and order, scholar that she is. Thank you to my favourite bow paddler.

As Kevin Schultz was my paddling mentor in Saskatchewan, so was Tony Shaw here in BC. Tony, a Master Canoe Instructor for the RCABC, took me under his wing when I moved to Vancouver Island. He and his family, long-time former residents of northern BC, used to own and operate Red Goat Lodge, the canoe outfitting business at Iskut. He also worked as a teacher in small communities such as Lower Post. Beyond his droll sense of humour and extremely caring nature, which make him a joy to teach paddling with, he is the best source of information on canoeing in northern BC I have ever found. Tony helped me research many of the rivers, edited numerous chapters and wrote the Foreword to this guide. The information, feedback, support and encouragement he gave me were invaluable.

A toast of great appreciation to my friend Mike Froese. I could not have asked anyone for the amount of time he so freely gave to editing the chapters and assisting with the index of this guide. Felicia Daunt did the same for me with my northern Saskatchewan guide, and Mike did a great job following in her wake. Many thanks to Karlene Gibson for paddling two of the routes with me and editing the Taku River chapter. "Dr. Livingstone" will always have a seat in my canoe.

My outrigger crew of the Comox–Strathcona Racing Canoe Club must also be acknowledged. I missed so many practices every season, yet the crew were nothing but supportive and excited about my work paddling and writing books. I first have to thank the remaining crew members of the Comox women's team that picked me up to race with them in 2001. They have now supported me through three book journeys and become my good friends over the years: Jackie Bell, Annie Boulding, Lyse Fortin and Michele Genge. Also, thank you to my other Comox teammates and friends that I've raced with in the years since, particularly the regulars: Tina Clarke, Rani Johns and Lisa Robertson. Lyse Fortin, Michele Genge and Lisa Robertson also helped me with both volumes of this guide, paddling a number of trips with me over the years. Additionally, Lyse and Michele edited hundreds of pages, and Lyse translated the meaning of French phrases for me. Merci!

I want to thank Sheila Achilles, Bruce Reeder, Liana Nolan and Greg Harling for the great trips on the Netson Creek/Rabbit River (volume one) and the Turnagain River (volume two). Those excellent adventures would not have been so great or easy without their company and skills. I also have to thank them for all the good food on those trips and for the feedback on the chapters that resulted from them. My appreciation to George Prevost for the use of his photographs and for being "Uncle" on the Lower Stikine in 2006! Also, my deepest thanks go to Brad Koop for all his support over the years in so many things.

My appreciation also goes to the following individuals and organizations for their help: Jacinta Sheridan, John Noble, Richard MacKellar and party, Peter Goetz, Libby Covernton, Phil Lamb, Richard Dugas, Blair Richardson, Bruce Partridge, Rick Gibson, Cory Pollock, Larry Pynn, Jay Neilson, Frank Knaapen, Dan Walker, Colin Leake, Erich Volkstorf, Kelly Knight, Larry and Lori Warren, Urs and

Marianne Schildknecht, Chris Moser, Bruce McNaughton, Dan Pakula, Jacquie Cunningham, Stan Boor, Johnny Mikes, Ian Kean, Bob Daffe, Dwayne Roberge, Jeff Brown, Jim Brooks, David Hett, John Elliott, Yvonne Lattie, Trudy Spiller, Tom Lee, Jim Allen, Neil Piller, Chris Joseph, Irene Collins and party, Dave Kirby and party, Michael Allender and Mark Scantlebury and party, Daniel Rabinkin and party, Chip (Charles) Head and party, Gordon Congdon and party, Leon Johnny, Joe Porter, Dave Falmer, Bruce and Anne Hill, Mia and Jimmy Rankin, Nancy Ross, Malcolm Edwards, Laurie Miller and the whole Boreal Rendezvous gang, CPAWS BC, CPAWS SK and CPAWS National Office, the Wilderness Canoe Association, the Saskatoon Canoe Club and the Vancouver Island Regional Public Library.

A special thank you goes to Jamie Boulding and Jim Miller at Strathcona Park Lodge for giving me the leeway in my COLT work that enabled me to write this guidebook and still make a living guiding and teaching paddling. I want to acknowledge the support of Paul Gordoko of Canada Portable Kayaks, the distributor of PakCanoes (PakBoats) in Canada, and Alv Elvestad, the manufacturer in the US. Thank you to Jason Schoonover for sponsoring my membership in the International Explorers Club, and especially for all his enthusiasm for my canoe explorations.

Finally, a toast to the wild rivers, for they have taught me what it means to be free.

FOREWORD

Selecting rivers for a guide to canoeing in northern BC that will represent the myriad choices that suffuse this vast area is a gargantuan task. There are so many waterways with wild and beautiful valleys and canyons that one can feel completely overwhelmed. It would take a lifetime to explore and document them all, and so some rivers will remain unsung – that is, until someone else comes along to add to the significant collection described in the volumes of this guide.

Laurel Archer has succeeded in providing the reader with such a variety of river trips that it is impossible to find a route that is not "perfect" for them. One nagging concern, as always, is that the very publishing of information about a river will lead to its overuse. On the flip side, this kind of exposure will lead to more people falling in love with northern BC's rivers, and it is likely that books like Archer's will be a vehicle for their preservation. I know the author has this firmly at the forefront of her mind.

In her first major literary undertaking, *Northern Saskatchewan Canoe Trips*, Archer left us with no doubt that her profound enthusiasm for canoe tripping is exceptional – equalled only by her love for all free-flowing rivers. This second project, the two-volume *Northern British Columbia Canoe Trips*, confirms Laurel as a passionate and dedicated advocate of that perfect combination: the canoe and the wild river.

An explorer at heart, Archer showcases several river trips in the guidebook series that have rarely been paddled. Many more were previously undocumented. Other rivers that have been previously written up by other notable authors are made to feel fresh, new and exciting. I have journeyed along a number of the routes described, and indeed supported Laurel in her exploration and research any way I could. I spent many years living, working and playing in the Cassiars and have an intimate knowledge of this land west of the Rocky Mountain Trench. In that regard, I can absolutely attest to the accuracy of information in the thorough river trip descriptions contained between the covers of these books. The rivers on the other side of the "divide" are less familiar to me but now have become firm friends in the reading, and I have shaped some resolute promises for future adventures. I am sure this exact and well-crafted production will do the same for you – and give you great joy in the process.

— Tony Shaw
Vancouver Island Representative, Recreational
Canoe Association of BC (RCABC);
Western Representative, Paddle Canada (PC);
Master Instructor, RCABC and PC

INTRODUCTION

ABOUT THIS GUIDEBOOK

The ideas and information contained in the two volumes of *Northern British Columbia Canoe Trips* are a product of over 20 years of canoeing and kayaking rivers, lakes and coastlines all over the world and hundreds of days paddling and researching the waterways of northern BC. After moving to Vancouver Island from northern Saskatchewan, I was eager to head up to BC's north and paddle its wild rivers. However, obtaining information about paddling northern BC's rivers was difficult, to say the least, except for the few popular routes. I soon realized there was even less information available for this area than there was for northern Saskatchewan, an area I'd written a guidebook for previously.

This lack of information, my love of paddling up north, and exploring and writing about wild rivers were reasons enough to write another canoeing guide, even though I really wanted to write a novel! Ultimately, it was my concern for the future of northern BC's magnificent and unique watersheds that finally convinced me of the need for this guide. Many of the rivers described in these two volumes are facing threats from projects detrimental to the northern ecosystem. People can debate the issues surrounding these development projects, but the rivers have no voice. I believe the health of river systems concerns everyone no matter where they live, and that rivers and ecosystems should be considered as entities in and of themselves, beyond the resources they provide to people. My comments about conservation are offered in that light.

Paddling the rivers in this guidebook was an absolute joy, though sometimes extremely nerve-wracking, given how little I knew about most of the routes. Researching the lesser-known rivers was a great adventure and challenge. Sometimes I only had maps and satellite images to determine whether a route was possible without horrible mountain-goat portages; on the river, I was always on my knees anticipating the unknown around each corner. Discovering a photo on the Internet of a canyon I had questions about running was better than finding a large gold nugget (though I'd have liked that too!). Panning for information on the difficulty of the rivers prior to paddling them was as difficult work as any prospector has ever undertaken. However, I believe I have managed in each of these volumes to provide paddlers with some gold-star routes that will suit varying skill levels.

Beyond the fact that it made good sense to me as a professional paddling instructor/guide and author to write this book, I truly believe we will lose our wild places if people don't know they exist and don't make them a part of their lives or dreams. It is often our experience of lands and waterways that encourages us to work to conserve them. What sense does it make to keep your favourite remote river a secret for the special few if it ends up being poisoned by an open-pit copper mine because nobody knows or cares? I also think some wild places can be overused and travelled in inappropriate ways, and that others are best left unvisited. However, all places are worthy of conservation, even if few people ever see them. That is an understanding that comes with travelling under your own power in remote places of great natural beauty, even if just for a few days a year. Hopefully, this guidebook will not only assist canoeists on their river travels and increase their appreciation of northern BC's wild lands and waterways, but will encourage them to work to provide more care for all that is wild, including these rivers.

My coverage of BC river routes north of 55 degrees latitude is by no means exhaustive. I chose these trips for numerous reasons: my familiarity with the rivers; the quality or uniqueness of the experiences available; to showcase the variety of ecosystems and landscapes of the region; for the popularity of the routes with canoe trippers, or just the opposite, because they are not commonly travelled; and, finally, to provide a range of difficulty for novice, intermediate, advanced and exceptional moving-water paddlers to choose from. Everyone will find a trip that will challenge her or him – I guarantee it.

Paddling northern BC rivers is not an enterprise to be taken lightly. My experience as a paddler and guide has led me to conclude that running a mountain river of intermediate difficulty in northern BC requires a higher level of river reading and running skills and knowledge than canoeing an intermediate level of difficulty drop-pool river in Precambrian Shield country. Many rivers in these volumes have hazards such as extremely cold water, large numbers of logjams, strainers, sweepers and deadheads, deep canyons, continuous moving water and very few portage trails. A couple of trips have tidal flats and open-ocean crossings or committing coastline to navigate. The variety and nature of northern BC's geography often makes for challenging trips, and some are definitely more difficult and hazardous than others.

Trip descriptions abound for many of the popular rivers in other Canadian provinces: you can find them online and in books and magazines. However, that is not true of the routes in northern BC, with the exception of its best-known river, the Stikine, and its tributary the Spatsizi. Northern BC is a different paddling environment than most eastern Canadian canoeists are familiar with, and a lack of information makes for a lack of choices and some paddling parties heading off down rivers unprepared. I cannot emphasize enough that you need to do your research on any canoe trip, whether by using this book or by some other means, in order to choose a suitable route that you can paddle as safely as possible.

That said, this is not a "how to" book, though I do give advice on what you need to know and the special equipment to bring with you on a given trip. There are many resources available to canoeists to develop their paddling and tripping skills: courses (the best certified moving-water courses are offered through the Recreational Canoe Association of BC, where you learn to paddle mountain rivers), books, videos and DVDs. I don't want to scare you off paddling some of these amazing routes, but it must be made clear that river tripping in northern BC requires solid moving-water and bushcraft skills, appropriate preparation and equipment and a lot of good judgment. These volumes are not about how to develop those skills and knowledge; instead they are designed to provide canoeists with the information they require in order to choose a river trip appropriate to their skill level and special interests while sitting in an armchair on a frosty December's eve.

Using the volumes of this guidebook in the manner they were intended, canoeists can measure their skill and knowledge against the information provided instead of against the reality of the river when it is too late to make another choice. Finally, the detailed Trip Notes are designed only to provide canoeists with information about what is around the next bend. They are not intended to be help canoeists run rivers they are not already capable of navigating safely.

DISCLAIMER

The information in this guidebook is intended only to assist canoeists in choosing and navigating a river suitable to their skill, knowledge, fitness level and interests. This book is just a guide, and as the author is human, its contents may unwittingly contain errors. Additionally, rivers are not static entities. Water levels vary extremely and wood hazards change. Adverse weather and local conditions can make a river trip much more difficult – it may be more physically challenging, a longer journey than expected or require a higher level of paddling and bushcraft skills. Canoeists are responsible for their own safety, using good judgment, erring on the side of caution and being constantly on the lookout for hazards. The author and publisher can accept no responsibility for any injury, loss or inconvenience sustained by any person as a result of the information found in this guidebook.

ABOUT CANOEING IN NORTHERN BC

Northern BC's rivers wind their way through an unbelievable diversity of landscapes and ecosystems, dropping through some of the most rugged country on the planet. Many tumble through either the Coast, St. Elias, Cassiar, Skeena, Omineca or Rocky Mountain ranges, providing unparalleled mountain scenery. Some traverse wild plateaus and wide plains, while others skirt foothills and dissect lowlands. The rivers in the Northwest flow through a land of ice into the sea. All northern BC rivers find their way to either the Arctic or the Pacific ocean. A number of them were used by First Nations, explorers, fur traders, gold miners and surveyors to traverse the remote interior or gain access to the northern coast. Navigating the waterway routes was not easy, and certainly neither was overland travel. However, given BC's topography, trails were more important for long-distance travel than in other provinces. From my seat in a plastic boat, I have often contemplated how mind-boggling it is that some of these rivers such as the Liard and the Finlay were run in bark, hide and dugout canoes. These early travellers certainly knew how to paddle and portage!

Today much of northern BC is still isolated and sparsely populated. The vast region north of the 55th parallel is approximately 45 per cent of the total area of BC, yet its people account for only about 2 per cent of the total population. That's around one person per 2100 hectares, or 5,200 acres, or 21 square kilometres. Three highways make up the main transportation infrastructure, along with logging and mining roads. There are a number of population centres scattered along the highways where canoeists can usually find the services they need.

The rivers of northern BC are some of the finest I have ever travelled. Whitewater thrills, unrivalled scenery, vast tracts of accessible alpine hiking, great wildlife viewing, solitude, hot springs, world-class salmon, steelhead, Arctic grayling and trout fishing, First Nations culture and fur trade and gold rush history make paddling in this region a one-of-a-kind experience.

The Setting

✳ Natural History

The natural history of BC is the basis for the smorgasbord of landscapes the canoeist travelling in northern BC will encounter. Cannings and Cannings's *British Columbia: A Natural History* provides a good explanation for the layperson of the natural processes that have shaped the province, and the following brief summary of them is from information found in that book.

Plate tectonics account for the extremely complex geology of BC. In a nutshell, much the province is composed of rocks from immigrant island chains and from the sea floor around them that collided with the existing continent of North America, starting about 200 million years ago. At that time there was no BC west of the Rocky Mountains. The island chains and rocks were squeezed, folded and then fused to ancestral North America, building the existing mountain ranges along southeast/ northwest lines and extending the continent's coastline to the west. The same dynamic processes – plate movement, mountain building, relaxation of the earth's crust, volcanic eruptions, earthquakes and water erosion – that created BC are continuing to shape the province today. For example, in the area where BC, the Yukon and Alaska meet, the St. Elias Mountains are growing higher by 4 cm per year.

Glaciation has also shaped the landscapes along the rivers of northern BC. Before the Pleistocene Ice Age, BC's mountains were high, but more rounded than today, and were separated by v-shaped valleys with few lakes. Over the last two million years, glaciers have sculpted the mountains, creating scalloped peaks, cirques and horns.

In valleys where large glaciers flowed, ice carried away the soft bottom sediments, and the rocky debris carved out the bedrock floors and sidewalls, making the valleys u-shaped. The bends were straightened in the process and these valleys became easier to travel. The debris from the erosive action of the glaciers was pushed along as the glaciers grew or deposited as they retreated. At the end of the Ice Age, this sediment either ended up in moraines or as outwash plains and kame terraces.

By 10,000 years ago the Cordilleran Ice Sheet, which covered most of BC, had melted, leaving only mountain icefields and scattered glaciers. Meltwaters in the valleys caused more erosion. Rivers, especially those with steeper gradients, cut deep into the sediments, quickly creating the floodplain levels we see today. Huge chunks of ice from the decaying glaciers sometimes jammed major rivers, changing the flow of meltwaters and creating lakes, some temporary, some not. Rivers continue to erode glacial sediment today, slowly changing the face of northern BC. The Rocky Mountains are wearing away at a rate of six millimetres every hundred years. Far away to the west the silt-laden Stikine River is building islands at its mouth.

✳ Environment and Climate

The rivers in northern BC can be grouped according to their three most defining characteristics: proximity to the ocean; location and elevation relative to the major mountain ranges, plateaus and plains; and environment and climate. A number of the rivers in this book run through two very different ecosystems, the scenery and nature of the waterways changing significantly as you descend.

Flowing through the Coast Mountains to the Pacific Ocean, the lower sections of the Taku, the Stikine and the Alsek are large, fast and silty (the Taku River is covered in volume one). Steep, rugged peaks line their icy waters. Many glaciers adorn the mountains, some reaching down to glacial lakes or even down to the river's edge, making for exceptional scenery. Technical rapids are uncommon, and the dominant vegetation is northern rainforest – hemlock, cedar, and even Sitka spruce near the sea. Forest fires are rare, but the old-growth forests are shrinking due to logging. You may see seals fishing for salmon along with the grizzlies. The climate is moderate, meaning the Pacific Ocean prevents extreme fluctuations in air temperature, but the paddler can expect cool summers and rain – cooler and wetter as you travel north and west into Alaska, where all three rivers flow into the Pacific. Daily temperatures in July will hover around 10–15°C on average. Precipitation in the Coast Mountains averages 1000–2500 mm a year or more.

The interior rivers described in this guidebook are predominantly characterized by their elevation and proximity to the Rocky, Cassiar, Skeena and Omineca mountains, various major plateaus and the Liard and Taiga plains. The mountain and plateau rivers are usually very fast and shallow, often dropping through canyons, and the significant rapids are often long and technical. The Omineca, Jennings, Dease, Toad and Turnagain are clear trout streams (the Omineca, Jennings and Dease rivers are covered in volume one). The Gataga and Tatshenshini's waters are silty right from the start (the Gataga is also covered in volume one). The foothills and plains rivers, like the Lower Muskwa, Fort Nelson and Lower Liard rivers, are often slower moving with few or no rapids of note, and their waters are silt laden (the Fort Nelson River is covered in volume one). Buttes and sandstone cliffs dominate the scenery.

Boreal forest vegetation dominates northern BC's interior. Forests of subalpine fir, white, Engelmann and black spruce as well as aspen and lodgepole pine are common, with balsam poplar and cottonwoods lining the floodplains. Forest fires are common in the drier areas, and new forests of aspen and pine are scattered like patchwork along many river valleys. The climate is continental, with dry air masses prevailing. The summers are short and warm; July daily temperatures average 20°c. However, the plains can be much hotter. In the higher elevations average annual precipitation is around 500–1000 mm, but in the rain shadows of the mountain ranges, it can be less than 500 mm and even as low as 300 mm a year in the Liard Basin.

Both volumes of this guide include rivers or sections of rivers in two transition zones between the coastal and interior climate. The Kispiox River (covered in volume one) lies in the low-elevation Nass Basin to the far south of the area described in the guide. The forest is mainly hemlock and cedar, becoming more boreal as you approach the Skeena River. It is cooler and wetter here than in the northern interior, and the richness of the vegetation, animal life and aquatic life is amazing. For instance, the Kispiox headwaters and upper stretches are home to one of the world's largest grizzly bear populations and the river hosts a world-class steelhead trout fishery. A portion of the Taku and Tatshenshini rivers and the Lower Stikine lie in the Yukon–Stikine Highlands, a more northerly transition zone between the coastal and interior climates (the Taku River trip is featured in volume one). This high-elevation area is much drier than the Coast Mountains to the west but wetter than the interior plateaus and plains to the east. The mix of vegetation is similar to that of the Kispiox River Valley, but the general environment is drier and the landscape more rugged.

Regardless of the type of river, canoeists can observe a variety of animals and birds. Most of the river valleys areas are home to moose, black and grizzly bear, wolf, fox, porcupine, river otter, mink, marten, fisher, beaver, snowshoe hare and squirrel. Deer, elk, mountain goat, Stone sheep, woodland caribou and bison also live in northern BC, along with cougar, lynx, coyote and wolverine. Marine environments provide the paddler with an opportunity to see seals, sea otters, sea lions and perhaps a humpback whale. Fish-eating birds such as the bald eagle and osprey are common. Ducks, mergansers, loons, gulls, terns and shorebirds are commonly seen in the estuaries. Tundra swans, hawks, kingfishers, dippers, grouse, ravens, jays, Canada geese, golden eagles, owls and numerous songbird species also may be seen, even though some of these birds are more common to interior routes. Fish are plentiful in many rivers, the most common species being whitefish, Arctic grayling, lake, rainbow and bull trout (known locally as Dolly Varden trout), northern pike and various salmon.

At these high latitudes, the long summer days and short nights make for many hours of enjoyment off the river, swimming, fishing and sitting around camp telling stories. Alpine hiking is an activity enjoyed by most BC canoe trippers – remember, I'm from Saskatchewan originally and prefer to use gravity, as in going downstream in my boat rather than uphill in my boots. That being said, even I can appreciate that there is truly amazing hiking to be done on many of the trips in this book. You can make day or multi-day treks to the alpine or take short expeditions to walk on glaciers or up creekbeds. You can also organize horse treks to really check out the backcountry, stopping in the middle of your canoe trip at an outfitter's lodge to hop on a steed and see the sights. There is a lot more to do on a canoe trip in northern BC than paddle the river, as if that weren't enough!

✳ Biting and stinging insects

In northern BC some areas and times of the year are worse for insects than others, depending on conditions that year. Normally, the farther north and inland and the lower the elevation, the worse the insects will be. On the Liard Plain after a wet spring, for example, the biting bugs will be very active on a warm day. Their numbers are significantly lower in the Coast and St. Elias mountains, in the marine environment and during a dry year. If you have paddled in the northern boreal forest elsewhere in Canada, and especially in the Arctic, you will not find the biting bugs nearly as bad in northern BC anywhere you go, except perhaps the far northeast in a wet year. Ticks are generally not found in BC north of the 55th parallel. Bees, wasps and hornets are found in the river valleys of northern BC. By far the most hornets I've encountered were on rivers east of the Rockies. They usually mind their own business, but medication for people with venom allergies should be carried at all times.

You can't completely escape blackflies, mosquitoes, no-see-ums (midges) and sandflies and horse, deer or snipe flies, but you can deal with them. Try using a bug net or hooded jacket with a face net, wear clothing that restricts the flies from crawling into it, or apply repellent with 40 per cent or more DEET. Avoid toiletries with strong odours, and wear light colours. Camping on gravel bars where there is a breeze and little for shade goes a long way toward being comfortable.

Blackflies come out in late spring, usually June in northern BC, and are at their worst in early July. Then they get active again in early fall for a short period. They are around during the day in shaded or partially shaded areas, and are busiest around sunset. The key is to protect those places where blood is close to surface of your skin: your face (especially around the hairline) neck, ears, wrists and ankles. Thankfully, blackflies do not bite inside a tent or late at night.

The peak season for mosquitoes is from early July to early August. They are most active on warm, humid mornings and again in the evenings. You'll find them anywhere there is shade – like on the portage trail and under your canoe when it's on your head! Mosquito populations are larger in wetter areas where there is standing or sluggish water, their prime breeding sites.

Up to the summer of 2007 there was no evidence of the West Nile virus reaching northern BC, even though researchers had predicted it would reach the province as early as 2005. According to health authorities, the reported incidence of West Nile in humans has plummeted since 1999, and most people will become immune to it once they are exposed to it the first time. Only one in 50 people, typically the elderly or those with weakened immune systems, will suffer serious symptoms once exposed.

No-see-ums and sandflies like the heat, and take burning bites that really get your attention. Their season is about the same as for mosquitoes. When it gets hot in July and early August you will encounter deer and horseflies and snipe flies (the tricky ones disguised as houseflies). They are a pain, and take out big chunks, but are usually only active in the heat of the day. I just hate when a horsefly bites the top of my head where my hair parts! A hat and repellent helps, but not much else. Just keep swatting them, hard.

By mid-August the insects have started to settle down. Normally, the later in the season you go on a trip, the less the bugs are a problem. However, proper insect repellent is a must on your equipment list no matter which river you choose at what time. If you won't use products with DEET, wear a head net or preferably a bug jacket with a hood and face net.

* Bears

People often ask me if I'm afraid of bears. I was pretty nervous about grizzlies when I first started camping in BC, but I'm now comfortable in grizzly and black bear country. This comes from reading about their normal behaviour and from my own observations of them in the wild. If you are careful about your behaviour, grizzly and black bears will usually give you a wide berth – provided you do not surprise or threaten them by coming between them and their cubs or a food cache.

Black bears tend to be more curious about people if they have never encountered them before. They are not programmed to prey on humans, but if they have begun to associate people with food, they can be dangerous. This is also true of grizzly bears, but because people are more often in black-bear country, negative encounters are more likely to occur. Therefore, black bears are usually more of a worry in populated areas than along remote rivers in northern BC. Grizzlies will normally give you an even wider berth in the wild and will not be aggressive unless surprised, provoked or habituated to human presence, or their programming is somehow messed up otherwise.

When in bear country, the goal is to avoid encounters: be alert; pay attention to your surroundings; and take precautions. Make lots of noise if approaching rapids where a bear can't hear you coming. Keep your distance if you spot a bear, and leave the area. Don't camp near a bear trail or where there is bear sign (droppings, tracks, digging, scratched trees etc.), or where food or garbage has been left (like a shore lunch spot for fishing parties or where hunters have camped or cut up carcasses). In camp, pitch your tent upwind and away from the cooking area. Keep the kitchen area clean of food scraps, and throw fish offal in deep water away from your camp. Burn leftover food and smelly waste products in a very hot fire. Hang your food, toiletries and other smelly items, or store them in bear-proof containers away from your tents. Never keep anything smelly in your tent, like the clothes you cook in, or anything bears may perceive as food, including toothpaste, deodorant, medications etc. Remember, a fed bear is a dead bear, and people travelling in your wake may be put at risk through your sloppy housekeeping.

The more you know about bears, the better off you will be if you do have a bear encounter. Identifying different species of bear and suggesting what to do if you have a negative encounter is beyond the scope of this guidebook. Take responsibility for being in bear country and read *Bear Attacks: Their Causes and Avoidance*, by Steven Herrero. In this excellent resource, Herrero describes the differences in black and grizzly bear appearance and behaviour, and, based on his considerable research, explains how to deal with a threatening bear. Interestingly, Herrero notes that grizzly bears are unlikely to attack groups of six people or more. The merits and use of bear repellents such as air horns and bear spray (pepper spray) are also discussed in the book.

The People and History

✳ The First Nations

Northern BC is a large area with a rich human history. It has been home to coastal and interior First Nations people for thousands of years. The rivers covered in the two volumes of this guide lie mainly within the traditional territories of the Coastal Tlingit, Inland Tlingit, Tahltan, Kaska, Sekani, Dene-thah (Slavey), Dunne-za (Beaver), Tutchone and Gitxsan. Their communities, traditional gathering places and hunting and trapping cabins dot the waterways. Traditionally, the First Nations people used dugout and spruce-bark canoes, rafts or frame boats covered with hides to travel water bodies for subsistence, transportation and trade. They also developed overland routes along waterways and between watersheds in order to move to their seasonal settlements and foraging, trapping and hunting grounds and to trade and socialize with other groups.

All the First Nations were at least somewhat semi-nomadic in prehistory. Their seasonal movements were based on the availability of food, established trading activities and social events. In summer, coastal people often travelled to salmon fishing spots and places where they could dry the catch for winter use, usually upriver in the dry interior. They would return to their settlements near or on the coast for the winter. Interior First Nations also moved seasonally, spending the spring and fall trapping, hunting, fishing and gathering in small groups. They would rendezvous in the summer at traditional places, coming together to trade and socialize with their own bands and with other First Nation trading partners. Come fall they would go off in small family units again to spend winters in subsistence activities.

Just before contact with European and American traders, the Coastal and Inland Tlingit, Tahltan, Gitxsan and Tutchone were living in the Pacific drainages covered in this guidebook. The Sekani, Dene-thah, Dunne-za and Kaska were living in the Arctic drainages. The marked differences between the coastal and interior environments were reflected in the cultures of the peoples. But they were not living in isolation, limited to the raw resources of their regions. Long before the fur traders arrived, trade routes between the two ocean drainages were very active. Rivers, mountain passes and heights of land between watersheds channelled social interactions and goods among the First Nations and later with the Euro-American traders.

Routes through the Coast Mountains facilitated trade between coastal and interior peoples. The major trading routes required travelling via rivers and land. The overland sections were called "grease trails," referring to the fish oil transported in wooden boxes dripping on the ground en route. Along with fish oil, products such as preserved eulachon (hooligan, ooligan, oolichan), dried seaweed, shells, seal skins and other maritime delicacies passed inland, while raw copper, obsidian, tanned elk, moose and caribou hides and other animal skins, babiche and sinew, land animal furs, quill work and lichen dyes were carried to the coast. Some interior groups benefited from trade going both ways through their territories.

Eventually, in the late 1700s, the coastal First Nations began to amass great power and wealth via new opportunities for trade. They had access to the sea otter furs the first Euro-American traders were looking for and "rights" to the river mouths on the coast, and they enforced control over their territory and trade routes. As such, they were first to acquire large quantities of the Euro-American trading goods few interior groups had access to. The Coastal Tlingit in particular started to dominate the First Nations summer rendezvous and "trading fairs." Their monopoly on trade with the fur traders plying the Pacific Coast and with First Nations from the east continued until Euro-Americans began to travel the interior in large numbers.

By the 1820s, the sea otter trade along the Northwest Coast was on the decline as the species neared extinction and traders then turned their sights to obtaining land animal furs. Trading became more intense with the increase in the interior fur trade, and the Coastal Tlingit benefited even more as middlemen. They obtained desirable merchandise such as guns, files, knives, axes and other metal goods from Russian, British and US ships arriving on the coast, while preventing interior First Nations from trading directly with the Euro-Americans. The indigenous summer rendezvous grew in importance and the coastal groups made more frequent summer and winter trading expeditions into the interior. The Tlingit monopoly on trade extended their range up rivers like the Stikine, Taku and Alsek, and they became a very rich and powerful culture. The interior nations to the west, such as the Tahltan, benefited from their close trading relationship with the Tlingit, as they could trade Euro-American goods to groups farther inland for a profitable return.

Later, with the development of the interior fur trade from the east and the building of Euro-American trading posts in north-central and northeastern BC, territorial boundaries and settlement, cultural and subsistence patterns changed again. A number of the interior First Nations became less nomadic and their rounds began to include stops at the fur trading posts. They would gather in the summer, move on to hunt and fish in the fall, and head off to the trapline or winter grounds for the coldest part of the year, often where there were good fishing lakes. In the spring they would head to the trading posts. Communities grew at the trading posts, with more and more traders, voyageurs and miners coming to northern BC. As the fur trade grew in importance in the First Nations' economies, they eventually permanently or semi-permanently relocated to settlements near the fur forts.

With more Euro-Americans coming to northern BC, their subsequent "country marriages" and the building of fur-trading forts often run by Métis employees of the fur-trading companies, the Métis population became a strong force in northern BC. They worked as traders, packers, trappers and guides.

Following the explorers and fur traders came the missionaries, with miners and surveyors fast on their heels. It was the Stikine and Cassiar gold rushes and the subsequent influx of independent travellers and traders into the interior from the west and east that finally broke the coastal First Nations monopoly on trade with the interior. These early gold rushes also got the attention of the government in Victoria, but it was the Klondike Gold Rush that resulted in money being directed toward developing transportation infrastructure such as the trails and the telegraph to the Yukon goldfields. Then large-scale projects, such as the Alaska and Cassiar highways and the W.A.C. Bennett hydroelectric dam, altered northern BC forever. Each of these influxes and projects brought more and more change to the First Nations' lives and to their relationships with their neighbours and the newcomers in the North.

✳ Early Explorations to Modern Day

Alexander Mackenzie, Samuel Black, John McLeod, Simon Fraser, Robert Campbell, George Mercer Dawson, Frank Swannell and Mary Henry, among other lesser-known explorers, all travelled northern BC's rivers. Their journeys through BC's wild northland would not have been successful without their First Nations guides, many of whom already had access to information about the best routes from the coast inland and throughout the interior. Old First Nations routes, which included the Stikine, Liard, Dease and Fort Nelson rivers, became especially key to explorers and fur traders. Trading posts were established along their banks. Both the Hudson's Bay Company (HBC, sometimes jokingly referred to as Here Before Christ) and the North West Company (NWC) opened and ran posts in northern BC along with numerous posts built and operated by independent fur traders. Roman Catholic and Anglican missionaries followed the traders, and the first missions were set up at Wrangell, Telegraph Creek, McDame, Fort Nelson and Fort Liard.

The greatest influx of non-aboriginals, however, was made up of gold seekers and those who followed in their wake to supply them. The first wave of hopeful "sourdoughs" came during the Omineca and Stikine gold rushes, which started in 1861. After the best claims in the regions had been worked and the excitement was over, many of the prospectors moved on to try their luck in the Cassiar Gold Rush, which really got rolling in 1873. The Klondike, the best known of the gold rushes, began in 1897, bringing exponentially more people to northern BC.

Many prospectors travelled the interior of northern BC to reach the Yukon (Klondike) goldfields. Many never made it. The "all-Canadian" routes were difficult, most of them horrendously so: up the Stikine River to Glenora/Telegraph Creek to Teslin Lake; from the Omineca region via Sifton Pass and the Kechika River to the Liard River or Teslin Lake following the Old Moodie and Police trails; from Quesnel up the Collins-Overland Telegraph Trail; and the Edmonton to Liard River route to the Yukon. A number of the gold seekers and their suppliers that did make it as far as the Yukon came back to northern BC to continue to prospect or trap, work as packers or set up shop. They made up the majority of the non-aboriginals in the North, along with HBC employees. Many men of Euro-American ancestry married northern women and stayed for the rest of their lives.

With the great number of people heading into the North during the gold rushes and the US expansionism of the day, the governments of BC and Canada realized they would have to do something to keep their territories intact. In 1863 the Stikine region, which included the Cassiar, became a territory of BC. In the early 1900s the border with Alaska was finally set.

Communication became central to running the Stikine and Yukon territories and establishing "good government." Two major telegraph initiatives were born, though many years apart. The Collins Overland–Western Union Telegraph Line (1865–1866) never got off the ground, but a trail was cut, much of it along ancient First Nations trade and travel routes. The Dominion Telegraph Line (Yukon Telegraph) was finished in 1901, also strung along First Nations grease trails for the most part. The trail from Ashcroft to Telegraph Creek and on to Atlin and the Yukon Territory was used for travel for many years after the Klondike Gold Rush ended and long after the telegraph line was shut down. Parts are still travelled by horse and foot today.

The Second World War also brought a huge increase in traffic to the North. In 1941, the Northwest Staging Route, a flyway of connected airports to supply military planes travelling to Alaska was completed. Watson Lake and Fort Nelson (which already had an airport that just needed improvements) were important links in the route. Watson Lake's airport had to be built from scratch, and the only feasible way to get building materials to these communities was to ship them via river and road. The Stikine–Dease rivers route to Lower Post on the Liard River once again became a busy "Trail to the Interior," having already been an important grease trail in First Nations trade and the main route to the Cassiar during its gold rush. The rough track between Telegraph Creek and Dease Lake was developed into a road that enabled the Watson Lake airport to be built from supplies and equipment shipped via the Pacific, up the Stikine and finally down the Dease.

"The Long Way Around" – the river/road route from Edmonton to Fort Nelson via the Waterways Portage and the Athabasca, Slave, Mackenzie, Liard and Fort Nelson rivers – once again became a significant travel route, as it had been during pre-Contact First Nations trade. This long route was used to bring equipment and materials to improve the airport at Fort Nelson. A winter road was also pushed through from Fort St. John to supply the project.

Right on the heels of the Northwest Staging Route came the construction of the Alaska Highway. Using the same two river-and-road routes, the highway was built to provide an overland military supply link to the airfields in Canada and Alaska. In 1942 the US Army Corps of Engineers finished what was basically only a track from Dawson Creek in BC to Delta Junction, near Fairbanks, Alaska. The following year, an improved road was completed. The Canadian section, then known as the ALCAN Highway, was turned over to Canada in 1946. In 1948 the entire route was opened to civilian traffic. Once the road – which crosses eight mountain ranges and 133 rivers and creeks – was complete and opened to all traffic, life in the North was changed forever. The new travel route impacted relationships among First Nations. Some groups lost contact with one another, while others developed new ties, and traditional lands were made more accessible to travellers and resource developers. Another megaproject, the building of the W.A.C. Bennett Dam in the 1960s, also altered the face of northern BC irrevocably. The dam changed the flow of numerous rivers and flooded a vast area, displacing many people. The resulting power source also encouraged further development in north-central and northeastern BC.

In the 1970s the Stewart–Cassiar Highway was finished, opening up the Stikine and Cassiar regions from the south as well. It joined the Alaska Highway near the Yukon boundary, and the road to Prince Rupert completed the main infrastructure now in place in northern BC. A railway from Fort St. James to Dease Lake was nearly completed before being abandoned in favour of trucking goods via the Cassiar Highway. It was thought during a low period in natural resource prices that any benefit from finishing the railway was no longer worth the expense. The railbed and bridges still remain, spectres of development plans gone awry.

Ironically, most of the economic activity in the North today involves tourism and resource extraction. The tourists come to hunt, fish, camp and see the natural-resource development wonders of northern BC, Yukon and Alaska, while companies look for more natural-resource development opportunities. First Nations are involved in both of these economic endeavours to varying degrees, and government land-use plans have been developed for all regions. There is no doubt that northern BC is open for business, yet a good number of First Nations and local people, plus others not living in the North, question the rate and sustainability of a number of the proposed developments. Many of the rivers in this guidebook are threatened by projects that are not environmentally sound. Each chapter provides more information on these issues, including how paddlers can get involved in related conservation initiatives.

WHAT YOU NEED TO KNOW TO GO

Many of the routes in this guidebook are on mountain rivers. Like plains and Shield rivers, mountain rivers have characteristics and hazards that you must become familiar with. However, mountain rivers require more moving-water skills and knowledge on average to descend them safely. The best analogy I can think of to illustrate the difference between paddling an average mountain river compared to an average Precambrian Shield river is that of driving on a highway through the Rockies in BC versus driving the Trans-Canada Highway through northern Ontario. On the mountain highway you consistently encounter steeper gradients with fewer chances to pull out and deal with any trouble. You need to pay very close attention to the road at all times. You must navigate sharp, blind corners that may be followed by hazards such as fallen trees or rock slides. You have to be able to stop abruptly. The weather can change faster and be more extreme in the summer months. The consequences of having an accident or leaving the road unexpectedly are often more severe. Ironically, to access a number of the rivers in this book, you may well drive mountain highways and logging roads, which can be a nerve-wracking experience (especially the road to Telegraph Creek and the logging road up the side of Williston Lake).

Putting the highway driving analogy aside, your greatest concern on BC rivers will be wood hazards: logjams, sometimes blocking the entire river or various channels, at the head of islands, on top of submerged gravel bars or reefs, or sticking out from riverbanks; and sweepers, strainers and deadheads. Precambrian Shield rivers do not have anywhere near the number of wood hazards found on an average BC river, and wood is most likely to be the cause of death for canoeists paddling mountain rivers.

Cold water, often glacially cold, is also a potential and serious hazard. In prime canoeing season on Shield rivers, the water is much warmer than on northern BC rivers. Most mountain rivers don't warm up much, as they are constantly being fed from snowmelt through much of the paddling season. In many cases glacier melt also accounts for a river's flow.

Combine these two major hazards with the characteristics of northern BC rivers described below and you will see why I say mountain rivers are potentially more dangerous to paddle than the rivers familiar to most canoeists in eastern Canada. Many northern BC mountain rivers host at least some the following features besides wood hazards and cold water: continuous sections of moving water and/or rapids, often with draining eddies; steep gradients with blind corners; canyons and mini-gorges with sheer sides and/or undercut rock; extreme fluctuations in water levels due to snowmelt, heavy rain and glacier melt; few places for a floatplane or helicopter to land if you need to be evacuated; very few established portages relative to the number of rapids on the routes; and on some river routes, tidal flats, open ocean crossings and committing coastlines to navigate.

This discussion is not meant to scare you off paddling the rivers in this guidebook, but to encourage you to be sure you are prepared in advance to paddle them safely. Note that not all the rivers in these volumes are mountain rivers either, but hazards such as rock features, hydraulics, sweepers, deadheads, strainers and logjams are present on all to some degree. Therefore, the minimum you need to know to safely attempt even the easiest of these trips, mountain river or not, is how to paddle a canoe proficiently in moving water. Canoeists should be able to paddle forward and in reverse in a straight line in current; ferry from one side of the river to the other; perform eddy turns and peel outs; and stop quickly. A solid understanding of how to read moving water and how rapids are classified is essential (see Appendix A for the system I use in this guidebook). And for most routes, you will need to be able to line, track and wade your canoe safely, and portage your gear and canoe efficiently. Last, but not least by any stretch of the imagination, you should also be competent in moving-water rescues and river rescue skills, especially with regard to assisted and self-rescue techniques, dealing with wood hazards, and pin or wrap situations. Self-rescue in the event of a capsize is usually faster than assisted rescue; add the cold-water factor and a few large pools below rapids and faster is definitely better. Preventing hypothermia is paramount. Take courses to upgrade your skills and increase your knowledge, and be sure you have the appropriate craft, equipment and gear for the trip you wish to do.

Competency in bushcraft is also required, and you must know how to pack for canoe travel and an extended stay in the wild. You should also have survival skills and emergency first aid training, especially with regard to dealing with hypothermia. You must be able to read topographic maps in various scales and navigate with them using a compass. As a minimum you will need to understand the basics of using the Universal Transverse Mercator (UTM)-based Grid Reference System (GRS) and latitude and longitude. For some trips you must also be able to use tide tables.

To preserve the natural values of the rivers, you must know how to practise low-impact camping. Of course we make a footprint on the land when travelling through it, but walk lightly and leave as little trace of your passing as possible. Read Appendix B and do your research. Remember that you will often be travelling through lands that still provide sustenance to the local people of the area. Harvest the bounty of the watersheds sparingly. If you are going to fish, you must have a valid licence for the species you are fishing and your location, i.e., Alaska or the Northwest or Yukon territories, as some of the river routes cross these borders. Obey regulations, including campfire bans that are applicable to the region or park where you are travelling. Be aware that all prehistoric and historic period sites and artifacts in BC are protected by law and should not be collected or in any way disturbed. In all ways, consider what you can do to help conserve the nature of these wild rivers and lands for the future.

Locating the River Routes

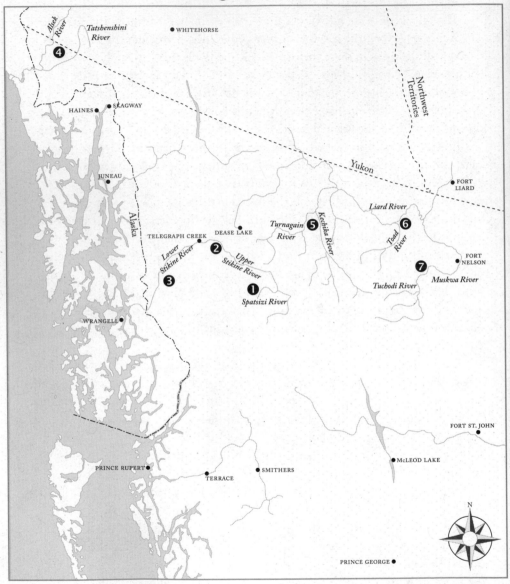

1. Spatsizi River
2. Upper Stikine River
3. Lower Stikine River
4. Tatshenshini/Alsek Rivers
5. Turnagain/Kechika Rivers
6. Toad/Liard Rivers
7. Tuchodi/Muskwa Rivers

HOW TO USE THIS GUIDEBOOK

FINDING THE RIVER ROUTE FOR YOU

This book will provide you with enough information about a particular canoe route so that you can choose a river trip that will suit your skill level and your interests. One chapter describes one route. A number of the routes involve multiple rivers.

Each trip is introduced with a map outlining the route, followed by a short summary of its attractions. Then the route is described in detail with reference to length, required topographic maps, logistics, when to go, difficulty level, the character of the river and region, historical values of the river, the degree of solitude to expect, wildlife-viewing potential, fishing, other activities that can be enjoyed on the route, and special equipment considerations. Finally, each chapter ends with Trip Notes that list topographic map coordinates of the route features, including put-ins and take-outs, road access, rapids, hazards, sources of emergency help, campsites and special attractions. The features are described briefly with regard to their location and nature. References to further reading material on the rivers, the route and the region are provided throughout each chapter and are listed at the end of the book. This information, along with the Directory of Services and Organizations and the appendices, should provide canoeists with what they need to know to decide on a suitable route and to organize and carry out the chosen trip.

The Logistics: Length, Maps, Access and When To Go

The length of the trip in kilometres is given, and in most cases options for shortening or extending the trip are suggested. Except for the most difficult trips – ones with many rapids that must be scouted, waded, lined or portaged – you can estimate travelling an average of 30 km per day. This is a pretty relaxing pace unless you encounter strong winds, extremely high or low water or other uncontrollable factors. Where deemed necessary, the minimum number of days for a particular trip is indicated.

In this section you will also find a list of required topographic maps for each trip. Maps at 1:50 000 scale are recommended for all the routes, but for a few the 1:250 000 will do. However, the Trip Notes will be less user friendly, and you need the 1:50 000-scale if you plan to do any longer hikes. Since you can now download and print NTS topo maps for free (with compatible mapping software like Ozi-Explorer) from Natural Resources Canada's Geogratis website (www.geogratis.ca/geogratis/en/download/scanned.html), why not use both scales? I like to use both for my river trips: I use the smaller scale 1:250 000 maps for understanding the big features of a region, like the mountain ranges and valleys, and the larger-scale

1:50 000 maps for looking at the river's features, like elevation drops and canyons, gravel bars and rapids.

If you do a shortened, custom trip, you can figure out from the Trip Notes what maps you won't need. If you lengthen your trip or do multi-day hikes that take you off the listed maps, you will need to consult the appropriate topographical map indexes to find out what you'll need. Optional maps, such as BC Forest Service Recreational maps, as well marine charts, are listed where relevant. All NTS maps are listed by index letter and numbers, for example, 74 K/10. United States Geological Survey (USGS) maps for trips that end in Alaska are also given by name to avoid confusion.

You can get all the NTS maps of both recommended scales by downloading them as digitals from the Geogratis website and then printing them; ordering E-topo digitals and then printing them; phoning or faxing for hard copies by post; or photocopying them from a library. Map and chart sources are listed in the Directory of Services and Organizations. Note that most of the rapids and waterfalls (a single drop of 1 m or more) are not marked on the topo maps and some that are indicated are marked in the wrong locations. Once you have your maps, use the Trip Notes at the end of the chapter to mark in all the features of interest on your chosen route so that you have at your fingertips the locations of the rapids, portages, sources of emergency help, campsites etc. while navigating the river. (Refer to the Trip Notes section of this introductory chapter for a brief explanation of the relationship between the NTS Grid Reference System and UTM coordinates.) Marking your maps with the important route features will also help you establish an itinerary and plan for each paddling day.

In terms of when to go, I specify the best and worst times to paddle the route in question. I must stress these are only recommendations based on a normal season. Water levels may fluctuate significantly from the historical averages and even from day to day depending on temperature and precipitation, especially on glacier-fed rivers. Additionally, global warming is having an effect on when the rivers peak, and the historical hydrometric data for each month may no longer be as helpful as it once was. From what I can tell, some rivers tend to peak at higher levels on average, earlier in some cases and later in others, while others have less water come the end of the season.

Generally, northern BC water levels are usually at their lowest in the late summer and fall, mid-August to the end of September. The rule of thumb is still that August is considered the prime canoeing month in northern BC, while June and early July are usually the times to avoid at all costs. You do not want to paddle a river in flood, and the early summer is when many of the rivers peak from snowmelt in what is known as the spring runoff, or freshet. That being said, anything can happen at any time when weather is involved, especially on a glacier-fed river. These watercourses can peak at any time with heavy rain.

Only some of the rivers described in this guidebook have active water-gauging stations. For those rivers (indicated in the trip descriptions), real-time and historical flows can be obtained from the Environment Canada and USGS hydrometric websites.

Snowpack and river level forecasts can be obtained for some routes if you want to keep an eye on how runoff is progressing in any given year.

In 1994/95 many of the province's real-time hydrometric data collection stations were closed down due to federal budget cuts. For the rivers in the book without active gauges, I provide you with archived material when possible so you can at least get a general sense of how the river normally fluctuates. However, before you go on your trip, you will have to collect current information on water levels from local sources such as BC Parks offices, outfitters and air services. Regardless of the information available in this book or online, I strongly suggest you always check on local conditions and hazards such as forest fires before setting out.

Do as much research as possible for any river trip, and always be prepared to change your plans. If the water level is very high or very low on your river trip of choice (especially when a route is water-level dependent), have an alternative route planned and do it instead. Water level affects the difficulty of a mountain river much more than it does a Taiga Plain or Precambrian Shield river. Some waterways can become virtually unnavigable at very low water or extremely dangerous at high water. You will also want to plan extra time in your itinerary to deal with the extreme daily fluctuations that are possible on glacier-fed or large-catchment, small-volume rivers. Obtaining local water-level information may also help with making equipment choices. You may need to take a canoe made from a plastic composite if the water is low. If it is high, you may want to take a spray cover – if you have the skill to run rapids that require their use.

Transportation options to the canoe trip's start and end points are given. Some trips can be accessed by driving your vehicle or catching a bus, while some require chartering a floatplane or boat. You may end up using a combination of all of these modes of transportation, maybe even with a maritime ferry thrown in! The topography of northern BC and the fact that some rivers end in Alaska make for some complicated logistics. Contact information for transportation services, canoe rentals and other potentially required services are listed in Directory of Services and Organizations.

If you haven't already looked into a PakCanoe (PakBoat), a fabulous folding/inflatable canoe with different models to choose from, I would suggest you do so, especially if you are planning to do some extensive tripping in northern BC. You will save money and some sweat. These boats fold and roll up into a duffel bag, so you can charter wheeled planes instead of floatplanes where there are airstrips. This is cheaper by far. And you can more easily get your canoe on scheduled jet flights, ferries, trains, buses etc. These craft are also lighter to carry than plastic boats.

One final aspect of logistics I discuss is safe parking. In some places you just do not leave your vehicle(s) unattended, while other places seem to be just fine. I note where safe parking is a sure thing – for example, aviation companies, outfitters, airports etc. For remote road-accessible put-ins you may want to make shuttle arrangements with canoe outfitters and long-distance taxi services in the area. These too are listed in the Directory of Services and Organizations.

Difficulty Rating: Is this Trip for You?

The trips are rated according to their comparative level of difficulty, much like ski runs are graded so that skiers can choose the run that best matches their skill level and terrain preferences. The rating system is based on the average difficulty of the whitewater that canoeists will encounter, i.e., what class of rapids to expect (see the Scale of Rapid Classification in Appendix A); the amount of whitewater to expect, i.e., the quantity of rapids and their nature (a few sporadic rapids versus continuous sections of rapids); the existence and condition of portages; the number of mandatory portages; and the number and type of special hazards, including wood hazards, long open-water crossings, glacially cold water, canyons without egress, tidal flats etc. The length, isolation, water-level fluctuations and weather patterns of the route are also factored in.

Remember, the route difficulty rating is only a generalization, but the star-rating system can give you a fair idea of what to expect. However, not all factors may be relevant to every river and at all times. High water or low water can significantly increase or lessen the difficulty of some river trips. That being so, in each chapter the basis for the rating and details on the nature of the challenges of the particular river trip are given based on water levels during the season.

Also, when considering the difficulty rating for a specific route, remember that rating the difficulty of rivers in general and rapids in particular is always a somewhat subjective exercise. My experience on the river with regard to weather, water levels and the skill level of the people I paddled the river with will no doubt be different from yours. Consider this and always err on the side of caution when choosing a trip, especially if you are the most skilled paddler in your party. You don't want to lead others into a situation that is too challenging for them. You likely will not enjoy yourself either if your group is stressed. (A tip: as well as reading the difficulty section in each chapter, also look closely at the Trip Notes for the number and types of portages, rapids, hazards etc. These specifics will help you understand my rating system.)

The following comparative system for rating the difficulty of the trips uses stars, with one star indicating the easiest routes to paddle and four stars the most difficult.

✳ Easiest: The moving water averages Class 1/1+ with possibly a few short, straightforward Class 2–/2 rapids; mandatory portages, where present, are on trails in good condition; some lining or wading may be required; there are few hazards and these are easily avoided; open-water crossings, if any, are short; the route is suitable for novice river-tripping canoeists.

✳ ✳ Average: The moving water averages Class 1+ to Class 2, with possibly some rapids approaching Class 3; there are portage trails in fair to good condition or there are other good options for getting around rapids you can't or don't want to run; mandatory portages, if any, are on paths of some sort; lining or wading may be required; there are wood hazards of concern, but these are easily avoided by trained paddlers; open-water crossings are few, if any, but may be committing; the route is suitable for intermediate river-tripping canoeists; novices should paddle in a party with more-skilled canoeists or go with a guide.

✳ ✳ ✳ Difficult: The moving water averages Class 2 to 2+, including long continuous rapids that must read on the run, including some sections of Class 3– rapids; there are Class 3 rapids in most cases and portage trails may or may not exist; bushwhacking, lining, wading or a combination of all three may be required to avoid running the more difficult rapids; there may be mandatory portages around waterfalls on game or horse trails; physical stamina is required; in some cases you may have to run challenging canyon rapids that cannot be scouted from land; there are numerous wood hazards of concern; open-water crossings and/or exposed coastline stretches, if any, are committing; these routes often run through remote areas without road access or sources for quick emergency help; these trips are suitable only for intermediate river trippers paddling in party with advanced and exceptional canoeists or on a guided trip; the routes are not recommended for novice river trippers in any scenario, except perhaps if they will be paddling tandem with an exceptional moving-water canoeist at lower water levels. Parties should be made up three canoes, equally matched in terms of abilities in paddling moving water and performing rescues.

✳ ✳ ✳ ✳ Most Difficult: the moving water averages Class 2 to 3, with long continuous read and run sections and stretches of more difficult rapids that may or may not be scoutable from land; there are many hazards to navigate, including any or all of the following: wood, canyon rapids that must be run, exposed and committing open-water crossings and/or coastline paddling; there are generally no portage trails, and bushwhacking is required to avoid rapids that parties decide not to run; physical and mental stamina is required; these routes are extremely dependent on water level, and the rivers run through isolated areas without road access or quick emergency help; the trip is only suitable for advanced and exceptional canoeists with excellent lining, portaging and river rescue skills. Three-boat parties are required.

You will note that skills levels are indicated in the river difficulty rating system. These are given so that you are aware of the skill and knowledge base required of paddlers to navigate the river in a reasonable amount of time and with maximum safety. However, safety is your responsibility and it is up to each canoeist to judge her or his ability to deal with what a particular trip requires in terms of skill and physical stamina. The following skill level definitions are used in recommending who should run a particular river and when, and are given in a mountain river context:

Novice: can read and run short and continuous Class 1+ rapids with another novice; scouts most rapids over Class 1+; only runs Class 2–/2 with another novice after scouting; can read and run up to Class 2–/2 continuous rapids with an intermediate partner; can perform basic moving-water manoeuvres such as side slipping, front ferries and eddy turns consistently with an intermediate partner in straightforward rapids; can self-rescue and understands assisted rescue techniques; has very little mountain river tripping experience, but has done some lake tripping.

Intermediate: can read and run continuous Class 2–/2 rapids; scouts most rapids approaching Class 2+; runs Class 2+ after scouting; may run short Class 3–/3 rapids with an intermediate partner empty, but usually walks around them; has taken at least one intensive whitewater course and can perform all basic moving-water manoeuvres with an intermediate partner in Class 2 water with an 80 per cent success rate; can perform self- and assisted rescues and has several seasons of river-tripping experience under their belt.

Advanced: can read and run continuous rapids up to Class 2+, even with a novice paddler; runs up to Class 3 with gear after scouting; has taken certification courses in tandem and solo whitewater paddling and can perform all moving-water manoeuvres and self- and assisted rescues in Class 2+ water with a 90 per cent success rate; and has at least five seasons of river tripping experience under their belt, including mountain river trips.

Exceptional: can read and run continuous rapids up to Class 3; will run Class 3 loaded with a novice partner after scouting; comfortably paddles Class 3/3+ rapids when paddling tandem with a skilled partner in a canoe with a skirt and up to Class 4– paddling solo in a playboat; performs precision manoeuvres and self- and assisted rescues in water that pushes the limits of open boating; has Instructor Trainer or Master Instructor certification in whitewater, plus extensive mountain river tripping experience.

The final piece of information given in the difficulty section is the gradient of the river(s). The elevation drop is given in metres per kilometre, e.g., the river drops 1.5 m/km. The details of gradient will be elaborated on with regard to what accounts for the drop in elevation – steady moving water, a canyon, a large waterfall – and in some cases the gradient of one route will be compared to that of another.

Character of the River and Region

The rivers are described in terms of the ecoprovinces and ecoregions they flow through, so you can visualize what the scenery and flora are like along the route and choose the environment that most intrigues you. See the Ecoprovinces of Northern BC map and the Ecoprovinces and Ecoregions of Northern BC table for a general overview.

The various landscapes the canoeist will paddle through are also described with reference to major topographical features such as the Skeena Plateau or Muskwa Ranges of the Rocky Mountains, as well as local features of interest or scenic sites, such as glaciers and moose-watching sloughs, along the whole route. Descriptions of the common or unique vegetation found along the river and in the forest and the alpine are provided. The geology of a region is noted generally and with regard to unique aspects of a region's natural history. A few trips, such as the Tatshenshini/Alsek, Stikine and Taku (covered in volume one), feature an incredible diversity of landscapes and you can pretty much experience most of the kind of scenery northern BC has to offer all in one trip!

(continues on page 30)

Ecoprovinces of Northern BC

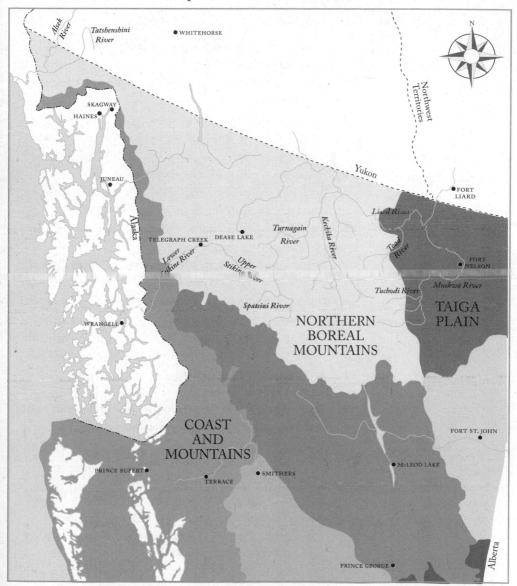

ECOPROVINCE	ECOREGION
Coast and Mountains	1. **Northern Coastal Mountains (NCM)**
	◆ A vast area of steep, rugged mountain ranges made up mostly of gneisses and granite
	◆ Fairweather and Boundary ranges characteristic of Northern Coastal Mountains ecoregion
	◆ Peaks range from 2100–3100 m ASL
	◆ Ranges are cut into several segments by large, steep-sided transverse valleys
	◆ Numerous fjords and glacial valleys
	◆ Main surface materials are colluvium and glacial deposits, with bedrock and ice common in higher elevations
	◆ High levels of precipitation (1000–2500 mm annually); cool and humid moderate climate
	◆ Alpine vegetation is mostly low-growing heather, dwarf birch, willow, grass and lichen
	◆ Subalpine forests are primarily subalpine fir and mountain hemlock
	◆ Closed-canopy western hemlock forests dominate at lower elevations; mixed with western red cedar and yellow cedar
	◆ Some Sitka spruce and alder occur in warmer, more humid middle and lower elevations near the coast
	◆ The lower reaches of the Tatshenshini/Alsek route and much of the Lower Stikine route lie in this ecoregion
Northern Boreal Mountains	1. **Liard Basin (LIB)**
	◆ A broad, rolling low-lying area covered with glacial drift and outwash deposits in which the Liard River is entrenched
	◆ The region is underlain by limestone and shale, and the basin lies at 620–930 m ASL
	◆ The climate is dry subarctic/continental with annual precipitation of 350–450 mm
	◆ Has extensive stands of boreal forest composed of lodgepole pine, white and black spruce and aspen
	◆ Dry sites support lodgepole pine; moist sites have black spruce and larch with a Labrador tea, horsetail and moss understorey

- The floodplains of the Liard River and its larger tributaries support white spruce, cottonwood and balsam poplar
- The lower reaches of the Kechika and Toad rivers as well as much of the Liard River lie in this ecoregion

2. Northern Canadian Rocky Mountains (NCR)

- The rugged Muskwa Ranges of the northern Rocky Mountains are the main feature of this ecoregion
- Peaks reach 3100 m ASL, and a number of glaciers skirt the higher peaks
- The mostly sedimentary rock forming the mountain ranges has been modified as a result of glaciation and erosion, among other natural processes
- Glacial drift, colluvium and bedrock outcrops are the main surface materials
- Precipitation ranges from 500 mm in the lower elevations to 800 mm higher up and in the mountain passes
- Alpine vegetation is common, consisting of dwarf willow and birch, alpine grasses and sedges
- Subalpine forests are dominated by subalpine fir and white spruce along with willow and birch shrubs
- Closed-canopy forests of lodgepole pine and white and black spruce dominate at lower, warmer elevations along with some aspen; balsam poplar grow on the floodplains
- Most of the Tuchodi River and the upper reaches of the Toad River lie in this ecoregion

3. Boreal Mountains and Plateaus (BMP)

- The ecoregion covers a vast area of northern BC and is composed of a complex of rugged mountains, high plateaus and lowlands
- Main features are the Cassiar and northern Omineca mountains; the Stikine and Yukon plateaus; and the volcanoes from the late Tertiary and Pleistocene, Mount Edziza and those of the Level Mountain area
- Both the Cassiar and northern Omineca mountains are older than the Rockies and are made up of a granitic core as well as metamorphic rock
- The highest peaks reach 2500 m ASL and carry a number of alpine glaciers

◆ The climate tends to be more moderate, warmer and wetter in the western half of the ecoregion, becoming more continental and drier with more extreme temperatures as you move eastward

◆ Temperature and precipitation vary with elevation, with average annual precipitation ranging from 400–700 mm

◆ Lichen alpine vegetation and bare bedrock dominate at higher mountain elevations

◆ Subalpine and middle elevation forests consist of subalpine fir with some white spruce and deciduous shrubs such as birch and willow

◆ Lower elevations and the plateaus are dominated by closed-canopy forests of lodgepole pine and white and black spruce, while floodplains host cottonwoods or balsam poplar

◆ The Turnagain, the Upper Kechika, the Spatsizi, the entire Upper Stikine route and the very beginning of the Lower Stikine route (around Telegraph Creek only) lie in this ecoregion

4. St. Elias Mountains (SEM)

◆ In northern BC the major feature of this ecoregion is the St. Elias Mountains

◆ The St. Elias Mountains are composed of Paleozoic and Mesozoic strata and characterized by vast regions of icefields and high-elevation peaks

◆ Peaks are serrated, with pinnacles ranging up to 6000 m ASL

◆ The main peaks stand as isolated blocks separated by broad icefields

◆ The few valleys that exist are in the eastern portion of the ecoregion and are dominated by morainal and fluvioglacial materials

◆ The surface materials are a combination of permanent ice and snowfields with minor areas of rock outcrop, rubbly colluvium and alpine tundra

◆ Alpine vegetation is composed of low-growing heather, dwarf birch, willow, grass and lichen, with wet sites hosting cottongrass and sedges

◆ On the sides of valleys that have vegetation there are subalpine forests composed of subalpine fir and white spruce; valley bottoms also host aspen, willow and alder

◆ Temperature and precipitation vary with elevation; average annual precipitation at low eastern elevations is around

300 mm and more than 1000 mm in the icefields to the west
- ◆ A portion of the Tatshenshini/Alsek route lies in this ecoregion

5. Yukon – Stikine Highlands (YSH)

- ◆ The ecoregion is a zone of climate transition from coastal to interior conditions lying in northwestern BC
- ◆ It falls within the rain shadow of the Coast Mountains and encompasses the mountainous areas leeward of the St. Elias and Boundary ranges
- ◆ Subdued mountains and wide valleys predominate
- ◆ Precipitation decreases moving inland, and temperatures are moderated throughout the year by the influence of the maritime air masses
- ◆ The mean annual precipitation is 500–600 mm
- ◆ Alpine tundra is dominated by low-growing heather, dwarf birch, willow, grass and lichen
- ◆ Subalpine forests consist of subalpine fir, white spruce and the occasional Engelmann spruce
- ◆ Closed boreal forests of black and white spruce are found at lower elevations
- ◆ Aspen and lodgepole pine regenerate after fire at mid- to lower elevations, and the river floodplains host cottonwood trees
- ◆ The lower Tatshenshini River and a short stretch of the Lower Stikine route lie in this ecoregion

Taiga Plain

1. Muskwa Plateau (MUP)

- ◆ The ecoregion lies in northeastern BC along the foothills of the Rocky Mountains and spans the border with NWT
- ◆ The southern section is a smooth upland, whereas the northern section forms part of the wide Fort Nelson Lowland
- ◆ Wetlands cover 25–50 per cent of the ecoregion
- ◆ The area is underlain with shales and sandstones, with elevations ranging from 760–975 m ASL
- ◆ Glacial till and organic deposits cover much of the sedimentary rock
- ◆ The climate is continental, with mean annual precipitation ranging from 400–500 mm
- ◆ Forests are mainly closed-canopy, with medium to tall stands of lodgepole pine and some tamarack; white birch and trembling aspen are common in the foothills and southern locales

- Poorly drained sites support black spruce and some white spruce
- White and black spruce are the climactic species of the area
- The nutrient-rich alluvial flats of the larger rivers host white spruce and cottonwoods, growing to sizes comparable to the largest in the boreal forests to the south
- There is a well-developed shrub component which includes dwarf birch, Labrador tea and willow
- Bearberry, mosses and sedges are the dominant understorey
- The very lower reaches of the Tuchodi, the middle Muskwa and a short stretch of the Liard upstream of the Fort Nelson River confluence lie in this ecoregion

2. Northern Alberta Upland (NAU)

- The area lies in the very northeastern corner of BC
- The uplands rise some 400–500 m above the surrounding lowlands and have steep scarps on their eastern sides
- The subdued relief is incised by major rivers and is composed of shales and some sandstone
- Wetlands cover 50–70 per cent of the region
- The ecoregion has a continental climate, with annual precipitation averaging 350–500 mm
- Rolling moraines are covered with organic deposits supporting open stands of stunted black spruce and some birch and shrubs
- Upland slopes that are free of organic blankets are mainly loamy glacial till supporting white spruce, balsam fir and aspen mixed forest
- The riverbanks host cottonwood trees
- The stretch of the Liard River from the Fort Nelson confluence to Fort Liard lies in this ecoregion

3. Hay River Lowland (HRL)

- The broad, level lowland plain that is drained by the Fort Nelson River and lower Liard River
- The area is underlain with shale, with surface deposits of organic soils, peat and glacial till on nearly level to gently rolling topography
- Average annual precipitation is 350–450 mm, in a continental climate

◆ Dry sites are characterized by closed-canopy mixed stands of trembling aspen, cottonwoods, white spruce, balsam fir and black spruce
◆ Poorly drained fens and bogs, about 30 per cent of the ecoregion, are covered with tamarack and black spruce
◆ The lower Muskwa River lies in this ecoregion

The rivers in this guidebook are also described according to type, e.g., a fast, shallow river flowing over a vast floodplain, such as the Tuchodi, versus a bouncy, hard-rock river with mini-canyons such as the Kispiox (covered in volume one) or a massive-volume coastal river in a wide valley such as the Lower Stikine. You can choose the kind of moving water you want to paddle. A few trips have it all, such as the Tatshenshini/Alsek route, the most difficult trip found in this volume, but most have a variety of rapids, from technical boulder gardens to wave trains through gorges and shallow, rocky fans made by glacial deposits.

The routes in this volume of the guidebook lie in three ecoprovinces and nine ecoregions. The following table outlines the ecoprovinces and ecoregions most relevant to describing the natural environment of the rivers in volume two of *Northern British Columbia Canoe Trips*. More-detailed information can be found on the Ecoregions of BC website. The website address and references for further research on the ecology and geology of the different regions are given in each chapter.

Local History

Often the trade-off for bumping into more people on the river is that the history of the route is much more varied and rich. The Stikine, Liard, Taku, Dease and Fort Nelson rivers were important waterways in prehistory (the latter three rivers are covered in volume one of this guide). Beyond providing First Nations with the necessities of life, as all the rivers covered in this guidebook did, they were the basis of vital travel and trade routes. They are still highways through the wild country. You will likely have the pleasure of meeting local people along these waterways who are enjoying the summer at their cabins or in boats pursuing traditional activities such as hunting and fishing.

A couple of the rivers saw voyageurs ply their waters, and a number of them were explored by fur traders and surveyors of note. Some became part of major routes to the goldfields that brought the first great influxes of Euro-Americans to northern BC. Some of the other rivers, like the Tuchodi and the Turnagain, were too rough to be travelled by canoe, and thus are missing the same extensive oral or written history. Many overland trails were established by First Nations for travel in these and other watersheds, and the explorers, traders, surveyors, prospectors, trappers, scientists and adventurers made great use of them throughout the historical era.

When travelling in the northern wilds, it is important to remember that you are in someone's ancient backyard. Leave everything you find just the way you found it, including antlers, rocks and other natural features. All prehistoric and historic period sites and artifacts are protected by law and should not be collected or in any way disturbed. Some trips pass through provincial parks and ecological reserves, where regulations to preserve fragile environments may be in force. This information, or a source for obtaining it, is given in the relevant cases.

The river trips are graded under the following star system according to their First Nations, exploration, fur trade and gold rush history values:

✳ Low: This route was not used by First Nations regularly for travel or trade, nor was it of importance in early explorations, the fur trade or gold rushes.

✳ ✳ Average: This route, or a part of it, has an oral and/or written First Nations history, but was not a major waterway for travel or trade; it was used by trappers and prospectors and explored by surveyors.

✳ ✳ ✳ High: This route, or a part of it, was a regular First Nations travel and trade route or was important in their culture and economy; it was explored by early fur traders and surveyors, and/or was important in gold rush and prospecting history.

✳ ✳ ✳ ✳ Very High: This river, or a part of it, was one of the most important waterways for First Nations trade and travel; famous explorers and surveyors documented the watershed; it was a major link in the fur trade routes; and it was an important waterway for gold seekers.

References for further reading about a river or area with significant prehistoric and historic values will be supplied in the local history summary and the References section.

Solitude

Each route's level of solitude is also rated. A couple of trips have fallen from favour or have never seen many canoeists, while others that were once paddled only by a select few have become quite popular. On the very popular trips it would be usual to see at least one or two other canoeing parties on a trip in August. Most routes have cabins, fishing and hunting lodges and local boat traffic to varying degrees. Some routes show more evidence of the modern world, including established campsites, bridges, mines etc. than others. The star rating indicates the level of solitude one can expect on a trip in peak season, as indicated in the When To Go section. The rating system is as follows:

✳ Low: Expect to see other canoeing and/or fishing/hunting parties and local boat traffic; there are lots of cabins, established campsites and significant evidence of the modern world.

✳ ✳ Average: You will likely encounter one or two canoeing and/or fishing/hunting parties and local boat traffic; you will see some evidence of the modern world almost every day.

✳ ✳ ✳ High: You may see one other party of canoeists or hunter/fishers, and local boat traffic is infrequent; signs of the modern world are comparatively few and are usually not intrusive.

✳ ✳ ✳ Very High: Expect to see no one for days, and very little evidence of the modern world.

Wildlife

Many people go on remote river trips in hopes of seeing wildlife. Grizzly and black bear, moose, elk, Stone sheep, mountain goat, caribou, lynx, wolverine and grey wolf are the big draws in northern BC and you will quite possibly see some of these species on a number of the routes. Smaller fur-bearing animals such as coyote, beaver, otter, muskrat, fisher, marten, fox, mink, snowshoe hare, squirrel, marmot and porcupines are also common. In some areas there are bison, mule and white-tailed deer, Dall sheep and cougar.

Bald eagles are particularly plentiful, and golden-eagle sightings are not uncommon. Ospreys, loons and mergansers are other common fish-eating birds. There are numerous dabbling and diving ducks, including mallards, pintails and harlequins. Owls, hawks, grouse, ptarmigan, swans, gulls, dippers, kingfishers, jays, flickers, ravens, snipe, flycatchers, redpoll, sparrows, warblers, siskin and chickadees are other commonly sighted birds. There are also many shorebirds to be seen, particularly in the marine environment.

You can also see seals a long way up the coastal rivers, and maybe a sea lion or even a humpback whale if you paddle from the mouth of the Stikine River to Wrangell. I have seen all these critters on the routes in this guidebook at some point, particularly bears, moose, dabbling and diving ducks, raptors and other birds.

Each trip has been assigned a comparative rating based on the potential for seeing the common fauna of the region:

✳ **Low:** Chances of seeing large mammals aren't good.

✳✳ **Average:** you will likely see some of the large and small mammals and bird species indigenous to the area.

✳✳✳ **High:** Chances are good you will see a variety of large and small mammals and numerous bird species.

✳✳✳✳ **Very High:** You have the best chance of observing a large number and variety of mammals and bird species.

Sources for further reading on the animals and birds of particular regions are listed in the chapters where particularly relevant and in the References section.

Fishing

Each river's fishing potential is comparatively rated on the star system from poor to excellent. The ratings are subject to seasonal cycles and natural fluctuations in fish populations, so don't necessarily count on fish for supper! However, some rivers are better than others for some species. The most common species angled for in northern BC waters are Arctic grayling, salmon, northern pike, and lake, rainbow and bull trout (known locally as Dolly Varden trout). There a couple of rivers to try for steelhead and kokanee as well. For each river, the species of fish most commonly caught will be listed, and the rivers will be assigned a comparative rating based on the ease of catching whatever species are found in its waters. The best time and location to catch a particular species will often be suggested, and recommendations for tackle will be noted where applicable. Further sources for finding out how to fish for certain species are also provided in the chapters where relevant and when that information is not within the author's realm of expertise.

✻ Poor: Few species of fish and few fishing spots; luck and a lot of time fishing are involved, but you'll probably catch something if you try hard enough.

✻ ✻ ✻ Average: You are bound to catch bull trout along the river if you try, and you may also have some luck with other common species, perhaps grayling or northern pike.

✻ ✻ ✻ Good: This river is known for its good fishing for at least two species, and you can catch them at a number of different spots along the route.

✻ ✻ ✻ ✻ Excellent: This river is known for its good fishing for two or more species; fish can be caught at points all along the route; and at certain spots you will have a great time catching big fish.

Be aware of the regulations you must comply with: you will need a BC fishing licence – two if you plan to fish in both fresh and saltwater – as well as one for the NWT, Yukon or Alaska depending on your route. None of the coastal routes have any great shellfish harvesting opportunities of note, but it is possible at some spots. Be sure to do your research on the special regulations for salmon and steelhead fishing.

Debarb your hooks and practise good catch and release technique. Keep only what you can eat. Conserving our natural resources is everyone's responsibility. For more information on angling regulations and licences, see the Directory of Services and Organizations for contact information for the BC Ministry of Environment's Fish & Wildlife Branch. Their website has all the information you will likely need.

Camping, Hiking and Other Activities

Camping is one of the great pleasures of a canoe trip. The river routes are rated on the availability and quality of the camping along the way, as well as other activities. Some rivers offer great opportunities for hiking, horse trekking, swimming or hot springs bathing – even shopping! Trust me: if I know of something interesting or fun to do along the route, it will be mentioned. Again, camping, hiking and other activities are rated according to the following star system:

✻ Low: the route is about the river experience itself; camping, wildlife viewing and fishing may be good or not, but there are few opportunities for other activities.

✻ ✻ Average: The route has decent to good camping and a couple of other activities to enjoy.

✻ ✻ ✻ Good: The camping is good and generally plentiful; there are a number of good hikes and perhaps some opportunities for horse trekking and/or swimming/hot springs bathing.

✻ ✻ ✻ ✻ Excellent: The camping is usually very good and generally plentiful; there are excellent opportunities for hiking, horse trekking and/or swimming/hot springs bathing.

Special Equipment Recommendations: What Else To Bring

Special equipment recommendations such as the type of canoe you will want to paddle and things you will want to bring in addition to the regular paddling, camping and safety equipment required on any river trip will be made for each route when relevant. For example, for rivers like the Tuchodi and the Jennings (covered in volume one) that are shallow and rocky, you should have a canoe made of plastic material such as Royalex; for northeastern BC rivers, you should seriously consider a hooded bug shirt with a face net; for some rivers, like the Turnagain, great whitewater fun can be had by advanced and exceptional paddlers who take along a spray cover for their canoe; and for hiking and long, open-water crossings you should bring a compass and know how to use it.

THE TRIP NOTES:
YOUR DETAILED GUIDE TO FEATURES ON THE ROUTE

In the Trip Notes you will find a list of map coordinates and descriptions for the route's notable features. Most of the coordinates are based on the Grid Reference System derived from the Universal Transverse Mercator (UTM) Grid marked on Canada's National Topographic System (NTS) maps. However, for trips that end in Alaska, you need United States Geological Survey (USGS) topo maps, and in this case I use latitude and longitude coordinates for features. I do this because the grid system drawn (sometimes not at all and sometimes with more than one grid!) on the USGS 1:63 360-scale topos is more cumbersome to use than on the NTS maps. Besides, you are going to end up in a maritime environment, where you should use latitude and longitude.

Because I generally use the NTS 1:50 000-scale topos for canoe tripping in Canada (this is the best scale for river running, as it shows the finest level of detail) and because these topos are most efficiently used with the Grid Reference System (GRS), I provide only six-digit coordinates for the features listed in the Trip Notes. The GRS coordinates are a shorthand version of UTM. This is the system the military uses and is more than accurate enough to locate features for canoe trippers on 1:50 000-scale topos.

A GRS coordinate is a simplification and conglomeration of a full UTM coordinate, which is made up of the easting point (think longitude) and northing point (think latitude) required to locate a spot on the UTM grid. A full UTM coordinate, therefore, consists of two long strings of numbers, one indicating the easting point, the other the northing point. That's a lot of numbers and they are not all required for finding a feature on a river when using topo maps, so I use the derivative GRS coordinate form suggested on the topo maps themselves. My Trip Notes coordinates are based on the GRS and consist of one set of six digits. The first three digits represent the easting point and the last three numbers represent the northing point. The third digit in both cases represents the closest tenth of a kilometre, or 100 m.

For example, according to the Trip Notes a rapid occurs at coordinate 045329. This means the rapid is 500 m east of grid line 04 and 900 m north of grid line 32. To find this rapid on the 1:50 000 map, you would put your pointer finger on the east grid line 04 (easting numbers run horizontally on your map) and go halfway over to the next grid line (05); then put your other pointer finger on the north grid line 32 (northing numbers run vertically) and move your finger toward grid line 33 until you have covered nine-tenths of the square between lines 32 and 33. Where your fingers meet is the approximate location of the rapid as described in the Trip Notes.

This is not meant to be a lesson in using NTS maps or the UTM system; it just an explanation of the derivative coordinates used in the guidebook notes. For a simple and practical example of using the GRS, look at the side of any 1:50 000-scale map. You will find a diagram of how to determine a GRS coordinate on an NTS map. There are many sites on the Internet you can consult for more information on UTM and using the GRS.

In the Trip Notes, the numbers and letters identifying the map being referenced are found in the far left column. Then a six-digit coordinate from that map is given in the Grid Reference column, indicating a feature of the river that is of importance or interest. A brief description of the feature is given in the far right-hand column. If the feature noted is a rapid, a difficulty classification is provided as well as a brief description of it and the location of a portage if any. Where relevant, an approximation of the length of the rapids and/or portage is given in metres. For example:

MAP NO.	GRID REF.	FEATURE	DESCRIPTION
74 K/15	042589	Rapid	There is a straightforward **Class 3** chute at the top of the rapid that runs into a **Class 2** rock garden. A good **portage trail (200 m) on RL** starts at the opening in the willows just above the head of the rapid.

Note that the GRS coordinates given are relevant only to the number and letter of the topo map they lie on; in the example above, the feature the coordinate locates is on the 1:50 000-scale map 74 K/15 only; the same coordinate, 042589, would locate something else entirely on some other topo. The topo map identifier is listed in the far left column each time a new map is introduced.

I use a number of standard abbreviations in describing river features and their locations: RL means river left, your left as you head downstream; RC means river centre, the middle of the river; and RR means river right, your right as you head downstream. Other common terms used include chute, hole, wave train, rock garden, cross-currents, sweeper etc. If you are not familiar with these terms, ask your paddling mentor what they mean. However, I believe the meanings will become evident as you become familiar with the guidebook and gain some experience using it on the river.

Do not expect the notes on the rapids and their classifications to help you run harder rapids than you would attempt normally. This is not their purpose. They are meant to provide you with information about what is around the next corner, assist you in assessing the difficulty of the rapids, and in particular cases outline some of the options available to you. If you read the Trip Notes carefully in advance, you will have a much better idea of the difficulty of the river trip, and I highly recommend you do this before committing to the route.

Hazards, campsites, natural attractions, side trips, trailheads and fishing holes are also briefly described and located using coordinates. Not every feature on the river is pinpointed, however. The river is not a static entity and will change from year to year. You must always be on the lookout for hazards. It is your responsibility to take care of yourself. An attempt has been made to cover most features of interest, except in the case of historic sites where it would not be possible to pinpoint and describe them all. However, the references I have supplied will help you find this kind of information.

Before your trip, I suggest you transfer the information from the Trip Notes to your 1:50 000-scale NTS maps (and in the case of trips ending in Alaska the USGS 1:63 360-scale topos) Then you'll have as much information as possible at your fingertips to help you navigate the river. Since many of the rapids and falls are not marked on the topo maps, you will want to at least mark in the difficult rapids and their associated mandatory or suggested portages. Likely you will want to plan your paddling days around good campsites, so mark those in too. If nothing else, I highly recommend marking sources of emergency help if there are any.

If you want to use your GPS with the GRS coordinates I give in the Trip Notes, set your position format to MGRS (Military Grid Reference System) and make sure your map datum setting is correct for the map you are using, e.g., NAD 27 Canada for the 1:50 000-scale maps for the Spatsizi River trip. For Alaska coordinates, change your position format unit setting to latitude and longitude in degrees, minutes and seconds in the same format I use. Be sure to also change your datum setting to what your USGS map indicates. Note that with any system there are sometimes anomalies and errors, and the topos are often old. If there is some question about the location of a feature, I have defaulted to the maps and the GRS coordinates rather than a GPS reading. That way we will all be on the same page. I have pointed out instances where there appears to be something weird going on. Not all cases will be noted, however.

THE RIVER ROUTES AT A GLANCE: A COMPARATIVE CHART

The chart on the next page summarizes some of the information provided in this guidebook. Its purpose is to allow you to quickly survey and compare the seven routes, made up of ten different rivers, for canoe trips that may be suitable to your pocketbook, skill level, time and interests.

The following abbreviations are used in the chart:

Length   the approximate length of the route in kilometres

Logistics   the standard or required mode of transport to the put ins and from the take-outs; options include:

> DI – drive in
>
> DO – drive out
>
> FI – fly in
>
> FO – fly out
>
> Various (jet boat, ferry, combination of driving, flying, ferry etc.)

When   the best months to paddle the route

Difficulty   the star rating indicating the difficulty of the route

Character   the route's primary type of ecological environment:

> BMT – Boreal Mountain
>
> TAP – Taiga Plain
>
> COA – Coastal
>
> TRA – Transitional

History   the star rating indicating the prehistoric and historic importance of the route

Solitude   the star rating indicating the potential level of solitude on the trip

Wildlife   the star rating indicating wildlife-viewing potential

Fishing   the star rating indicating fishing potential

Other   the star rating indicating the quality and quantity of camping, and the quality and variety of other non-paddling activities on the route

Table 2: The River Routes at a Glance

River Route	Length	Logistics	When	Difficulty	Character	History	Solitude	Wildlife	Fishing	Other
Spatsizi River (and Upper Stikine)	97 km (249 km)	DI/FO (DI/DO)	Mid-July to Sept.	* ½ (** ½)	BMT	** ½	**	*** **	** (** ½)	*** ** (* ** ½)
Upper Stikine River	284 km	FI/DO	Mid-July to Sept.	** ½	BMT	** ½	**	**	** ½	*** ½
Lower Stikine River	247 km	Various	Mid-May to Oct.	**	BMT, TRA and COA	****	*	* ½	**	** ½
Tatshenshini and Alsek rivers	214 km	DI/FO	Mid-Aug. to Sept.	** **	BMT, TRA and COA	** *	** ½	**	**	** ½
Turnagain River (and Kechika)	215 km (310 km)	FI/Various (Various/DO)	Late July to Sept.	*** (** ½)	BMT	**	** (**)	** (* *)	*** ½ (** ½)	*** (**)
Toad and Liard rivers	308 km	DI/DO Various	Aug. and Sept.	** **, ½	BMT and TAP	**, ***	**, **	**	**	** ½, **
Tuchodi and Muskwa rivers	239 km	FI/DO Various	Mid-July to Sept.	***, ½	BMT and TAP	**	**	**	**, *	**, ½

CHAPTER ONE:

SPATSIZI RIVER

The Spatsizi is the river to paddle to if you want to see red goats and do multi-day hikes on the famous Spatsizi Plateau. Situated in a region known as BC's Serengeti of the North, the plateau is home to many species of large mammals and hosts great alpine hiking. The river, the plateau and the provincial parks protecting the region all bear the same name: Spatsizi is derived from the Tahltan words for red goat and refers to the "Land of the Red Goats." On your canoe trip you paddle by the base of Red Goat Mountain. Its ridges are covered in iron oxide and this is where the local mountain goats roll in the dust that stains their coats red. You can also hike up the shoulder of this landmark to the alpine to look more closely for these creatures if you choose.

The Spatsizi is a short little float with no portages after reaching the river. Once you finish the long carry to put in you can make many other treks, or not. You can also fly in to the Spatsizi, saving your legs for the great multi-day hiking. Reaching the alpine is not difficult from the river. There are numerous trails that make getting up above treeline to the tundra ridges a lot less work.

Many canoeists choose to paddle the Spatsizi to access the Stikine River and thus avoid some of the more difficult rapids and portages of the Upper Stikine route while not sacrificing too much alpine hiking potential or peak scenery. The Spatsizi River clips along at its beginning with some fun rapids in the first few kilometres to get your heart rate up. The middle of the run is slower, with moose meadows to enjoy. Before flowing into the Stikine the river picks up again and you are at historic Hyland Post.

A combination of enjoyable paddling, hiking and great wildlife viewing make this river trip one of the most popular and accessible in northern BC. Don't let the ghost of a railway and long portage down to the river scare you away, though you may shiver at the spectres of development that continue to haunt this spectacular area.

Length: The drive-in and fly-out trip described in detail in the Trip Notes is approximately 97 km long. This figure indicates paddling kilometres only. It does not include the 5-km portage from the railway grade to the put-in at the confluence of Didene Creek and the Spatsizi, the most common way to access the river. The Spatsizi is a short tributary of the Stikine River, and though one can take out by

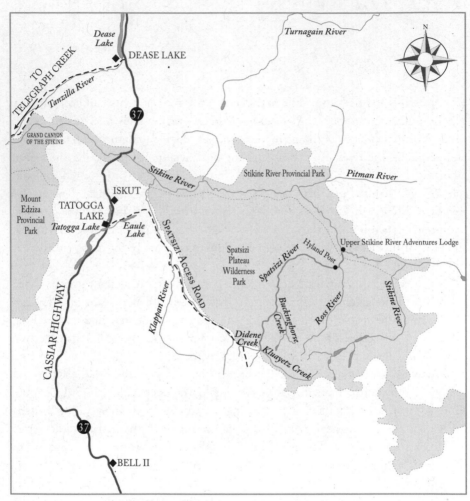

Spatsizi River

flying out from the confluence of the Spatsizi and Stikine rivers, many canoeists choose to carry on down the Stikine to where there is road access, making for a drive-in and drive-out trip.

You drive and portage to the most common put-in for the Spatsizi using the abandoned BC Rail grade and the Spatsizi River Access Trail (the 5-km portage trail from the railway grade to the river, maintained by BC Parks). The BC Rail grade is reached by driving the Cassiar Highway (Hwy. 37) to the north end of Tatogga Lake, then turning east onto the Ealue Lake Road. This road is subject to closure; there have been washouts and blockades in the past. Contact the Iskut First Nation in Iskut or the BC Parks Stikine Area office in Dease Lake to be sure you will have access. See the Directory of Services for contact information.

To run just the Spatsizi River, you normally fly out from the confluence of the Spatsizi and the Stikine via floatplane. However, if you have a folding or inflatable craft, you may be able to charter a wheel plane to pick you up at Hyland Post (missing the last 10 km of the river trip). You will need to arrange for permission from the owners, the Collingwood brothers of Spatsizi Wilderness Vacations, before your pilot will be willing to land there to pick you up. I have to say, a flight over the Spatsizi Plateau is something you will never forget. The land is so green and gentle, and the creeks and rivers and clumps of darker green trees that decorate it look like they have been drawn on, they contrast so greatly. From above, the scenery is unreal. It's got to be an IMAX production!

If you don't wish to drive and portage to run the Spatsizi, you may be able to fly to a very small lake known locally as Canoe Lake (noted as Airplane Lake in the BC Parks literature) and do a short portage into the Spatsizi. Or you can fly to the river itself, where a floatplane can land near Red Goat Mountain. Canoe Lake is located about 3.5 km downstream from where Buckinghorse Creek flows into the Spatsizi. The river is only a short carry from the lakeshore (less than 500 m from any spot on the western or northern shore of the lake). Flying to Canoe Lake to put in takes about 30 km off your trip; most people would carry on down the Stikine River to drive out at the price. Pilots may not want to land there, either, because the lake is so small. Check with the floatplane charter services first if you are considering this put-in option.

The other fly-in option is to a spot on the river near Red Goat Mountain. From what I've been told, you will need to fly from Smithers in this scenario. Apparently you must charter a floatplane larger than a Beaver to land on the river here, but do your research to be sure. This option shortens your river trip by about 40 km, which may be an attractive option only for those wanting to hike rather than paddle and those who want to avoid all rapids. This and the Canoe Lake option make for a trip with no rapids to navigate and lots of hiking opportunities. They are the best options for paddlers without the moving-water skills required to paddle the significant rapids of the Stikine River.

The whole Spatsizi route alone will only take about four or five days, including the time you need to do the 5-km portage to the put-in. You will only need three days maximum if you fly in to Canoe Lake or Red Goat Mountain to start your trip. The current is slow in the middle of the trip, but doing 25 km a day is not a stretch for most groups. You won't want to do this trip in such a short time, however. The big draw of the Spatsizi River is that you can easily get up to the alpine tundra of the plateau to hike around and look for wildlife. You can also do several multi-day hikes in the area. I am not really an avid hiker, but this is one river trip where even I would support the idea that paddlers should spend as much time travelling on land as they do on the river! To just paddle the river would be missing the real nature of the Spatsizi Plateau.

To lengthen the trip, paddlers often continue another 153 km on the Stikine to take out at the Cassiar Highway, where a bridge crosses the Stikine south of Dease Lake. The classic Spatsizi/Stikine trip is about 249 km long. You will want five more days to do the Stikine leg. Nine days is a good amount of time to do the whole Spatsizi/Stikine trip if you don't do any major hikes. See the Upper Stikine River chapter for more information on extending your Spatsizi trip this way.

Red Goat Mountain to Stikine confluence*	59 km
Canoe Lake to Stikine confluence*	66 km
Access Trail to Stikine confluence*	97 km
Red Goat Mountain to the Hwy. 37 Bridge via the Stikine**	211 km
Canoe Lake to the Hwy. 37 Bridge via the Stikine**	218 km
Access Trail to the Hwy. 37 Bridge via the Stikine**	249 km

* These trips are described in detail in the Trip Notes section of this chapter.
** The Stikine leg of this route is described in detail in the Trip Notes section of the Upper Stikine River chapter.

Topographic Maps: NTS 1:50 000- and 1:250 000-scale topo maps are recommended for the Spatsizi trip, especially if you plan on doing any serious hiking – particularly the multi-day routes. The 1:250 000-scale will do, but the coordinates listed in the Trip Notes will not be as user-friendly. If this is one of your first extended river trips and you are not familiar with using the Grid Reference System (GRS) on the 1:50 000s, you should take the opportunity to practise on this route. As well, using this larger scale of map, you can also learn more about the nature of rivers and how their features are represented on topos. I say why not take both scales along? The 1:250 000-scale topos will help you identify the plateau's larger features, which really helps when you are hiking. This is also a good trip for paddlers to practise using a GPS in conjunction with topos. Make sure you set your GPS map datum to NAD 27 Canada for use with the 1:50 000 topos, and set the position format to MGRS (Military Grid Reference System).

See the discussion on topographic maps, the UTM and Grid Reference systems and use of a GPS in the How To Use this Guidebook chapter.

The 1:50 000-scale topos you will need for the Spatsizi River trip are 104 H/2 (only necessary if you want your map set to cover the entire Spatsizi River Access Trail), 104 H/7 (the map with the actual put-in on it), 104 H/9 and 104 H/10 (the map with the Stikine confluence on it). If you fly to Canoe Lake or to the river near Red Goat Mountain you will need 104 H/7, 104 H/9 and 104 H/10. See the Upper Stikine chapter Trip Notes to figure out which maps you will need if you plan to continue down to the Cassiar Highway bridge take-out. The 1:250 000-scale map you need for the Spatsizi River trip is 104 H.

I suggest you purchase or print your topo maps in advance. Not only will you be able to plan your paddling days, but by using the coordinates in the Trip Notes you can mark in sources of emergency help, potential campsites, trailheads for hikes and other sites of interest so that you'll have the information at hand when navigating the river.

Note that the list of maps does not include the 1:50 000-scale maps you will need for doing extended hiking trips. To figure out what you need, look at the Spatsizi Plateau Wilderness Provincial Park map discussed below for the standard hiking routes and then consult the index of NTS topographic maps for BC online at www.maptown.com/canadiantopographical/bcntsindex.html.

BC Parks publishes a map called Spatsizi Plateau Wilderness Provincial Park (a 1:280 000-scale sketch without contour lines) that will give you a good overview of the park and the hiking/horse trails you could access from the river. It is not a substitute for the topo maps but it is useful as a planning guide, especially for the multi-day hikes (it shows campsites on the trails). The map can be found online at www.env.gov.bc.ca/bcparks/explore/parkpgs/spatsizi/spatsizi.pdf.

Getting There and Away: To run just the Spatsizi you can access the river either by driving or flying, but you must fly out. The Upper Spatsizi is road accessible via the abandoned BC Rail grade, so this is usually a drive-in and fly-out trip. However, some parties fly in as well. Many parties carry on to paddle the latter part of the Upper Stikine River route down to the bridge where the Cassiar Highway (Hwy. 37) crosses the Stikine, a classic drive-in and drive-out trip.

To reach the Spatsizi River Access Trail (the 5-km portage trail to the put-in), drive the Cassiar Highway to the north end of Tatogga Lake, where there is a sign and a turnoff to head east on Ealue Lake Road. Drive about 22 km on this road, crossing the Klappan River, and then turn right to head south on the BC Rail grade. The grade, newly refurbished in 2008, basically follows the southwestern boundary of the Spatsizi Plateau Wilderness Provincial Park. Approaching the Spatsizi River Access Trail, you will see the park sign on the left indicating the trailhead, approximately 126 km from the intersection of the Cassiar Highway and the Ealue Lake Road. Count on about a three-hour drive for the shuttle one way. For this drive-in option, you will need to use either two vehicles minimum or an outfitting service. Note that you likely want four-wheel drive and that there are no vehicle rental options north of Smithers and Terrace. Finally, the BC Rail grade has been washed out and blockaded in the past, so you would do well to call the BC Parks office in Dease Lake or Smithers or the Iskut First Nation's office in Iskut ahead of time to make sure it is open for public travel before making your final shuttle plans.

The most time-efficient way to do the shuttle if you are doing a drive-in and fly-out trip is to contract a driver, or a driver and vehicle, from one of the canoe outfitters or air services in the Tatogga Lake/Iskut/Dease Lake area. They will drop you off at the put-in and you can fly from the Spatsizi and Stikine confluence or Upper Stikine River Adventures' lodge right back to your vehicles. You will want to charter a floatplane from Tatogga Lake or Dease Lake in this case. Both are located on the Cassiar Highway (km 390.2 and km 488.3 respectively). Be sure to ask your pilot where he or she would prefer to pick you up: from a gravel bar right at the edge of the Stikine's flow or at the lodge just downstream on the Stikine. You should get permission to fly out from Upper Stikine River Adventures' lodge. Contact information for outfitters offering shuttle services, air charter companies and Upper Stikine River Adventures is listed in the Directory of Services and Organizations.

For some, chartering a floatplane to Canoe Lake (called Airplane Lake in BC Parks literature) or to a stretch of the Spatsizi near Red Goat Mountain and then flying out from the Spatsizi and Stikine confluence or at the Upper Stikine River Adventures lodge may be the best options. These alternatives are best for those parties with very little time, those wanting to hike more than paddle and/or those who want to avoid any rapids.

To fly in to Canoe Lake you will likely want to use an air service in the Tatogga Lake/Iskut/Dease lake area. Note that some pilots may not want to land at Canoe Lake because it is so small. From what I understand, you will need to charter a larger floatplane out of Smithers to put in on the river near Red Goat Mountain. Check with the charter services first if you are considering either of these put-in options.

For the fly-in and fly-out Spatsizi trip the logistics are simple. Fly to one of the two possible put-ins and then fly out from the confluence of the Spatsizi and the Stikine or from Upper Stikine River Adventures' lodge. You will end up right back at your vehicle(s) no matter what location you fly from.

If you wish to travel without vehicles or canoes, you can either charter a small aircraft or take a scheduled flight to Dease Lake. At the moment, Northern Thunderbird Air has flights to Dease Lake from Smithers on Mondays, Wednesdays and Fridays. However, as of 2008 there were no canoe or vehicle rentals available right in the community of Dease Lake. However, canoe rentals and shuttles can be arranged via the canoe outfitters in the Iskut area, Dease River Crossing and Telegraph Creek. A number of airlines have scheduled flights to Smithers, Terrace or

Whitehorse. You can rent vehicles in all three communities, but there are no canoe rentals in Terrace as far as I know. If you are coming from the south and you wanted to do a fly-in and fly-out trip with the least hassle, you could drive or fly to Dease Lake, Smithers or Whitehorse, rent canoes and fly out with the local floatplane service. No shuttle required, but this would be an expensive undertaking!

Parties skilled enough to paddle the Upper Stikine River from the Spatsizi–Stikine confluence may want to carry on down the Stikine to the bridge on the Cassiar Highway over the river, arranging for a pick up or vehicle shuttle ahead of time. If you want to do the classic drive-in and drive-out Spatsizi–Upper Stikine route, you can do the shuttle yourself or a have an outfitter shuttle your vehicle(s). You need to get your gear and canoes to the Spatsizi River Access Trail and then your vehicle(s) to the bridge over the Stikine south of Dease Lake (km 437.2 on the Cassiar Highway). It's about a 160-km shuttle drive one way from the head of the Spatsizi River Access Trail to the take-out at the bridge. I haven't heard any reports of vehicles being broken into at the trailhead or the parking area below the bridge to date. However, using an outfitter for this long shuttle will save you a lot of time. It may be even cheaper for you not to do the shuttle yourself, and you also avoid any consequences of having left a vehicle(s) unattended at the take-out. Consider having an outfitter drive to the bridge take-out and either leave your vehicle there for you shortly before you plan to arrive, or pick you up with it, or pick you up with their vehicle (and trailer if necessary) and take you back to yours. Finally, you can always hitchhike to complete your shuttle. A friendly local will likely stop and give you a ride. I've never had much luck with the RV tourists.

In conclusion, you have a lot of options for making the logistics of a Spatsizi River or Spatsizi–Stikine canoe trip work for you. You will likely come up with more than I have suggested. See the Directory of Services and Organizations for contact information for the services you will need to make your plan work.

You can set up camp at the head of the Spatsizi River Access Trail off the railway grade if you arrive too late in the day to make the 5-km carry to the river. There is also a free park campsite at the river put-in. See the Camping, Hiking and Other Activities section for more on these camping options. The gravel bars at the confluence of the Spatsizi and Stikine rivers make for great camping if you have to wait for your floatplane pick-up. You can also camp for free in the clearing at the bridge take-out on the Stikine.

When To Go: Mid-July to the end of September. The Spatsizi usually sees its freshet, or peak runoff, in June, sometimes as late as early July. You do not want to paddle the river at these high water levels unless you are very skilled moving-water canoeists. In a normal year you will also not be able to drive on the abandoned BC Rail grade before the end of June, as it will still be covered with snow or too sloppy. In the early summer there will also be lots of snow at higher elevations, limiting your hiking opportunities, and creeks will likely be running high, making crossings on foot dangerous.

Only parties of experienced moving-water paddlers not interested in long, multi-day hikes will want to paddle the Spatsizi in mid-July. Gravel bar camping sites will be fewer, and you will need to be more vigilant about wood hazards if the water is still up. The bonus of higher water is that the swift current will help you make good time on the route, leaving you more hours to relax, do day hikes and take in the sights. The wildflowers in the alpine and along the river will be coming out in full force. However, so will the insects! They really come out as the heat turns on in the long hours of daylight. On the other hand, frost is possible at night in any month in this area.

July daily highs in Dease Lake can reach 20°c; nights are cool, which brings down the mean daily temperature to 14°. You can expect the daily temperatures on the plateau to be closer to the average because of the elevation. You will likely have some sun, but July can also be rainy. Apparently July sees an average of 10–13 days with measurable precipitation, but annual rainfall totals are relatively low because the Spatsizi Plateau is in the rain shadow of the Coast and Skeena mountains. It doesn't usually pour for days on end as it does on the coast in this region, but I did have a relatively wet trip in the end of July 2002, with some rain almost every day for a week. I have also been on the plateau in other years in July and had mostly sunny weather.

On boreal river mountain rivers in northern BC, water levels usually drop come the end of July. August is normally a much lower-water month on this route and is the best time for less-experienced moving-water paddlers to run the Spatsizi. Normally, the gravel bars are more exposed in August, making for good camping sites. The insects start to die off with the cooler nights later in the month. The berries are out and fishing picks up as the river clears. The hiking will be good at this time of year as well. Life is generally as good as it gets on the river in this usually drier month.

You will likely have slightly lower flows in September. It will often be frosty in the mornings, and snow is definitely possible. You may also get cold, northern headwinds. On the other hand, you could get very warm sunny days throughout your journey. You will need to pack for any weather; expect the worst and enjoy what you get! The joys of a fall trip are the changing colours of the deciduous trees and shrubs in this region, and the later you do a Spatsizi trip the more wildlife you will see if you go hiking and the better the fishing will be. The bugs will also have really calmed down, making camping and hiking even more pleasant.

I love an autumn trip. But if you are not experienced fall canoe trippers, consider a late August/early September trip rather than at the end of the season so you don't have to deal with the more significant weather challenges while working on your outdoor living skills. The other drawback of a late-season trip down the Spatsizi is that the hunters will be out in full force. You may not see the wildlife you usually would along the river as a result. However, if you do some hiking side trips you may see more than earlier in the season.

The table below shows average monthly mean flows for May to September derived from archived data from two hydrometric stations no longer operating. Many federal water survey stations were decommissioned after 1994 due to cuts in the budget of the Environment Canada. You can see how much of a difference there is in water levels over the paddling season and why you want to avoid June's peak flows and a potential late spring runoff in July.

Average Monthly Mean Flows, m³/s

	Spatsizi near its mouth	Stikine below the Spatsizi
May	90	200
June	225	500
July	170	350
August	75	160
September	65	130

Source: Jennifer Voss, *Stikine River: A Guide to Paddling the Great River*, Rocky Mountain Books, 1998.

Since there are no longer any active water survey stations on the Spatsizi or the Upper Stikine or any other relevant waterways in the area, you can only determine general water levels on the Spatsizi at any given time by contacting local sources. Try calling the BC Parks office in Dease Lake or Bruce at BC–Yukon Air. See the Directory of Services and Organizations for contact information.

You can check how any given year's water levels are shaping up by monitoring the snowpack on the Environment Canada River Forecast & Snow Survey website, at www.env.gov.bc.ca/rfc. On the website is a snow survey (snowpack and water supply outlook) bulletin that is published in January and updated eight times per year. The publication includes data gathered from snow and hydrometric measuring stations, and the regional snowpack and water supply forecasts basically tell you whether water levels are expected to be lower or higher than normal in a region come the summer, as well as how much of the snow has melted and how fast. This is good general information, useful in deciding when to schedule your trip. If there is lots of snow on the plateau and it is not melting rapidly, you may want to delay your trip to August to avoid a late runoff. You could have high flows throughout July. However, I suggest that if you are less-experienced canoe trippers working on your moving-water skills, do not plan to go before August at all.

Finally, be aware that the Spatsizi and the Stikine both respond to rainfall. If it has been wet for some time in the spring and early summer the rivers will stay up longer. They can also rise again quickly from heavy rains any time of year.

Difficulty of the River: ✳ ½ The Spatsizi River route gets this difficulty rating mostly because the first 10 kilometres have a few rapids approaching Class 2 to navigate. The rapids are usually shallow with rocks to avoid and the river also braids, making for places where wood can gather and create hazards. For the entire length of the run, the major river hazards are sweepers and strainers, deadheads and partly submerged logs in the shallows. Wood collects midstream on the submerged gravel bars and at tight bends with strong current where the bank is eroding, making for dangerous logjams, sweepers and strainers. You must have the moving-water skills to be able to avoid rocks and wood hazards.

The Spatsizi is a small-volume river and not pushy at normal summer water levels. After the rapids at the beginning of the route there is only continuous moving water to deal with. There are no portages after the biggie at the start and there are no big lake crossings, making it a nice float. However, the route is relatively isolated and the water is cold.

If you do not take out at the confluence of the Spatsizi and Stikine and carry on down the Upper Stikine to the bridge on the Cassiar Highway, you are looking at a more difficult route by quite a margin. The Upper Stikine is rated at 2½ stars for difficulty; it is a much larger-volume river and has more rapids and some canyons that must be paddled. There are portages so you can avoid running the larger rapids, except one. There is no trail for the long Jewel Rapids, which can rate Class 2+ at some water levels. At lower water levels, canoeists can likely do some combination of paddling, lining and wading to avoid running the whole rapid; a bushwhack portage would be strenuous. See the Upper Stikine River chapter difficulty section and Trip Notes for further information on the difficulty of the stretch of the Stikine from the Spatsizi confluence to the Cassiar Highway bridge take-out.

The Spatsizi route is a good trip for paddlers that already have some remote-river tripping and moving-water skills and experience, particularly if they are interested in combining paddling with hiking in the wilds of BC's north country. This is not a difficult trip compared to many in the two volumes of *Northern British Columbia Canoe Trips* given that you just don't go when the river is high. It's a great solo trip for those inclined to try that or those who enjoy a solitary experience. Carrying on down the Stikine is an undertaking that should not be taken lightly and paddlers must have solid moving-water and tripping skills. Novices should not consider running the Stikine leg unless they will be paddling in a party with advanced or exceptional moving-water paddlers.

The gradient of the Spatsizi is 1.2 m/km and the beginning few kilometres and the last 20 km of the river account for much of the elevation drop. The gradient of the Spatsizi is similar to that of the Gataga/Kechika route (covered in volume one), but the rapids on that route are more challenging.

Character of the River and Region: The small Spatsizi winds north from its head-waters in the Skeena Mountains, turning east to cut through the Spatsizi Plateau and finally making a short run north again to join with the Upper Stikine River. The Spatsizi Headwaters and Spatsizi Plateau Wilderness provincial parks spread across the Skeena Mountains and the Spatsizi Plateau. The Eaglenest Range of the Skeena Mountains dominates the northwest of the area and the range's highest peak, Mount Will (part of a large massif) at 2500 m ASL, towers above Gladys Lake.

Ecologically speaking, this canoe route lies in the Northern Boreal Mountains ecoprovince, and the length of the Spatsizi flows through the Boreal Mountains and Plateaus ecoregion. The huge Stikine Plateau (of which the Spatsizi Plateau is a part) is made up of open, gently rolling plateaus and highlands transitional to the rugged terrain of the Skeena Mountains and the Cassiar Ranges. This vast upland stretches from the headwaters of the Finlay–Stikine divide almost 500 km northwest to the headwaters of the Taku River and Atlin Lake. Elevation ranges from 1600–2000 m ASL, extending in a broad curve broken by wide U-shaped valleys. The area is mantled with glacial drift and underlain largely by sedimentary and volcanic rocks.

Boreal forest covers the valley bottom of the Stikine River and those of its principal tributaries, such as the Spatsizi and Klappan rivers. Frequent fire history has created a mosaic of white spruce, lodgepole pine and aspen-dominated forests in a variety of seral age classes and vast areas of deciduous shrubland. Extensive wetland habitats, fens, marshes, swamps and bogs are also common along the valley bottoms. Subalpine fir and scrub birch and willow dominate in the subalpine elevations, and the alpine plateaus are characterized by low scrub deciduous and heath vegetation, grassy meadows and "lichen-grasslands."

The Spatsizi Plateau has a northern interior climate similar to that in the subarctic. The temperature in the summer can reach 35°C, with the same location experiencing –50° in the winter. Annual precipitation is low, ranging from 350–650 mm on average, and relatively evenly distributed throughout the year. Prevailing westerly winds bring coastal air to the region, but it has generally lost most of its moisture by the time it reaches the plateau. Summertime surface heating produces convective showers. Cold air ponding in subalpine valleys is a common occurrence.

On the Spatsizi canoe route you pass through some diverse landscapes and a couple of different bioclimatic zones. The river starts as a small-volume stream, running fast through shallow, braided channels. The riverbed is gravel and silt. The minor rapids in the first 10 km have small and large rocks to avoid. The water of the Spatsizi can be either murky grey or an aquamarine colour, depending on whether the river is still clearing from the freshet or from heavy rains. Silt from feeder creeks running at high flows causes the murkiness, while glacial flour makes for the milky-green colour when the river clears. The forest in the upper valley is typical of the Spruce-Willow-Birch bioclimatic zone, and the mountaintops are alpine tundra.

After Buckinghorse Creek joins the Spatsizi from the east to downstream to where Kliweguh Creek flows in from the west, the river constantly grows larger and the valley opens up. This section of river offers some of the most scenic mountain views and hosts great wildlife-sighting potential. Once you reach Red Goat Mountain you have dropped into the White-and-Black-Spruce bioclimatic zone.

From Kliweguh Creek to its confluence with the Stikine River, the Spatsizi flows through a wide valley of lodgepole pine flats and semi-open grasslands. The banks steepen and the river flows faster. There is some braiding after the Kliweguh Creek confluence to Hyland Post, then after a fast stretch the Spatsizi spits its flow into a wonderfully large and open area of gravel bars dotted with shrubs and wildflowers. Here its distinct waters run side by side for a ways with the normally clear blue waters of the Upper Stikine.

For more information on the ecology and natural history of the area, consult The Ecoregions of British Columbia website: www.env.gov.bc.ca/ecology/ecoregions/province.html. Environment Canada's Ecological Framework document, at http://atlas.nrcan.gc.ca/site/english/maps/environment/ecology/framework/1, provides more detail about BC's ecological classifications. A good website for ecological information specific to the Spatsizi is at www.spacesfornature.org/greatspaces/spatsizi.html.

An excellent book to consult for general information on BC's natural history is *British Columbia: A Natural History*, by Cannings and Cannings. Jennifer Voss's guidebook *Stikine River: A Guide to Paddling the Great River* is also a good source of information on the Spatsizi and Stikine rivers' natural history. There is also an article by Patrick Mahaffey about the classic Spatsizi–Stikine canoe trip in *Paddle Quest: Canada's Best Canoe Routes*.

Local History: ✳ ✳ ½ Much of the Spatsizi Plateau lies in the hunting grounds of the Tahltan and Iskut First Nations and is an important area for these people. The region has a history of big-game hunting and conservation. Though management of the area's ecosystem is taking place as a result of the creation of the provincial parks and associated protected areas, it is under siege all around from natural resource extraction threats.

The Spatsizi Plateau is called "Land of the Red Goat." Spatsizi is an anglicized name said to come from two Tahltan words meaning "red goat." Mountain goats have a habit of rolling in dust, and the iron-oxide-coloured dust found on Red Goat Mountain on the Spatsizi River makes their normally white coats turn red.

The Tahltan are part of the Dene-na or Na-Dene (Athapaskan-speaking people). According to written sources they moved onto the Spatsizi Plateau some 2,000 years ago, and later centralized in an apparently unpopulated area of the Lower Stikine watershed some 300 years ago. This migration precipitated close trading relationships and subsequent cultural ties to the Tlingit along the coast. By the beginning of the 20th century, the Spatsizi Plateau also became home to a group of Sekani and Gitxsan descent, originally from Bear Lake to the south and east, that eventually joined with some local Tahltan to become the Iskut First Nation, part of the Tahltan Central Council.

The Iskut First Nation has an interesting history and it is intimately related to the Spatsizi Plateau and Stikine River watershed. Their ancestors were likely the people Black met on his 1824 explorations of the Finlay River headwaters in search of a route to the Stikine. In his journals Black describes meeting with a group of Sekani, who actually accompanied him to the Chuckachida confluence, and by travelling with them he also met the Thloadennis, a clan of Tahltan. This clan eventually moved farther west, closer to their cousins; and the Sekani and Gitxsan "Bear Lakers" (a few families from the villages of Kuldo and Kispiox) moved into Groundhog Plateau country, the grassy plateau region between the Upper Stikine and Skeena rivers vacated by the Tahltan.

Sometime after 1890 when the HBC closed Fort Connelly (established in 1826) on Bear Lake, the Bear Lakers began to headquarter on the banks of the Upper Stikine at the village of Caribou Hide, which got its name from the caribou hides they used for clothing and tents. They sporadically traded at Telegraph Creek (approximately 250 km west), but mostly did their commerce at Fort Ware in the Rocky Mountain Trench, the nearest supply centre about 130 km to the east. After a flu epidemic in the 1920s they relocated a short way east to Metsantan Lake, along with a few more families from Bear Lake.

The Spatsizi Plateau was seldom visited by outsiders after the few initial explorers, fur traders, surveyors and gold seekers passed through until sometime after the flu epidemic. It is thought that the Hyland brothers opened the first trading post, still called Hyland Post and located up the river left bank of the Spatsizi near its confluence with the Stikine. By 1929 they were trading for furs with the First Nations people trapping in the area. According to Tommy Walker, a big-game outfitter to later operate out of Hyland Post, a competitor soon set up shop near the Hylands but there wasn't enough trade for two outfits so both businesses folded. Another account says there was a "silver frost" and ice coated the grasslands in the area causing the death of many horses and the end of the Hyland brothers' enterprise.

The buildings at Hyland were being taken back by the land when Walker came through in 1948, but the area around it was still being trapped by a family of Bear Lakers/Caribou Hiders from Metsantan Lake. The post area had been a seasonal camp of the people from Caribou Hide, and likely before them the group of Tahltan who had moved farther west. Confluences have always been important gathering places for First Nations in northern BC, though neither the Tahltan of the west nor the Bear Lakers normally used canoes for long journeys. They preferred to walk, though rafts were used for river and short lake crossings. Occasionally they would build spruce bark canoes for longer water journeys.

On the Walkers' 1948 overland trip to set up their Cold Fish Lake camp, they met the band at Metsantan Lake and there were only 39 remaining members. Metsantan Lake was fished out (ironically, Metsantan meaning "full belly" in Sekani) and game was scarce. The people were in dire straits. Walker reports in his book *Spatsizi* that the Indian Agent wanted the band to move to Telegraph Creek; they wanted to remain free to live their semi-nomadic subsistence lifestyle, the reason they had moved from Bear Lake to the Upper Stikine watershed in the first place.

After Tommy and Marion Walker set up their hunting camp at Cold Fish Lake on the Spatsizi Plateau, some of the people from Metsantan Lake worked for them – at Cold Fish Lake during the guiding season and at Hyland Post during the winter to look after the horses. A number moved to Telegraph Creek in 1949, as did Tahltan families from the Klappan and Sheslay river and Dease Lake area bands that had been decimated by disease.

Eventually, in the early 1950s, still dogged by disease and economic hardship, the majority of the original Bear Lake families settled across the Stikine River from Telegraph Creek. This location, so close to the main Tahltan headquarters, was not ideal. A decade later most families moved into the Eddontenajon and Kluachon lakes area, the headwaters of the Iskut River at the head of the Iskut River Valley. The present-day village of Iskut is near Kluachon and the lake is sometimes referred to as Iskut or Skoot Lake. It gets its name from Klue Cho, which means "big fish" in Tahltan. Kluachon Lake drains into Eddontenajon Lake and this name has been translated as "Place where the little boy drowned."

Prior to the new settlement, a small Catholic mission existed at Kluachon Lake, with priests travelling the Telegraph Trail from Telegraph Creek to hold services when the few Tahltan families in the area gathered there as part of their seasonal rounds. One priest, Father Doetzel, helped the Bear Lake/Caribou Hide/Metsantan Lake families relocate from their community across the river from Telegraph Creek to their new home by the Kluachon Lake mission (called Eddontenajon Village – I know, it is all very confusing). A few families of Tahltan settled permanently there as well.

According to Walker, the fact that some of the Bear Lakers had worked on the construction of the Stewart-Cassiar Highway (Hwy. 37) from the Stikine River to the old mission prompted the community to leave the isolation of the "wrong" side of the Stikine at Telegraph Creek. By 1972 the bridge over the Stikine was complete and the Cassiar Highway provided much easier access to and from traditional Tahltan country. There was an increase in the population in the Telegraph Creek and Iskut areas in the 1970s as homesteaders came from southern BC and the US. The village near the mission site was now near the highway, and a new village site, called Iskut, ended up being on the east side of the Cassiar Highway. Ironically, the descendants of the Bear Lakers living at Iskut were now the least-isolated group of the Tahltan Council.

In the 1990s local people in the region became more directly involved with mining in their traditional territories by providing services such as road construction and maintenance and camp catering. Now there are several large mining exploration and development projects underway in the region. Both the Telegraph Creek and Iskut communities appear to be internally divided on the issue of development in their territories. A number of people question the rate and sustainability of development in the region and assert that the community and elders must participate in decision-making about such issues.

In 2006, a group of Iskut First Nation elders formed the Klabona Keepers Elders Society. Their goal is to ensure the long-term sustainable stewardship of their territory, especially the Sacred Headwaters, the area of the Skeena Mountains that gives rise to the Nass, Stikine and Skeena rivers. The group, along with other supporters, hosted a large gathering in the Sacred Headwaters in August 2006 to discuss and consolidate efforts to protect the region. Joining the Iskut Nation elders were hereditary chiefs of the Haida, Gitxsan, Wet'suwet'en, Taku River Tlingit and Haisla Nations, as well as non-aboriginal allies, including Rivers without Borders. Since that time there has been a groundswell of support for the group's goals and for the Klabona Keepers and their many supporters in protecting the Sacred Headwaters from coalbed-methane mining. The coalition achieved at least a temporary victory as of December 2008, when the BC government declared a two-year moratorium on that activity in this extremely special place.

The major threats to the Spatsizi Plateau region and its people are numerous and include the following:

- BC Metals' Red Chris copper/gold mine and road project is located on the Todagin Plateau between Ealue and Kluea lakes, approximately 18 km southeast of the village of Iskut. Mine activity, especially frequent blasting, would threaten the Stone sheep populations on Todagin Mountain. The tailings impoundment would impact fish habitat and likely end a 55-year-old traditional Tahltan guided hunting enterprise. The project has received regulatory approvals, but BC Metals cannot operate without a viable source of power.
- Fortune Minerals' proposed Klappan open-pit coal project is just on the edge of the Spatsizi Plateau Wilderness Provincial Park, with the haul road to go from the headwaters of the Little and Big Klappan drainages of the Stikine through the headwaters of the Nass and Bell-Irving rivers.
- Shell Canada is exploring for coalbed methane and has drilled four test wells near the head of the Little Klappan and Spatsizi rivers. This type of industrial activity requires numerous access points and drill sites and the energy it would produce would contribute to climate change. This project would be especially harmful to water quality given its proximity to the Sacred Headwaters. (Source: Rivers without Borders, at www.riverswithoutborders. org/about-the-region/iskut-stikine)

The combined impacts of all of the projects (including a major power line and cargo road) currently proposed in the Stikine watershed would definitely affect the environment and local communities. Besides obvious issues of water quality and salmon habitat, the Klappan River Valley is a traditional hunting ground for the Telegraph Creek and Iskut people. The name Klappan comes from the Tahltan phrase "good food for animals here" – as in meadow or wide open valley.

For more information on the Sacred Headwaters and other Spatsizi/Stikine watershed conservation issues and campaigns, go to the following websites:

Klabona Keepers Elders Society, at www.sacredheadwaters.com;
Dogwood Initiative, at http://dogwoodinitiative.org/campaigns/sacred-headwaters;
Citizens Concerned about Coalbed Methane, at www.ekcbm.org;
First Nations Land Rights and Environmentalism in BC, at www.firstnations.de/mining.htm?05-3-tahltan.htm;
Rivers without Borders, at www.riverswithoutborders.org/about-the-region/iskut-stikine;
Friends of the Stikine, at www.panorama-map.com/STIKINE/stikine.html (case-sensitive URL); and
CPAWS BC, at www.cpawsbc.org.

The following websites also provide good information and opportunities to take action to protect the Stikine River region from harmful development:

www.skeenawatershed.com;
www.ecojustice.ca;
www.miningwatch.ca;
www.dogwoodinitiative.org;
www.spacesfornature.org/greatspaces/spatsizi.html; and
the Pembina Institute site at http://bc.pembina.org/mining.

Contact information for the Cassiar Watch Society, a locally based conservation organization active in the region, can be found in the Directory of Services and Organizations. Their point person suggests canoeists need to make their voice heard in the management committees for the Stikine and Spatsizi area provincial parks.

There is a long history of conservation in the region. On December 3, 1975, Spatsizi Plateau Wilderness Provincial Park was established, due to pressure from outfitters and conservationists. It is a large and significant park in Canada, at 696,160 ha. It was designated to conserve the area and encompass a large enough part of the ecosystem to maintain the system's ability to support large wildlife populations. The intent was also that the public could enjoy the outstanding scenery and varied terrain with hiking, photography and nature study as well as canoeing. Hunting is allowed in the park, but the Gladys Lake Ecological Reserve in the central part of the park, just south of Cold Fish Lake, has a hunting ban. The reserve was established in 1975 to study Stone sheep and mountain goats in undisturbed alpine and subalpine habitat. The only unregulated public access is by hiking trails. Besides hunting being banned in the reserve, camping, fishing, aircraft and fires are not permitted either.

Apparently one of the first things BC Parks did after the Spatsizi Plateau Wilderness Provincial Park was created was to burn down all the old buildings and cabins of the people who had been living off the land. The hunting lodges were excluded from this policy, however. Small wonder why some First Nations are leery of park status for their lands.

Spatsizi Headwaters Provincial Park, at 427 ha, is a postage-stamp-sized addition to the Spatsizi Plateau Wilderness Provincial Park. The park was designated in 2001 to protect the headwaters of the Spatsizi River and the upper elevation glacial lakes and alpine meadows around the headwaters. The management plan mainly focuses on protecting natural values, but also Tahltan cultural and harvesting sites as well as maintaining the hiking, camping and wildlife viewing values in this area of the Skeena Mountains. Quite noticeably, the Stikine headwaters, as well as the headwaters of other rivers born in the Sacred Headwaters area – the Nass and the Skeena – are not protected. Though they are located hardly a stone's throw from the Spatsizi's headwaters, they happen to sit in the area targeted for mining and fossil fuel projects. The government of BC has been involved in conserving significant parts of the Spatsizi Plateau by establishing parks and protected areas, but obviously the ecosystem is still at risk and there are many issues on the table.

For some on the river reading about the history of the Spatsizi River and Plateau try *Notes from the Century Before: A Journal from British Columbia*, by Edward Hoagland. He recounts the history of numerous places, interviews with old timers and his own travels in the area. Stories from the descendants of the "Bear Lakers" and the Tahltan at Iskut can be found in "*'Kuji K'at Dahdahwhesdetch' (Now I Told All of You): Stories Told at Iskut, British Columbia, by Iskut Tahltan Elders*, a self-published booklet edited by Thomas McIlwraith and funded by the Endangered Languages Fund. Tommy Walker's book *Spatsizi* is an account of his time as a big-game outfitter in the region and the fight for protected status for the Spatsizi Plateau. A recent book on the area, *In the Land of the Red Goat*, by Bob Henderson, is about Bob's four decades of wrangling, guiding and fishing in the rugged Spatsizi and Stikine country. He tells many stories about the region and its characters and describes his journeys on the horse trails that make for such good hiking.

Level of Solitude: ✳ ✳ This is one of the most popular river trips in northern BC, so you might see another canoeing party during prime paddling season from late July to the end of August. You will not feel overcrowded on the route, but you will probably see signs of human activity nearly every day and even when hiking, be it signs, cabins or aircraft overhead. This canoe trip lies in a park and the area sees more visitors than many other remote regions. That said, fewer than 1,000 people visit the Spatsizi Plateau Wilderness Provincial Park each year and that number includes all visitors, not only canoeists.

During the prime hunting season, from August 1 into September, you are very likely to encounter motorized boat traffic around the confluence of the Spatsizi and the Stikine. Thankfully, there is usually little traffic on the Spatsizi until late in the canoeing season, as the use of motorized boats is restricted upstream of Hyland Post until September 1.

Wildlife: ✱ ✱ ✱ The best time for wildlife viewing on the Spatsizi Plateau is said to be during September and October, when species are preparing for winter and moving to lower elevations. However, the Spatsizi River is a great trip for seeing large mammals even in the summer, especially if you throw a couple hikes in the alpine into your itinerary. Mountain goats, red or not, are certainly around. Other characteristic species of the Spatsizi Plateau are grizzly and black bear, caribou, Stone sheep, moose, wolf, coyote, lynx and wolverine. Smaller critters such as red fox, beaver, otter, marten, fisher, mink, porcupine, hoary marmot and snowshoe hare are common.

Of note, the Spatsizi Plateau provides habitat for a large population of woodland caribou. In summer the caribou appear to be organized into three herds, each associated with the Spatsizi, Upper Stikine or Finlay river valley. These herds share a common winter range along the low-elevation, forested slopes of the Stikine River. The lichen-rich boreal forest is the most critical feeding area for the caribou. Thin snowcover in the rain shadow of the Eaglenest Range make it one of the most important habitats for woodland caribou in BC.

We saw grizzlies and woodland caribou on the Upper Spatsizi in late July, as well as many moose around the confluence with the Stikine. Wolves are frequent visitors to the gravel bars of the Spatsizi. You can see their tracks in the silt, and parties may also be treated to an actual sighting of this elusive species. Frank Knaapen and Jay Neilson saw a group of three black wolves just across the river from them on their July 2008 trip.

Eagles, both bald and golden, can be found on the Spatsizi Plateau. Other potential raptor sightings include hawks, osprey, northern harrier, merlin, kestrel, gyrfalcon and peregrine falcon. A number of species of owls can be seen, including the great grey owl and great horned owl. Loons, Canada geese and many species of shorebirds and ducks can be seen on the river and shore. Waterfowl species include mallard, gadwall, blue-winged teal, canvasback, bufflehead and grebe. Ptarmigan and grouse lurk on the ground in the alpine and in the forest: willow, rock and white-tailed ptarmigan occur throughout the alpine tundra, while Franklin's grouse, ruffed grouse and blue grouse occur at lower elevations. There are at least 149 bird species found in the Spatsizi Plateau Wilderness Provincial Park alone, so I highly recommend you bring a field guide in order to identify the large number of birds you will likely see on your trip. A couple of guides are listed in the References section.

Fishing: ✱ ✱ It is possible to catch rainbow trout, bull trout (known locally as Dolly Varden trout) and Arctic grayling on a Spatsizi River trip. I've never heard of anyone getting skunked. Rainbow trout are found in the clear, cold headwaters creeks. Fishing for Arctic grayling and bull trout is usually fairly good at the mouths of clear creeks where there waters mix with the silty Spatsizi. Your chances of catching more fish are greater later in the summer when the river clears.

Camping, Hiking and Other Activities: ✳ ✳ ✳ ✳ You can camp at the trailhead of the BC Rail grade if you arrive too late in the day to make the carry to the put-in. Water can be obtained from the creeks the grade crosses or brought with you on the shuttle. There is a pit toilet located down a short path just left of where the portage trail starts, but no other infrastructure as of 2008. The better park campsite is at the end of the Spatsizi River Access Trail, 5 km down by the river put-in. There is a pit toilet, fire ring, bear-proof food cache (a big metal cabinet that can hold four large canoeing barrels) and a creel survey and visitor registration box. Do use the facilities; the campsite sees more use than any other and you will leave less of an impact on the site. Also, the site is user-maintained, so pack out what you pack in.

Once on the river most groups will choose to camp on gravel bars. There are some really nice spots with big mountain scenery. Only a couple of stretches on the route lack good camping sites and they are described in the Trip Notes. Most of the gravel bar sites will be pristine, the spring floods having washed them clean. Do not rely on this, however, and no trace your campsite as much as possible. I'm sure the canoeing party behind you will appreciate not seeing any evidence of you. If you do camp at a spot with more than footprints of previous campers, leave the site cleaner than it was when you arrived. See Appendix B about camping with minimal impact on the environment. Campfires are allowed in the park, but BC Parks encourages campers to conserve wood by keeping their fires small and only using driftwood and cooking on stoves. See www.env.gov.bc.ca/bcparks/explore/whatyou.html#campfires for more information on campfires in the park. Check for the Fire Danger Rating and possible campfire bans at http://bcwildfire.ca or by contacting the BC Parks office in Smithers or Dease Lake. If you are hiking into the Gladys Lake Ecological Reserve, please note that camping is not allowed and fires are not permitted there.

The hikes that can be made from the banks of the Spatsizi River are one of the main attractions of this trip. Most trails below treeline evolved from game trails that were later used as horse trails. The majority of these trails are blazed or marked and have relatively low gradients. The alpine areas have excellent terrain for hiking and you can usually go where you wish quite easily. However, obey signs and use designated trails where they exist, for your own safety and to minimize your impact on the fragile vegetation. Multi-day hikes should only be undertaken by fit, experienced and well-equipped hikers.

The trailheads for day hikes from the river – the Red Goat Mountain ridge hike; the Plateau Trail north of Hyland Post; and a couple hikes on park trails you could do from camp – are located with coordinates and briefly described in the Trip Notes.

Multi-day hikes such as the Cold Fish Lake Trail beginning at Mink Creek or Hyland Post are not described, though the trailheads are noted. For more information on the multi-day trail hiking opportunities, get the online map of the Spatsizi Plateau Wilderness Provincial Park, as it shows the trails that make for numerous day and multi-day hiking options including some campsites. Also check out the following Spatsizi Plateau park websites: www.env.gov.bc.ca/bcparks/explore/parkpgs/spatsizi /hiking.html and www.env.gov.bc.ca/bcparks/explore/parkpgs/spatsizi/canoeing.html.

Horse trekking is another option for off-the-river adventure. The Cold Fish Lake and Hyland Post areas in particular have a significant history and the photography and wildlife-viewing opportunities are simply too great to miss. Contact Spatsizi Wilderness Vacations run by the Collingwood brothers, Upper Stikine River Adventures run by Gerry Geraci or Stikine Trail Rides run by Willy Williams to add a day or multi-day trail ride to your itinerary. See the Directory of Services and Organizations for contact information for these outfitters.

Special Equipment: On the Spatsizi canoe route you will want to use a canoe that you are comfortable running rapids in and that you can repair or get back into shape to carry on downriver in the event of a wrap or punching a hole in your boat (this is particularly true if you are carrying on to run the Upper Stikine down to the Cassiar Highway bridge take-out). A throw bag with a towing/quick-release system you can easily reach on your canoe is required on any trip, but even more vital if you are on a one-boat or solo trip. You are better off with this system when swimming your boat to shore in the event of a capsize.

You will likely want a two-wheeled canoe cart if you do the 5-km portage on the Spatsizi River Access Trail down to the common put-in. The trail is about five feet wide in most places, except where it goes down the steep hill. It is maintained by BC Parks and is not all that rough, but it is wet in places. The ideal width of the cart axle is about 50 cm and if you plan on doing one trip with your cart heavily loaded, you will want to bring one capable of carrying 180 kg. The standard one will do if you make two trips or people carry some of the gear. Whichever cart you bring, be sure it can be dismantled after use if you are unable to leave it with your vehicle(s). There are a few canoe rests along the trail if you choose to portage the traditional way.

A water filter is necessary on this trip. You can get rid of the silt by letting water in a pot stand for a while, but the possibility of "beaver fever" needs to be dealt with. Take extra water bags for filling up at the clear streams to save your filter some hard work.

The Spatsizi Plateau has an active bug population in the warm summer months, though it usually dies down by late August. You will want to take a head net, bug jacket, repellent or some combination of the three. I never go anywhere up north without my hooded bug jacket with a face net and repellent with lots of DEET, and this is one of the trips where I have used them both, especially while hiking.

I would also carry pepper spray and/or an air horn to deal with potential bear encounters. There are lots of grizzly bears in this region and if you are hiking you are more likely to surprise them. Make lots of noise when walking, and be aware of your surroundings and places where you may not be seen well, such as when bushwhacking up to the alpine. Take a food-hanging kit if you are doing multi-day hikes. (Climbing pulleys make a great addition to carabiners and this equipment can double as a wrap kit on the river, something you should always carry on a river trip with rapids like those you will find on the Upper Stikine River route.)

Sturdy footwear and proper backpacks will be obvious additions to your gear if you are doing multi-day hikes. For any hiking you should carry a compass and appropriate topo maps and know how to use them. Because the hiking is so superb and the potential for seeing wildlife so great, you will want to maximize your experience by taking a good set of binoculars.

The park authorities encourage hikers to limit their use of wood for campfires and to keep fires small. Cooking on stoves is recommended, particularly when hiking (you will likely want a backpacking model if you are doing multi-day routes). Fritz Handel, the maker of the Bushbuddy stove, lives just outside Iskut. His small, efficient wood-burning stoves are sold at the Iskut gas station convenience store on the Cassiar Highway or you can order them online. See the Directory of Services and Organizations for contact information.

Trip Notes:

MAP NO.	GRID REF.	FEATURE	DESCRIPTION
104 H/2	147442	Trailhead; Camping	The Spatsizi River Access Trail begins here. There is an obvious sign and the start of the 5-km portage is easily seen. You can camp at the trailhead if you arrive too late to make the carry, but the better site is at the river put-in.
104 H/7	187474	Put-in; Camping	The put-in for the river trip is the gravel bar at the confluence of Didene Creek and the Spatsizi. The BC Parks campsite is at the end of the portage trail beside the creek. Didene is said to mean "young caribou" in Tahltan.
	185478	Rapids	The river is fast and braids for the first 10 km or so.
	186511		The first 4 km host shallow, rocky rapids from **Class 1 riffles up to easy Class 2 sets with rocks to avoid**. Watch for wood hazards where the river braids and on the outside of sharp bends. Depending on water levels, some

tricky spots may be found at grid reference coordinates **185478, 185483 to 186490, 181499** and from **186507 to 186511. Class 1** riffles will be your constant companions for the rest of the trip!

187524	**Camping**	A nice gravel bar camp can be made on RL below the Eaglenest Range.
184524	**Cabin**	There is a rundown cabin on RL near the mouth of the creek.
187600	**Camping**	On RL the gravel bar just below the creek outlet makes for a spot to camp with views of the valley opening up. Try fishing at the mouth of the creek.
192618	**Rapid**	As you come around the bend there is a bouldery **Class 1+** ledge on RR that is easily avoided by running RL of RC.
217631	**Camping**	On RR is a gravel bar where you can make camp with a view.
230642	**Camping**	On RR there is a nice, large gravel bar upstream of a small creek, with a good view of Denkladia Mountain to boot. Apparently Denkladia means "person who walks with spear" in Tahltan.
245660	**Camping**	Where the river widens there is a large gravel bar on RR that provides a camping spot with huge views down the open valley and a snye in behind with wildlife sighting potential.
247674	**Camping**	There is a nice, big gravel bar "island" for camping on RR downstream of Buckinghorse Creek. A slow, swampy section of river follows with lots of wildlife sighting potential and gaga scenery.
239710	**Canoe Lake put-in**	This small lake is just big enough for a Beaver to put down in and take off again! It's noted as Airplane Lake in the BC Parks Literature. The lake is unnamed on the topos, and for those wanting the lat/long coordinates, it is approximately 57° 29' north latitude and 128° 36' west longitude. It's a short carry to the river. Ask your pilot to drop you off at 128° 36' west longitude. It's a short carry to the river. Ask your pilot to drop you off as close as possible to the best spot to portage over to the river. There is a campsite on the Spatsizi

about 3 km downstream of the north end of the lake if you arrive late in the day. See the next entry.

104 H/10	238737	Camping	On the gravel bar at the head of the treed island there is good camping. Beware of wood hazards when choosing a landing spot, however. There are nice views of the Eaglenest Range and Red Goat Mountain. The river really slows and meanders from the base of Red Goat Mountain to Mink Creek.
	248773	Camping	On the RL gravel bar a camp can be made with good views of Red Goat Mountain and the river valley downstream.
	244774	Camping	There is a gravel bar "island" that makes for a small, breezy camp with views.
	240776	Red Goat Mtn. hike	To hike the flank of Red Goat Mountain with a minimum of bushwhacking, start your hike downstream of the small creek coming in on RL at GR 214775. The current will be swift and the embankment high, so you will need to securely tie up your canoe(s). Zigzag your way northwest up the flank until you can head southwest up the ridge to the top. There is no trail up the ridge. The trail on the shoreline is a game trail and will not lead you uphill.
	246792	Camping	On RR there is a large gravel bar for making camp. **Note**: This is the last good camping site for about 12 km.
	258867	Hiking	Downstream of the last outlet of Mink Creek in the far RL channel behind the island is access to the trail that goes all the way from the BC Rail grade at the Klappan River to Upper Stikine River Adventures' lodge via Cold Fish Lake and Hyland Post. It is called the Cold Fish Lake Trail and you can access all the other trails in the park via this main trail. This is one of the spots you will most likely plan to start a multi-day hike from. There might be flagging tape at the trailhead. The beginning of the trail is hard to follow, as it starts off in low, swampy ground.
	265876	Camping	Just upstream of an unnamed creek on RR a gravel bar island with trees makes a good camp.
	271894	Camping	On RR across from creek outlet on RL is a large sand/gravel bar that makes a good camp.

	284911	Camping	On RL is a large sand/gravel bar that makes a good camping spot. You may see evidence of it also being used as a wolf pack rendezvous site!
104 H/9	308918	Camping; Hiking	There is a nice, treed gravel bar camp to be made at the outlet of Kliweguh Creek on RL. After dinner you can hike on the trail that joins the Cold Fish Lake Trail at Mink Creek to Upper Stikine River Adventures' lodge via Hyland Post. You could also start a multi-day hike on the park trails from this location. **Note**: There are few good spots to camp from about 5 km downstream from here to just downstream of Hyland Post, about 25 km from Kliweguh Creek. The river braids a bit after the confluence and depending on water levels some of the gravel bars will do. However, eventually the banks start to steepen and there are few places to stop and get out of the boat. The river also speeds up and you are flying once you pass the Dawson River confluence.
	469896	Confluence; Rapids	The Dawson River comes in on RR and around the upcoming s-bend some bluffs make for interesting scenery. The current also picks up and there may be some **Class I/I+** waves. Be alert, the river is peppy all the way to the Stikine confluence!
	500893	Hyland Post	On RL you will see the dock and the path leading up to the cabins of this historic trading post and ranch. There is also an airstrip, which you will see if you go on the hike up to the alpine of the plateau. See the next entry for details on access to the trail for this hike.
	515893	Camping; Hiking	You can camp on the gravel bar on RL across the Spatsizi from the creek mouth on RR. This is where you want to stop if you are day hiking the Plateau Trail or carrying on farther to do a multi-day hike in the park. The area around Hyland Post is private property.

Plateau Trail Access: From the campsite follow a light trail heading back upstream to Hyland Post. At the Post, just past the cabins, you should stop and ask permission to cross the property. Continue west on the obvious dirt horse track on the airstrip to where the three teepee posts stand (GR 495895). From here the trail goes north through chest-high willows. The horse track splits at GR 494897; |

go east up the ridge that eventually backtracks west. Eventually you reach a not-so-obvious junction at 490900 where the Plateau Trail begins to your right. There may still be a dark wooden sign saying PLATEAU and some flagging tape. The trailhead may be hard to see due to logs placed there to discourage horses. Take this narrow, well-used path heading northeast and then north to the plateau. It will likely take about three hours to reach the edge of the plateau. Once there, you can wander for hours or days at will. There is a cairn at the top of the plateau, 360-degree views and spots to camp.

531899	**Bluffs**	Just before the Ross River confluence there are some bluffs on RR.
531900	**Camping**	A camp can be made on RR just downstream from the Ross River outlet with its sentinel rocks. Ross River is also called "Willow River" by the Tahltan.
	Hiking	You can hike on the trail toward Upper Stikine River Adventures' lodge to stretch your legs if you haven't already had enough hiking! **Note**: you will have to swim the Stikine if you plan on actually reaching the lodge. It's on the RR side of the Stikine.
527906	**Camping**	There is also camping on a large gravel bar about 1 km downstream from the mouth of the Ross River on RR. You can also access the trail heading to the lodge found in back of this site.
530917	**Camping**	On RL there is a gravel bar to camp on that hosts the morning sun.
544940	**Hunting camp**	On RR there is an established campsite on the trail to Upper Stikine River Adventures' lodge.
538958	**Campsite**	On RR, on the point at the mouth of the Spatsizi, is a fairly established campsite with "furniture."
536962	**Confluence; Camping; Take-out**	At the confluence of the Spatsizi and the Stikine there are many gravel bars to camp on. For shade keep RR and pick one of the ones upstream of the Stikine's flow. If you are flying out you will have to move to where your pilot has agreed to pick you up. Upper Stikine River Adventures' lodge is on RR downstream about 2.5 km from where the Spatsizi flows into the Stikine.

The confluence of the rivers was burned in 2002 and as a result the area was teeming with moose in 2003. It's really cool to see the contrast between the clearer, bluer water of the Stikine and the often siltier water of the Spatsizi here.

*** Go to the Upper Stikine River chapter for the Trip Notes from the confluence of the Spatsizi and the Upper Stikine to the bridge take-out on the Cassiar Highway (Hwy. 37).

CHAPTER TWO:

UPPER STIKINE RIVER

The Stikine River is the best known and most popular river for canoeing in northern BC. There are two classic trips that include much of the 600+ km stretch between Happy Lake and the Pacific Ocean, and they draw paddlers from all over the world. The river hosts a great diversity of landscapes, flowing from the dry boreal mountains through the Coast Mountains and temperate rainforest to the tidal flats at the Stikine's mouth on the Pacific Coast. The Grand Canyon of the Stikine, which separates the Upper Stikine canoe route from the Lower, is unrunnable but well worth taking a peek at by driving the crazy road to Telegraph Creek or by hiking or a horse trek.

Highlights of paddling the Upper Stikine include alpine hiking at the headwater lakes and multi-day hikes across the famous Spatsizi Plateau. Often called BC's Serengeti of the North, the plateau's valleys and rolling alpine ridges offer excellent wildlife-viewing opportunities. Grizzlies and caribou flourish along with wildflowers. Fishing is also good right from the get go in the small headwater lakes.

The whitewater along the route will keep paddlers alert. Some rapids must be portaged, such as Fountain Rapids, a lovely series of drops. At certain water levels the bulk of the current hits a large midriver rock, sending up a great fountain-like plume of water. Chapea Rapids will have even the most skilled whitewater paddlers seriously considering their options. Beggarly Canyon may provide some thrills or a carry. With the exception of Jewel Rapids, a boulder garden that requires good manoeuvring skills, and the S-Bend, a snaking wave train, the significant rapids have portage trails that are usually in reasonable to good condition. The fact that there are trails meant for canoeists (with canoe rests in some places!) is a novelty for most northern BC rivers. The confluence of the Spatsizi and Stikine rivers is a marvellous place to moose-watch and camp, and there are many camping sites with mountain views along the route.

The Upper Stikine run is not the historic route the Lower Stikine is, but while paddling the upper river one can imagine northern BC as it once was, a vast land travelled lightly by people living off its bounty. The Spatsizi Plateau Wilderness and Stikine River provincial parks protect the Upper Stikine River route, an indication of its great recreational and scenic values.

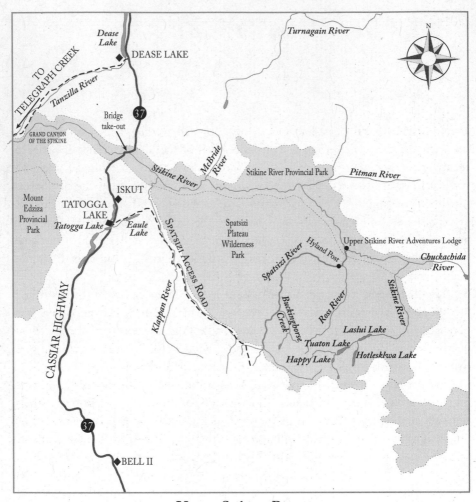

Upper Stikine River

Length: Tuaton Lake, the second of the three headwaters lakes, is the most common put-in for the Upper Stikine River route. The usual take-out is just downstream of the bridge on the Cassiar Highway (Hwy. 37) that crosses the Stikine south of Dease Lake, a distance of 276 km. This is normally a fly-in and drive-out trip with straightforward logistics.

To paddle this route in a relaxed manner, allow yourself nine days on the river. If you want to do some significant hikes, then add more days to your itinerary. I really recommend you spend a good amount of time up in the headwaters lakes area. This is one of the best river trips for alpine hiking in a high-elevation environment. You should plan for an extra day in case you cannot fly in due to bad weather. There is a high pass that must be navigated, and if the cloud is too low, you won't be getting to Tuaton.

The longest trip on the Upper Stikine route, from Happy Lake to the bridge take-out, is approximately 284 km. The alpine hiking and scenery are great and there is more solitude. This option adds one paddling day, as you must navigate Happy Creek to where it joins the Stikine River upstream of Tuaton Lake. From there it is smooth sailing down to Tuaton. You will want to take a couple days to fully enjoy the alpine hiking at either or both of these headwater lakes.

To shorten the Upper Stikine route, you can fly in or out at either the Stikine–Spatsizi confluence or Laslui Lake. The latter cuts off one short river day and is your best option if you go late in the season or in a very low-water year, as the creek section between Tuaton and Laslui may be too shallow to paddle. The distances between the potential put-ins and take-outs are listed in the table at the end of this section. To calculate how many days you will need for any of them, experienced canoe trippers can count on doing about 30–35 km a day once on the Stikine River and not being rushed.

Note that if you are not into whitewater, flying out at the confluence is your best option. You will avoid three significant rapids this way, two of which do not have portage trails. However, you will still have to run numerous smaller rapids. If you decide to egress the river at the Stikine–Spatsizi confluence, be sure to ask your pilot where you will be picked up. The pilot may want to pick you up from a gravel bar at the confluence or downstream a couple kilometres at Upper Stikine River Adventures' lodge.

Laslui Lake to Stikine–Spatsizi confluence*	118 km
Tuaton Lake to Stikine–Spatsizi confluence*	123 km
Happy Lake to Stikine–Spatsizi confluence*	131 km
Spatsizi confluence to Cassiar Highway (Hwy. 37) Bridge*	153 km
Laslui Lake to Cassiar Highway (Hwy. 37) Bridge*	271 km
Tuaton Lake to Cassiar Highway (Hwy. 37) Bridge*	276 km
Happy Lake to Cassiar Highway (Hwy. 37) Bridge*	284 km

* These trips are described in detail in the Trip Notes section of this chapter.

Topographic Maps: 1:50 000-scale NTS topo maps are highly recommended. The 1:50 000s you require for the classic route starting at Tuaton Lake and ending at the bridge take-out are 104 H/8, 94 E/5, 94 E/12, 104 H/9, 104 H/16, 104 H/15, 104 H/14, 104 H/13 and 104 I/4. If you start at Happy Lake, you will also need 104 H/1. If you want to use the 1:250 000-scale maps as well, the ones you need are 104 H, 94 E and 104 I. Look at the Trip Notes at the end of this chapter to come up with the list of maps you will need if you do a shorter version of the route.

I suggest you purchase or print your topo maps in advance. Not only will you be able to plan your paddling days, but using the coordinates in the Trip Notes you can mark the locations of sources of emergency help, potential campsites, trailheads for hikes and other sites of interest so you'll have the information at hand when navigating the river. This is a good trip for paddlers to practise using a GPS in conjunction with topos. Make sure you set your GPS map datum to NAD 27 Canada for use with the 1:50 000 topos and the position format to MGRS (Military Grid Reference System). See the discussion on topographic maps, the UTM and Grid Reference systems and use of a GPS in the How To Use this Guidebook chapter.

Note that the list of maps does not include the 1:50 000-scale maps you will need for doing extended hiking trips. If you plan on doing any serious hiking, especially any of the multi-day routes, you will need the 1:50 000 and 1:250 000-scale topos of the area you plan on hiking in. To figure out what you need, look at the Spatsizi Plateau Wilderness Provincial Park map discussed below for the standard hiking routes and then consult the index for NTS topographic maps for BC online at www .maptown.com/canadiantopographical/bcntsindex.html.

BC Parks publishes a map called Spatsizi Plateau Wilderness Provincial Park (a 1:280 000-scale sketch without contour lines) that gives a good overview of the park and the hiking/horse trails you could access from the river. It is not a substitute for the topo maps but it's a useful planning guide, especially for the multi-day hikes (it shows campsites on the trails). The map can be found online at www.env.gov.bc.ca/bcparks/explore/parkpgs/spatsizi/spatsizi.pdf.

Getting There and Away: The classic Upper Stikine route is a fly-in and drive-out trip. The only drive-in option is to paddle the Spatsizi River to its confluence with the Stikine, then carry on to the bridge take-out (see the Spatsizi River chapter for more information). The only road-accessible take-out for the Upper Stikine route is the bridge on the Cassiar Highway (Hwy. 37) over the Stikine. If you only want to run the Upper Stikine River to the Spatsizi confluence, you must fly out. You can also do a fly-in and fly-out trip, making logistics very simple.

To fly in to Tuaton Lake or one of the other headwater lakes, you have choices for local air charter services, and canoeists normally begin their trips from two convenient staging areas: Tatogga Lake and Dease Lake. Paddlers can arrange for shuttles by contacting the canoe outfitters in the region. The charter air services in these communities may also help you with your shuttle and will also pick you up if you want to egress the route at the Spatsizi confluence.

Tatogga Lake and Dease Lake are both on the Cassiar Highway (km 390.2 and 488.3 respectively) and home to the air services you will likely want to use. If time as opposed to money is the concern, flying from Smithers will save you driving the Cassiar Highway (though I must say it is a scenic route). To stage your trip from Tatogga Lake or Dease Lake, the logistics are simple and the shuttle short. To do your own shuttle with two or more vehicles, you drive to the air service, drop off your canoe and gear, then shuttle your vehicle(s) to the bridge take-out (km 437.2 of the Cassiar Highway) and head back to the air service to fly out. You paddle to the take-out, drive back for your vehicle parked at the air service, and Bob's your uncle!

The distance between Tatogga Lake Resort, where the North Pacific Seaplanes (formerly Harbour Air) base is, and the bridge over the Stikine is 47 km one way. The bridge is about a 45-minute drive north from the resort. The distance from Dease Lake to the bridge over the Stikine is 51 km one way and also about a 45-minute drive from the community of Dease Lake. BC–Yukon Air and the other air charter bases are actually out of town on Dease Lake itself, adding about 5 km or so to your drive.

Canoe rentals and shuttles can be arranged via the outfitters near Iskut, about 10 km north of Tatogga Lake. There are accommodation facilities right in Dease Lake, but you can rent canoes from Stikine River Song in Telegraph Creek and the outfitter at Dease River Crossing and they will also do shuttles for you. If you only have one vehicle you can arrange for a driver from one of the outfitters (or maybe the air service will help you) to shuttle your vehicle to the bridge take-out so it will be waiting for you when you go to take out. Or, you can have the outfitter come and pick you up with their vehicle and take you back to yours. I haven't heard any reports of vehicles being broken into at the parking area below the bridge, but you may want to have the shuttle driver bring your vehicle to the take-out just before you plan to arrive there. Finally, you can always hitchhike to complete your shuttle. A friendly local will likely stop and give you a ride. I've never had much luck with the RV tourists.

If you wish to travel without vehicles or canoes, you can charter a small aircraft on wheels to fly in to Dease Lake or you can take a scheduled flight. At the moment, Northern Thunderbird Air offers scheduled flights from Smithers to Dease Lake on Mondays, Wednesdays and Fridays. A number of airlines offer scheduled flights to Smithers, Terrace or Whitehorse. You can also rent vehicles and canoes in these communities, with the exception of Terrace. There are no canoe outfitters in Terrace that I know of. You can also charter a floatplane from all three communities for a fly-in and fly-out trip, making logistics simple but expensive. You will need to ask your pilot where on the river they can pick you up. They likely will not want to taxi under the bridge to the usual take-out!

In conclusion, you have a lot of options for making the logistics of an Upper-Stikine-only route or a Spatsizi–Stikine canoe trip work for you. You will likely come up with more than I have suggested. See the Directory of Services and Organizations for contact information for the services you will need to make your plan work.

If you arrive too late in the day to fly out, there are campgrounds at Tatogga Lake Resort, Dease Lake, Smithers, Terrace and Whitehorse. There are also camping spots where the plane drops you off at the Happy Lake and Tuaton Lake put-ins. The gravel bars at the confluence of the Spatsizi and Stikine rivers make for great camping if you choose to put in or take out there. You can also camp in the large clearing just off the Cassiar Highway at the bridge take-out.

When To Go: Mid-July to September. You can't get in to the headwater lakes early in the season, because they will still be frozen. The railway grade in to the Spatsizi will also still be impassable due to snow and/or thawing. You do not want to run the Upper Stikine route during peak runoff, which usually happens in June but can be as late as July. Less-experienced moving-water paddlers should only plan trips in August, when water levels normally drop significantly. If the multi-day hikes are your prime objective, you will also want to go later in the summer. You don't want to walk and camp in the snow, and on some routes you must make creek crossings on foot that could potentially be dangerous at early-season high water. Note that if you go late in the season, especially in a low-water year, you may not be able to paddle the shallow section of river between Tuaton and Laslui lakes, but you can still put in at Laslui. The Collingwood brothers of Spatsizi Wilderness Vacations own the lodge at Laslui Lake (as well as Hyland Post) and you could contact them about water levels and get permission to land at their dock.

Paddling remote rivers in high water or flood conditions is not recommended. On the Upper Stikine route, besides the fact that the rapids will be pushier, it is the wood hazards made by slumping clay cliffs and bank erosion during runoff and very wet conditions that are of concern. When I paddled the route in mid-July of 2003, the freshet had been late and large, making for flood conditions a week or so before we set off. It had also been raining quite steadily. The high water was not an overly significant problem in regard to the rapids or camping availability – we were a small and very skilled group of moving-water paddlers – but it certainly was problematic for navigating all the new wood hazards. At one point the river flow had changed due to a large landslide that had blocked the main channel, making for a sharp corner and new channels thrashing through the forest. We were suddenly committed to running a narrow Class 2+ rapid obstructed with stumps and strainers. A mistake in that descent would have had Class 5 consequences and I never want to be in a situation like that again. The river has since returned to its former course and this spot is no longer a problem.

My experience suggests that only parties of experienced moving-water paddlers not interested in the multi-day hikes will enjoy the challenge of a mid-July trip on the Upper Stikine. You will need to be extra-vigilant about wood hazards and be able to navigate very strong hydraulics. Camping sites will be smaller, fewer and farther between if the river is still up. The bonus of higher water, though, is that the swift current will help you make good time on the route, leaving you more hours to relax, do day hikes and take in the sights. The wildflowers in the alpine and along the river will be coming out in full force. But so will the insects! They really come out as the heat turns on in the long hours of daylight. On the other hand, frost is possible at night in any month in this area.

July daily highs in Dease Lake can reach 20°c; nights are cool, which brings the mean daily temperature down to 14°. You can expect the daily temperatures during at least the first part of your Upper Stikine trip to be closer to the average because of the elevation. It could be very chilly up at Tuaton Lake. There are only 60 frost-free days on average in the Stikine headwaters area!

You will likely have some sun, but July can also be rainy. Apparently July sees an average of 10–13 days with measurable precipitation, but annual rainfall totals are relatively low because the Spatsizi Plateau is in the rain shadow of the Coast and Skeena mountains. So, the weather at the headwater lakes will be colder and wetter, but as you descend, precipitation and frost are normally less likely. Cold northern headwinds can occur when the weather is unsettled. It doesn't usually pour for days on end the way it does on the coast, but I did have a relatively wet trip at the end of July 2002, with showers every day for a week. I have also been in the region in July in other years and had mostly sunny weather. On an Upper Stikine River run you need to pack for any weather; expect the worst and enjoy what you get!

On boreal mountain rivers in northern BC, water levels usually drop come the end of July. August is normally a much lower-water month on this route – the best time for less-experienced moving-water paddlers to run the Spatsizi. Normally, gravel bars are more exposed in August, making for good camping sites. The insects start to die off with the cooler nights later in the month. The berries are out and fishing picks up as the river clears. The hiking will be good at this time of year as well. Life is generally as good as it gets on the river in this usually drier month. If you go at the end of August or later, be sure on your flight to your preferred put-in to check whether there is any water in the river between Tuaton and Laslui lakes. If not, land at Laslui to begin your trip.

September will be chilly and frost is guaranteed. It will likely snow instead of rain at the higher elevations. You will not make as good time on the river with the normally lower water, but the wildlife viewing is at its peak in the fall and the changing colours of the deciduous trees and shrubs will make for a scenic trip. The bugs will have pretty much packed it in for the season, making hiking and camping even more pleasant (unless it is warm, in which case the blackflies may make a significant appearance again).

I love an autumn trip. But if you are not experienced fall canoe trippers, consider a late August/early September trip rather than at the end of the season so you don't have to deal with the more significant weather challenges while working on your outdoor living skills. The other drawback of a late-season trip down the Upper Stikine is that the hunters will be out in full force. You may not see the wildlife you normally would along the river as a result. However, if you do some hiking side trips you may see more than earlier in the season.

The table below shows average monthly mean flows for May to September derived from archived data from a hydrometric station on the Upper Stikine route that is no longer operating. Many Environment Canada water survey stations were decommissioned in 1994/95 due to budget cuts. You can see the significant differences in water flows over the paddling season and why you want to avoid the June freshet or a late spring runoff in July.

Average Monthly Mean Flows (m³/s) Stikine River below the Spatsizi Confluence

May	June	July	August	September
200	500	350	160	130

Source: Jennifer Voss's *Stikine River: A Guide to Paddling the Great River*, Rocky Mountain Books, 1998.

Since there is no longer an active water survey station on the Upper Stikine route or any other relevant waterways in the area, you can only determine general levels at any given time by contacting local sources. Keep in touch with your air service and/or canoe outfitter about water levels or call the BC Parks Stikine Area office in Dease Lake at (250) 771-4591. BC Parks officers float the river in mid-July to check the route. We met them in 2003. Hopefully, they will have done their tour by the time you hit the river and can tell you what to expect for water levels and any new hazards or park regulations you should know of.

You can check how any given year's water levels are shaping up by monitoring the snowpack on the Environment Canada River Forecast & Snow Survey website, at www.env.gov.bc.ca/rfc. On the website is a snow survey (snowpack and water supply outlook) bulletin that is published in January and updated eight times per year. The publication includes data gathered from snow and hydrometric measuring stations, and the regional snowpack and water supply forecasts basically tell you whether water levels are expected to be less or more than normal in a region come the summer and how much of the snow has melted and how fast. This is good general information, useful in deciding when to schedule your trip. If there is lots of snow in the Skeena Mountains and on the Stikine Plateau and it is not melting rapidly, you may want to delay your trip until August to avoid a late runoff. You could have high flows throughout July. If you are less-experienced canoe trippers working on your moving-water skills, do not plan to go before August in any year.

Finally, be aware that the Upper Stikine responds to rainfall. If there is wet weather for some time in the spring and early summer the river will stay up longer, and it can also rise again quickly from heavy rains any time of year.

Difficulty of the River: ✳✳½ The Upper Stikine route gets a 2½-star difficulty rating, mostly because of the wood hazards and the Class 2 rapids and one set of Class 2+ rapids (Jewel) that do not have portages. After the Pitman River confluence you can expect riffles and Class 1+ rapids at every bend. There are also tricky cross-currents in a number of places. Intermediate moving-water paddlers will likely enjoy the challenges of the route, but should avoid higher water levels. Novices should only paddle this route at lower flows and with advanced or exceptional moving-water paddlers in their party.

There are no big lake crossings, so wind is not a factor, though you may encounter headwinds that will slow you down. The route is relatively long and remote, and the water is cold. The most potentially dangerous sections of the river are where it braids. Wood gathers and creates hazards. For the entire length of the run, the major hazards are logjams, sweepers and strainers, deadheads and partly submerged logs in the shallows. There are often wood hazards at tight bends with strong current. You must have the moving-water skills to be able to avoid midstream hazards on the submerged or partially exposed gravel bars and to stay to the inside of the corners to avoid trees that have come down due to erosion of the banks. Additionally, paddlers need the skills to safely stop in eddies to scout and land at the head of portage trails.

The route is not overly strenuous. There is only one mandatory portage, around Fountain Rapids, though most parties will carry around the ledges in Chapea Rapids and perhaps the main drop in Beggarly Canyon. If you decide not to run Jewel Rapids, and water levels are too high to line and wade it safely, you will have to bushwhack portage around it. This carry will be long and hard work.

The Stikine begins as a small-volume stream. Most of the rapids in the very upper reaches of the river are shallow and rocky but not difficult to navigate. The Stikine gathers volume steadily, and with the exception of Fountain, the upper rapids are small and easily run. The rapids leading into Chapea Rapids are the exception. These Class 2−/2 rapids need to be navigated carefully. A capsize in them may result in your canoe going down the meat of Chapea and getting beat up.

The Upper Stikine doubles in volume after the Spatsizi joins it. It becomes a medium-volume river there and just keeps on growing with each major tributary's inflow. Jewel Rapids, Class 2+, are likely the most difficult set of rapids a less-experienced party will run on the Upper Stikine route, since they are not easily lined except in lower flows and there is no portage trail. This long boulder garden will challenge moving-water paddlers still working on their basic manoeuvring skills. Sideslipping and backpaddling are required to avoid the obstacles scattered throughout the run. Good river-reading skills are required to identify rocks, waves and holes and pick a safe route between them. At average August flows, paddlers can avoid the running the main flow of the rapids by eddy-hopping down far river right. You can boat-scout or hop out on shore to walk ahead and take a look and likely line the sections you don't want to run. Beggarly Canyon, Class 2+ and maybe even 3− at some water levels, can be portaged in part or entirely. Large waves and strong hydraulics and strong eddy lines make this rapid trickier at higher water. If you run the lower part of the canyon there is some really swirly water with cross-currents and boils in the squeeze between the canyon walls. S-Bend is the final rapid of note that must be run. There is no portage trail and you can't line. It can be Class 2 at certain water levels, with standing waves, strong hydraulics and eddy lines and tricky currents.

There are numerous sets of Class 1+ to 2- rapids throughout the route, especially after the Pitman River confluence. Depending on water levels, these may or may not be there or may be different in character. Standing waves are common in constricted parts of the river. Corners and squeezes in the hard-rock canyons and where the channels converge after islands are most likely places to encounter tricky cross-currents and boils. There are no big lake crossings, so wind is not usually of great concern on this trip; however, the Stikine becomes quite wide and it is possible that headwinds will slow your progress considerably at times, particularly lower down on the route.

In conclusion, the Upper Stikine is a river trip for paddlers who already have canoe-tripping experience and intermediate moving-water skills. Novices should only do this trip with advanced or exceptional moving-water paddlers in their party. This is not a particularly difficult trip compared to many in the two volumes of this guide, given that you don't go when the river is running high. It is a very good choice for those wanting a trip that combines whitewater with excellent hiking.

The gradient of the Stikine River from Happy Lake to the bridge take-out is 2.7 m/km, taking the lake distances out of the equation. The gradient from Tuaton Lake down is somewhat less than that, given there is a significant drop in elevation between the Happy and Tuaton lakes over a short distance. The gradient of the Upper Stikine route is similar to that of the Kispiox River (covered in volume one), and where hard rock outcrops, they both have bouncy rapids.

Character of the River and Region: The Upper Stikine River winds northeast, from its headwaters in the Skeena Mountains, across the Spatsizi Plateau. On the plateau it zigzags for a stretch, then turns northwest and finally west to flow along the southern edge of the Stikine Ranges of the Cassiar Mountains. After the bridge take-out the river drops through the Grand Canyon of the Stikine, a place you don't want to be in a canoe, or any other craft for that matter – except maybe in an aircraft on a scenic flight!

Ecologically speaking, the Upper Stikine canoe route lies entirely in the Northern Boreal Mountains ecoprovince and the Boreal Mountains and Plateaus ecoregion. On the canoe route you can experience three different bioclimatic zones, two just paddling the river and a third if you hike up to the alpine. The Upper Stikine boasts a number of very diverse landscapes.

The headwaters of the Stikine River flow out at the base of the far northeastern ranges of the Skeena Mountains. The trip starts in the subalpine in the high elevations of the Spatsizi Plateau, which is part of the much larger Stikine Plateau. The plateau country is transitional to the rugged terrain of the Skeena and Cassiar mountains.

Stretching from the headwaters of the Finlay River almost 500 km northwest to the headwaters of the Taku River and Atlin Lake, the Stikine Plateau is a huge, rolling upland. Elevation ranges from 1600–2000 m ASL and the plateau extends in a broad curve broken by wide U-shaped valleys, like the Stikine River Valley. The plateau is mantled with glacial drift and hosts drift-filled valleys with numerous lakes. The glacial deposits are underlain largely by sedimentary and volcanic rocks, including shale, sandstone, granite and conglomerate rock. The valley bottoms of the Stikine River and its principal tributaries, including the Spatsizi and Klappan rivers, are occupied by boreal forest. Frequent fire history has created a mosaic of white spruce, lodgepole pine and aspen-dominated forests in a variety of seral age classes and vast areas of deciduous shrub land. Extensive wetland habitats, fens, marshes, swamps and bogs are common along the valley bottoms. Subalpine fir and scrub birch and willow dominate in the subalpine elevations, and the alpine plateaus are characterized by low deciduous scrub, heath vegetation, grassy meadows and "lichen-grasslands."

At the headwater lakes where the Upper Stikine River route begins, the mountaintops are bedrock and alpine tundra. The subalpine forest on the slopes and in the upper valley is typical of the Spruce-Willow-Birch zone. Willow and birch shrubs, along with subalpine fir and white spruce dominate the open subalpine forest. The shrub vegetation is anywhere from one to three metres high on average, with patches of grassy meadows. It can take anywhere from one to two hours of bushwhacking to get to the alpine tundra of moss, lichen and herbs.

The trees are stunted even in the valley bottom. Cold air ponds in the valley, making for harsh growing conditions. Tuaton Lake sits at 1275 m ASL, and frost and snow are possible at any time. There are less than 60 frost-free days in this area, so be prepared for cold in the high elevations. There is not much for firewood at the headwaters and it is illegal to cut trees in the park, so be sure to have a good stove for cooking and use only driftwood for small fires.

The plateau country has a northern interior climate, similar to that in the Subarctic. The heat in the summer can reach 35°c, with the same location experiencing –50° in the winter. Annual precipitation is low, ranging from 350–650 mm on average, and relatively evenly distributed throughout the year. Prevailing westerly winds bring coastal air to the region, but it has generally lost most of its moisture by the time it reaches the Spatsizi Plateau. Summertime surface heating produces convective showers.

From its outlet at Tuaton Lake, the Stikine River is a small-volume stream, running first through a swampy area and then on through shallow, braided channels to Laslui Lake. The riverbed is sand and gravel, and the water is usually clear here in the prime canoeing season. This section of river, between Tuaton and Laslui lakes, offers some of the most scenic mountain views along the route, as well as great wildlife sighting potential because there are no trees lining the riverbank. We saw a caribou right next to the river and it hung around unconcerned with our efforts to stop the canoe and quickly get a good picture. It posed for us for a long time! I also love the upper stretches of the Stikine's floodplain because from the gravel bars to the base of the mountain slopes there are masses of wildflowers, especially in July. The esker landscape around Laslui Lake is also attractive, but say goodbye to the Skeena Mountains. You leave their vistas behind as you carry on across Spatsizi Plateau to Fountain Rapids.

Once you reach Fountain Rapids, you can admire the open lodgepole forest the portage trail runs through. The volcanic, cheese-grater rock of the rapids is quite something, as is the plume of water the rapids get their name from. At certain water levels a midstream rock shoots up a jet of water that looks like a fountain. The stretch from Fountain to Caribou Hide is the steepest section of the Upper Stikine on average and you will encounter a number of rapids from riffles to approaching Class 2 in difficulty. Rocks are your main concern.

Nearing Chapea Rapids you drop into the White-and-Black-Spruce bioclimatic zone. Interesting to note here that Chapea is an anglicized version of the Tahltan word meaning "poplar tree." Because though the forest along the river is often spruce with a moss understorey, balsam poplar groves begin to show up and you may see lupine, larkspur and monkshood in the forest clearings. In sandy areas there are often lodgepole pine and understorey plants that like drier climes, including lichen, crowberry and kinnikinnick. Strawberries, broadleaf willow herb, cow parsnip, cinquefoil, fireweed, buttercup, arnica, Indian paintbrush, columbine, saxifrage, mountain avens and yarrow can be found along the riverbanks and gravel bars.

The rock walls at Chapea make for a mini-canyon prelude to the Pink Granite Canyon to come. The river is still quite clear here, even though it has gained volume and now runs through a wide valley with an old burn. You can see the Omineca Mountains to the east on your approach to Caribou Hide. There is some nice open country here. Numerous kinds of berry bushes can be found in the forest, including blueberry, raspberry, currants, gooseberry, huckleberry, bunchberry, cranberry, chokecherry and bearberry.

After Caribou Hide the valley widens even more and the river slows and begins to braid. Before you hit a difficult stretch of braiding to navigate, you could stretch your legs at Adoogacho Falls. About 10 km upstream from the Chuckachida you get into a stretch of significant braiding and meanders. Bank erosion makes for lots of wood hazards. Be alert and ready to manoeuvre.

The views near the Chuckachida's mouth are great, once you have a chance to look around, no longer focusing on avoiding wood hazards! After the Chuckachida River joins the Stikine the volume of the river and the speed of the current increase noticeably, but the river is open and more easily navigated. You pass Mount Albert Dease on your right, apparently named for the son of Peter Warren Dease, the Métis HBC fur trader and Arctic explorer for whom the Dease River is named. The Dease is covered in volume one of this guidebook.

The confluence of the Spatsizi and Stikine is a marvellous place to camp. The often silty Spatsizi flows through a wide valley of lodgepole pine and poplar flats and semi-open grasslands and meadow to its mouth, where there is a plethora of gravel bars hosting shrubs and wildflowers. Unfortunately the confluence area was burned in 2001 or 2002. But it's still beautiful and the moose are happy. We saw four in a bay to the north when we paddled up to view the mixing of the then silty grey Spatsizi waters with the blue Stikine flow. Ironically, the fire was a result of a prescribed burn in the area getting out of control. Apparently there was some concern it was going to burn Hyland Post! From just downstream of the confluence, you can hike to the Post and then onward up the Plateau Trail to the alpine.

Heading downstream on the now doubly wide and much murkier Stikine, you will pass Upper Stikine River Adventures' lodge on river right. The highlight of the next stretch of river is Jewel Rapids, a long boulder garden without a portage trail. Following the rapids there is good current through the wide valley. There is not much for mountain views, but the conglomerate rock walls of Schreiber Canyon are pretty. You can explore up the creek in the steep-sided canyon for a few kilometres.

The river picks up steam as you approach the Stikine Ranges. They bring a different flavour to the river setting. The rugged mountains are dissected by widely flaring valleys, mantled with glacial drift. Typical of the Cassiars, the peaks you see on the latter section of the Upper Stikine route are comprised of Cassiar batholith, granitic rocks folded into volcanic and sedimentary rocks, with a significant component of limestone/dolomite in some places. Ridges and summits are rounded below 1800 m ASL and sharply scalloped above that elevation due to glaciation. The highest peaks in the Cassiars reach 2500 m ASL. There is bare bedrock at elevations above treeline, and the alpine vegetation below consists of heath and tundra as well as willow, birch and other dwarf shrubs, alpine grasses, sedges and mountain avens.

The climate of the Cassiar Mountains is influenced by Pacific weather systems. Considered northern continental, it is somewhat warmer and wetter than that of the Spatsizi Plateau. Before you get any great mountain views, however, you go through a section of river with high, slumping clay cliffs. This is where we had our adventure with the new channels cut through the forest. The main channel had been blocked by a mudslide from one of these eroding steep faces. Watch for wood hazards. The river is siltier and can be lively. There are standing waves at a number of bends.

The Stikine Ranges finally make a good showing at the Kehlechoa and McBride river confluences, which are good places to camp. The outcropping of hard rock at Beggarly Canyon is also a highlight of the scenery on the lower part of the route. My favourite campsite lies in a sandy cove halfway down the canyon, just before the vertical canyon walls really squeeze the river.

The valley opens up again after Beggarly and you suddenly see the abandoned railway bridge over the river. It looks very odd. Then the muddy-brown Klappan enters on river left and the Stikine just keeps getting murkier and wider until S-Bend

Rapids, another hard-rock gorge. After being compressed there, the Stikine flows along at a good pace though the open valley. Eventually, you will see the Cassiar Highway coming down the river right side of the valley from Dease Lake and then in front of you the bridge over the Stikine. There is no way you can miss the take-out. If you do, say hello Grand Canyon, bye-bye life!

This amazing section of the Stikine has been successfully run by only a handful of extreme kayakers. There are Class 5+ cataracts within vertical cliff walls of up to 300 m and the river is squeezed at one point to 2 m in width. Salmon can't get up the canyon and that tells you something. The canyon walls are made up of sedimentary and volcanic rock, including sandstone, granite and columnar basalt. Mountain goats grace the clefts of this stunning 100-km-long natural wonder. The canyon can be appreciated on foot, on a horse trek or by scenic flight. Jet boats go a short way up the lower part of the canyon from Telegraph Creek as well. To add a Grand Canyon adventure to your canoe trip itinerary, see the Directory of Services and Organizations for contact information for businesses offering excursions.

For more information on the ecology and natural history of the ecoregions of the Stikine, consult The Ecoregions of British Columbia website: www.env .gov.bc.ca/ecology/ecoregions/province.html. Environment Canada's Ecological Framework document, at http://atlas.nrcan.gc.ca/site/english/maps/environment/ ecology/framework/1, provides more detail about BC's ecological classifications. Web pages for ecological information specific to the Spatsizi Plateau and the Stikine River can be found at www.spacesfornature.org/greatspaces/spatsizi.html and www. spacesfornature.org/greatspaces/stikine.html.

A good book to consult for general information on BC's natural history is *British Columbia: A Natural History*, by Cannings and Cannings. Jennifer Voss's guidebook *Stikine River: A Guide to Paddling the Great River* is also a good source of information on the Stikine's natural history. There are three great coffee table books to enjoy as well: *Alaska to Nunavut: The Great Rivers*, by Neil Hartling with photographs by Terry Parker; *Roll On! Discovering the Wild Stikine River*, by Bonnie Demerjian; and *Stikine: The Great River*, by Gary Fiegehen.

For some articles on canoe trippers' experiences of the Upper Stikine route try "The Magic of an Old Friend," by Tony Shaw (one-time owner/operator of Red Goat Lodge at Iskut) in *Kanawa* magazine, and Patrick Mahaffey's "Spatsizi and Stikine Rivers" in the book *Paddle Quest: Canada's Best Canoe Routes*. To vicariously run the Grand Canyon in a whitewater kayak, read the chapter on Ken Madsen's descent in *Wild Rivers, Wild Lands*. See the References section for bibliographical information on all the suggested reading.

Local History: ✳ ✳ ½ Most of the Spatsizi Plateau lies in the hunting grounds of the Tahltan and Iskut First Nations, and their heritage sites are widespread over the area. There were two historical-period settlements in the area: Caribou Hide, on the banks of the Upper Stikine, and another just east of the river at Metsantan Lake. The Stikine region also has a history of big-game hunting and conservation. Though management of the area's ecosystem is taking place as a result of the creation of the provincial parks and associated protected areas, it is under siege all around from natural resource extraction threats.

The Spatsizi Plateau is called "Land of the Red Goat." Spatsizi is an anglicized name said to come from two Tahltan words meaning "red goat." Mountain goats have a habit of rolling in dust, and the iron-oxide-coloured dust found on Red Goat Mountain on the Spatsizi River turns their normally white coats red.

The meaning of Stikine is not so certain. Most sources say the word means "the river" as in the sense of "the great river" in Tlingit. The BC Geographical Names Information System (BCGNIS) online notes that Stikine comes from "Stahankane" meaning "grande rivière" and was the First Nations name for the river: "From a Tlingit word meaning "the river," in the sense of "the definitive, or great river" as reported in 1799 by Captain Rowan, commander of the *Eliza* of Boston. The Stikine was labelled "Ryka Stahkin" on a Russian chart of 1848 and its spelling is varied on many maps and documents from Shikene, Stachine, Stachin, Stah-Keena, Stahkin, Stakeen, Stickeen, Stickienes, Stikeen, Stikin and Sucheen. The river's name was amended to its present spelling in 1869.

However, in the online encyclopedia Wikipedia, the entry states the name is an approximation of the Tlingit words Shtax' Héen, meaning "cloudy river (with the milt of spawning salmon)" or, alternatively, "bitter waters (from the tidal estuaries at its mouth)." This second meaning seems likely, as a Tlingit Traditional Territory map and poster on the Alaska Native Knowledge Network, www.ankn.uaf.edu, shows the name of the Wrangell tribe as Shtax'héen Kwáan, or Bitter Water Tribe. The tribe is also referred to as the Stikine Tlingit or Indians in other literature.

The Sekani that Samuel Black met around Metsantan Lake called the Stikine "Schadzue." This name may indicate the Sekani referred to the Stikine River in terms of its size and power, as one of their names for the Liard River was Itzehadzue, meaning "great current river." Apparently the Stikine is also known to some Iskut First Nations people as "The Uncle of Rivers" and I have read that the Tahltan also referred to it as "Muddy River." The river was called the St. Francis River in "Purchase of the Russian Possessions in North America by the USA," a letter from Mr. Collins to Mr. Seward, dated New York, April 4, 1867. The Stikine has even been referred to as Pelly's River, making it very confusing if you were looking for the Pelly River in the Yukon!

It is also not clear when the Tahltan, a Dene-na or Na-Dene group (an Athapaskan-speaking people), moved into the Upper Stikine region. It is thought the Tahltan's ancestors were living in northwestern BC 2,000 years ago, that they had moved west from the Subarctic interior into an apparently unpopulated area of the Pacific Basin, which included the Upper Stikine River drainage, some 300 years ago. They then expanded their annual rounds to include the lower reaches of the

Stikine. There is strong evidence that by the early 1700s the Tahltan were trading with the Tlingit from the Wrangell area, yet still remaining semi-nomadic, hunting and trapping in the interior in the winter. The Tahltan's profitable trade with the Tlingit and the salmon-rich environment of the Pacific Basin encouraged them to become more sedentary, centralizing in the Lower Stikine River drainage. When the first Europeans arrived they were already based there, and salmon fishing, hunting and inter-First Nations trading were the basis of their economy.

Relationships with the Kaska, Sekani and Bear Lake/Caribou Hide (Sekani and Gitxsan) groups to the east were generally commercial and peaceful. Marriages between members of the groups were not uncommon, but the Tahltan were to become greatly influenced by the culture of the coastal Tlingit from communities near the mouth of the Stikine River. The Tahltan eventually developed very close trading ties with the Tlingit on the coast and intermarried extensively. In September, the annual rendezvous with the Tlingit was the climax of the trading and social calendar.

The Stikine River was part of an important inter-native trading route, or grease trail. In the early days the Tahltan traded as near-equals with the Wrangell, or Bitter Water Tribe, of the Coastal Tlingit. Tahltan products such as cured hides, furs, robes, leather goods, babiche, quillwork and obsidian (flakes of which made for very sharp cutting tools) were valued on the coast. The Tahltan traded these interior goods for hooligan (oolichan or eulachon) and salmon oil and eggs, shells, copper plates, ceremonial clothes and blankets. The Tahltan would then trade some of these coastal goods to the Kaska and Sekani to the east. They had middleman advantage in the coastal–interior trade in the region.

Relations with the Tlingit intensified once the Tlingit made contact with the Russian, British and American fur traders coming to the Northwest Coast, beginning in 1799. The Euro-American traders wanted sea otter pelts to trade in China, and the Tlingit supplied them. The Tlingit's location at the mouth of the main rivers and end of the grease trails along the coast made for exclusive trading rights with the newcomers, which they guarded fiercely. This enforced monopoly on the trade of western goods from the coast to the interior shifted the Tlingit–Tahltan balance of power. The Tahltan adapted by establishing closer social ties with the Tlingit through increased trading relationships and intermarriage. Disease epidemics devastated the Tahltan population after Contact, also resulting in further assimilation into the Tlingit way of life. (See the Lower Stikine River chapter for more on the Coastal Tlingit from around Wrangell.) A sound economic strategy was to be part of the clan (Tlingit), so to speak, and to increase production of valued animal products. The changes in Tahltan culture reflected this.

Once the sea otter were extinct, the demand for furs from the interior increased. The Tlingit, as well as the Tsimshian farther south, pushed more aggressively into the interior in search of furs to trade. The Tahltan stepped up their trapping and trading activities to the east in the Spatsizi Plateau and northward to Dease Lake and beyond, putting them in competition with other interior groups who had either migrated into the areas the Tahltan used to hunt and gather in or those that had traditionally been based in areas the Tahltan were now active in. There is still some dispute about traditional territories with regard to the interior plateaus near the Taku headwaters and the Dease River region. See www.stikine.net/Tahltan/tahltannations.html and the Taku River and Dease River chapters in volume one of *Northern British Columbia Canoe Trips* for more on this topic.

The HBC's search for an overland route to the Pacific Coast from interior northern BC resulted in the establishment of a network of trading posts from the Lower Liard River to Dease Lake, but trade was skimpy to the west. This network never reached its potential because of the Tlingit trading monopoly over the Stikine's lower reaches and the trading with posts on the Coast. Neither Samuel Black's 1824 journey overland from Fort St. James to find a route to the Stikine, nor the establishment of Fort Halkett on the Liard in 1829 and 1832 (two different locations), nor John McLeod's 1834 exploration of the Dease, nor Robert Campbell's success in making contact with the Tahltan and Tlingit in 1837 or 1838 at their annual rendezvous and his establishment of the short-lived Dease Lake Post made much impact on the Tahltan way of life or on the First Nations coastal–interior trading relations.

The European trading rights along the coast passed from Russian to English hands in 1839 and the HBC stepped up its maritime operations, basically abandoning efforts to conduct trade from the interior. The change in the traders' nationalities did not change the Tlingit's powerful position as middlemen or the position of the Tahltan as traders to the interior Nations. In fact, trade to the interior intensified and the Tlingit's power and wealth grew. The Tahltan threw their lot in with them to an even greater extent, and even some Kaska bands to the east began to take on cultural characteristics of the Tlingit (likely via their trading relations and intermarriage with Tlingitized Tahltan).

It was the gold rushes that eventually brought these trade monopolies to an end. The 1861/62 Stikine River Gold Rush was short-lived and inconsequential from a gold perspective, but it marked the first major influx of non-Tahltans into Tahltan territory in the Pacific drainage. In 1862 the supply needs of the gold seekers led to the advent of riverboat service from Wrangell, Alaska, to Glenora and Telegraph Creek, effectively destroying the trader/middleman role the Tahltan had enjoyed for centuries and it cut heavily into the Tlingit monopoly of trade and shipping up the Stikine. In 1863 Governor James Douglas claimed all land north to the 60th parallel as part of British Columbia. This further opened up Tahltan country to outsiders. Riverboats began to ply the Stikine in earnest, bringing gold seekers, suppliers and others looking to make their fortune.

In 1865/66 there was an attempt by Perry McDonough Collins and the Western Union Company to establish a transcontinental telegraph connection between North America and Russia. Telegraph Creek became a staging area for the crews clearing the trail and stringing the line, and independent newcomers began to take up the majority of the trade in European-American goods in the area.

It was the Cassiar Gold Rush of 1873 to 1876 that finally broke the Tlingit's control over trade to the interior. By 1878 most of the Stikine region had been explored by prospectors. The huge influx of gold seekers and the traders setting up shop to service the gold diggings could not be controlled, and interior groups had access to trade items previously only obtainable through the Tlingit via the Tahltan.

The change in trading relationships, the participation of the Tahltan in packing and freighting in the Cassiar boom (around 1875 the first horses were introduced as a transport mode and Tahltan people quickly become adept handlers), along with the epidemics of disease that accompanied increased contact with Euro-Americans, altered First Nations lives and territories. The Tahltan population was decimated by disease by 1875 and the remnants of several bands joined together to form one tribe under one chief. They built a village called Tahltan on a high terrace about 2.5 km downstream of the Stikine from the Tahltan River mouth and it became their headquarters until 1920, when they abandoned it and moved to Telegraph Creek.

The Klondike Gold Rush in the Yukon (1898–1903) made Telegraph Creek an even busier place. Though Glenora was the main staging area, the trailheads for the Collins Overland–Western Union telegraph line and the Teslin Trail to the Yukon could be accessed at Telegraph Creek, the farthest navigable point of the Stikine River. There was a huge wave of prospectors coming through Tahltan country via these routes to the Klondike and sundry others in their wake. Sundry others included big-game hunters. Andrew Stone led an expedition into the Cassiar region to collect specimens of animals for the American Museum of Natural History and with his announcement of the "discovery" of several new species such as the Stone sheep (named after him), the area became a major destination for trophy hunters.

Telegraph Creek became a major transportation hub. In 1901 the Dominion Telegraph was completed. The line stretched from Ashcroft, BC, to Dawson City, Yukon, via Telegraph Creek. During construction of the line, Telegraph Creek was the staging area for the project and for the aborted railway and wagon road planned for the Teslin Trail (the head of this traditional First Nations trail was at Telegraph Creek). The Klondike Gold Rush and the major government-funded projects associated with the huge influx of people into the North brought even more activity into Tahltan territory. They also brought the wage economy, and the traditional trading and subsistence economy of the Tahltan fell in importance. Though the Tahltan still basically lived off the land, this period presented more opportunities for working as packers, wranglers and guides than ever.

Wires in the Wilderness: The Story of the Yukon Telegraph, by Bill Miller, is an excellent source of historical information on the history of northern BC from the late 1800s and into the mid-1900s. The book includes descriptions of the booms and busts of Telegraph Creek, the characters of the times, and stories of interesting journeys taking place on the trails associated with the telegraph lines to Atlin and the Yukon. For instance, Miller tells the tale of Simon Gunanoot (a Gitxsan from the Kispiox area) and his brother-in-law Peter Haimadan, accused of murdering two men. The outlaws were known to frequent the eastern edge of the Spatsizi Plateau and were helped by telegraph line workers while eluding police. Gunanoot, a construction worker and packer on the Yukon Telegraph Line, remained free for 13 years, roaming the terrain he knew so well before giving himself up and being acquitted of the murders. Apparently one of his sons is buried near Laslui Lake.

In 1910, in response to rumours that the British Columbia government had claimed all land outside of federal reserves as Crown land, the Tahltan joined other tribes in BC in the Indian Rights Movement. The Tahltan claimed rights over their traditional territories with a formal document, the "Declaration of the Tahltan Tribe," signed by Chief Nanok (Nanook or Nanuk) and 80 other tribesmen, and urged the formalization of a treaty to address all matters regarding these rights. No such treaty has ever been made, and the Tahltan Indian Band and Iskut First Nations are not participating in the BC Treaty Process. Their stand is that aboriginal title lands can only be surrendered to the federal Crown and converted to non-title lands. However, the two groups have undertaken discussions outside of the treaty process with provincial treaty negotiators on a wide range of topics, including addressing concerns associated with development in their asserted traditional territories.

The First Nations people predominantly associated with the Upper Stikine River are comprised of two groups, the Tahltan Indian Band (with headquarters at Telegraph Creek) and the Iskut First Nation (with headquarters at Iskut), each with an elected council. The overarching Tahltan Central Council (with offices at Dease Lake) is comprised of representatives of ten families from each band. The council links the Tahltan bands and has represented them on issues of joint concern, specifically on asserted inherent rights and title. Apparently the Tahltan Indian Band and the Iskut First Nation are regarded as separate, unaffiliated bands by the Canadian government.

Like the Tahltan Indian Band, the Iskut First Nation has an interesting history and it is intimately related to the Upper Stikine River. Their ancestors were likely the people Black met on his 1824 explorations of the Finlay and Stikine headwaters. In his journals Black describes meeting with a group of Sekani who actually accompanied him to the Chuckachida confluence. While travelling with them, he met the Thloadennis, a clan of Tahltan. This clan eventually moved farther west, closer to their cousins and the "Bear Lakers," a few families of Sekani and Gitxsan descent (from the villages of Kuldo and Kispiox) who moved into Groundhog Plateau country, the grassy plateau region between the Upper Stikine and Skeena rivers vacated by the Tahltan. See the Turnagain chapter in this volume for more information on the Sekani and Gitxsan First Nations. (The Omineca and Kispiox chapters in volume one cover more of the history of the Sekani and Gitxsan and the Bear Lakers.)

Sometime after 1890 when the HBC closed Fort Connelly (established in 1826) on Bear Lake, the Bear Lakers began to headquarter on the banks of the Upper Stikine at the village of Caribou Hide, which got its name from to the caribou hides they used for clothing and tents. They sporadically traded at Telegraph Creek (approximately 250 km west), but mostly did their commerce at Fort Ware in the Rocky Mountain Trench, the nearest supply centre, about 130 km to the east. After a flu epidemic in the 1920s they relocated a short way east to Metsantan Lake along with a few more families from Bear Lake.

The Spatsizi Plateau was seldom visited by outsiders after the few initial explorers, fur traders, surveyors and gold seekers passed through until sometime after the flu epidemic. It is thought the Hyland brothers opened the first trading post, still called Hyland Post and located up the river left bank of the Spatsizi near its confluence with the Stikine. By 1929 they were trading for furs with the First Nations people trapping in the area. According to Tommy Walker, a big-game outfitter who later operated out of Hyland Post, a competitor soon set up shop near the Hylands and there wasn't enough trade for two outfits so both businesses folded. Another account says there was a "silver frost" and ice coated the grasslands in the area, causing the death of many horses and the end of the Hyland brothers' enterprise.

A provincial government survey of the Stikine River was commissioned in 1935, led by P.M. Monckton. But the area was so wild and remote that one survey was not enough, and Jim Morgan was still surveying and exploring the upper river in the 1960s. Edward Hoagland travelled with Morgan on the Stikine for a few days and wrote about him and the river in his book *Notes from the Century Before*. Hoagland mentions in the book that Morgan pointed out to him how the Stikine's tributaries coming in on river right are clear, while those flowing in on the left are siltier. Take a look at the Chuckachida and Pitman rivers versus the Spatsizi and Klappan, and you will see what he means.

The building of the Northwest Staging Route and Alaska Highway brought another wave of activity to the Telegraph Creek area. Many gold seekers on their way to the Cassiar travelled the "Trail to the Interior," boating up the Lower Stikine River to Glenora or Telegraph Creek, then going overland to Dease Lake and finally heading north down the Dease River by watercraft. To deal with the increasing numbers of gold seekers and their suppliers, the trail from Telegraph Creek over to Dease Lake was upgraded in 1874/75. In the 1940s this was the main supply route for the building of the Northwest Staging Route and then the Alaska Highway. Goods shipped up the Stikine were trucked over from Telegraph Creek and then floated down the Dease to Lower Post to be hauled from there to Watson Lake and beyond. More wage labour opportunities drew the Tahltan off the land and further concentrated the population of the Stikine River Valley.

The buildings at Hyland were being taken back by the land when Walker came through in 1948, but the area around it was still being trapped by a family of Bear

Lakers/Caribou Hiders from Metsantan Lake. The post area had been a seasonal camp for the people from Caribou Hide and likely before them the group of Tahltan who had moved farther west. Confluences have always been important gathering places for First Nations in northern BC, though neither the Tahltan of the west or the Bear Lakers normally used canoes for long journeys. They preferred to walk, though rafts were used for river and short lake crossings. Occasionally they would build spruce bark canoes for longer water journeys.

When Walker's party, on their overland trip to set up their Cold Fish Lake camp, met the band at Metsantan in 1948, there were only 39 band members. Metsantan Lake was fished out (ironically, Metsantan means "full belly" in Sekani) and game was scarce. The people were in dire straits. Walker reports in his book *Spatsizi* that the Indian Agent wanted the band to move to Telegraph Creek; they wanted to remain free to live their subsistence, semi-nomadic lifestyle, the reason they had moved from Bear Lake to the Upper Stikine watershed in the first place.

After Tommy and Marion Walker set up their hunting camp at Cold Fish Lake on the Spatsizi Plateau, some of the people from Metsantan Lake worked for them – at Cold Fish Lake during the guiding season and at Hyland Post during the winter to look after the horses. A number moved to Telegraph Creek in 1949, as did Tahltan families from the Klappan and Sheslay rivers and Dease Lake area bands that had been decimated by disease. This was the second Tahltan amalgamation in the Lower Stikine River Valley. See the Lower Stikine River chapter for more Tahltan history in this region.

Eventually, in the early 1950s, still dogged by disease and economic hardship, the majority of the original Bear Lake families settled across the Stikine River from Telegraph Creek. This location, so close to the main Tahltan headquarters, was not ideal. A decade later most families moved into the Eddontenajon and Kluachon lakes area, the headwaters of the Iskut River at the head of the Iskut Valley. The present-day village of Iskut is near Kluachon and the lake is sometimes referred to as Iskut or Skoot Lake. It gets its name from Klue Cho, which means "big fish" in Tahltan. Kluachon Lake drains into Eddontenajon Lake and this name has been translated as "Place where the little boy drowned."

Prior to the new settlement, a small Catholic mission existed at Kluachon Lake, with priests travelling the Telegraph Trail from Telegraph Creek to hold services when the few Tahltan families in the area gathered there as part of their seasonal rounds. One priest, Father Doetzel, helped the Bear Lake/Caribou Hide/Metsantan Lake families relocate from their community across the river from Telegraph Creek to their new home by the Kluachon Lake mission (called Eddontenajon Village – I know, it is all very confusing). A few families of Tahltan settled permanently there as well.

In the 1950s and '60s a number of people from Telegraph Creek and Iskut worked in the mineral exploration industry. In the 1960s the increasingly common use of aircraft led to Smithers becoming the staging point for exploration in Tahltan

Country, rather than Telegraph Creek. Tahltan involvement in exploration activities in their homelands declined as a result.

By the 1960s, most communities had lost their traditional economies for good. With government financial assistance and compulsory education, many of the First Nations people in the area became more sedentary and more reliant on the purchase of food from stores. Though subsistence through trapping, hunting and fishing was still important to the economy, wage labour was becoming much more so. Tahltan began to work at the Cassiar asbestos mine (1952–1992), the construction of the Cassiar Highway and the northern extension of BC Rail (Pacific Great Eastern) to Dease Lake. Increased wage labour and access to the south brought modern problems to the First Nations communities.

By 1972 the bridge over the Stikine River was completed and the Stewart–Cassiar Highway provided easy access to Tahltan country. There was an increase in the population in the Telegraph Creek/Iskut area in the 1970s, with homesteaders coming from southern BC and the US. The Bear Lakers that had relocated to the mission site were now near the highway. In fact, a new village site, called Iskut, ended up being on the east side of the Cassiar Highway. According to Walker, the fact that some of the Bear Lakers had worked on the Cassiar Highway from the Stikine River to the old mission prompted the community to leave the isolation of the "wrong side" of the Stikine at Telegraph Creek. Ironically, the descendants of the Bear Lakers living at Iskut were now the least isolated group of the Tahltan Council.

In the 1990s the people of Telegraph Creek and Iskut became more directly involved with mining operations in their traditional territory by providing services such as road construction and maintenance and camp catering. Now there are several large mining exploration and development projects underway in the region. Both communities appear to be divided within on the issue of development in their territory. A number of the people question the rate and sustainability of development and assert that the community and elders must participate in decision-making about such issues.

In 2006, Iskut First Nation elders formed a group called the Klabona Keepers Elders Society as a step to ensure the long-term sustainable stewardship of their territory, especially the Sacred Headwaters, the area of the Skeena Mountains that gives rise to the Nass, Stikine and Skeena rivers. In August 2006, the group hosted its first large gathering in the Sacred Headwaters valley. Joining the Iskut Nation elders were hereditary chiefs of the Haida, Gitxsan, Wet'suwet'en, Taku River Tlingit, and Haisla Nations, as well as non-aboriginal allies, including Rivers without Borders. Since that time there has been a groundswell of support for the group's goals, and as of December 2008 the Klabona Keepers and their many supporters had achieved at least a temporary victory in protecting the Sacred Headwaters from coalbed methane mining. The BC government put a two-year moratorium in place on that activity in this extremely special place.

The major threats to the Upper Iskut–Stikine region and its people are numerous, including:

◆ BC Metals' Red Chris copper/gold mine and road project is located on the Todagin Plateau between Ealue and Kluea Lakes, approximately 18 km southeast of the village of Iskut. Mine activity, especially frequent blasting, would threaten the Stone sheep populations on Todagin Mountain. The tailings impoundment would impact fish habitat and likely end a 55-year-old traditional Tahltan guided hunting enterprise. The project has received regulatory approvals, but BC Metals cannot operate without a viable source of power.

◆ Fortune Minerals' proposed Klappan open-pit coal project is just on the edge of the Spatsizi Provincial Park, with the haul road to go from the headwaters of the Little and Big Klappan drainages of the Stikine through the headwaters of the Nass and Bell-Irving rivers.

◆ Shell Canada is exploring for coalbed methane and has drilled four test wells near the head of the Little Klappan and Spatsizi rivers. This type of industrial activity requires numerous access points and drill sites, and the energy it would produce would contribute to climate change. This project would be especially harmful to water quality given its proximity to the Sacred Headwaters. (Source: Rivers without Borders, at www.riverswithoutborders.org/about-the-region/iskut-stikine)

The combined impacts of all of the projects (including a major power line and cargo road) currently proposed in the Upper Stikine watershed would definitely affect the environment and local communities. Besides obvious issues of water quality and salmon habitat, the Klappan River Valley is a traditional hunting ground for the people of Telegraph Creek and Iskut. The name Klappan comes from the Tahltan phrase "good food for animals here" – as in meadow or wide open valley.

For more information on the Sacred Headwaters and other Stikine watershed conservation issues and campaigns, visit the following websites:

Klabona Keepers Elders Society, at www.sacredheadwaters.com;

Dogwood Initiative, at http://dogwoodinitiative.org/campaigns/sacred-headwaters;

Citizens Concerned about Coalbed Methane, at www.ekcbm.org;

First Nations Land Rights and Environmentalism in BC, at www.firstnations.de/mining.htm?05-3-tahltan.htm;

Rivers without Borders, at www.riverswithoutborders.org/about-the-region/iskut-stikine;

Friends of the Stikine, at www.panorama-map.com/STIKINE/stikine.html; and

CPAWS BC, at www.cpawsbc.org.

The following websites also provide good information and opportunities to take action to protect the Stikine River region from harmful development:

www.skeenawatershed.com;

www.ecojustice.ca;

www.miningwatch.ca;

www.dogwoodinitiative.org;

www.spacesfornature.org/greatspaces/stikine.html; and

the Pembina Institute site at www.afterthegoldrush.ca.

Contact information for the Cassiar Watch Society, a locally based conservation organization active in the region, can be found in the Directory of Services and Organizations. Their wild-river director suggests canoeists need to make their voice heard in the management committees for the Stikine and Spatsizi area provincial parks.

For some on-the-river reading that will provide you with history and background on the Stikine River, try the previously mentioned *Notes from the Century Before: A Journal from British Columbia*, by Edward Hoagland. He recounts the history of numerous places in the Stikine watershed and interviews with old timers besides telling stories about his own travels in the area. Stories by the descendants of the "Bear Lakers" and Tahltan at Iskut can be found in *Kuji K'at Dahdahwhesdetch (Now I Told All of You): Stories Told at Iskut, British Columbia, by Iskut Tahltan Elders*," a self-published booklet edited by Thomas McIlwraith and funded by the Endangered Languages Fund. Tommy Walker's book *Spatsizi* is an account of his life as a big-game outfitter and of the fight for protected status for the Spatsizi Plateau. In a recent book on the area, *In the Land of the Red Goat*, author Bob Henderson recounts his four decades of wrangling, guiding, flying and fishing in the rugged Stikine country. Henderson tells many stories about the area and its characters and describes his guiding journeys on the horse trails that make for such good hiking.

The fact that big-game hunting was and still is such an important activity on the Spatsizi Plateau is obvious from these books. On December 3, 1975, Spatsizi Plateau Wilderness Provincial Park was established, due to pressure from outfitters and conservationists. It is a large and significant park in Canada at 696,160 ha, or 7,000 km². It was designated to conserve the area and encompass a large enough part of the ecosystem to maintain the system's ability to support large wildlife populations. The intent was also that the public could enjoy the outstanding scenery and varied terrain with hiking, photography and nature study as well as canoeing. Hunting is allowed in the park, but the Gladys Lake Ecological Reserve in the central part of the park just south of Cold Fish Lake, has a hunting ban. It was established in 1975 to study Stone sheep and mountain goats in an undisturbed alpine-subalpine habitat. The only unregulated public access is by hiking trails. Besides hunting being banned in the reserve, camping, fishing, landing aircraft and fires are not permitted either.

Apparently one of the first things BC Parks did after the Spatsizi Plateau Wilderness Provincial Park was created was to burn down all the buildings and cabins of the people who had been living off the land. The hunting lodges were excluded from this policy, however. Is it any wonder why some First Nations are leery of park status for their lands?

Established in 1987, the Stikine River Provincial Park was originally designated only as a recreation area. It was upgraded to a provincial park in 2001. A corridor of 217,000 hectares, it covers the Upper Stikine River Valley from the boundary of the Spatsizi Plateau Provincial Park to below the Grand Canyon of the Stikine. In the 1970s there was a feasibility study done on a proposal to dam the river in the canyon. By the early '80s plans were well underway, but due to intense public pressure (including from the US because of the impact on salmon stocks in Alaska) the project was dropped. Class A provincial park status protects an area from any hydro dam development, so a significant stretch of the Stikine River is now safe, but the same cannot be said of its larger tributaries.

In 2001, two protected areas were created along the Stikine, one covering the lower reaches of the Chuckachida River and another covering the lower Pitman River. These areas were designated as protected to provide connectivity to high-water habitat in those areas adjacent to Stikine River Provincial Park, key corridors for caribou, grizzly, fisher wolverine (blue listed) and moose. Protecting fish habitat and fishing opportunities was also a reason for the areas' designations. Stikine River Provincial Park and the Chuckachida and Pitman protected areas together made for the first fully protected area in BC that encompasses contiguous streams, large rivers and lakes believed to support the species of bull trout (blue listed) in the full diversity of its life history.

Spatsizi Headwaters Provincial Park, at 427 ha, is a postage-stamp-sized addition to the Spatsizi Plateau Wilderness Provincial Park. The park was designated in 2001 to protect the headwaters of the Spatsizi River and the upper elevation glacial lakes and alpine meadows around the headwaters, mainly focusing on maintaining the hiking and wildlife-viewing values in the area. Quite noticeably, the Stikine headwaters, not so far away, are not protected, and happen to lie in the area targeted for mining and fossil fuel projects. The same is true of the Nass and Skeena headwaters – thus the Sacred Headwaters campaign discussed previously.

The Stikine River has been designated a BC Heritage River and has been nominated for Canadian Heritage River status. However, neither program has the muscle politically or practically to do much for the river without a management plan in place. On the Outdoor Recreation Council of BC's (ORCBC) list of the ten most endangered rivers in the province for 2010, the Stikine is tied for first place because of the threat of the coalbed methane project in the Sacred Headwaters. See the ORCBC website, at www.orcbc.ca. Despite all the protection already afforded the Upper Stikine River watershed, its health is still in jeopardy.

Level of Solitude: ✱ ✱ The two classic Stikine River routes are the most popular canoe trips in northern BC. I expect you will see at least one other canoeing party if you go on the Upper Stikine route during prime paddling season. There are several commercial canoe and raft companies currently offering trips on the Upper Stikine route, but not all the advertised expeditions go in a given season.

On Tuaton and Laslui lakes you may see parties fishing from small motorboats. At the Stikine and Spatsizi's confluence you may also see people in motorboats from either Hyland Post or Upper Stikine Lodge. Stone sheep hunting season begins August 1. Resident jet boat hunters come up the Stikine later in the season to hunt moose. There has been a problem with some of them leaving moose carcasses and garbage around.

You will not feel overcrowded on the river, but you will likely see signs of the modern world nearly every day, even when hiking – be it signs, horse trails, lodges, cabins, bridges or aircraft overhead. The parks protecting the Stikine watershed have lots of visitors besides paddlers. Happy Lake is likely the place you will find the most solitude.

Wildlife: ✱ ✱ ✱ Chances of seeing large mammals on an Upper Stikine canoe trip are good, especially if you do some hiking in the alpine. Hiking on the alpine ridges around the lakes and on the plateau you are almost certain to see caribou. The Spatsizi Plateau provides habitat for a large population of woodland caribou. In summer the caribou appear to be organized into three herds, each associated with either the Spatsizi, the Upper Stikine or the Finlay river valley. These herds share a common winter range along the low-elevation, forested slopes of the Stikine River. The lichen-rich boreal forest is the most critical feeding area for the caribou. Thin snowcover in the rain shadow of the Eaglenest Range makes it one of the most important habitats for woodland caribou in BC.

Other likely wildlife sightings include grizzly bear, moose, wolverine, wolf, lynx, beaver and hoary marmot. Stone sheep also reside in the upper elevations of the Spatsizi Plateau. If you stop at Laslui Lake and do the hike up to Hotlesklwa Lake you could see mountain goats. Mule deer can be seen in the lower elevations. Mink, ermine, otter, muskrat, porcupine, snowshoe hare, Arctic ground squirrels and other small rodents can also be seen anywhere along the route. On our 2003 trip in the third week of July we saw grizzlies and woodland caribou in the stretch from Tuaton to Lasuli and four moose at the confluence of the Stikine and Spatsizi alone.

Eagles, both bald and golden, are found in the Upper Stikine River watershed. Other potential raptor sightings include a number of species of hawk, osprey, northern harrier, merlin, kestrel, gyrfalcons and peregrine falcon. Owls can be seen, including the great grey owl and great horned owl. Loons, Canada geese and many species of shorebirds and ducks, including mallard, gadwall, blue-winged teal, canvasback, bufflehead and grebe, are visitors to the Stikine. Grouse and ptarmigan lurk on the ground in the alpine and in the forest. There are over 140 bird species found in the

Spatsizi Plateau Wilderness Provincial Park alone. Bring a field guide to identify the many you will see. A couple of guides are listed in the References section.

Fishing: ✳ ✳ ½ You can catch rainbow and lake trout in the headwater lakes and bull trout (known locally as Dolly Varden trout) and Arctic grayling on the river. Fishing is often good below rapids, particularly in the eddies below Fountain Rapids. You can also catch bull trout and grayling at the mouths of clear streams flowing into the Stikine. Look for creek or river mouths with deep pools or channels and eddies where the outflows of the clear water mix with the river. This is your best bet for finding fish when the Stikine becomes silty. Grayling in particular prefer clear, cold water. I've never heard of anyone getting skunked on this river. Be conservative with your catch, as bull trout are blue-listed in this region.

Camping, Hiking and Other Activities: ✳ ✳ ✳ ½ There is a somewhat established campsite at the Tuaton Lake put-in near the park sign. There are a couple of others at key spots along the route: Fountain Rapids and Beggarly Canyon Rapids. Both of these have pit toilets. There is a pit toilet at the bridge take-out and you can camp in the clearing there.

Most camping spots are natural and found on gravel bars. There are some really nice sites with big mountain scenery. There are only a couple of stretches on this route where good campsites are lacking and they are identified in the Trip Notes.

Most of the gravel bar campsites will be pristine, the freshet having washed them clean. Do not rely on this, however; instead, be sure to "no trace" your campsite. I'm sure the canoeing party behind you will appreciate not seeing evidence of you. If you do camp at a spot that shows signs previous campers, leave the site less impacted than it was when you arrived. See Appendix B for tips on camping with minimal impact on the environment.

Campfires are allowed in the park, but BC Parks encourages people hiking in the park and camping at the headwater lakes to conserve wood by keeping their fires small and cooking on stoves. See www.env.gov.bc.ca/bcparks/explore/whatyou.html#campfires for more information on campfires in the park. There is lots of driftwood for fires along the most of the route, the exception being the headwater lakes and some of the established and well-used camping spots. Check for the Fire Danger Rating and campfire bans at http://bcwildfire.ca or by contacting the BC Parks office in Smithers or Dease Lake. If you hike into the Gladys Lake Ecological Reserve, please note that camping is not allowed and fires are not permitted there.

There are many alpine and subalpine hiking opportunities in the headwaters and lower down river on the Spatsizi Plateau. The alpine areas have excellent terrain for hiking and you can usually go where you wish quite easily – once you bushwhack through the stunted trees and thick shrubbery! The trails below the treeline evolved from game trails that were later used as horse trails. You can also do a tour of the headwater lakes and across the Spatsizi Plateau. The majority of trails are marked on the Spatsizi Plateau Wilderness Provincial Park map put out by BC Parks.

The long, multi-day hikes outlined on the park map can be accessed from Tuaton and Laslui lakes, from just below the confluence of the Spatsizi and the Stikine or from near the Klappan River mouth, where you can access the trailheads via the railway bed (note that this access point is a long way from any alpine hiking). The majority of the trails are blazed or otherwise marked. Established campsites and other sites of interest are also marked on the park map. Obey signs and use designated trails where they exist, for your own safety and to minimize your impact on the fragile vegetation. Multi-day hikes should only be undertaken by fit, experienced and well-equipped hikers. For more information on the multi-day trail-hiking opportunities, get the online map of the Spatsizi Plateau Wilderness Provincial Park and check out the following Spatsizi Plateau park websites:

www.env.gov.bc.ca/bcparks/explore/parkpgs/spatsizi/hiking.html; and
www.env.gov.bc.ca/bcparks/explore/parkpgs/spatsizi/canoeing.html.

There are also day and shorter hikes all along the Upper Stikine: up the Hotlesklwa River to see mountain goats, to Adoogacho Falls, Caribou Hide to Metsantan Lake or the Edozadelly Plateau, the Plateau Trail at Hyland Post, up Schreiber Canyon and Beggarly Creek, along the rail grade from the bridge by the Klappan River and from the bridge take-out to Entrance Rapids in the Grand Canyon. The trailheads or starting points for these are indicated in the Trip Notes.

Horse trekking is another option for off-the-river adventure, especially for those who want to check out the alpine but don't enjoy hiking. On horseback, you can see lots of the plateau country and its wildlife. Contact Spatsizi Wilderness Vacations (the fishing camp at Laslui Lake and Hyland Post are part of their operation), Upper Stikine River Adventures (their lodge is the one just downstream of the confluence of the Spatsizi and Stikine) or Stikine Trail Rides (their base is just west of the bridge take-out).

You may also want to add a Grand Canyon adventure to your canoe trip itinerary. Parts of the 100-km-long canyon can be appreciated on foot, by horse trek or on a scenic flight. Jet boats go a short way up the lower part of the canyon from Telegraph Creek as well. See the Directory of Services and Organizations for contact information for the outfitters offering a variety of excursions in the Upper Stikine area.

Special Equipment: On the Upper Stikine route you will want to use a canoe that you are comfortable running up to Class 2+ rapids in and that you can repair or get back into shape to carry on downriver in the event of a wrap or pin on rocks or punching a hole in your boat. Chapea and Jewel rapids are potential boat-breaker and wrap rapids.

A water filter is necessary on this trip. You can get rid of the silt by letting water in a pot stand for a while, but the possibility of "beaver fever" needs to be dealt with. Take extra water bags for filling up at the clear streams to save your filter some hard work.

The Spatsizi Plateau and Stikine River Valley have active bug populations in the summer months, though they usually die down by the end of August. You will want to take a head net, bug jacket, repellent or some combination of the three. I never go anywhere up north without my hooded bug jacket with a face net and Muskol, a repellent high in DEET. I have used them both on trips in the Stikine region, especially while hiking.

I would also carry pepper spray and/or an air horn to deal with potential bear encounters. There are lots of grizzly bears in this region and if you are hiking you are more likely to surprise them. Make lots of noise when walking, and be aware of your surroundings and areas where you may not be seen well such as when bushwhacking up to the alpine. Your pin/wrap kit, something you should always have on a remote river trip with rapids like the Upper Stikine route, can double as a food-hanging kit. Climbing pulleys make a great addition to carabiners, minimizing friction and maximizing mechanical advantage. Hoisting your goodies will be much easier with pulleys.

Sturdy footwear and proper backpacks will be obvious additions to your river gear if you are doing multi-day hikes. Because the hiking is so superb and the potential for wildlife viewing so great, you will want to maximize your experience by taking a good set of binoculars. For any hiking you should carry a compass and appropriate topo maps and know how to use them.

Park authorities encourage campers to limit their use of wood for campfires and to keep fires small. Firewood is limited at Happy and Tuaton lakes, so a stove for cooking is necessary if you are going to spend much time at the headwater lakes. Fritz Handel, the maker of the Bushbuddy stove, lives just outside Iskut. His small, efficient wood-burning stoves are sold at the Iskut gas station convenience store on the Cassiar Highway or you can order them online. See the Directory of Services and Organizations for contact information. You will likely want a backpacking model if you are doing any serious hiking.

Trip Notes:

MAP NO.	GRID REF.	FEATURE	DESCRIPTION
104 H/1; 104 H/8	515450	Put-in; Camping	Happy Lake is the put-in for the longest trip possible on the Upper Stikine. Your pilot will likely drop you at the camping spot at the narrows north of the large island. This is one of two possible camping spots. The other is also on the west shore, but farther south.

Hiking in the alpine is what you have come for, so pick a ridge and look for a route that has the least distance through the subalpine. Whichever route you choose, you will have to bushwhack for some way, usually from one to two hours through the forest and then shrubs to above treeline to reach the alpine tundra. There are also two horse trails heading east and south of Happy Lake that will take you through some valley scenery. See the BC Parks Spatsizi Plateau Wilderness Park brochure/map.

Navigating to Tuaton Lake includes a combination of portaging, lining and wading Happy Creek. Following the creek, you can usually paddle the river stretch to Tuaton.

The exit rapid out of the northeast end of Happy Lake (GR 529455) can usually be lined down the RR channel around the island or you can use the **portage trail (about 100 m on RR)**.

At the first falls you will find another **portage trail (700 m) on RR**. It takes you past a second falls and through to a small, unnamed lake. There is a tiny campsite at the start of the portage trail, and the trail is fairly good through thick bush.

Once at the small lake you can head left and go down the creek in some manner or carry on down the portage on RR. We were able to paddle and wade down the creek all the way to the confluence of Happy Creek and the Stikine. At this point you can likely paddle the remaining distance to Tuaton Lake.

104	558488	Put-in;	Your pilot will likely drop you on the east

104
H/8

558488 **Put-in;** Your pilot will likely drop you on the east
         Camping shore of Tuaton Lake, where there is a park
                 sign and camping. This camping site is marked
                 incorrectly on the park map. There were fresh
                 grizzly beds at the site when we arrived there
                 in 2003. A group we saw later told us there
                 was a bear hanging about for a number of days
                 before we arrived there!

         Hiking From the campsite by the BC Parks sign you
                 can hike on a horse trail (not that obvious in
                 places) on the east side of the lake. It heads
                 south to the headwaters of the Stikine (the trail
                 is not marked on the park map). You can also
                 head straight up to the alpine from the campsite
                 to view the amazing valley hosting the Stikine's
                 upper headwaters.

                 There is a semi-permanent cabin (GR 545949)
                 on the west side of Tuaton where there used to
                 be a camping spot. You could camp near it, but I
                 suspect bears find it interesting, so would avoid
                 it myself. The other possible campsite is also on
                 the west shore of the lake, on the south side of
                 the southernmost creek mouth (approximately
                 GR 541487).

                 You can also hike on horse trails on the west
                 shore of Tuaton. One goes south toward the
                 Stikine's uppermost headwaters, the other
                 north all the way to Hyland Post. (See the BC
                 Parks map.) The west side of the valley also has
                 some good options for getting up to the alpine.
                 You can start a tundra ridge hike from the cabin
                 or the camping spot by the creek.

566500 **Narrows;** The narrows coming out of Tuaton Lake
         Fishing hosts some fast water, and fishing for trout
                 or grayling can be good here. Hop out on the
                 grassy bank and try your luck.

                 From the narrows to near where topo map
                 104 H/8 ends there are wonderful alpine
                 meadows and great mountain views. The gravel
                 bars are lined with masses of flowers in July.
                 We saw caribou in this stretch too.

600525 **Riffles** There are approximately 400 m of shallow,
                 rocky rapids from **Class 1 riffles up to Class
                 1+** with a few rocks to avoid.

The most interesting section is at the end, following the tiny island at the corner. There are some small standing waves at higher water.

94 E/5	639551	**Lodge; Hiking**	On the east shore of Laslui Lake there is a hunting and fishing camp (owned by Spatsizi Wilderness Vacations) tucked into the corner of a bay. Laslui Lake gets its name from the Tahltan phrase meaning "muddy fish lake."

You can do a day hike (about 4.5 hours return) from the camp to Hotlesklwa Lake on a good horse trail. (See the BC Parks map.) It is possible to see mountain goats up on Mount Terraze. |
	658569	**Camping**	A nice gravel bar camp can be made on the west shore of Laslui Lake, just upstream of the creek mouth.
	667565	**Camping**	At lower water you can camp on the beach here on the east shore of the lake.
	672573	**Camping**	On the point on the east shore of Laslui you can make camp on the gravel stretch by the trees.
	716581	**Camping**	On RR there is camping on a lodgepole pine bench. At the north end of the cutbank there is a trail up to a flat, forested area where you can stretch your legs after dinner
	733584	**Rapids**	About 150 m downstream of an obvious, grassy hill on RL there are **Class 1+** rapids. They start at the narrows upstream of the one bar marked on the topo and are about 300 m long. They are rocky at the beginning, with only moving water at the end. The yellow "Pullout" sign for Fountain Rapids is obvious on RR after this small rapid.
	738584	**Portage; Campsites; Fishing**	The **portage trail (1000 m) for Fountain Rapids is on RR** and starts just before the river bends to the left. It is a very good trail through open forest, with a canoe rest on a knoll about halfway down on your right. Fountain Rapids is **Class 4+**, so you will portage. If you still want to stretch your legs after the carry, check out the small falls at the top of the rapids. Talk about cheesegrater rock. Fountain gets its name from the large, midstream rock in the rapids farther downstream that makes a great rooster tail at some water levels.

There are two camping sites at Fountain: one is about 100 m from the end of the trail, the other at the very end. There is a latrine by the larger site. The grayling fishing can be good in the eddy where you put in after the portage.

755590	**Rapid**	At the narrows, right after the put-in, there is a set of **Class 1+** waves in higher water. The following stretch of river downstream to Chapea Rapids has numerous rapids, some of them approaching **Class 2**. Be alert!
779581	**Rapids**	The rapids between the two bars marked on the map (about 200 m apart) are **Class 1+** and rocky.
785583	**Rapids**	The next marked rapids are **Class 1+/2−** (harder in lower water, as there are more rocks to avoid). The first set is marked by two bars and has rocks to avoid. The second set, also marked by two bars, has three big boulders that must be navigated.
793580	**Rapid**	The next three bars marked represent a straightforward **Class 1+** rapid.
800579	**Rapid**	Another marked **Class 1+** rocky rapid.
813576	**Rapid**	An unmarked straightforward **Class 1+** rapid.
818577	**Rapids**	The one marked bar represents another **Class 1+** set of rapids that is about 300 m long and has some big boulders to avoid.
823579	**Rapids**	From just before where Chapea Creek comes in on RR to just after the yellow pullout sign on RL for Chapea Rapids, there are rocky rapids with some standing waves. The rapids sweep right around the bend and range up to **Class 2−/2**, depending on water level. **To scout these unnamed rapids upstream of Chapea Rapids, stop on RL upstream of where Chapea Creek comes in on RR.** There is a trail along the RL bank, which makes for an easy look. Stopping will allow you to make a route plan for reaching the head of the portage trail for Chapea Rapids proper. In my opinion, **the best pullout for scouting Chapea Rapids proper is from an eddy on RL behind a large boulder just before the pullout sign**. You can then choose to line or run the rapids down to where the portage trail comes close to the river again downstream of the sign.

Chapea Rapids are **Class 3/3+** at some water levels and are full of ledges. Depending on water level, some combination of lining, wading, pulling over and running may be possible.

The portage trail is about 1000 m long from the RL pullout downstream of the sign (it is a 1.5 km carry if you portage the unnamed Class 2−/2 rapids before the pullout). The trail around Chapea Rapids crosses a creek and is wet in places. There is a canoe rest about 650 m into the carry. The trail ends at a small beach in a low-walled, hardrock canyon.

There is not much for camping before, on or after the portage trail, especially in high water. In low water you can camp at a couple places in the next five kilometres.

After Chapea Rapids comes 10 km of fun rapids ranging up to **Class 2−**. Stay alert and enjoy! You will end up in a long, pink-granite canyon with some standing waves at its bends and then the river will settle down.

853615	Camping	On RL there is a grassy area that will make do for a camp if you really want to stop for the day or need to dry out.
865639	Camping	On RR there is a lodgepole pine bench up on the bank. The landing isn't easy and the bank is steep to carry up, but the forest floor is flat and spacious.
869639	Camping	On RL there is also a pine bench with the same access difficulties, but if you need to stop it is nice up top.

There is an old burn coming up and the river braids for a stretch.

867673	Campsite	There is a camping site on RL on a pine bench in the RL channel around the island. You will see some moose antlers nailed to a tree. This site has probably been used for a very long time, given its location near Caribou Hide and the trail to Metsantan Lake. You can access the campsite by parking your canoe in the big eddy above the tiny island next to the big island. There is a trail up the shoulder of the pine bench. This area is not burned.

		Hiking	The site of the village of Caribou Hide, once home to the "Bear Lakers," is upstream of Moyez Creek on RR. You can't see any remains of the village, as the buildings were burned. The trail to Metsantan Lake, about 10 km up Moyez and Metsantan creeks, makes for a good hike.

You can also hike up to the Edozadelly Plateau south of Metsantan Creek for views of Metsantan Lake and the Omineca Mountains to the east. Voss indicates it will take about two hours of bushwhacking to reach the alpine.

	842725	**Camping**	Double blazes on a tree indicate a camping spot up on the bench on RL.
94 E/12	021749	**Camping**	On RL, the upstream gravel bar at the mouth of Chili Creek is a camping spot. Fishing can be good at the creek mouth.

Downstream of Chili Creek the current picks up again and there are some riffles here and there for about 5 km.

	818754	**Camping**	After a riffle there is a gravel bar at the foot of the island where you could make camp.
	813768	**Camping**	A potential camping spot on the foot of another island.
	812778	**Rapid**	There is a **Class 1+** rapid with a big boulder to avoid.
	809788	**Camping**	On RL, across from the mouth of Adoogacho Creek, there is a large area to camp back in the trees. You can ferry over to hike to the falls from here.
	810789	**Waterfall hike**	As I understand it, the best way to see Adoogacho Falls fully is to hike up the west side of the creek. You can't get up to the top of the falls if you take a route on the east side of the creek up what starts as a trail unless you cross the creek at some point. The distance to the falls is about 1 km, and the hiking is difficult and potentially dangerous as you climb up the steep gorge. If you get up to the top, the view of the falls and the Stikine behind you is awesome.

Adoogacho is an anglicized version of the Tahltan phrase meaning "big den," perhaps because the creek's canyon looks so much like a cavern.

807790	Camping	About 200 m downstream of the Adoogacho Creek mouth there is a sandy beach area on RR. If you camped here you could hike to the falls at your leisure.
799797	Rapid	On RR there is an undercut cliff and **Class I/I+** standing waves at the bend.
799802	Camping	On RR there is a sandy area at the head of an old side channel that makes for a small camp.
783864	Cabin	On RL there is an old log cabin. About 2.5 km downstream from the cabin watch for sweepers in the RL channel around the island.
795885	Camping	There is an okay camping spot in the spruce trees on RR.
800895	Camping	The open pine forest up the bank on RR makes for a potential camping spot.
805903	Camping	At the lowest point of the RR bank there is a path leading up to a camping spot in the trees. **Hazards:** Watch for sweepers and strainers on the bends for the next 5 km. There are dangerous logjams in the shallows just upstream of the Chuckachida confluence. You must be very careful choosing your route.
836925	Camping	An exposed camp can be made on the large, marked gravel bar on RL.
843940	Logjam	A logjam blocked all but far RL in 2003. Approach this bend very carefully.
843945	Logjams	This was the worst section for wood hazards on the river in 2003 (except the new channel we ran because of the landslide!). The strainers, sweepers and logjams just before the Chuckachida confluence are really bad. Pick your way through them on this sharp bend with extreme caution.
831949	Camping; Old cabin	On RL, across from the tiny island at the opening of the tiny side channel, is a great campsite. There is an old cabin and the view up the Chuckachida is amazing. You can also walk on the game trail along the side channel behind your camp. There are a few minor riffles to the end of map 94 E/12, but nothing above **Class I/I+**.

765966	**Camp**	A horse camp can be seen on RR just after Park Creek.
756965	**Camping**	A sandy point on RR, just about 500 m down from a riffle and at the end of a tiny side channel, can suffice as a small camping spot.
723943	**Riffle**	A **Class 1** riffle with a rocky ledge on RR to be avoided.
720947	**Camping**	On RR is a gravel bar with some sandy tent spots.
677948	**Camping**	On RL is a great camping spot just downstream from the Sanabar Creek mouth. The gravel bar has sandy areas that make for good tent spots. So does the flat bench in behind. You can walk down the game trails to stretch your legs after supper.
645957	**Camping**	A typical gravel bar camp can be made on RR. There are sandy spots for tents and trees for the tarp.
605957	**Hunting Camp**	On RL is a hunting camp sits. You can see the hanging poles from the river and a horse crossing marked by flagging tape just downriver.

You will see evidence of new and old burns as you approach the confluence of the Stikine and the Spatsizi. They are from purposely set, controlled fires (well, mostly controlled; I heard one got away on them and almost burned Hyland Post!) in an effort to increase wildlife populations in the area.

Here the Stikine picks up its pace again and **Class 1/1+** waves and riffles are pretty much your constant companion to the confluence.

536962	**Confluence; Camping; Potential take-out/ put-in**	At the confluence of the Spatsizi and the Stikine there are many gravel bars to camp on. If you are flying out from here, pick a downstream one. Upper Stikine River Adventures' lodge is downstream on RR about 2.25 km.

The old burn you see here was from a fire in 2002. The area was teeming with moose as a result in 2003. It's really cool to see the clear, bluer water of the Stikine run alongside and eventually take in the often grey and silty or milky, aquamarine-coloured flow of the Spatsizi here. The Stikine now doubles in size and plateau scenery surrounds you.

			Hiking	If you want to hike the Plateau Trail on a day trip or start a multi-day trek on foot or by horse, you will first have to hike 10 km to Hyland Post on the horse trail on the RL side of the Spatsizi. (See the BC Parks map.) You will have to ferry over to RL and find a spot to leave your canoe(s). Directions for getting to the trailhead of the Plateau Trail from Hyland Post are found in the Spatsizi River chapter Trip Notes. Note that it will take you three hours to hike up to the edge of the alpine on the Plateau from Hyland Post one way, and that does not include the time it will take you to get to Hyland Post from the confluence.
104 H/9	531990	Lodge		Upper Stikine River Adventures' lodge sits on RR. It is possible to take out or put in here with permission. You may also want to arrange for a horse trek ahead of time. There are horse corrals on both sides of the river here.
	527994	Cabin		On RL is a cabin I believe is used by BC Parks staff while working in the area and on their trips down the Stikine.
	515008	Camping		On the gravel bar at the head of the midstream island is a green spot out of the burn that makes for a good camp.
104 H/16	506027	Riffle		At the bend and in the narrows there are **Class 1** waves.
	506030	Camping		On the RL gravel bar at the mouth of Diamond Creek (also called Marion Creek after Tommy Walker's wife) there is a nice camping spot at lower water. At certain water levels there may be some riffles below the creek's outlet.
	495072	Camping		This "island" with the W marked on it makes for a good camp. There are small aspen for your tarp and a bit of cover, with lots of room for tents on the gravel all around. Pick your spot. The view across the river of the aspen forest is much better than one of the old burn in the area. This is the last good spot to camp or batten down the hatches before Jewel Rapids, which is coming up in approximately 7.5 km.

506110	**Swallow nests**	There are swallow nests on the RR bank 2 km before Jewel Rapids. This landmark will put you on course if you have lost track of where you are. In a dry year or later in the season the small creeks dry up, making it hard to use them to pinpoint your location.
450121	**Jewel Rapids**	This potentially **Class 2+** rapid can be up to 2 km long, depending on water levels. In July 2003 we saw the yellow warning sign thrown up in the bush (by flooding or ice, I suppose) on RL, just before the boulders. This is where the "meat" of Jewel Rapids begins. The boulders are large and not too close together. But if the river is up, things will happen a lot faster and you will need to be more proficient at manoeuvring your canoe. There are standing waves that will splash into the boat at any water level, but, there are a number of choices for lines, so you can stay dry if you work at it. In normal August water levels you can eddy-hop on far RR, boat-scouting or jumping out as spotters walk ahead and look. You may also be able to line or wade parts of the drop at low water. In most places the forest is not too thick, so the potential is there for **a bushwhack portage** on either side of the river.
424136	**Riffles**	There are **Class 1+** waves around the island, peaking in height and irregular in shape where the channels converge.
407146	**Camping**	On RL just before the bend with the clay cliffs is a large gravel/sandbar you could camp on.
405144	**Riffles**	There are **Class 1+** waves for 200 m around the clay cliff bend.
403152	**Riffles**	In the RR channel around the island there are some **Class 1/1+** waves.
403154	**Camping**	The gravel point at the foot of the midriver island provides a camping spot.
399161	**Camping**	On RL, on the upstream side of the unnamed creek, you can camp on gravel with a nice view of the red rock cliffs across the river.

There is fast water around this pretty bend that ends at the pink-granite rock cliffs on RR. |

	396167	**Riffles**	There are some **Class 1+** waves at the narrows.
	385168	**Riffles**	There are more **Class 1+** waves at this narrows.
	380176	**Riffles**	In the RL channel around the gravel bar island there are some **Class 1/1+** waves at certain water levels.
	366190	**Riffles**	At the bend there are some **Class 1+** waves.
	354195	**Riffle**	After the rock bluff on RR there is a **Class 1+** riffle in the left channel of what looks like an island on the map. A ledge on RL is exposed in lower water.
	320223	**Riffles**	There are some **Class 1+** riffles as the river bends left and then right before the big rock outcrop on RR at GR 313229. At the outcrop another riffle follows. An old burn (from 1992) eventually appears on RR, and as you approach the Pitman River confluence the valley really opens up with great views.
	300243	**Riffles**	Another set of **Class 1+** riffles occur on the bend to the right.
	297253	**Riffle**	You encounter yet another **Class 1+** riffle before the Pitman confluence.
104 H/15	292265	**Camping**	On RR just below the Pitman's mouth is a small beach landing spot with a small camping area behind. Not a good choice for a camp in heavy rains, as flooding is possible. The site would be very small in high water, but it's nice in low water, with good fishing potential. However, watch for the very soft, sandy areas that almost swallowed up my friend Tony!
	290264	**Camping**	On RL there is a large gravel bar that would make a good high-water camp. It is just across from the Pitman's mouth. Choose your spot; there's lots of room.
			From the confluence of the Pitman and the Stikine to the bridge take-out there are **Class 1** waves at nearly every bend and narrows and between gravel bar islands. The riffles are too numerous to list and all can be seen well in advance, so only the rapids Class 1+ or greater will be described.

273261	Scenic site; Hiking	Schreiber Canyon is up the creek mouth on RR. It is a pretty site to explore. You can land on the tiny beach at the creek and wade and scramble your way up the narrow creek over fallen trees to the canyon proper. It's about a 25-minute expedition up between multicoloured conglomerate rock walls that become more tan-coloured as you reach the end of the scenic gorge.

The Stikine downstream is fast and braided, with a few easy riffles to navigate where the river narrows or channels converge. You will want to keep your eyes peeled for logjams and wood hazards piled up on the many sand and gravel bars. |
266243	Camping	On RL there is a large gravel bar where you can set up camp.
155231	Riffle	At the narrows there are **Class 1+** standing waves. This is usually the largest of the riffles from Schreiber Creek to Kehlechoa River.
139233	Riffle	At the bend there are **Class 1+** standing waves.
114225	Camping	On the RL wooded island just upstream and across from the Kehlechoa River confluence (which is not obvious at all), there is a site where hunters appear to have camped.
098224	Camping	The north end of the island RR, after that not at all obvious Kehlechoa River confluence, makes for a camp with good views.

By this juncture the Stikine has become very murky due to the silt-laden waters of the major feeder rivers and creeks flowing in on RL. The major feeder streams coming in on RR are usually clear, however. Interesting! |
| 055220 | Hazards | In July 2003, when we were on the Upper Stikine in high water, heavy rains caused the already slumping cliff on RR to collapse, blocking nearly half the river with earth and making for horrendous wood hazards. By August 2008 the river had regained its normal course and the wood hazards had been moved in past freshets. I don't know what the situation is now; **be cautious from GR 055220 through to 045205**. |
| 001204 | Camping | On the "island" on RR there is good camping. |

After the Cullivan Creek mouth on RL there is evidence of an old burn from 1992.

912202	**Riffles**	On the bend where the river is squeezed there are **Class 1+** standing waves.
903216	**Riffle**	Midway around the next bend there is a point of land on RR that makes for some funky hydraulics and even whirlpools at higher water. Stay to the inside of the turn and react to the eddies for a conservative (dry) line.
		The burn is no longer evident along the river here.
897205	**Riffles**	There is some funky water following the island gravel bar RR of RC, then some **Class 1+** standing waves through the narrows.
882217	**Camping**	On RR just before the creek there is a camping spot on a gravel bar.
880220	**Riffles**	On the bend where the river is squeezed there are **Class 1+** standing waves.
855239	**Camping**	On RL at the beginning of a snye there is a sandy site at the start of the gravel bar that makes a nice camp with a view of Mount Sister Mary.
855245	**Cabin**	A nice, well-secured cabin sits on RR.
839249	**Camping**	You can camp right next to the McBride River on the upstream gravel bar of its mouth. Stay far RR through the islands to get there. The views are better on the RL island across from the confluence, but you can't get clear water on foot.
838243	**Camping**	On the gravel bar on the island across from the mouth of the McBride there is a nice camping spot.
833239	**Camping**	On the foot of the RL "island" there is another good camping spot.
816220	**Camping**	Yup, another good spot to camp near the head of the wooded island on RL.
814213	**Camping**	Okay, here's one more spot to try – a gravel bar near the head of the RR wooded island.
755196	**Hunting camp**	On RL there is a hunting campsite in the back of the gravel bar. A floatplane can land here if you need to take out for some unexpected reason.

You will see another old burn on RR as you come out of this straight stretch of river.

	734195	Camping	A camp can be made on RL on the downstream gravel bar at the mouth of this unnamed creek.
104 H/13	663194	Camping	On RR, the gravel bar at the foot of the wooded island makes for a camping site. This is the second last chance to camp or stop and batten down the hatches before Beggarly Canyon.
	652203	Camping	You can camp on the RR shore, on a large gravel bar.

The next stop is the portage trail for Beggarly Rapids. You will see yellow BC Parks signs. The rapids are not death-defying by any means, but do stop at the head of the portage trail to get out and take a look. The rapids may be too much for your group and should be scouted by everyone. Besides, the suspension bridge over Beggarly Creek on the portage trail is cool.

635211 **Beggarly Canyon; Portage; Rapids; Camping; Hiking** — You will see the Parks warning sign and the **portage trailhead on RR**. The river is fast here at any water level so stay tight RR after you see the first sign. Be ready to pull into the RR eddy behind the big boulders where there is a sandy landing spot. (If you decide to run Beggarly Canyon Rapids after scouting, it is best to line back upstream so that you have more time to ferry out toward RL to set up for your run.)

The main **portage trail** is about **1100 m** long and bypasses the largest set of rapids in Beggarly Canyon, but not the swirly water and boily chutes through the rest of the canyon.

This trail ends at a small but very pretty established campsite in the canyon by the river (GR 630215). There is a pit toilet nearby. You could also camp up on the treed bench along the portage trail or in the grassy flats by the creek. (In lower water, to shorten your carry you may choose to line down to GR 633214, making for a portage of 250 m. There are large boulders to tie up to and you can also camp at the sandy flat section about 5 m up from the river.)

If you don't feel comfortable running the rest of the canyon, you can continue to portage on a less-trod trail that climbs up the canyon wall and then down to the river in a bay (GR 627218), adding about 550 m of carrying. The view of the canyon is great from this high trail, so hike up here anyway to enjoy this great spot on the Stikine. At lower water you can also hike a short way up the Beggarly Creek bed.

Beggarly Rapids rate a **Class 2+/3−**, depending on water levels. The main set of Beggarly is at the sharp bend and has an obvious, deepwater "V" located RL of RC, with significant standing waves to follow which can swamp canoes without decks. There are strong hydraulics associated with this first large drop, including whirlpools; then there can be tricky water in the rest of the canyon, strong hydraulics, pushy cross-currents and whirlpools. This is especially the case at high flows.

625219	**Camping**	You could camp or dry out after Beggarly on the small gravel bar on RL just below the canyon if you had to.
615232	**Bridge; Hiking; Camping**	The abandoned rail grade to Dease Lake crosses the river here. The bridge is spooky, inhabited by cliff swallows. Be careful when walking on the bridge, as the wooden planks are rotting. You can hike pretty much anywhere on the Spatsizi Plateau from here via this ghost railway line and the horse trails that join with it, but only on multi-day hikes. There are better access points to get to the alpine quicker. See the Spatsizi Plateau Wilderness Provincial Park map put out by BC Parks for the trails you can access from the rail grade. You can camp on RL just downstream of the bridge (GR 614231) if you do decide to hike.

After the bridge you will encounter funky riffles at nearly every bend in the river. The current picks up and there are **Class 1+/2−** rapids beginning in earnest around GR 587256, where the river narrows. S-Bend Rapids, about 5 km down from the silty Klappan's flow coming in on RL, is the trickiest of the sets downstream from the rail grade bridge to the take-out.

	576273	**S-Bend Rapids**	When high cliffs appear in the distance downstream, you are entering S-Bend Rapids, rated **Class 2**. The standing waves on RR can be large. Running the inside of the bend (RL) is the most conservative and driest line; but the eddy lines are strong, so be wary of your angle. There are no portaging or lining options for this set of rapids.
			More **Class 1+/2−** rapids follow S-Bend Rapids for at least 1.5 km. Keep your focus.
	548281	**Camping**	There is a flat, grassy spot on RL to camp on with a sand beach in front for landing. You can collect clear water at a creek about 100 m downstream. The Stikine is very murky after the Klappan adds its silt to the flow.
104 1/4	497311	**Camping**	On RR there is a large, treed, sandy bench with an established campsite on it, i.e., there is "furniture" here.
	482330	**Riffles**	There are riffles at the sharp bend to the left upstream of Tees Creek. Strong hydraulics and cross-currents can be found for 200 m or so at lower water.
	439338	**Hwy 37 Bridge; Take-out; Camping**	The bridge spanning the Stikine signals you are coming to your take-out. The best spot to take out is on RR about 40 m downstream from the bridge at the large gravel bar/parking lot/camping area with access to the Cassiar Highway. The death notices for the Grand Canyon downstream will get your attention.

You can camp on the gravel bar in a pinch, but it's loud being by the highway and not very pretty. However, there is good clear water to be had from the creek at GR 436338 and there is a pit toilet at GR 439339.

The private property to the west is the Willy Williams ranch, home of Stikine Trail Rides. You can go over and ask permission to hike up his horse trail to the beginning of the Grand Canyon. An amazing bird's-eye view of Entrance Rapids can be had for a hike of 2.5 hours one way. You could also arrange for a horse trek in the area, but I would plan this ahead of time so you aren't disappointed if you can't get on one by dropping in.

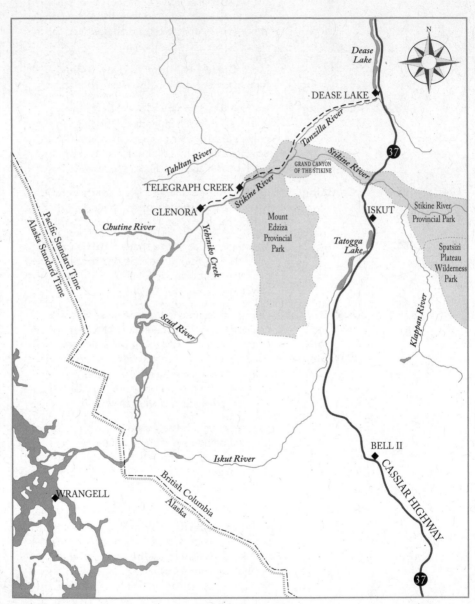

Lower Stikine River

CHAPTER THREE

LOWER STIKINE RIVER

The Stikine River is the best known and most popular river for canoeing in northern BC. Two classic trips make for over 500 kilometres of prime paddling and these routes draw canoeing enthusiasts from all over the world. A sleeping giant with a few ticklish spots up her sleeve, this river at prime canoeing water levels in August is one of the most accessible, scenic and historic river trips in this guide.

From Telegraph Creek, downstream of the unfathomable and unrunnable Grand Canyon, the Stikine flows through a dry valley in the boreal highlands, gaining volume from tributaries large and small through a rich transitional ecosystem displaying interior and coastal vegetation, to push its way through the Boundary Ranges of the Coast Mountains to the temperate rainforest and marine environment of the Pacific Coast. The highlight of this canoe route is the incredibly beautiful and diverse landscapes you encounter. Basalt columns line deep canyons, volcanoes overlook the river valley, glaciers glisten among sharp peaks and tidal flats stretch across a vast delta at the Pacific – all this and more in one trip. The icy scenery of the Coast Mountains is reason enough to paddle this route. You can even canoe a glacial lake or two, though neither Great Glacier nor Shakes Glacier will fit in your camera's viewfinder from water level!

This mother river is one of the great salmon streams of the Pacific, and the angling for numerous species can be very good. The Lower Stikine run is a big-water experience, as in large volume. The river is not a whitewater run and there are no portages. However, Scatter Ass Flats will keep even the best canoeists on their knees and on the edge of their seats. You can stretch your legs hiking up ridges and creekbeds or on your short trek to bathe in Chief Shakes Hot Springs!

The history of this waterway will boggle the minds of those with an interest in bygone days. Tahltan and Tlingit legends, old fur-trading posts, gold rush sites and homesteads are your constant companions through this mighty corridor joining interior northwestern BC to the Alaskan Panhandle.

Length: The Lower Stikine route from Telegraph Creek to Wrangell, Alaska, is approximately 247 km in length. The minimum number of paddling days you will want for the route is seven. However, headwinds and water levels will make a big difference as to how strenuous a one-week trip can be. If you are less experienced canoe trippers and/or have a larger group, you should plan for at least eight days of paddling in August. If you are putting in or taking out via a jet boat near the mouth of the Stikine or paddling all the way to Wrangell, tides must also be accounted for in your paddling itinerary and shuttle logistics. The Stikine delta is very shallow: at lower tides paddlers will be dragging their crafts in spots and navigation is impossible for jet boats. Additionally, if you plan on flying back to Telegraph Creek, bad weather may delay your flight. Finally, if the weather brings low cloud and heavy rain, you will miss some of the best scenery. I would add some extra days to your itinerary in order to really relax and see the sights and not have to worry about tight timelines. Rushing can lead to bad decisions and you do not want to push the weather on this trip.

There is no way to lengthen this route unless you run the Upper Stikine and arrange for transport of you and your outfit around the unrunnable Grand Canyon to Telegraph Creek or carry on paddling on the Pacific Ocean if you have the seamanship and skills.

You can shorten a Lower Stikine trip fairly easily. There are three good options. One, you can get picked up by jet boat or floatplane at the border of BC and Alaska, avoiding US Customs. Two, you can go as far as the Tongass National Forest Shakes Slough cabins and get picked up by a jet boat there. Or you can paddle as far as the TNF Garnet Ledge cabin near the mouth of the Stikine and get picked up by boat there instead.

See the list of distances below for the length of these trip options. To figure out the number of paddling days you will need, my rule of thumb is that if you are experienced canoe trippers and not going to do much hiking, you can count on doing 35 km a day on the river and not being rushed. It is worth mentioning again that if you encounter strong headwinds and/or water levels are down, you will have to work harder to make this distance every day.

Telegraph Creek to US border*	187 km
Telegraph Creek to Shakes Slough cabins*	203 km
Telegraph Creek to Garnet Ledge cabin*	228 km
Telegraph Creek to Wrangell*	247 km

*These trips are described in detail in the Trip Notes section of this chapter.

Topographic Maps: NTS 1:50 000-scale topo maps are seriously recommended for the BC portion of the Lower Stikine route, and you'll need USGS 1:63 360-scale topo maps (a similar scale to 1:50 000s where one square inch equals one square mile) for the Alaskan stretch. The braiding on the Lower Stikine will confound the best navigator at times, and you will want to know where you are, particularly as you approach and run through Scatter Ass Flats. The larger-scale USGS maps will enable you to navigate the many channels of the very wide and braided Alaskan stretch of the Stikine and the river's massive delta and tidal flats. If you want to do some serious hiking and exploring, you'll also need this larger scale, along with the 1:250 000 to see the larger features of the region. You will also have to have a compass and know how to use it, not just for any extensive hiking, but if you paddle across to Wrangell you must have a bearing to follow in case of fog.

The NTS 1:50 000-scale maps you need are 104 B/12, 104 B/13, 104 G/4, 104 G/5, 104 G/11, 104 G/12 and 104 G/14. The NTS 1:250 000-scale maps you might want to carry as well are 104 B and 104 G. I use this smaller scale of topo to identify and locate myself with regard to the larger features of the region a river runs through, as well as for planning extended hiking expeditions.

The USGS maps in 1:63 360-scale you will need are PETERSBURG C-1, PETERSBURG C-2, BRADFIELD CANAL C-6 and PETERSBURG B-2. At the mouth of the Stikine there are serious mudflats and sandbars that are difficult and potentially unsafe for paddlers to navigate at lower tides. There are large variations between high and low tides in southeast Alaska. The Stikine delta's tidal range is over 7 m (23 ft.). You must understand how tides work and take a tide table with you so can plan when to paddle from the mouth of the Stikine to Garnet Ledge and/or Wrangell. See the Special Equipment section for obtaining the correct tide table.

There is a recreation map of the Lower Stikine River region available from the BC Forest Service (BCFS) that is a useful planning tool. Even though it has some outdated information on Forest Service campsites that no longer exist and the route to Chief Shakes Hot Springs is not depicted accurately, it does give you a good overview of the sites of interest along the river on one map. There is also a similar Tongass National Forest (TNF) map, "Stikine River Canoe/Kayak Routes," that covers the Alaskan portion of the Stikine trip. This map shows the TNF cabins and campsites along the very lower reaches of the river. See the Directory of Services and Organizations for contact information for purchasing these two optional maps.

I suggest you purchase or print your topo maps in advance. Not only will you be able to plan your paddling days, but using the Grid Reference System (GRS) and latitude and longitude coordinates in the Trip Notes you can mark in sources of emergency help, known hazards, potential campsites, trailheads for hikes and other sites of interest. Then you will have this information at hand when navigating the river.

A GPS will really help you on this river trip and on your crossing to Wrangell. The Stikine braids so much it is difficult at times to determine exactly where you are. It is almost impossible in fog, in my experience. If you are at a loss as to where you are exactly, taking a GPS reading will be very helpful. Note that in the Trip Notes I use GRS coordinates based on the NTS 1:50 000-scale maps for the route features located in BC and latitude and longitude format for those found in Alaska. The UTM grids on the USGS 1:63 360-scale topos can be confusing and sometimes are not even marked, so I revert to using the maritime position format. Make sure at the start of your trip that your GPS map datum setting is NAD 27 Canada to match the 1:50 000 topos and the position format is set to MGRS (Military Grid Reference System). Once in Alaska switch your map datum setting to NAD 27 Alaska and your position format setting to latitude and longitude, using the same format for degrees, minutes and seconds found in the Trip Notes. For a discussion on topographic maps and the use of a GPS see the How To Use this Guidebook section.

You will also need to know the current magnetic variation for Wrangell – the difference between magnetic and true north (which changes by a given amount every year) – if you will be crossing from the mouth of the Stikine to Wrangell. You must calculate an accurate bearing to follow in case of fog. You can use a GPS for following a compass bearing as well. I never use my GPS as my sole source for navigating, however; too many things can happen to electronics in a wet environment, and batteries run out. If for any number of reasons you can't use your GPS for the crossing, you could potentially be in trouble.

Getting There and Away: The Lower Stikine route is often done as a drive-in and drive-out trip, though you have some other good options as well. Your logistics for egress will depend on how you get to Telegraph Creek and where you want to take out. Some common scenarios and brief notes for variations on the options for transport follow. Because there are so many options for logistics and so many transport services available, you have the luxury (or chore, depending on how you look at it) of being creative in making up logistics that will suit your party. The factors for most parties include the number of people on your trip, whether you bring your own canoes or rent, time constraints and how much money you are willing or able to spend.

You have two put-in options. One is the public dock at Telegraph Creek, kitty-corner from the Anglican church. The other is the riverbank in front of Stikine RiverSong, a hotel/café/canoe outfitter/jet boat service owned by a local family located just downstream of the public dock. You have at least four take-out options, three of which are for shortened versions of the classic Lower Stikine canoe trip. The classic take-out is the public dock at Wrangell. You can shorten your trip by getting picked up by jet boat or floatplane at the border of BC and Alaska, avoiding US Customs, or by getting picked up by boat at the Tongass National Forest Shakes Slough cabin or Garnet Ledge cabin.

Options for staging your trip include the communities of Telegraph Creek, Wrangell, Dease Lake, Smithers and Whitehorse. You can drive the 113 km (about two hours) from Dease Lake to Telegraph Creek on a gravel road that is quite good in places and steep, crazy and then very crazy in others. Driving RVs and pulling large canoe trailers on this road is very challenging and not recommended at all. You can rent canoes, arrange for safe parking and a jet boat shuttle, camp or stay in a hotel, and buy a meal, groceries and souvenirs at Stikine RiverSong in Telegraph Creek. This outfitter will also shuttle canoes and people to and from Dease Lake if you choose to stage there. If you rent canoes from them, you can arrange to leave them in

Wrangell and have them picked up later. There is another grocery store on the reserve up from Telegraph Creek that sells gasoline and there is a small airstrip at Telegraph Creek. In the past, you could charter a floatplane from the air service located at a small lake close to Telegraph Creek, but you will have to see if there is a company currently operating there. Service has been on and off over the years.

To get to or from Wrangell you must use the Alaska Marine Highway ferry system or fly via a charter float or wheel plane or a scheduled jet. You can rent canoes in Wrangell and arrange for a jet boat or aircraft shuttle to Telegraph Creek. Wrangell has many tourist services and you can pretty much get anything you need there.

Dease Lake is easily accessible by driving, chartering a small plane or taking one of Northern Thunderbird Air's scheduled Monday, Wednesday and Friday flights from Smithers. From Dease Lake you can drive, charter a float or wheel plane to Telegraph Creek or get picked up by the outfitter in Telegraph Creek, Stikine RiverSong. Dease Lake has basic tourist services, but as of 2008 there was no canoe outfitting service operating or canoe or vehicle rentals available in the community. There is an outfitter that rents canoes and offers shuttle services at Red Goat Lodge near Iskut on the Cassiar Highway south of Dease Lake. There is another outfitter north of Dease Lake at Dease River Crossing on the Cassiar Highway that also rents canoes and offers shuttle services.

You can drive or fly via scheduled jet service to Smithers. From there you can drive or fly via a charter float or wheel plane to Telegraph Creek and possibly Wrangell, though since 9/11 some air services have found the hassle of crossing the border not worth it. You can rent vehicles and canoes in Smithers and it has all the tourist services you could expect from a larger community. If you drive from Smithers you could rent canoes from Red Goat Lodge near Iskut on your way north instead of driving all the way to Smithers with them, but the most convenient is to rent canoes from Stikine RiverSong in Telegraph Creek.

Whitehorse is the largest of the potential staging communities and has the most services for canoeists. You can drive or fly via scheduled jet service to Whitehorse. From there you can fly via wheel or floatplane (taking your canoes with you) to Telegraph Creek or rent a vehicle. You can rent canoes and arrange for shuttles from canoe outfitters in Whitehorse. You could have them shuttle you to Skagway to catch a ferry to Wrangell, rent canoes from them or in Wrangell, and then have them pick you up again from Skagway.

There is BC Ferries service from Port Hardy on northern Vancouver Island to Prince Rupert. The Alaska Marine Highway starts its ferry service in Bellingham, Washington, and ferries go to Wrangell and beyond, as far north and west in Alaska as you can go. I must say that taking the ferry is one of the highlights of a Lower Stikine trip for me. It is very relaxing and comfortable and you can really enjoy the maritime environment.

So, you have many options for putting together logistics that suit your party's interests and needs. See the Trip Notes for coordinates for the take-outs and consult the Directory of Services and Organizations for contact information for the services you will need to execute your plans.

If you are paddling all the way to Wrangell you will need to bring a compass and know how to set and follow a bearing in fog. If you don't know what a compass bearing is or why you must adjust your compass for the variation between true north and magnetic north, you need to learn more about using a compass. There are many sources for this, so do your homework and then practise following a compass bearing while paddling a canoe before you attempt it on this trip. Be sure you have the current variation (what is called declination when navigating on land) for the Wrangell area before starting off. Your pilot or jet boat charter operator will be able to tell you.

You will also need to know how the tides work and how to use a tide table. It is normally around a 90-minute to two-hour crossing to Wrangell from the TNF Garnet Ledge cabin, and for paddling the Stikine delta's tidal flats, you want a tide of at least three feet throughout the duration of your navigation. There is a calculation for determining how high or low the tide will be at any given hour of the day called the Rule of Twelves. Once again, if you don't know what that means, find out. Using this general rule, you can calculate when the rising tide will be three feet or greater. That is when you can start paddling to Wrangell, assuming the weather is alright, of course. Note that though you will be paddling against the tide, it is better to go on a rising tide than a falling one in terms of making it across and not getting stranded. That said, if you are experienced ocean canoeists and the weather is appropriate, you may decide to cross when the tide is approaching its maximum. That way, the falling tide will give you a push, making for a faster crossing. Be aware, though, that Alaska time is one hour earlier than BC time. If it's noon in BC, it's only 11:00 a.m. in Alaska.

You can set up camp on the riverbank in front of Stikine RiverSong for a minimal fee if you arrive too late in the day to get on the river. And they have rooms and you can get meals at the cafe. It would be a courtesy to spend a few dollars at the Stikine RiverSong cafe or store if you camp out front but are not using any of their other services. I seriously recommend booking one of the TNF cabins for your last night on the river. See the Camping, Hiking and Other Activities section in this chapter for a further discussion on this recommendation.

There is no camping near the take-out at the public dock at Wrangell. There are campsites in Wrangell, one of which you can paddle to. Otherwise, you will need to take a cab to any accommodations. The ferry terminal is in the same harbour as the public dock and you can paddle to it.

Be sure to call US Customs as soon as you arrive and they will come down to the public dock. You absolutely must have passports to show and go through all the formal customs procedures. If you fax your itinerary and particulars, including the names and passport numbers of your party ahead of time, that will speed up the process.

When To Go: Mid-May to October. That said, you want to avoid flood stage and the higher flows of the freshet, which normally happens in June or July, depending on the snowmelt. However, it is the nature of a glacier-fed river in a maritime climate, such as this stretch of the Stikine, to fluctuate significantly with air temperature and rainfall. The fact is the Lower Stikine could reach its peak annual flow in any month during the paddling season. Parties of advanced and exceptional paddlers will be able to deal with the challenges of high flows, but it is nerve-wracking and I can tell you that from experience. Less-experienced parties should only plan to paddle this route when the river is most likely to be at low flows. You also want to avoid as much rain and fog as possible, though those are always a factor in coastal country. Bad weather makes it difficult to see the glaciers in all their glory and you don't want to miss that! Based on archived hydrometric data and normal weather patterns, the prime canoeing time on this route is usually mid- to late August.

I must emphasize that you can experience high water at any time when on a river influenced by glacier melt. Sometimes the water level will rise steadily but it can also rise quickly and dramatically. This is how it works. If you have cold, very wet weather, the river will rise steadily and significantly from the rain. But if you have warm, very wet weather, the rain runs off and the snow and ice of the glaciers melt, adding to the runoff, and this combination makes for abrupt and extreme increases in the river's flow. Less of a worry, as the river will rise more gradually, is when the weather is sunny and hot. The snow and ice melt and the river will rise with the runoff and stay up until it cools off. In short, flows on glacier-fed rivers are especially influenced by weather systems, and given the normal weather patterns of northern BC and Alaska, you have to be prepared to deal with high water at any time.

As on the Taku River (covered in volume one), a May trip is possible for experienced, well-equipped canoeists. Water levels are normally still low, but May can also see high flows from snowmelt if it is an early spring. Snow and cold weather are drawbacks to a trip in this month. Camping will be a challenge if the snowpack was large and snow is still piled high along the riverbanks. Tony and Neil's trip in May 2006 had them camping on 6-m-high (20-ft.) snow banks! However, May is usually the driest month on this route with regard to rainfall. You should definitely be wearing appropriate immersion paddling gear for a trip in this month. Less-experienced paddlers and solo parties should wear immersion gear at all times on glacier-fed rivers. The water is icy cold.

June usually hosts the freshet, the major annual snowmelt-induced runoff. No group should plan a trip for this month except parties of advanced and exceptional canoeists. Archived USGS surface water streamflow data from 1977 to 2004 shows that out of 28 years of data collection, annual peak flows occurred during June in 12 of them. You will certainly have a good push from the current in this month, and the bugs will likely not be out en masse yet. Wood hazards are your biggest concern. Scatter Ass Flats will be extremely difficult to navigate. Finding campsites will also be a challenge. Most of the gravel bars on the lower reaches will be underwater. You are advised to plan your paddling days on this stretch with regard to the forest service camping sites and TNF cabins.

You can also have very high water from the freshet and glacier melt in July. According to the aforementioned USGS streamflow statistics, nine of the 28 years recorded saw peak annual flows in this month. Only parties of experienced canoe-trippers with strong moving-water skills should plan for a July trip. The gravel bar camping will be scarcer in higher water, and you will need to be especially vigilant about wood hazards if the Stikine is up, particularly in Scatter Ass Flats. The bonus is that the fast current will help you make good time on the route, leaving you more time to relax, hike and take in the sights. The wildflowers in the alpine and along the river will be coming out in full force, and so will the bugs. They really get going as the heat turns on in the long hours of daylight.

July daily highs at Telegraph Creek can reach 23°c, with nights being cool. You are more likely to have sun during the first days of your trip than the last few. Telegraph Creek is in the dry, boreal climate of the Tahltan Highland. This ecoregion lies in the rain shadow of the Coast Mountains, so it doesn't usually pour for days on end like it does closer to the coast. Lower down on the Stikine the daytime temperatures will not be quite so warm, but night temperatures will be more moderate. Frost is much less likely the closer you get to the coast, even in September and October. Around Telegraph Creek, daily highs in those months usually range from around 10–15° and the coastal temperatures will likely be similar. It can rain for days on the lower reaches of the Stikine as you approach the Pacific. It's the temperate rainforest, what do you expect!

Come the end of July, water levels on the Stikine will normally start to drop. August is normally a lower-water month on average compared to June and July, with levels coming down significantly toward the end of the month. This is the time for less-experienced moving-water paddlers to run the Lower Stikine. The exposed gravel bars make for good camping, insect populations have usually started to decrease with the cooler nights and the berries come out in this normally drier month. Life is generally as good as it gets on a river trip by the third week of August. Rain is less likely than in July and the glacier-viewing potential is higher as a result. Headwinds and less current will increase the amount of time you will be on the water, but you will still have lots of daylight to work with.

Headwinds can be really fierce in the summer months because of daytime heating and the nature of the topography of the Stikine River Valley. One day on our July 2006 trip (one of the two sunny days we actually had) we had a 12-km/h current giving us a push and though we were paddling as hard as we could (four of the six of us were competitive canoe racers), we were barely making headway. The wind also makes steering, especially around wood hazards and in tricky currents, even more difficult. Plan on paddling in the morning and perhaps again in the evening if headwinds become an issue. Tony Shaw told me later that the Tlingit used to sail their large dugout canoes up the Stikine. Yes, I can see that!

You will have the lowest water flows of the canoeing season in September and October, so you will not be getting as much of a push from the current as you would earlier in the season. Have some extra time built into your schedule in case you get behind. The days will be much shorter, and headwinds are still quite likely. Be warned, it will also be frosty in the mornings on the upper stretch and snow is definitely possible. On the other hand, you could get relatively warm, sunny days throughout your journey. You will need to pack for any weather; expect the worst and enjoy what you get!

The joys of a fall trip are the changing colours of the deciduous trees and shrubs along the river, and the later you do a Lower Stikine trip, the more wildlife you will see and the better the fishing. The bugs will also have really calmed down, making camping and hiking even more pleasant. I love an autumn trip. If you are not experienced fall canoe trippers, consider a late August/early September trip rather than at the end of the season, so you don't have greater than normal weather challenges while working on your outdoor living skills. You won't have as much daylight, so make sure your itinerary has some leeway to deal with contingencies.

The table below gives you average monthly mean flows from May to October at the water-gauging station in Alaska. The data is from the USGS website and the table I've created shows volume in both cubic feet per second (this is all you will get on the USGS website) and then in cubic metres per second, a conversion I have supplied for those who have a better sense of that measure. Yes, this is huge-volume river!

USGS 15024800 Stikine River near Wrangell
Average Monthly Mean Flows 1977–2004

	ft³/s	m³/s
May	66,940	1896
June	135,200	3828
July	134,600	3811
August	107,000	3030
September	80,130	2269
October	57,330	1623

Source: USGS Surface-Water Monthly Statistics, June 2007

The following story from 2006 will give you some context for understanding monthly water levels on the Lower Stikine and the extreme fluctuations of levels on glacier-fed rivers. When Lisa, Lyse, Michele, Libby, George and I paddled the route from July 19 to 26, we started out in sun; by the evening of the second day it was raining, and it rained for days (we experienced all kinds of precipitation from pouring rain to blanketing fog). The rain was associated with a Pacific warm front and the river went into full flood. It was not the annual snowmelt runoff that brought the river up so quickly; the freshet had already happened in mid-June. It was the combination of rain and warm-weather-induced glacier snow and ice melt that sent the water levels shooting up in such an extreme and abrupt fashion. This is the coastal bomb that I have been warning you about.

When we put in at Telegraph Creek, the river was somewhat low for that time of year: 105,000 ft³/s (2973 m³/s), more like an average August flow. By day three, after a night of rain, the flow had jumped to 121,000 (3426); by day four it was at 156,000 (4417), way up from normal levels for June or July. It kept pouring and the river was in the trees by day six, flowing at 179,000 (5069). The river stayed up the rest of the trip even though the air temperature actually went down. This was due to steady light rain mixed with some heavier showers. This account depicts concretely how a glacier-fed river fluctuates, how much and how fast. The difficulty of the route jumped from two stars to three plus, just like that. Scatter Ass Flats was a nightmare in flood. Just to add to the fun, we were running it in the thickest fog I have ever experienced. Finally, we had to stop on a mushy, ever-shrinking patch of mud and horsetails and wait for hours for the fog to clear. We could not navigate at all. Wood hazards came out of nowhere in the extremely fast current. Other canoeing parties were also stranded. Some called for evacuation via jet boat charters. Some parties never put in at all.

The point is, even if you are monitoring the Stikine's water levels and go in a low-water month, you may get much more than you bargained for. It is normal for the river to fluctuate, but you want to stop and wait out the high water if things get too crazy. We were a strong group of paddlers so we carried on, got flooded out of our campsite beside the Flood River (ha, ha!) and generally had an epic trip, though lots of fun anyway. However, other parties that did not stop and wait for better conditions had serious troubles, including capsizes.

To find out what the water levels are currently doing on the Stikine, go to the USGS website, waterdata.usgs.gov/usa/nwis, click the "Real-time data" button and in the "Select sites by number or name" slot, enter 15024800. The real-time flows can be obtained in graph or table form. There are a number of output parameters, discharge being the main one you want. Choose the "Graph w/stats" option to compare the real-time flows to the historical average. You can see a whole month's worth of data if, under "Days," you enter 31. Looking at the longer period will help you decide if you are looking at a high-water year or just an unusual spike from some warm weather with lots of rain. If it appears to be a high-water year so far, and the river is still rising continuously, you might consider bumping your trip to a later date. But remember, the bomb can drop at any time and the river can rise by more than 30 cm, or one foot, per hour!

You can check how any given year's water levels are shaping up by watching Environment Canada's River Forecast & Snow Survey at www.env.gov.bc.ca/rfc. On the website is a snow survey (snowpack and water supply outlook) bulletin, which is published starting in January and updated eight times per year. The publication includes data gathered from snow and hydrometric measuring stations, and the regional snowpack and water supply forecasts basically tell you whether the water levels are expected to be less or more than normal in a given region come summer, and how much of the snow has melted and how fast. This is good general information, and again useful in deciding when to schedule your trip. For instance, if there is a large snowpack in the Coast Mountains, a June or July trip would not be a good idea, even for very skilled moving-water canoeists.

Difficulty of the River: ✳✳ The Lower Stikine River route gets two stars for difficulty. Inexperienced moving-water canoeists often think this is an easy trip because there is little for whitewater on the route. That is not the case. There are actually a few rapids that have some haystacks that will get your attention and there are hazards on the Lower Stikine that can get you into more trouble than any straightforward rapids. The river is very large volume and there are a number of places with very tricky current and long stretches of fast-moving water laced with dangerous wood hazards. The river can increase in flow significantly and quickly, making nearly all the tricky spots more difficult to navigate. Finally, the water is glacially cold, making the consequences of capsizing in this wide river or on the ocean crossing even more dangerous.

This is not a trip for parties of paddlers who do not have solid moving-water skills. Novice paddlers should be in tandem boats with more advanced paddlers and only paddle at lower water. The difficulty of this route increases greatly at higher water, and flows can increase significantly and quickly given certain conditions. Finally, if you paddle all the way to Wrangell you must deal with the extensive tidal flats at the mouth of the Stikine and a committing open-water crossing to Wrangell Island, which has strong currents and boat traffic. Weather is of utmost importance, with wind and/or fog your primary concerns.

This not an overly strenuous trip in terms of portages, as there are none. But you will exert yourself paddling if you get headwinds, and you should paddle the crossing to Wrangell at your fastest pace. Running a large-volume river such as the Stikine often means a free ride (if there isn't a headwind of any account), but the fast and powerful current also makes for places where things get tricky. You will encounter boily water with strong cross-currents where the river is squeezed or hits a headwall and where flows converge around islands or gravel bars. The Lower Stikine braids significantly, even extremely in a number of sections, making for shallows where wood can gather and create hazards. There can be wood hazards at tight bends with strong current. For the entire length of the run, the major hazards are sweepers, strainers, logjams, deadheads and partly submerged logs.

You must have the moving-water skills to be able to avoid midstream hazards on the gravel bars, which at high water will be submerged in very strong current making them even more difficult to navigate. You will also need the river-reading skills to locate deepwater channels in the face of many channels to choose from, a number of which may be blocked or at least obstructed by wood hazards. You will have to make your choices on the fly and quickly in many places, and with a vengeance in Scatter Ass Flats. You must be able to deal with strong eddies and avoid trees that have come down due to erosion of the banks. These wood hazards may actually be multiplying before your eyes as the banks where there is strong current slump, taking the trees into the river with them. This is often the case on the outside of sharp bends in the river. These hazards caused by erosion will also be harder to navigate in high flows. The water will be siltier as well, so you must look for submerged hazards and determine the deepwater channel by water features and current lines, with little in the way of colour clues. See the Character of the River and Region section and the Trip Notes for more detailed information on where you are likely to encounter navigation challenges on the Lower Stikine route.

Hypothermia is always a danger because the water is glacially cold. Wearing immersion paddling gear is recommended and you must be prepared for quick rescues. If there is a capsize, you must know how to swim aggressively away from wood hazards and what to do if you come up against one in your canoe or while in the water. All paddlers should know how to do assisted and self-rescues. Self-rescue by righting and scrambling back into your canoe should be practised before going on the trip. It is the quickest way out of the water. You should have your canoe set up with a throw bag in position with a quick release strap to tow other canoes to shore if the swimmers can't climb back in their boats. Self-rescue and swimming your boat to shore are your only options if you are on a solo boat or solo voyage trip (neither is recommended, except for the most skilled and safety-conscious paddlers). For the ocean crossing, a canoe-over-canoe rescue would be your only option. In rough seas with loaded boats, this will be difficult. Paddlers should be able to perform self-rescues so they can right and scramble back into their canoe unassisted if necessary.

In conclusion, the Lower Stikine route is a good trip for paddlers who already have canoe tripping, moving-water and river and deepwater rescue skills and experience and are interested in paddling a coastal river. The Lower Stikine is the easiest of the three routes covered in this guidebook series where you can paddle to the Pacific. The Tatshenshini requires exceptional whitewater skills and the Taku (covered in volume one) has more wood hazards and a stretch of ocean canoeing that is much more intense. There is much to be learned about large-volume river paddling and navigating and this is not a difficult trip compared to many in this book (assuming you aren't on the river in high water or flood conditions). However, less advanced moving-water paddlers should plan to paddle the Lower Stikine in August, when river and weather conditions are normally at their best, and should also consider taking a guide.

The gradient of the Lower Stikine run is 0.72 m/km (3.80 ft./mi.), similar to the lower reaches of the Taku River. This does not give you a picture of the power and speed of the current, however, especially in high water. In 2006 I clocked our floating speed at 20 km/h at times. I have read that the Stikine in its lower reaches is the fastest navigable free-flowing river in North America. The major fast-water sections occur in the first 80 km or so of the route, with a few exceptions indicated in the Trip Notes.

Character of the River and Region: The Lower Stikine River route begins just downstream of the final rapids of the Grand Canyon. At Telegraph Creek the river is about 200 m across and flows quickly southwest off the Tahltan Highland, taking in many creeks as it enters the Boundary Ranges of the Coast Mountains (called the Coast Range in Alaska). There, it is bumped by great ice-covered peaks to run south in wide, braided bends collecting glacier melt from huge low-elevation glaciers and large tributaries to make a great turn to the west to flow into Alaska. The Stikine then heads northwest and then southwest in a big s turn to spread out into a massive delta (27 km across at its widest point) of islands and mud flats to its mouth at the junction of Frederick Sound, Sumner and Stikine straits and the Eastern Passage in the Alexander Archipelago of the Pacific Ocean.

Ecologically speaking, the Lower Stikine River route lies in two ecoprovinces made up of smaller ecoregions. In the big picture, the upper reaches of the route lie in the Northern Boreal Mountains ecoprovince, while the middle and lower reaches are in the Coast and Mountains ecoprovince.

The first stretch of river, from Telegraph Creek to just before it drops into the Boundary Ranges, runs across the Tahltan Highland through the Boreal Mountains and Plateaus ecoregion, a subsection of the larger Northern Boreal Mountains ecoprovince. The Tahltan Highland sits on the western edge of the Stikine Plateau, a huge and open, gently rolling region of plateaus and highlands, transitional to the rugged terrain of the Cassiar Ranges and the Skeena Mountains.

The Stikine River Valley where it incises the Tahltan Highland is the driest area of the Stikine Plateau. Precipitation is light, ranging from 400–700 mm per year on average, depending on elevation. Average daily temperatures in summer reach 22°c. The area around Telegraph Creek has a long growing period for this far north, and there are homesteaders that farm on a small scale. The glacial-drift-filled valley bottom of the Stikine River and that of its principal tributary in the highland, the Chutine River, are occupied by boreal forest. Frequent fire history has created a mosaic of white spruce, lodgepole pine and aspen-dominated forests in a variety of seral age classes, and vast areas of deciduous shrubland. Wetland habitats, fens, marshes, swamps and bogs are common along the valley bottoms.

Subalpine fir and scrub birch and willow dominate in the subalpine elevations, and the alpine is characterized by low deciduous scrub, heath vegetation, grassy meadows and "lichen-grasslands." Sharp bedrock peaks and volcanic cones characterize the Tahltan Highland ecoregion downstream from Telegraph Creek. To the east, Mount

Edziza, once known as Ice Mountain, is a volcano and the highest peak in the region at almost 2800 m ASL.

The Lower Stikine River is fast and silty at Telegraph Creek, and the river bottom is gravel, with cobble, gravel and sand beaches along its banks. The valley is steep-sided and goes through mini-canyons with high cliffs lined with basalt columns in places. As you descend this dry valley dotted with cabins, you encounter some rapids with standing waves and squirrelly water where the river bounces off cliff walls, converges again around gravel bars or takes in large creeks. Depending on water levels, there are usually four significant sets of such riffles: one before Kunishma Creek, one at the creek mouth, one at Buck's Riffle and a final set a couple of kilometres downstream from Buck's.

Three Sisters Rapids are created by three midstream rock outcroppings that lie in a very pretty canyon. The rapids in high water can be interesting. There are boils, small whirlpools, strong eddy lines and reflector waves off the river left wall, followed by cross-currents where the channels around the large midstream outcroppings converge. After Three Sisters a minor final drop occurs: Bad Rapids. The waves and hydraulics aren't too hard to avoid in higher water, but in lower water it is harder to skirt the large bedrock reef and avoid the standing waves.

As you approach Glenora, Mount Glenora dominates the landscape to your right. Glenora, once a bustling tent city, has been almost totally reclaimed by the land. Only the long beach now lined with uniform-size poplar trees and a falling-down cabin in behind gives you a sense of the ragtag settlement of 5,000 prospectors that was camped here at one time during the Klondike Gold Rush. I tried to imagine the steamboats chugging up the river to land here, disgorging hundreds of hopeful sourdoughs, but I had a hard time. You should read John Muir's account of his hike up Mount Glenora in his book *Travels in Alaska*. He loves the natural world he encounters in northern BC, as you will note from his effusive text, but has a bit of an epic walkabout on Mount Glenora. His companion dislocates both shoulders in a fall.

From Glenora to the Chutine River confluence the river doesn't braid all that much, even though the Stikine's valley widens considerably. There are some big mountain views, and deciduous trees – birch, aspen, balsam poplar – line the floodplain. Downstream of Glenora, Dutch Charlie's Riffle is just a fast run of small standing waves over a gravel riverbed.

At the Chutine River mouth, which is hard to discern because it has a large delta, you are in an open valley setting and the river begins to braid. It comes together again at Jacksons, and just before Dokdaon Creek comes in on river left there is a tricky corner. The river flows into a headwall rock cliff on river right, making for some very funky water, with small whirlpools, big boils and serious cross-currents. The best idea is to avoid the messy water by eddying out high on river left and then paddling the slow water downstream. There are some good views of the snow-capped peaks of the Boundary Ranges following the tricky corner.

You will now paddle a short stretch of river lying in the transition zone between the dry interior and wet coastal climate. Like the Boreal Mountains and Plateau ecoregion, the Yukon–Stikine Highlands ecoregion falls within the rain shadow of the Coast Mountains. The mean annual precipitation is only 500–600 mm, much drier than one would expect so close to an inlet of the Pacific Ocean. This amount increases and temperatures moderate as you travel toward the Pacific and come under the influence of maritime air masses. Subalpine forests consist of subalpine fir and white spruce, with occasional Engelmann spruce. Aspen and lodgepole pine are common in areas where the forest has burned. At lower elevations, old-growth forest of black and white spruce prevails, with clumps of cottonwoods and/or balsam poplar lining the gravelly floodplain.

The Stikine River Valley becomes more thickly forested in this transitional area. Where the river flows around a large, wooded island, Missusjay Mountain hunches over Steamboat Channel, and Grand Rapids heads up the river left channel. Grand Rapids are not grand, just a long gravel riffle with some minor standing waves. More interesting is the water where the channels converge downstream of the large island. The valley narrows here for a short time, then widens and the views are great. The Stikine braids around gravel bars to Devil's Elbow, and from there you may have tricky currents at sharp corners and as you enter Klootchman Canyon. Here the river is squeezed into a canyon with vertical rock walls you just know mountain goats love. The canyon has mild fast water.

Then the Stikine braids again past thickly forested mountain slopes. Sandy gravel bars are common and the views of the Boundary Ranges are great. There is a tricky spot after a very shallow, braided area before the river narrows approaching Little Canyon. Boily water and cross-currents where the channels converge will catch the unaware canoeist by surprise.

Little Canyon is a beauty, even in the pouring rain. In high water the Stikine really gets squeezed here, and there are boils, strong cross-currents and whirlpools. Stay loose and paddle through smoothly. At low water navigation is easy and you can take your time and enjoy this last canyon of note.

The river widens and braids as you pass Cone Mountain. Now the Boundary Range mountains and glacier views start to come into their own. The Boundary Ranges of the Coast Mountains lie in the Coast and Mountains ecoprovince. The highest mountains in the Boundary Ranges reach up to 3100 m ASL, and granitic rock prevails. Rugged, glaciated topography, steep slopes in numerous valleys, and hanging glaciers and icefields characterize the mountains. Surface materials are colluvium and glacial deposits.

The scenery just keeps on coming in this section of river, glacier after glacier. Obviously, with all this ice around, precipitation levels are high. The lowest levels, 1000 mm annually, are found in the eastern Boundary Ranges, while the annual mean is 2400 mm on the Stikine Icecap. The climate of the Coast Mountains is moderate and very humid from proximity to the Pacific. Alpine vegetation includes heather, dwarf birch, willow grass and lichen. Below the tundra, subalpine fir and mountain hemlock forests dominate. At lower elevations mountain hemlock is replaced by western hemlock. Western yellow and red cedar trees prevail along the coast and at lower elevations in the inlets. Sitka spruce grows in the warmer, more humid middle and lower elevations near and along the coast. Rainfall is heavy in the Sitkan biotic zone along the Alaskan coast.

As you approach Patmore Creek and all the way to Flood Glacier you will need to keep your eyes peeled for wood hazards, which is unfortunate because starting with the views of Commander Mountain and Glacier you are into really gaga scenery. This is a difficult section of river to navigate in high water, as the midstream gravel bars are mostly submerged and finding the deepwater channel and avoiding the wood all over the place is tricky. The water is much siltier now as well, so you must look for submerged hazards and the deepwater channel by water features and current lines, with little for colour clues. Scud River comes in on river left and is very silty.

There is another difficult section as you approach Flood Glacier, with one corner where the deep water takes you far river left. The river then turns sharply to the right and there is a rock outcrop on the river left shore where there may be wood hazards. There are strong cross-currents and whirlpools as you make the turn.

The Stikine stops braiding for a short stretch before the mouth of Flood River. Steep, heavily forested slopes line the river. Flood Glacier is magnificent, and you can walk to the outwash lake from the upstream side of Flood River. After Flood River the Stikine starts to braid again past the Anuk River confluence. Anuk is really only a creek, and its outlets can even be dry after a long period without rain. The delta has great camping and the floodplain is quite hikeable. We saw two wolves in 2006 when we were camped here drying out after being flooded out of our Flood River campsite.

Just downstream of Anuk you are into a huge graveyard of trees. Stumps, logs, branches and all sorts of wood hazards are hung up on gravel bars through which the river snakes in many shallow channels. This is the tricky approach to the very tricky section of the Stikine known locally as Scatter Ass Flats. This will be the greatest test of your river-reading and manoeuvring skills yet. You will be navigating the scary flats from downstream of the Anuk River confluence to around the Sterling River confluence. The river is wide, extremely braided, and lies in a huge U-shaped valley. I'm sure there are great views, but I saw nothing but strainers, sweepers and logjams tangled on gravel bars, poking out of the water, caught on submerged gravel bars and lining the shore, especially around the delta of the Porcupine River. It was actually hard to see anything at all because of the extremely thick, low-lying fog! The day we paddled Scatter Ass Flats was one of the most bizarre and nerve-wracking days I've ever had canoeing. And I've canoed a lot of days.

From the Sterling River on past Mud Glacier, once called Dirt Glacier for its load of black moraine, navigation becomes much easier and you can look around at the great scenery as you float. The river is more or less one channel and prettier, lined with thick vegetation. The trees are mostly western hemlock and they get bigger as you approach the coast. There is a hot springs up a creek about 1 km upstream of Choquette Creek, but it's a muddy scramble up to it. The hot springs seep from granitic rocks at the base of the valley wall and in the mud just beyond. It's an interesting place with some history, but the muddy "warm" pools can't compete with the big draw across the river: Great Glacier. Great Glacier is huge, thus its name. It used to be called Big Stickeen Glacier in Muir's time.

You will want to walk through the mossy rainforest up to the lake below Glacier Lake to get a good view of the glacier. First you have to get to the Great Glacier Provincial Park campsite. This requires navigating some potentially tricky cross-currents as you approach the river draining Outwash Lake, and then there is a strong ferry to be made across it to the eddy, where you can access the landing site. When we were crossing to the campsite in the flood of 2006, chunks of ice were rushing down the outflow river, and the ferry over to the almost non-existent eddy and the paddle up to the landing site was a challenging exercise all in all. Only the fact that river water was running through the bushes gave us enough respite from the current to attain upstream. I call the eddy you want to reach to get to the campsite "Leaf Eddy."

The trail from the Great Glacier campsite to Outwash Lake is very pretty. The trees and ground are covered with a plethora of mosses. Huge mushrooms and many ferns and blueberry plants can be found on the lush forest floor. The trail is usually in good condition and you can easily carry your canoe up to paddle on the lake. When we were there, the trail became a river and we couldn't get to the lake on foot! Normally it will take you about 30 minutes to stroll the trail (just over 1 km), and it will be about a 45-minute portage.

Great Glacier has bridged the Stikine in the past, joining up with the much smaller Choquette Glacier on the other side of the river. There are Tlingit and Tahltan legends about the ice bridge, and Muir notes the physical evidence of it in his writing. It is hard to imagine that a glacier could be so big or that it could recede so much. You will notice that the topo map (derived from aerial photographs from the 1940s) shows the glacier outwash lake much smaller than it is now. That's because Great Glacier has receded so much. Both Great Glacier and Le Conte Glacier are fed by the Stikine Icecap/Icefield, one of the few remnants of the once-vast ice sheets that covered much of North America during the Pleistocene. It covers 7511 square kilometres along the crest of the Coast Mountains that separate BC and Alaska and extends 190 km from the Whiting River to the Stikine River.

After Great Glacier the Stikine slows and you paddle through a wide valley with sloping, forested banks to the Iskut River confluence where the views are magnificent. Your next feature of note is the fish-processing plant, where you can learn much about international salmon fishing conflicts, not to mention buy a fish for supper.

Back on the river you are soon at Boundary House, perched on a hill overlooking the Stikine. Once the customs office called Stikine, it is now privately owned. We were lucky enough to get an invitation to spend the night there on our 2006 flood trip – there were no gravel bars left to camp on, so it was a very good thing. The house is really old and ghostly and looks great from the river.

Now you are on a stretch of the Stikine where sloughs are the norm. As you come around a wide, sweeping turn you will see the cutline on the thickly forested slope to your left that indicates the Alaskan border. At the base of Mount Flemer the views are huge. The river widens and runs almost straight west, but you need to head off north into Ketili River/Hot Springs Slough to bathe in the very enjoyable Chief Shakes Hot Springs. It can be a challenge to find the hot springs. Navigate carefully so you don't miss it.

Warm and clean, you will come to the first of the Tongass National Forest (TNF) recreation cabins at the entrance to Shakes Slough. It's worth a paddle up the slough to Shakes Lake to view the glacier, especially if you didn't make it to the outwash lake of Great Glacier. The side trip is strenuous in places, but the rock cliffs and the water-level view of the glacier are worth the effort.

After the passing the cabins, you continue for a straight stretch on the Stikine with little braiding. Waterfalls grace the steep slopes to your left and then there is a majestic massif rock outcropping on your right.

Andrew Island on your left is a sandy esker feature you can hike around on. This was a camping/staging area for prospectors on their way to the gold fields. At this juncture you will have to decide whether you will go left or right around Limb Island. If you are booked at the TNF Garnet Ledge cabin for your last night on the river, stay in the farthest left deepwater channel all the way to the mouth of the Stikine, to Point Rothsay and beyond. If you are booked at TNF Twin Lakes cabin and/or are going to Le Conte Glacier as a side trip, stay right.

Time your navigation of the entire Stikine delta so that you will be paddling on a tide of three feet or more. Do not attempt to navigate the delta at low tide. You can get stranded on the miles of tidal mud flats. This marine estuary is teeming with birds, but keep your eyes peeled for shallows and wood hazards. For more about navigating the tidal flats and crossing to Wrangell see the Trip Notes.

The Stikine delta will only get bigger as more silt from glacial deposits is brought down by the river's flow. In fact, the delta has grown substantially since the international boundary survey in 1901.

For more information on the ecology and natural history of the area, consult The Ecoregions of British Columbia, at www.env.gov.bc.ca/ecology/ecoregions/province .html. Environment Canada's Ecological Framework document, at http://atlas.nrcan .gc.ca/site/english/maps/environment/ecology/framework/1, provides more detail about BC's ecological classifications. A good book to consult for general information on BC's natural history is British Columbia: A Natural History, by Cannings and Cannings. Jennifer Voss's Stikine River: A Guide to Paddling the Great River is also a good source of information on the natural history of the Stikine. The Tongass National Forest website has some interesting articles on the Stikine's ecology, at www.fs.fed.us/r10/tongass/forest_facts/resources/fauna_flora/life.shtml. For information on glaciers see www.fs.fed.us/r10/tongass/forest_facts/resources/geology/icefields.htm. Two great books about glaciers you may want to read are Julie Cruikshank's *Do Glaciers Listen?* and John Muir's *Travels in Alaska*. The books are very different, giving contrasting views of "wilderness" and humans' connection to it.

Local History: ✳ ✳ ✳ ✳ I would wager the Lower Stikine River has seen more people ply its waters throughout time than any other river in this guidebook and maybe all of them put together. Lying in the traditional territories of the Tahltan and the Tlingit, the Lower Stikine River provided a gateway to interior northern BC via trails radiating out from its farthest upstream navigable point, Telegraph Creek. The Stikine River Valley is one of the few passable corridors through the Coast Mountains to the interior, and the river and ancient First Nations grease trails connected the Pacific Ocean to Arctic Ocean watersheds. In the historic era, travellers coming up the Stikine could reach the Cassiar region goldfields and the Liard watershed via a trail to Dease Lake and then by navigating the Dease River. They could also reach the Yukon goldfields via the Teslin Trail to Teslin Lake, then paddling the lake and the Teslin and Yukon rivers. Though the sea otter pelt trade brought the first wave of Euro-Americans to the coastal waters around the Stikine's mouth, it was gold that brought the region into the province of BC. Ore rather than fur is what made this river so famous, unlike many great eastern waterways. Today it is in the news because of opposition to numerous resource-extraction projects on its major tributary, the Iskut, and in both the Iskut and the Stikine rivers' headwaters.

There are some differing interpretations of the meaning of the name of this important waterway. Most sources say Stikine means "the river," as in the sense of "the great river," in Tlingit. The BC Geographical Names Information System (BCGNIS) online notes that Stikine comes from Stahankane, meaning "grande rivière," and was the First Nations name for the river: "From a Tlingit word meaning 'the river,' in the sense of 'the definitive, or great river' as reported in 1799 by Captain Rowan, commander of *Eliza* of Boston." The Stikine was labelled "Ryka Stahkin" on a Russian chart of 1848 and its spelling varied on many maps and documents from Shikene, Stachine, Stachin, Stah-Keena, Stahkin, Stakeen, Stickeen, Stickienes, Stikeen, Stikin to Sucheen. The river's name was amended to its present spelling in 1869.

However, the Wikipedia entry states the name is an approximation of the Tlingit words Shtax' Héen, meaning "cloudy river (with the milt of spawning salmon)," or alternatively "bitter waters (from the tidal estuaries at its mouth)." This second meaning seems likely, as a Tlingit Traditional Territory map and poster on the Alaska Native Knowledge Network website shows the name of the Wrangell tribe as Shtax'héen Kwáan, or Bitter Water Tribe. The tribe is also referred to as the Stikine Tlingit or Indians in other literature.

The Sekani that Samuel Black met around Metsantan Lake called the river "Schadzue." This name may indicate the Sekani referred to the Stikine River in terms of its size and power, as one of their names for the Liard River was Itzehadzue, meaning "great current river." Apparently the Stikine is also known to some Iskut First Nations people as "the Uncle of Rivers" and I have read that the Tahltan also referred to it as "Muddy River." The river was called the St. Francis River in "Purchase of the Russian Possessions in North America by the USA," a letter from Mr. Collins to Mr. Seward, dated New York, April 4, 1867. The Stikine has even been referred to as Pelly's River, making it very confusing if you were looking for the Pelly River in the Yukon!

It is also not clear when the Tahltan, a Dene-na or Na-Dene group (an Athapaskan-speaking people), moved into the Upper Stikine region. It is thought the Tahltan's ancestors were living in northwestern BC 2,000 years ago and that they had moved west from the Subarctic interior into an apparently unpopulated area of the Pacific Basin, which included the Upper Stikine River drainage, some 300 years ago. They then expanded their annual rounds to include the lower reaches of the Stikine.

Just as there appears to be some question about the origin of Stikine, the same seems true in the case of the name of one of the First Nations so intimately tied to it. Tahltan has been translated to mean "something heavy in the water," as in migrating salmon moving up the Tahltan River. Another source claims Tahltan is derived from the Tlingit name for the low, flat area at the mouth of the Tahltan River that was an important trading site for the two groups. Apparently the Tahltan refer to themselves as the people of the village built at the confluence of the Tahltan and Stikine rivers.

Once an exclusively hunting-based interior culture, the Tahltan are said to have moved farther west to utilize the salmon runs of the Lower Stikine River and its tributaries. There is strong evidence that by the early 1700s they were trading with the Tlingit from the Wrangell area. The Tahltan migration west precipitated close trading relationships and subsequent cultural ties with the Tlingit along the coast. Their profitable trade with the Tlingit and the salmon-rich environment of the Pacific Ocean drainage encouraged them to become more sedentary and they began to centralize along the Stikine River upstream of where the Boundary Ranges begin.

When the first Europeans arrived in the Stikine region, the Tahltan economy was based on salmon fishing, hunting and First Nations trade. Relationships with the Kaska, Sekani and Bear Lake/Caribou Hide (a mixed group of Sekani and Gitxsan) groups to the east were generally commercial and peaceful and there was intermarriage between the First Nations, but the Tahltan were closely tied by trade and marriage and eventually culture to the coastal Tlingit from communities near the mouth of the Stikine River. The Tahltan called the Tlingit from the Wrangell area To-tee-heen, meaning "people of the stinking (salt) water."

The name Tlingit comes from their name for themselves. Tlingit is a Euro-American approximation for the Tlingit words meaning "human being(s)." The

Tlingit from the Wrangell area had several principal settlements of longhouses made of cedar planks where they wintered. These villages were deserted in the summer when families moved to their fishing and hunting camps. The Tlingit moved upriver to catch and process salmon, as the interior was a much better environment for drying and smoking fish.

There was an arrangement between the Tahltan and the Tlingit with regard to the use of the Lower Stikine for fishing in summer. The Tlingit had their summer sites downstream of Telegraph Creek, while the Tahltan had theirs upstream from there, but the exact location of the boundary between the two First Nations' traditional territories was, and still is, a matter of debate. The Tahltan claim their traditional territory goes at least as far downstream on the Stikine as Great Glacier Provincial Park. Apparently there is evidence of rock cairns strung along the mountain ridges downstream of Little Canyon that may at one time have been a Tahltan–Tlingit territorial boundary. However, there was a fish-drying site at a creek named Shakes (a hereditary Chief name of the Wrangell Tlingit) upstream of Little Canyon, and a Tlingit petroglyph still lies just downstream of Hudson Bay Flats. At some point, at least some Tlingit were summering on the river much farther upstream than Little Canyon.

Territories must certainly have changed as the balance of power in trade tipped in favour of the Tlingit after Contact. The Tlingit were able to monopolize the Euro-American trade with their traditional use of and "rights" to the mouth of the Stikine. They forbade interior First Nations from trading with the newcomers and their power increased with their lucrative position as the exclusive middlemen in trading Euro-American goods. Despite two smallpox epidemics prior to 1840, Tlingit culture flourished with the increased trade until the late 1860s.

When the first waves of Euro-American traders came looking for sea otter furs, an infrastructure of grease trails and fleets of canoes was already in place supplying an extensive intertribal trading network among the Tlingit, Eyak, Tsimshian and Haida as well as interior First Nations. Important trade items included Tsimshian carvings, dentalia from the south, Chilkat blankets, copper and obsidian obtained from the interior and Haida canoes. The coastal clans, such as the Tlingit, traded among themselves and their direct trading partner freely, while there were protocols for trading with outsiders.

Canoes were by far the most important vehicles for transportation for the Wrangell-area Tlingit. The most common type of canoe was a dugout made of a local red cedar with extra pieces attached to form the bow and stern and thwarts set in to hold the stretched sides apart. Called "the spruce," it was used mainly for hunting, fishing and travel by small parties.

After Contact, sails were rigged for canoes, at first made of cedar matting and later of cloth. As my friend Tony Shaw notes, the fact the canoes could sail upstream against the very strong Stikine current is testimony to the velocity of the upstream winds on this route!

Tlingit tribes preferred the great Haida canoes for long trips and for carrying trade goods. At 20 m long with two masts and sails, they could carry six to eight tons of freight. Wealthy Tlingit headmen, such as Chief Shakes of the Wrangell Tlingit, purchased these canoes in trade with the Haida and they were used to haul large loads up and down the Stikine. The canoes were often decorated with carvings and paintings of clan crests and were given names. Both men and women paddled canoes and some sources say it was the women who did the tricky navigating. Normally, paddles of yellow cedar were used.

The rich maritime environment of the coastal Tlingit homelands made for a vibrant artistic culture, as evidenced by the totem poles and ceremonial garments of the Tlingit as well as their bone carving and metal work. After the summer provisioning was done, much of the winter was spent carving, singing, dancing and storytelling in the longhouse villages. When the rivers were frozen the Tlingit also made short trading trips into the interior. See the Tatshenshini/Alsek rivers chapter for more on Coastal Tlingit culture, prehistory, Euro-American relations and political activism and for sources for further reading.

With the move to the rich Lower Stikine environment, the Tahltan became less nomadic and annually converged upon a fixed headquarters in the summer. Hunting was very important for the Tahltan, who were big-game eaters traditionally. October to June was spent in small groups in their customary hunting grounds, while the summer season was spent at their salmon fishing sites fishing, feasting, visiting and trading. The summer season started with an annual gathering, but it was the September trading rendezvous with the Tlingit that was the climax of the commercial and social calendar. Later, when Euro-American trading posts were prospering and the monopoly the Tlingit had on western trade goods was broken, the Tahltan would return from their hunting grounds to the village of Tahltan for Christmas.

The Tahltan in prehistory did not travel much by water. They mainly travelled overland in all seasons, making river and small lake crossing by raft. Bark canoes were rare and only built for short-term use. With their move to the Stikine River region and the adoption of Tlingit culture the Tahltan began to use dugout canoes, but the Tlingit did most of the lucrative canoe-freighting up and down the river in prehistory and at the beginning of the gold rush era. Eventually steamboats undercut their business transporting goods on the Lower Stikine.

In prehistory the Tahltan are thought to have traded as near equals with the Tlingit from the Wrangell area. The Stikine River was part of an important grease trail from the coast to the interior. Tahltan products such as furs, cured hides, robes, quillwork, leather goods and babiche, as well as obsidian from the Mount Edziza area, were valued on the coast. The Tahltan traded their interior goods for hooligan (oolichan or eulachon), salmon oil and eggs, shells, copper plates, ceremonial clothes and blankets. They then retraded some of these coastal goods to the Kaska and Sekani to the east. They had the middleman's advantage in the coastal–interior trade in the region.

Does an evening on Alsek Lake get any better than this? Tatshenshini/ Alsek Route, 2004

The Stikine in flood near the mouth of the Iskut. Lower Stikine Route, 2006

Triumphantly on the ice against all advice. Tatshenshini/Alsek Route, 2004

Setting the net for the heli-portage of Turnagain Falls. Turnagain/Kechika Route, 2005

Rainforest hiking on the Stikine. Lower Stikine Route, 2006

Loading the lunch bucket from the Raft of Plenty. Tatshenshini/ Alsek Route, 2004

Ice jam manoeuvres on Alsek Lake. Tatshenshini/Alsek Route, 2004

The PakCanoe in the pack ice of Alsek Lake. Tatshenshini/Alsek Route, 2004

Camp at Melt Creek, just upstream of the Tatshenshini and Alsek confluence.
Tatshenshini/Alsek Route, 2004

Mini-gorges are one of the attractions of the
Turnagain River. Turnagain/Kechika Route, 2005

Gravel bar cum heli-pad for the Turnagain Falls
portage. Turnagain/Kechika Route, 2005

Rain shower over the Kechika Ranges. Turnagain/Kechika Route, 2005

Autumn colours on the Tatshenshini River. Tatshenshini/Alsek Route, 2004

The campsite at Beggarly Canyon is fit for royalty. Upper Stikine Route, 2003

The mouth of the Stikine at the Pacific Ocean. Lower Stikine Route, 2006

Perfect August paddling day on the Tuchodi River. Tuchodi/Muskwa Route, 2005

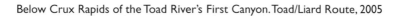

Below Crux Rapids of the Toad River's First Canyon. Toad/Liard Route, 2005

No wonder the Muskwa is so murky!
Tuchodi/Muskwa Route, 2005

Turkey dinner with all the fixings to celebrate
a successful and very easy heli-portage of
Turnagain Falls. Turnagain/Kechika Route, 2005

An eagle tops off an iceberg's beauty on Alsek Lake. Tatshenshini/Alsek Route, 2004

Tahltan relations with the Coastal Tlingit intensified once the Tlingit made contact with American, Russian and British traders. The Euro-American traders wanted sea otter pelts to trade in China and the Tlingit supplied them. The Tlingit's location at the mouth of the main rivers and the beginning of the grease trails along the coast made for exclusive trading rights with the newcomers, which they guarded fiercely. The Tlingit's enforced monopoly on the trade of western goods from the coast to the interior shifted the balance of power with the Tahltan, and the Tahltan adapted by establishing closer social ties with the Tlingit through increased trade and intermarriage. A sound economic strategy was to be "part of the Tlingit clans," so to speak, and to increase production of valued animal products, and Tahltan culture reflected this. Disease epidemics decimated the Tahltan population after Contact, also precipitating further assimilation into the Tlingit way of life.

Once the sea otter were nearing extinction in the early 1820s, the demand for furs from the interior increased. The Tlingit and Tsimshian pushed more aggressively into the interior in search of furs to trade. The Tahltan stepped up their trapping and trading activities to the east in the Spatsizi Plateau and northward to Dease Lake and beyond, putting them in competition with other interior groups who had migrated into or been traditionally based in those areas. Apparently, in the 19th century, increased competition for resources such as fishing sites, hunting ranges and traplines – and rights as middlemen in trade along the coast-to-interior trade routes – made for conflict in Tahltan dealings with the Inland Tlingit, originally from the Taku River region, and with the Tsimshian to the south. The Level Mountain area and the headwaters of the Sheslay and Nahlin rivers were contested by the Taku River Tlingit, as was the Upper Nass River region by the Tsimshian-speaking groups to the south. According to www.stikine.net/Tahltan/tahltannations.html, there is still some dispute about Tahltan traditional territory with regard to the interior plateaus near the Taku headwaters and the Dease Lake and Dease River region.

The HBC's search for an overland route to the coast from interior northern BC resulted in the establishment of a network of trading posts from the Lower Liard to Dease Lake. But neither Samuel Black's 1824 journey overland from Fort St. James to find a route to the Stikine, nor the establishment of Fort Halkett on the Liard in 1829 and 1832 (two different locations), nor John McLeod's 1834 exploration of the Dease, nor Robert Campbell's success in making contact with the Tahltan and Tlingit in 1838 at their annual rendezvous and his establishment of the short-lived Dease Lake Post made much impact on the Tahltan way of life or on the First Nations coastal–interior trade. The status quo with regard to trading relations in northwestern BC remained.

The Euro-American history of the northern Pacific Coast began with the first encounters between European explorers and the Tlingit in the 1700s. The Russians first came into contact with the Tlingit in 1741. Bering reached as far east as Kayak Island. Chirikov travelled to the Alexander Archipelago, where he met the Tlingit from the Wrangell area, but he felt they were hostile so he returned west. In 1774, the first of three Spanish forays, called the Bucareli expeditions, explored to 60° north latitude, and a priest, Father Savaria, made a number of drawings that recorded Tlingit life in the era before the fur trade. By 1775, the Russian traders and trappers had begun to settle in Tlingit territory.

In 1778, Captain James Cook became the first British explorer to reach the northern Pacific Coast. He had maps from the first two Bucareli expeditions, and they inspired him to investigate the coast of America on his third voyage in search of the Northwest Passage. What resulted from this voyage was a demand for sea otter pelts in China. Once word got out, European and American fur traders flocked to the area, hoping to get in on the otter pelt trade.

In 1794, while surveying the north coast, Captain George Vancouver passed by the mouth of the Stikine. He did not investigate it, however, and only the channels and shoals of the delta mudflats were marked on the maps of his journey. In fact, by the end of the 1700s most expeditions focused on finding more sources of sea otter pelts rather than on surveying or exploring. More and more traders made contact with the Tlingit up and down the coast and by 1825 the sea otter populations were devastated.

The Russians were the major trading partners of the Tlingit in the early days of the fur trade, and in 1799 the Russian American Company was granted full trading privileges along the north coast. They established Fort (Redoubt) Dionysius at the present townsite of Wrangell in 1834 and the Tlingit of Wrangell Island and area moved to live near the fort. The Russians' strong trading presence in the Stikine River region gave great power to the Wrangell Tlingit as middlemen. Furs were generally traded for blankets, beads, steel traps, tobacco and cloth. Peter Skene Ogden tried to open an HBC trading fort inland on the banks of the Stikine but the Tlingit and the Russians more than frowned upon his enterprise.

Eventually, however, the European trading rights along the coast passed from Russian to English hands in 1839. The HBC then stepped up its maritime operations, basically abandoning efforts to conduct trade from the interior. In 1840 the HBC took over at Wrangell and renamed the trading hub Fort Stikine. However, the change in the traders' nationalities did not make much difference to the Tlingit's powerful position as middlemen or the Tahltan's as traders to the interior First Nations. In fact, trade intensified. HBC wool blankets became the medium of exchange, the value of trade items being converted to worth expressed as numbers of blankets. Fort Stikine was closed in 1849 and HBC trade was carried on by steamship, expanding the company's coastal trading network substantially.

The 1861/62 Stikine River Gold Rush was short-lived and inconsequential from a gold perspective but it marked the first major influx of non-native people inland into Tahltan traditional territory. In 1862, the supply needs of the gold seekers led to the advent of riverboat service from Wrangell to Glenora. In 1863, Governor James Douglas claimed all land north to the 60th parallel as part of British Columbia, which included the Stickeen Territories designated as part of Canada the year before in order to deal with the influx of Americans during the gold rush. This further opened up Tahltan country to outside interests.

The abortive attempt by Perry McDonough Collins and the Western Union Company in 1865/66 to establish a transcontinental telegraph connection between North America and Russia also affected the Tahltan. Sternwheelers began to ply the Stikine, and Telegraph Creek became a staging area for the crews clearing the trail and stringing the line. Independent newcomers were taking up the trading of European-American goods, once the sole right of the Tlingit and the Tahltan down the line. An HBC post was built near the mouth of the Anuk River and another at Hudson Bay Flats. You can still see where the forest was cleared there in the uniform second growth. The Stikine RiverSong buildings were originally located there and floated up the river to Telegraph Creek at a much later date. The HBC's lease with the Russians lasted until 1867, when the sale of Alaska to the United States for $7.2-million took place. Now ensconced upriver, the HBC was well placed to carry on with its fur trading in the Stikine area.

It was the Cassiar Gold Rush of 1873 to 1876 that finally broke the Tlingit's control over trade in the interior. By 1878 most of the Stikine/Cassiar region had been explored by prospectors. The huge influx of prospectors and the traders setting up shop to service the gold diggings at Dease Lake and on the Dease River and its tributaries could not be controlled, and interior groups now had easy access to goods previously obtainable only through the Tlingit. (See the Dease River chapter in volume one for more on the history of the Cassiar Gold Rush.)

The change in trading relationships, the participation of the Tahltan in packing and freighting during the Cassiar boom (the first horses were introduced as a transport mode around 1875 and Tahltan people quickly become adept handlers), along with the epidemics of disease that accompanied this increased contact, altered territorial boundaries. By 1875 the Tahltan population had been decimated by contagious diseases and the remnants of several bands had joined together to form one tribe under one chief. They built a village called Tahltan on a high terrace along the Stikine about 2.5 km downstream from the mouth of the Tahltan River. It became their headquarters until 1920, when they finally abandoned it and moved to Telegraph Creek. The large annual trading rendezvous between Tlingit and Tahltan became a thing of the past. Eventually, the smaller rendezvous with the families from Metsantan Lake who came to fish the Stikine for salmon also lost its importance.

In 1885 the Canadian and US governments enacted a potlatch ban, which directly affected the Tlingit and other First Nations such as the Tahltan, who had by then made it a part of their culture. The law stated that every Indian engaging in a potlatch or Tamanawas (spirit) activities was deemed guilty of a misdemeanour and subject to imprisonment for up to six months. Despite the ban, potlatching continued clandestinely for decades. Numerous nations petitioned the governments to remove the law against a custom they saw as no worse than Christmas, when friends were feasted and gifts were exchanged. As the potlatch became less of an issue in the 20th century, the ban was dropped from Canadian law in 1951.

Anglican missionary activity was really stepped up among the Tahltan with the arrival of Rev. Frank Palgrave in 1897. The mission was called the Upper Stikine Mission, and a church, called St. Mary's, was built at Tahltan. Eventually Anglican missionary activity was headquartered at Telegraph Creek, where St. Aidan's Church was built in 1924. In 1900 the St. Theresa Catholic Mission Church was built at the end of a row of Tahltan log houses overlooking the Stikine River in Telegraph Creek.

The Klondike Gold Rush in the Yukon (1898–1903) made Telegraph Creek an even busier place. Though Glenora was the main staging area, the old Collins Overland–Western Union telegraph line trail and the Teslin Trail to the Yukon could be accessed at Telegraph Creek, the farthest navigable point on the Stikine River. There was a huge wave of prospectors, and sundry others in their wake, travelling through Tahltan country on their way north to the Klondike.

In 1901 the Dominion Telegraph was completed, stringing together Ashcroft, BC, and Dawson City, Yukon, via Telegraph Creek, a major staging area for its construction. This project and the aborted railway and wagon road planned for the Teslin Trail, an ancient grease trail to the Yukon River, brought even more activity to the interior. Telegraph Creek became a major transportation hub. *Wires in the Wilderness: The Story of the Yukon Telegraph*, by Bill Miller, is an excellent source of information on the history of northern BC from the late 1800s and into the mid-1900s. The book includes descriptions of the booms and busts of Telegraph Creek, the characters of the times, and stories of interesting journeys taking place on the trails associated with the telegraph lines to Atlin and the Yukon.

From the Tlingit and Tahltan perspective, this period was characterized by waves of sickness and the introduction of the wage economy. Their trade and subsistence economies were failing. The Tlingit began shipping goods for Euro-American traders instead of for themselves and they began to work for wages in the growing commercial fishing and sawmill industries on the coast. Small settlements were abandoned, the people moving to major towns and in summer to the canneries. Though the Tahltan still basically lived off the land, the Klondike Gold Rush and the building of the Dominion Telegraph presented more opportunities for working for wages as packers, wranglers and guides than ever.

In 1898, joining the men with gold fever, Andrew Jackson Stone of the American Museum of Natural History went in search of his own treasure. He headed up the Stikine, down the Dease, then down the Liard River to Fort Liard and eventually the Mackenzie to Fort McPherson, collecting specimens of northern plants and animals. He travelled with Tahltan guides, and thanks to their tracking skills Stone "discovered" two new big-game species. These he described in scientific papers: "A New Mountain Sheep" (1897), "The Mountain Caribou of Northern British

Columbia" (1900), "Results of a Natural History Journey" (1901) and "New Caribou from the Cassiar Mountains" (1902). The new mountain sheep species was given the formal Linnaean name *Ovis dalli stonei*, shortened to Stone sheep.

On his 1879, 1880 and 1890 journeys to Alaska and northern BC, American naturalist John Muir travelled with Tlingit guides from Wrangell. His observations on the Wrangell Tlingit he travelled with and the other First Nations they met illustrate the changes in the Tlingit and Tahltan cultures during this time. Muir brought the human and natural history, particularly the glaciers, of southeast Alaska and the Lower Stikine River region to the attention of the public through his book *Travels in Alaska* (see www.gutenberg.org/etext/7345), but his most well known book at the time was *Stickeen, the Story of a Dog* (see www.gutenberg.org/etext/11673). This hugely popular story, published in 1909, is about a Tahltan bear dog.

Tahltan bear dogs were especially adept at winter hunting because of their lightness and small size, which enabled them to run on top of the snow. They could track animals or help herd them back to the Tahltan hunter. The little dog was bred to be a hunter and was especially known for its bravery in attacking and chasing off bears or holding them at bay for the Tahltan hunter. As Europeans and Americans moved into Tahltan territory, bringing a variety of other dogs, the Tahltan bear dog became increasingly of mixed race. The breed was first documented by ethnographer James Teit during his study of Tahltan culture in the early 20th century. At that time he believed the breed was on its way to disappearing. The Tahltan bear dog was declared extinct in 1974, and in 1988 Canada honoured the breed with a commemorative stamp. See www.everythinghusky.com/features/beardog.html for more information on this amazing canine.

The large number of miners travelling to the goldfields aggravated the long-standing controversy concerning the boundary between the Alaska Panhandle and British Columbia. In 1903, a six-man tribunal composed of American, Canadian and British representatives finally decided upon the border. The decision was generally favourable to the US. It gave the river mouths along the coast to Alaska and the rivers inland to BC, an action that has long caused international conflict over salmon fishing rights, especially along the Stikine.

Relations between the Tlingit and Tahltan and the governments of the day were altered by the final demarcation of the international border. The coastal Tlingit lost their fishing rights to certain areas on the Taku and Stikine rivers as a result of the rivers being in Canadian territory. They fought to retain their political rights and control over their subsistence resources in Alaska by organizing the Alaska Native Brotherhood/Alaska Native Sisterhood in 1912. In 1929, the Tlingit in Alaska began a struggle to regain more control of their natural resources, which ultimately resulted in the Alaska Native Claims Settlement Act of 1971. The Act gave roughly 44 million acres (17.8 million ha, or 10 per cent of the state) and almost US$1-billion to Alaskan native peoples in exchange for renunciation of all aboriginal claims to land in the state. For more information on Tlingit prehistory, culture and recent events, see the Tatshenshini/Alsek chapter, the References section and the following sources: Aurel Krause's *The Tlingit Indians: Results of a Trip to the Northwest Coast of America and the Bering Strait* and F. de Laguna's article "Tlingit" in *The Handbook of North American Indians, Volume 7, Northwest Coast.* Also, I highly recommend two books previously referred to: Julie Cruikshank's *Do Glacier's Listen?* and John Muir's *Travels in Alaska.*

In 1910, in response to rumours that the BC government had claimed as Crown land all land outside of federal reserves, the Tahltan joined other tribes in BC in the Indian Rights Movement, and Chief Nanook (Nanok or Nanuk) and 80 other tribal council members signed a formal "Declaration of the Tahltan Tribe." This document asserted the Tahltan's rights over their traditional territories and urged the formalization of a treaty to address all matters regarding these rights. No such treaty was ever made and the Tahltan are currently not participating in the BC Treaty Process. Their stand is that aboriginal title lands can only be surrendered to the Crown and converted to non-title lands. However, provincial treaty negotiators have undertaken discussions with the Tahltan Indian Band and Iskut First Nation outside of the treaty process on a wide range of topics, including addressing concerns associated with resource development in their asserted traditional territories.

The building of the Northwest Staging Route and the Alaska Highway brought another wave of activity to the Lower Stikine River and the Glenora/Telegraph Creek area. Many gold seekers on their way to the Cassiar travelled the "Trail to the Interior," boating up the Stikine to Glenora or Telegraph Creek, then going overland to Dease Lake and finally heading north down the Dease River by watercraft. To deal with the increasing numbers of gold seekers and their suppliers, the trail from Telegraph Creek over to Dease Lake was upgraded in 1874/75. In the 1940s this was the main supply route for the building of the Northwest Staging Route and then the Alaska Highway. Goods shipped up the Stikine were trucked over from Telegraph Creek and then floated down the Dease to Lower Post, to be hauled from there to Watson Lake and beyond.

A shipyard was built at Lakehouse. The three tunnel boats and the diesel-powered sternwheeler constructed there could hardly navigate the tight bends, logjams and shallows of the Dease, especially along the upper river. Snaggers, men who cleared the rivers of wood, were hired to keep the run as clean as possible, just as they did on the Stikine. For a lively account of a canoe trip made in 1948 and some history of this ancient grease trail, read R.M. Patterson's *Trail to the Interior.* It's absolutely required on-the-river reading and one of his best books, in my opinion.

There are many written accounts of historic and modern journeys on the Stikine River that you may want to read before or on your canoe trip. Campbell, Ogden, Choquette, Thibert, Moore, Pike, Muir, Dawson, Hyland, Henry and many more explorers, surveyors, prospectors and adventurers travelled the Lower Stikine route. The following are recommended reading: Pike's *Through the Subarctic Forest*, Hoagland's *Notes from the Century Before: A Journal from British Columbia* and Pynn's *The Forgotten Trail*. Many stories and interesting tidbits of information on the names and history of places can be found in these works. There are three great coffee table books to enjoy as well: *Alaska to Nunavut: The Great Rivers*, by Neil Hartling; *Roll On! Discovering the Wild Stikine River*, by Bonnie Demerjian; and *Stikine: The Great River*, by Gary Fiegehen.

In 1949 the "Bear Lakers" from Caribou Hide who had eventually moved to Metsantan Lake became neighbours of the Tahltan. They relocated, in dire straits, from Metsantan Lake to the banks of the Lower Stikine across from Telegraph Creek (the IR you see on the map across from Telegraph Creek was the reserve created for them). As well, members from bands in the Klappan and Sheslay rivers areas and Dease Lake moved to Telegraph Creek, amalgamating with the Tahltan already based there. The permanent move to Telegraph Creek was partly because their children were required to attend school and there were no schools in the tiny, far-flung settlements established at annual gathering places and fur-trade posts.

At present, many people in the Lower Stikine region with Tahltan ancestry belong to two bands, each with an elected council: the Tahltan Indian Band and the Iskut First Nation. The overarching Tahltan Central Council is comprised of representatives of 10 families from each band. The Central Council links the Tahltan bands and has represented them on issues of joint concern, specifically on asserted inherent rights and title. The Tahltan Indian Band and the Iskut First Nation are recognized as separate, unaffiliated bands by the Canadian government. For more information on the Tahltan, see the Reference section and the Dease Lake community website, www.stikine.net, including the Tahltan Nation CD-ROM created by School District 87, which is based on interviews with Tahltan elders. See the Upper Stikine River and Spatsizi River chapters of this book for more information on the Iskut First Nation. Sources for further reading are listed in the References section.

Northern BC was surveyed and mapped more thoroughly in the 1950s, followed by an explosion of mineral exploration. Many Tahltan worked on the surveys and for the exploration companies. In the 1960s the increasingly common use of aircraft resulted in Smithers, rather than Telegraph Creek, becoming the staging point for exploration in Tahltan country. Tahltan involvement in exploration activities in their homelands declined as a result.

By the 1960s most communities had lost their traditional economies for good. With government monetary assistance and compulsory education, many of the First Nations people in the area became more sedentary and more reliant on purchasing food from stores. Though subsistence trapping, hunting and fishing were still important to the economy, wage labour was becoming much more so. Tahltan people began to work at the Cassiar asbestos mine (1952–1992) and on the construction of the Cassiar Highway and the northern extension of BC Rail (the Pacific Great Eastern) to Dease

Lake. Wage labour and road access to the south brought modern problems to the First Nations communities.

By 1972 the bridge over the Stikine was completed and the Stewart–Cassiar Highway (Hwy. 37) provided easy access to Tahltan country. There was an increase in the population in the Telegraph Creek/Iskut area in the 1970s, with homesteaders coming in from southern BC and the US. The Bear Lakers who had relocated to the Kluachon Lake mission site were now near the highway. In fact, a new village site, called Iskut, ended up being on the east side of the Cassiar Highway, on the opposite side of the road from the old mission and the lake. See the Upper Stikine River chapter for more on the history of the Iskut First Nation.

In the 1990s the local First Nations people became more directly involved with mining operations in their traditional territory by providing services such as road construction and maintenance and camp catering. Now there are several large mining exploration and development projects proposed or under development in the headwaters of the Stikine and the Iskut and on the Iskut River proper. The communities of Telegraph Creek and Iskut are internally divided on the issue of development in their territory. A number of people question the rate and sustainability of development and say the community and elders must participate in decision-making about such issues.

In 2006, Iskut First Nation elders formed a group called the Klabona Keepers Elders Society as a step to ensure the long-term sustainable stewardship of their territory, especially the Sacred Headwaters, the area of the Skeena Mountains that gives rise to the Nass, Stikine and Skeena rivers. In August 2006, the group hosted its first large gathering in the Sacred Headwaters valley. Joining the Iskut Nation elders were hereditary chiefs of the Haida, Gitxsan, Wet'suwet'en, Taku River Tlingit and Haisla Nations, as well as non-aboriginal allies, including Rivers without Borders. Since that time, there has been a groundswell of support for the group's goals in protecting the Sacred Headwaters from coalbed methane mining. The Klabona Keepers and their coalition achieved at least a temporary victory as of December 2008 when the BC government put a two-year moratorium in place on that activity in this extremely special place. See the Upper Stikine chapter as to the Sacred Headwaters and for links to more information on conservation campaigns in that area.

In 2007 the Stikine and Iskut rivers were tied for ninth place on the list of most endangered rivers put together by the Outdoor Recreation Council of BC (ORCBC). Threats include the use of the lower reaches of the Stikine and the Iskut for dilution of effluent from open-pit copper mining. There are many potential mine sites in the Iskut–Stikine volcanic belt, a rich source of metal deposits. NovaGold has permits to build a mine on Galore Creek, 20 km from the main stem of the Lower Stikine River. Potentially they could also put in a hydro dam in Forrest Kerr Canyon on the Lower Iskut, which would dewater a significant portion of the river. Skyline Gold is exploring the Bronson Slope deposit on the Lower Iskut, near the old Johnny Mountain and Snip mines. See the following website for more information: http://

riverswithoutborders.org/about-the-region/iskut-stikine. On the ORCBC list of the ten most endangered rivers in BC for 2010, the Stikine is tied for first place because of the threat posed by the coalbed methane project in the Sacred Headwaters, as discussed previously.

The Stikine has been designated a BC Heritage River and has been nominated for Canadian Heritage River status as well. However, neither program has the muscle politically or practically to do much for the river without a management plan in place. At present the only protection afforded the BC stretch of the Lower Stikine below Telegraph Creek is from two small provincial parks. Choquette Hot Springs (48 ha) and Great Glacier (9300 ha) provincial parks, both established in 2001, lie almost opposite each other across the Lower Stikine. The last 60 km of the river lies in the Stikine–Le Conte Wilderness Reserve of Alaska's Tongass National Forest, established in 1902 by President Theodore Roosevelt.

Choquette Hot Springs was protected in recognition of the uncommon plant, algae and bacteria species associated with the warm water, and the hot springs and surrounding thermal wetland and riparian area are considered biologically and physically exceptional. Alexander (Buck) Choquette, the first prospector to find gold on the Lower Stikine in the early 1860s at Buck's Bar (probably near what is now known as Buck's Riffle), built a trading post on the flats near the hot springs in 1879. A long-time resident of Stikine country, he married Georgina, daughter of one of the Chief Shakes of the Tlingit First Nation. The name was taken by a succession of Tlingit leaders, as was the norm in northwest coast cultures and still is.

The Great Glacier park designation was based on the recognition of the scenic nature of the river-level glacier and its glacial lake and the associated recreational values, glacier viewing, camping, hiking and canoeing on the lake. It also protects uncommon plant species and old-growth forest associated with the low elevation periglacial ecosystem found there.

The Lower Stikine in Alaska is completely within the Tongass National Forest and is one of the highlights of the Stikine–Le Conte Wilderness Reserve of the protected area. According to the US Forest Service website, the Tongass is home to about 75,000 people who are dependent on it for their livelihoods. Several Alaskan First Nations live throughout the area: the Tlingit, Haida and Tsimshian. Thirty-one communities are located within the forest, the largest being Juneau. The forest is named for the Tongass group of the Tlingit people, who inhabited the southernmost areas of the Alaska Panhandle near what is now Ketchikan. Bald eagles, five species of salmon and both grizzly (brown) and black bears abound throughout the forest. The health of the forest is evident in that there are no threatened or endangered species to be found in the forest or the streams, in large part due to the fact the region is so remote and inaccessible.

Despite the lack of park protection along the BC stretch of the Lower Stikine River, there is a history of conservation activism with regard to it. A hydro dam project for the Stikine's Grand Canyon proposed in the 1970s was canned, deemed unprofitable in the end. It clearly would have affected the salmon habitat on the lower river. The upper reaches of the Stikine down to its Grand Canyon finally became a Class A provincial park, called Stikine River, in the late 1990s. For more on the history of the conservation of the Stikine River and the provincial park, see www .spacesfornature.org/greatspaces/stikine.html#history. The large park – 217,000 ha – was not achieved without a fight.

Another conservation victory was the cessation of hovercraft activity on the Lower Stikine. In 1996, a hovercraft travelling from Wrangell up the Stikine to the Iskut confluence and then upstream on the Iskut to supply Cominco's Snippaker gold mine was made to cease operation, as it was proved damaging to fish habitat. Pressure to stop those projects came in large part from the organization Friends of the Stikine (see www.panorama-map.com/STIKINE/stikine.html) and the US and Alaskan governments because of the impact on fishing interests. The public also rallied. There is hope for sustainable and less harmful resource extraction practices, but until they are applied to projects, it is up to us to keep up the good fight and make sure river ecosystems are not destroyed irreparably. See the Directory of Services and Organizations for contact information for finding out more about conservation issues and initiatives in the Stikine region.

Level of Solitude: ✳ I believe this is the most popular trip in northern BC. You can expect to see at least a couple of other canoeing parties if not more during the height of the paddling season. You may even feel a bit crowded if you camp at Great Glacier or stay at one of the two Shakes Slough cabins. You will likely see signs of human activity every day: canoeing parties, jet boats, evidence of previous campers, and cabins and other human-made structures. This is a historic and well-used waterway. It is the route with the least solitude in this book, but the incredible beauty of the diverse landscapes you encounter goes a long way toward making up for that.

Wildlife: ✳ ½ Large-mammal sightings are unlikely in the main channels, except perhaps the odd bear along the shore or mountain goat high on a cliff. There is lots of traffic on the river. However, side trips down sloughs and hikes up creekbeds provide some better opportunities for wildlife viewing. Mammal species commonly found in the ecosystems of the Lower Stikine are grizzly and black bear, moose, mountain goat, deer, wolverine, wolf, fox, mink, otter, beaver, muskrat and squirrel. Seals have been seen over 200 km up from the mouth of the Stikine! In 2006 we saw two wolves near our camp by the Anuk River and a beaver near the Iskut River confluence. Tony Shaw, who does this trip year after year in May, says he always sees mountain goats up on some cliffs on river left (see the Trip Notes).

Bird enthusiasts will be happy on this trip. Bald eagles are plentiful all along the river. Other likely raptor sightings include hawks and osprey. There are a number of species of owls in the area, including great grey and great horned. Loons, mergansers, Canada geese, Arctic terns and many species of shorebirds and ducks, including mallards, buffleheads and grebes can be seen on shore or on the river. The lower reaches of the route are a migratory corridor for numerous species of birds and waterfowl, and there is a resource page on the Tongass National Forest website outlining the species you may see: www.fs.fed.us/r10/tongass/forest_facts/resources/fauna_flora/chklststkn.html.

Fishing: ✳ ✳ Fishing for bull trout (known locally as Dolly Varden trout) is fairly good at the mouths of the clear creeks flowing into the upper stretches of the Lower Stikine. They are usually found around eddies where the outflow streams mix with the silty river water. They strike at anything moving and shiny. Spoons and spinners work well. It is also possible to catch Arctic grayling in the clear, cold creeks and where they flow into the Stikine. Grayling will bite at tiny spoons and spinners, but fly fishing is often the best method for catching them. Salmon fishing in a river like the Stikine takes a lot of know-how and the right equipment and tackle. This enterprise requires more expertise than I can provide. Do your research or stop at your friendly neighbourhood fish-processing plant to shop for a salmon for dinner!

Camping, Hiking and Other Activities: ✳ ✳ ½ Camping is good on the BC portion of the Lower Stikine route, but once you enter the low areas in Alaska, finding a natural site is more difficult, particularly at high water. I strongly advise you to plan your itinerary with regard to where you can camp along that stretch and especially where you want to be, and when, to start your crossing to Wrangell. I also strongly recommend booking at least one Tongass National Forest recreation cabin on your trip. If it's been very wet or the tides aren't in your favour, you will be sorry you didn't.

You can camp at the put-in on the riverbank down from Stikine RiverSong for a minimal fee. There are no campgrounds in the community of Telegraph Creek. There are some in Wrangell, though, and you can even paddle to one of them. For other accommodations it's a long haul from the public dock. You'll have to take a cab.

There are two established campsites on the route. One is the BC Forest Service Recreation Site at Glenora, which is free and has road access, outhouses and numerous camping sites with fire rings and picnic tables. The other site with "organized" camping is at Great Glacier. Before being made part of the provincial park, this was a BC Forest Service Recreation Site. The camping is still free, and there is an outhouse, fire rings and two picnic tables. The site can be crowded. Be sure to use the outhouse, fire rings and the obvious tent sites. This site sees too many people to make any more impact on it than necessary. Also, the site is user-maintained, so pack out what you pack in. You will need a stove for cooking here. There will be very little for firewood, if any, and I will put money on it being wet if there is.

Once on the river, most groups will choose to camp on gravel bars along the route, especially at creek mouths that provide a source of clear water – the Lower Stikine is very silty. There are some really nice spots with big mountain scenery. Note that at high water some of the gravel bars will be washed out and you will need to find higher land. Wooded gravel bar sites will usually still be dry and there are grassy terraces that will make do in places. If you are paddling at high water, make sure you plan each of your days with regard to where you can camp. The Trip Notes will really help you with this, as I have paddled this route in very high water. In a pinch, where safety is an issue, I don't think anyone will hassle you about camping in the clearings around the Tongass National Forest recreation cabins.

I would book either the Garnet Ledge cabin or the Shakes Slough cabin for your last night on the river. These are two good starting points for your last day of paddling. Look up the tides first to see when you can paddle the tidal flats. You want to be at the mouth of the Stikine on a rising tide or start your crossing to Wrangell from Garnet Ledge at high slack. You cannot navigate the mouth or the delta of the Stikine at lower tide. You can't get to Garnet Ledge on a low tide, either, and there is little for good camping near the mouth of the river. You could find a spot that will do, but I wouldn't want to be looking in the pouring rain or high wind and be worrying about getting stranded on the mud flats. If the wind comes up on those flats, you have no way to get off them quickly and you will be in a dangerous situation. Do your research and planning ahead of time. Listen to the weather forecast and be conservative in your decisions so you do not end up in an unsafe situation.

There is hiking potential on the Lower Stikine route, but the region is not known for its alpine hiking. Most of the popular hikes are short and at lower elevations. If you are looking for a multi-day challenge, try travelling a distance on either the Telegraph or Teslin trail from Telegraph Creek before or after your canoe trip. You could also hike in the Mount Edziza area, accessible from Telegraph Creek, Glenora and the Yehiniko (Bear) Creek camping spot. Multi-day hikes should only be undertaken by fit, experienced and well-equipped hikers who have done their research.

On the river trip itself, you can do an easy hike on the track from Glenora back toward Telegraph Creek; for a scratchy, StairMaster torture session you can bushwhack up into the alpine of Mount Glenora like Muir did. If you stop at Hudson Bay Flats you can hike the old trail back to Glenora. Most of the larger creek floodplains provide short hikes. There is a strenuous hike to be made up Missusjay Mountain and more pleasant jaunts up to the glacial lakes below Flood and Great glaciers. Andrew Island gives you a chance to easily stretch your legs once more before reaching the Pacific. The trailheads or start points for the more popular hikes are described in the Trip Notes.

Horse trekking is another option for off-the-river adventure. You can view the Grand Canyon from horseback, ride in the alpine or do both in one trip. Willy Williams of Stikine Trail Rides will do custom tours. You can also experience a short stretch of the Grand Canyon's whitewater by jet boat with Dan Pakula of Stikine

RiverSong. See the Directory of Services and Organizations for contact information for these and other outfitters offering tours in the area.

If you have the time and inclination while in Wrangell, there are petroglyphs, totem poles, Chief Shakes Island and the Clan House to see. Shopping is good for locally made arts and crafts. Visit the Nolan Center, housing Wrangell's museum and visitor centre, for more information on these and other attractions.

Special Equipment: You must have a valid passport to enter Alaska, and US Customs will ask you to produce yours upon arriving in Wrangell. You are expected to remain at the public dock until an officer comes down to clear you through. You will also have to have a passport to get out of Alaska by plane or ferry.

On the Lower Stikine route the kind of canoe you use is not as much of an issue as it is on rivers with significant rocky rapids. Smashing up your boat is not likely unless you really mess up. You want a canoe in good condition that is large enough to handle the volume of the river and associated strong hydraulics and carry your gear easily. It must also be manoeuvrable enough so you can run Scatter Ass Flats safely, and be seaworthy if you paddle to Wrangell. Outfitting your canoe with a throw bag with a towing/quick-release system you can easily reach is vital for this wide, large-volume river, especially if you are on a single boat or solo trip. You are better off with this system when towing another canoe or swimming yours to shore in the event of a capsize.

Dressing for immersion, i.e., wearing a wetsuit and paddling or dry top or a dry suit, is recommended, especially for trips early or late in the season and for less-experienced and solo paddlers. You are paddling glacially cold water.

A water filter is necessary on this trip. You can get rid of silt by letting water in a pot stand for a while, but the possibility of "beaver fever" needs to be dealt with. Take extra water bags for filling up at the clear streams to save your filter some hard work.

Bring a stove for cooking. On the lower reaches of the route, finding dry firewood and lighting a fire will likely be a challenge, particularly if it's been wet for days and there is no cedar driftwood around.

Insects are not usually as much of a problem on coastal rivers as they can be on interior rivers. However, this route starts in the interior and the bugs can be bad in camp in the warmest months. You will want to take a hooded bug jacket with a face net or a head net and/or repellent, especially if you want to do some hiking.

If you are paddling to Wrangell or doing any extensive hiking, you will absolutely need to bring a compass and know how to use it. You must have a bearing for the crossing to Wrangell Island in case of fog (take your bearing from some point on the mainland out of the tidal flats – the compass won't help you navigate the mud flats in the fog and you will want to stay close to shore until your bearing starting point). To prepare in advance for your crossing (if you have to start in the fog, this is the only way you will have a bearing), you also need the variation for Wrangell so you can use your topo map to come up with a magnetic bearing to follow. If you don't know what I am talking about, you need to learn more about using a compass before you do any ocean crossings. Also, I recommend you get some practice at following a bearing while paddling before you set off on this trip. A GPS is a great addition, as following a bearing while paddling is easier using it than a compass. However, I never rely completely on electronics or anything battery powered, especially in a wet environment. That said, bringing a VHF radio is also very important. You need to listen to the weather forecast to decide whether you should attempt your planned crossing, and it is a valuable marine communication device in case of emergency.

A tide table for the Stikine's delta is also a must. You can obtain one from www .tidesandcurrents.noaa.gov/tides06/tab2wc2a.html#144 by clicking on "predictions" beside "Stikine River Entrance, Point Rothsay." If you don't know how the tides work or how to calculate tide height at any given hour by using the Rule of Twelves, find out. Then do your homework, working out exactly when you can cross to Wrangell on an appropriate tide to navigate the Stikine's mud flats.

I would also carry pepper spray and an air horn to deal with potential bear encounters (the horn is also a good idea for the crossing to Wrangell, in case of fog). There are a fair number of bears in this region and if you are hiking you are more likely to surprise them. Make lots of noise when walking and be aware of your surroundings and areas where you may not be seen or heard well. Obviously, if you are planning on doing some extended hiking trips, bring the proper equipment. If you're a birder, it would be well worth taking some binoculars. Maybe you will also spot some mountain goats on high.

Trip Notes:

MAP NO.	GRID REF.	FEATURE	DESCRIPTION
104 G/14 East	718195	Put-in	You can put in at the riverbank right below Stikine RiverSong or upstream at the public boat launch kitty-corner from the Anglican church.
	710192	Cabins	There are cabins high on the RR bank across from IR 7.
	684175	Rapids	There is a big rock on RL in the RL channel around the island. In higher water there are some good-sized **Class 2−** standing waves which are easily avoided by taking a line at the inside of the bend. In low water the waves are not so easily avoided and the RR channel around the gravel bar island may be dry.
			There is a homestead at Kunishma Creek just downstream on RL. At lower water there are significant standing waves in front of Kunishma Creek. You can easily skirt them by staying RR.
	675163	Camping	On the gravel bar on RL there is a treed bench with sandy tent spots that makes for a good camp if you get on the water late. It is just before the bend to the right that hosts Buck's Riffle.
	672160	Riffle	At lower water **Buck's Riffle** is a **Class 1+/2−** set of standing waves on the bend. The riffle is virtually non-existent in high water.
104 G/14 West	657164	Rapids	In high water there are more significant **Class 1+/2−** standing waves at the bend to the left following Buck's Riffle.
	656160	Camping	A nice camp can be made on the RL gravel bar following the bend described above.
	650158	Cabins	On RR upstream of Dodjatin Creek there is a group of cabins. Note: There is no longer a Forest Service campsite at Dodjatin Creek.

	Fishing hole	Fishing for bull trout/Dolly Varden can be good at the mouth of the creek, but please respect that this is a local fishing spot traditionally used by Tahltan families.
638157	**Cabins**	There are cabins on RR overlooking the river.
621160	**Camp**	On RR, Winter Creek is a traditional Tahltan camping spot used while fishing for sockeye and just enjoying the summer in general. Note: there is no longer a Forest Service campsite here anymore either.
596141	**Rapids**	**Three Sisters Rapids** are **Class 2–** in high water, but they hardly exist at lower flows. The islands come up fast in any case, so be prepared if you want to take pictures. You obviously want to avoid broaching on these pretty rock outcrop islands. A tricky aspect of this section of river is that the currents converge after the islands, making for cross-currents and very swirly water, especially in the RL (main) channel. Run RR at high water, but RL is fine at lower flows.
593135	**Rapids**	**Bad Rapids, Class 1+/2–**, are right around the corner. There is a midstream gravel bar island, and in the RL channel, on RL, there is a rock island (GR 592130), a large boulder and some large standing waves at high water. In high water, the rock and associated hydraulics and waves can be avoided by taking the RR channel or staying far RR in the RL channel. It is harder to avoid the rock and standing waves on RL at lower water. You may have no choice but to run the RL channel. Be on your knees!
	Camping	A nice camp can be made on the large gravelly island between the channels. Landing is good at the foot of the island approaching from the RL channel.

581126	**Historic site**	Glenora was a large staging town for the gold rushes in northern BC and the Yukon, as well as for the building of the Yukon Telegraph and Alaska Highway. Nothing much remains but some old rotting cabins as evidence of how important this once busy community was in history. But, you can imagine the flats in front of the river denuded of trees and lined with hundreds of watercraft, including steam sternwheelers, and thousands of gold seekers moving about through a tent city. "Glenora" is a combination of the Gaelic word for valley, "glen," and the Spanish word for gold, "oro." There are still some interesting homesteads in the area, with road access but no services.
	Hiking	From here you can bushwhack up to the alpine of Mount Glenora. Maybe read Muir's account of his epic hike in *Travels in Alaska* first! Across the river you can see the road up to the historic Diamond B Ranch at Callbreath Creek.
	Camping	There is organized camping at the Glenora Forest Service Recreation Site if that is what you prefer. A burn starts a couple kilometres downstream on RL, but there is good natural camping at Tsikhini Creek regardless.
580090	**Camping; Short hike**	On RL, on the upstream side of Tsikhini Creek there is great camping in the trees on the floodplain flats. You can fish at the creek mouth and hike up about 30 minutes to where the creek cascades off a cliff. You can't see the waterfall from creek right, but the walking is easy to the cliff base.
	Hiking	Across the river is the site of an HBC trading post, now called Hudson Bay Flats. The site is in fact very flat and you can see why the post was located there. The uniform trees indicate the clearing made for the post. There is a trail leading upstream to Glenora that you can hike.

	579083	Tricky water	In high water there is a section of strong cross-currents and significant whirlpools about 800 m downstream of Tsikhini Creek. If you stay left you may be able to avoid the worst of this tricky spot. In low water there is nothing to worry about here.
	571067	Petroglyph	On RL at lower water you can see a carving in a large rock that lies on a beach. To help you locate the beach with the petroglyph, look for the cabin across the river on RR at the mouth of Damnation Creek. The beach is basically across from the cabin, and there is a tree back on the beach with an arrow carved into it that points to the petroglyph. The carved rock may be covered with sand if no one has dug it out since the last high water. To find it, walk exactly 10 paces toward the river from the tree with the arrow on it. If you don't see it, start digging! If you are in the river after pacing out the distance, you're paddling the Stikine at high water. As if you didn't already know that!
	555055	Camping; Short hike	A very nice camp can be made on RL on the gravel bar on the downstream side of the mouth of Yehiniko Creek (known locally as Bear Creek). There is fishing potential here and a nice view of the cliffs. There are more sheltered sites up the creek a ways too. You can walk up the creekbed to stretch your legs after dinner or hike up the hills in the burn to get a view of the river.
104 G/11	530027	Riffle	**Dutch Charlie's Riffle** has some **Class 1** waves and is just barely a riffle. The burn ends in this area.
104 G/12	502003	Cabins	Cabins sit up on the RL bank.
	477954	Cabin	There is another cabin on RL on the upstream side of Snipper Creek.
			On RL you may also be able to spot some mountain goats up on the cliffs.

466948	Camping; Fishing	On RL there is a large area for camping on the downstream side of the mouth of Helveker Creek, even at very high water. The flat area next to the creek is exposed, but there are sheltered sites in the trees. Fishing is usually good at the creek mouth. Helveker Creek was named by the surveyor Forrest Kerr for his wife, Helen Vicars Kerr.
		Note: Headwinds generated by daytime heating can be very strong in the braided section of river starting upstream of the Chutine River confluence (they can be strong all the way to Wrangell from Telegraph Creek, mind you!). This is also a confusing section to navigate, but pretty! Watch for wood hazards.
458946	Cabin	There is a cabin on RR where the map indicates Lease 3572.
449929	Cabins	On RL, on the upstream side of Kirk Creek, there is a group of cabins.
411908	Camping	A small, sheltered camp can be made on RR at the creek mouth found at the 350 m elevation mark. There is a larger site to come at Jacksons Flats.
398895	Tricky water	In high water especially, there are some serious cross-currents and boily water where the river bends toward the left at Jacksons. The main flow hits the cliff on RR and causes the tricky water. You can eddy out high on RL after the point and avoid all the "confused seas." At low and average water it is not difficult to run the left side of the main chute, staying away from the headwall.
394888	Camping	An excellent camp can be made on the downstream side of Dokdaon Creek, on RL. The floodplain is huge and there are some small trees for cover. The cliff across on RR is nice to look at, too.

| 393884 | Riffle | **Grand Rapids** is a **Class 1+** riffle of small standing waves and fast water at most water levels. These minor rapids lie in the RL channel around the big island. The rapids are not very grand but they are somewhat long, reaching down to where the two channels converge after the island. There may be more interesting water here than in the rapids! |
| | Hiking | In Steamboat Channel, the RR channel around the big island, you may find the starting point for the Missusjay Mountain hike. The trailhead is not obvious, and I don't know how good the trail will be, if you can find it. People do hike the ridge, according to Dan Pakula from Stikine RiverSong. This may be the adventure you have been looking for! |

From Devil's Elbow to the end of Klootchman Canyon there can be tricky currents at corners and in the narrows. In high water we found some strong cross-currents just before entering Klootchman.

The canyon itself is usually just fast water without too much action. Klootchman is supposedly a Chinook word for "a woman or wife." There must be some interesting water here at some water levels, as, according to Warburton Pike, on the way upstream the Tlingit men put down their paddles here and the women took complete charge of navigating this canyon.

| 356793 | Camping | On the island on RL is a gravel bar that makes for a good camp. |
| 350788 | Rapids | Approximately 1 km downstream of Klootchman Canyon the river takes a sharp turn toward a headwall. There can be good-sized waves along the cliff that can be skirted by staying to the right side of the main channel. The huge flood runoff in 2007 changed the run of the river here. |

	330771	**Camping; Short hike**	A really nice camp, known locally as "Whitesands," is on RR and the upstream side of Vekops Creek. There's a sandy beach with camping up behind and trees for shelter. There is a nice hike from the camp up to two waterfalls.
104 G/5	346746	**Tricky water**	Where the river narrows again after spreading over some large gravel bars there is boily water and strong cross-currents, especially at higher water.
	351740	**Water survey station**	On RL is an inactive water-gauging station.
	331706	**Camping**	At low water you can camp on the gravel bar on RR at the mouth of the small creek.
	330690	**Camping**	Another low-water camp can be made on RR at the mouth of Jonquette Creek.
	328670	**Little Canyon**	There can be very boily water, strong cross-currents and whirlpools in Little Canyon at high water. Stay loose and paddle through smoothly. At low levels the water is much less interesting. This is a lovely canyon.
	326646	**Camping**	You can camp on the left side of the island (which may not be an island at low water). There are large trees for shelter. Tricky currents may be found around the corner, depending on water levels.
	325622	**Camping**	There is a large floodplain gravel site on RR downstream of Deeker Creek. In the next wide and shallow section of river, wood hazards are of concern. Be alert and on your knees. The glacier views are astounding now, starting with Commander Glacier all the way to Mud Glacier. It will be difficult to keep your eyes on the water!
	274553	**Camping**	On RR there is a huge floodplain camping area downstream of Patmore Creek. Camping for millions with amazing glacier views! You can stretch your legs after dinner with a walk up the creek. You can also camp on the many large gravel bars

			downstream past the Scud River confluence at normal water level
	282514	Camping	This is a site on RL with large trees for shelter. Good in high water and bad weather especially.
			There are more wood hazards in the next section to Flood River. Be cautious. There is a tricky corner where the main channel swings far RL and the current bumps up against a rock outcrop on shore, making for a sharp turn to the right. Wood hazards are possible and there can be whirlpools in the eddy on RR and following the sharp turn.
104 G/4	310427	Camping; Short hike	On RR you can camp on either the upstream or the downstream side of Flood River. This is the second-last good spot to camp before Scatter Ass Flats. The upstream camping spot has the bonus of about a one-hour hike (one way) to Flood Lake, with great glacier views. Be warned you will get your feet wet crossing two small creeks unless you have rubber boots. The downstream side has a pretty spot to camp, with trees and great views back upstream. **Note:** You could get flooded out of this site in very high water like we did. It was Flood Camp!
	315417	Cabin	There is a fairly new cabin on RR about 1 km downstream of the mouth of Flood River.
	329373	Cabin	On RR by the small creek mouth there is a cabin below a large, steep mountainside.
			CAUTION: Now you are approaching the most hazardous section of the Lower Stikine with regard to wood hazards. It is known locally as **Scatter Ass Flats**. You will be constantly looking for the channel with the most water and constantly manoeuvring away from wood hazards. It's confusing and difficult to navigate these flats. You must be on your knees and navigating with your 1:50 000 maps (a GPS with maps will be useful here.

for knowing where you are and not getting off on some unnavigable side channel). Old riverboaters have called this section of the Lower Stikine route a death trap in high water. The mid-channel gravel bars are submerged under fast-moving water, making it even more difficult to avoid the wood piled on them.

	368335	Camping; Short hike	To take a break from the tricky paddling, you can have lunch and explore the site of an old HBC post once located on RR 500 m or so upstream of the Anuk River mouth (the river is a trickle in dry conditions). There is also a great camp spot at the coordinates given. The actual mouth of the Anuk is hidden from view from the main channel by islands and the river can actually be dry in low water. We saw two wolves here in 2006.

CAUTION: The river is clearer of wood for a short stretch, but the guts of **Scatter Ass Flats Is Just downstream, all the way to the Sterling River confluence**. This is going to be the greatest test of your moving-water and river-reading skills yet, especially at high water. Things will happen fast and you must make quick decisions on your best route through the many channels laced with wood.

Note: There is only mediocre camping in this section of river to Great Glacier, and only at lower water. The few good spots are in out-of-the-way places. There is almost nothing for gravel bar camping when the river is very high. If it is very high, I would plan to camp by the Anuk River confluence and at the established campsite at Great Glacier the next night.

104 B/13	319025	Hot springs	Don't get too excited about the Choquette Hot Springs. They are not that hot, and you have some muddy wading and clambering over beaver dams to do to get to a pool of just

barely warm water. But it's an adventure if you have the time. The springs are at the base of a rock cliff up a creek 1 km upstream from Choquette Creek on RL. The creek you want for the hot springs is directly across the Stikine from the Fowler cabin, which sits on RR. If you can't see the Fowler cabin across the river from the creek mouth, you are at the wrong one.

313024	Cabins	There are two cabins (one is the Fowler cabin) on RR as you approach Great Glacier Provincial Park campsite.
301996	Camping; Short hike	There is a provincial park campsite at the trailhead to walk in to Outwash Lake below Great Glacier. There are two picnic tables, an outhouse and lots of room for tents.

The site is on RR, just downstream of the river draining Outwash Lake. To land there you must ferry across the outflow of the lake to a narrow eddy below the rock point. The landing for the campsite and trail is a small nook, and it is a steep path up. You have to land your canoes one at a time.

The approach to the landing is tricky. In medium to low flows there are three channels formed by two gravel islands that are submerged at high flows. When the Stikine and the outflow from Outwash Lake are high you need to stick tight to RR of the Stikine to get into the eddy beside the outflow. The front ferry over to the campsite landing is pushy, the current is fast and there are standing waves in the outflow stream you must cross.

At low to medium flows the RR channel of the Stikine has some big waves that could swamp open canoes, so the far left channel around the gravel bar islands is the best route even though it looks like you won't be able make it over to the campsite. The middle channel is an option if it's not too shallow.

The hike to the lake takes about 25–30 minutes one way without a canoe.

We could not hike the whole trail, which is usually in good condition, on our July 2006 flood trip. The lake was starting to drain down it!

Caution: If you do decide to portage up the trail and paddle on Outwash Lake, do so early in the morning. Afternoon outflow winds create large waves. Also, stay a good distance from the glacier. Anything can happen with a huge piece of ice like that. People have died from tipping in this lake and being unable to rescue themselves. The water is deathly cold – go figure.

	305996	**Camping**	Across the Stikine from the Great Glacier campsite is a very nice, treed island gravel bar to camp on, at least at more normal flows. It was flooded in the third week of July in 2006.
	301984	**Camping**	At lower water, you can also camp on the gravel bar on RR on the point.
	294954	**Cabins**	There are a number of cabins up the snye.
104 B/12	294925	**Cross**	There is a white cross on the RR point across from the Iskut River confluence. I was told it was erected in memory of Francis Gleason's father, who died somewhere up the Iskut River.
	286875	**Salmon plant**	The Great Glacier salmon plant is on RR. It has been here since the '70s. Stop in to buy fresh fish for supper, get the lowdown on the salmon wars from Bob and see the state-of-the-art processing plant.
	285873	**Cabin**	This is a Fisheries Department cabin, on RR.
	277850	**Historic site**	Boundary House (also known as Stikine) was where river travellers stopped to clear Canada customs in bygone days. It is privately owned now.

	254830	**US Border**	Welcome to the State of Alaska. **Note:** the coordinates for the Trip Notes are now in latitude and longitude format.
C-6 Bradfield Canal	**56° 39' 06" 131° 55' 00"**	**Cabin**	On RL is the Flemer cabin.
	56° 40' 22" 131° 56' 25"	**Turnoff: Ketili River**	This is the turnoff to paddle the Ketili River/Hot Springs Slough to Chief Shakes Hot Springs. You need to keep your eyes peeled for this nondescript opening on RR. First you will see a creek on RL, then an island ahead and then the turnoff to the Ketili River on RR about 300 m before the midriver island. There is a lone pine tree at the entrance. The river/slough does not have much current compared to the Stikine.
C-1 Petersburg	**56° 43' 10" 132° 01' 55"**	**Turnoff: Hot springs**	From the Ketili River you must turn north deeper in the wilds of the slough at these coordinates. You will now paddle for about 700 m (about 200 m past a likely turnoff which leads to a waterfall) before seeing the **first**
			landing site of two for visiting the hot springs (**56° 43' 10"/132° 01' 14"**). This platform takes you to the hot springs via a short path up a creek and then through the forest. **You can also land at the dock** about 300 m farther east (**56° 43' 08"/ 132° 01' 00"**). From the dock you follow the boardwalk that takes you to the outdoor tub. From the outdoor tub you will see the path to the indoor tub and then the forest trail out to the other landing.
		Camping	In the grassy meadow near the outdoor tub is a potential camping spot – if it's not too wet.
			Note: Be alert for jet boats speeding along in the slough. Get off to the side as soon as you hear one!

56° 34' 18" 132° 06' 20"	TNF cabins; Camping	On RR, hidden from view by trees until you get close, are the two Shakes Slough cabins. If you haven't booked one, likely they won't mind if you camp in the clearing at the cabins if you are really stuck for the night. It's not great camping, but it is sheltered. **Note:** there is no water source near these cabins except the river.
	Side trip	You can paddle up Shakes Slough to Shakes Lake on a day trip. This is a pretty trip and usually worth the time and effort. You will do some strenuous upstream paddling and tracking but the rock canyon and Shakes Glacier are spectacular. Paddle the lake with caution and avoid strong afternoon outflow winds and going too close to the glacier's base. **Note:** In high water, it is not possible to get up to the lake.
56° 42' 29" 132° 07' 42"	Water survey station	On RR is a USGS water-gauging station. It is active and the real time readings are available online.
56° 42' 15" 132° 11' 00"	Cabin	On RR is a private cabin.
56° 41' 30" 132° 42' 15"	Camping	On RL on Andrew Island is a large sandy area that once housed many campers desperate to get up to the gold fields via the Stikine. You can definitely find something that works for a camp for your group here. The sandy flats up the bank are much better than some swampy spot, even if it is a bit of a hump up.
56° 41' 45" 132° 20' 00"	Cabin	There is another private cabin on RR after Kakwan Point.
56° 39' 52" 132° 14' 21"	TNF cabin	You may well want to consider booking the Mount Rynda cabin at the confluence of Andrew Creek and Andrew Slough instead of the busy Shakes Slough and Garnet Ledge cabins. Camping will only get harder to find as you approach the ocean.
56° 38' 30" 132° 19' 30"	Float- house	Just before Hooligan Point proper is a floathouse. You're nearly at the Pacific Ocean! From Hooligan Point, head for Point Rothsay.

C-2 **Petersburg**	56° 36' 57" 132° 20' 28"	**Cabin**	A private cabin sits on the west side of the most northwestern of the Cottonwood Islands.
			Note: Be sure at all points to take the RL channel that has the most flow. Then keep to the mainland shore to Point Rothsay and Garnet Ledge. You can see on the USGS map where there is a passage through the mud flats.
	56° 34' 35" 132° 21' 57"	**TNF** **cabin;** **Camping**	You should seriously consider booking the Garnet Ledge cabin for your last night before crossing to Wrangell. It sets you up for a short paddle the next day, and you can take advantage of a calm morning, as the wind on a fair day will pick up during the day. You will also be able to more easily time your travel on a rising tide. From here it is about a 1½- to 2-hour paddle to Wrangell Island, depending on winds and tide. Ocean travel in a canoe is not to be taken lightly. You must be prepared with a compass bearing in case of fog.
			Take your bearing from a point on the mainland out of the mud flats. Do not cross in bad weather or with an iffy forecast or on a falling tide. Note that Eastern Passage also has boat traffic and significant current.
			You are not supposed to camp in the clearing around the cabin, and it's pretty low and wet except for the beach in fair weather and at lower tides. However, if it comes down to a question of safety, stop here. Just be respectful of the party using the cabin if there is someone there. Note there is a hefty fine of up to $5,000 for staying in a TNF cabin without a booking. If you have a satellite phone, you can call the TNF district office in Wrangell and explain your predicament.
B-2 **Petersburg**	56° 29' 01" 132° 22' 54"	**Wrangell**	You can take out at the public dock at the marina.

*** Don't forget to call US Customs on your arrival at Wrangell!

CHAPTER FOUR

TATSHENSHINI/ALSEK RIVERS

Some people will question why I have included the Tatshenshini/Alsek route in this guidebook when it is a trip suitable only for exceptional whitewater canoeists fully trained in river rescue and with many years of river-tripping experience. I concur with something I read somewhere that goes along the line of "If you only *think* you are good enough to paddle the Tat, you probably aren't." But canoeing the Tatshenshini and Lower Alsek rivers is a trip of a lifetime and those paddlers who take their skills to the highest level so they can achieve their dreams have my support. The route is normally travelled by raft, and much of the river-running information found in the public sphere is from a rafter's perspective, so I'm passing along what I know about paddling it in a canoe in order to assist canoeists ready to make this run and to inspire those who can only dream for now.

The Tatshenshini River is a tributary of the large-volume Alsek River and together they form one of the largest drainages in the Americas. The delights of making this journey from the dry boreal mountains of the Yukon through BC's Coast Mountains into the land of ice and then out to the Gulf of Alaska are many. There is no doubt that the steep-creeking experience of the boisterous and technical whitewater of the Tatshenshini canyon will make you quiver in your booties, and you will not be daydreaming on the rest of the route by any means. Camping is good nearly everywhere, with the floodplains of clear creeks making ample flat spots for tents. Hiking up these gravel highways is pleasant and there is a walk for everyone after dinner or on a day off. Those looking for more than stretching their legs can hike up to the alpine in places and even walk on a glacier!

The scenery as you approach the Alsek confluence causes what rafters call SOS, or "Scenic Overload Syndrome." It is sure to infect even the most jaded travellers who think they have seen it all. Walker Glacier provides the first chance to get up close and personal with the cause of the disease. Ironically, for as much as I love mountain rivers, it is Novatak Glacier that is my favourite – it's a prairie of ice and I'm a Saskatchewan girl at heart.

Your last incomparable treat is Alsek Lake. This glacial lake, in the early evening sun, dappled with icebergs of gel-toothpaste blue, charcoal grey and snow white, fringed with massive glaciers and ringed by rugged peaks, is probably the most beautiful sight I have ever seen. Considering I have been lucky enough to visit so many magical places, that is saying a lot.

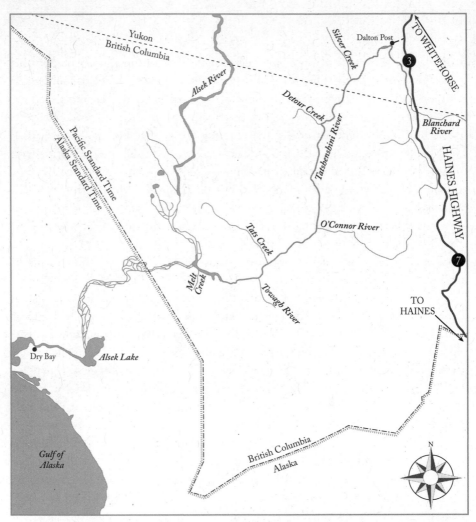

Tatshenshini/Alsek Rivers

From the whitewater thrills of the canyon, Monkey Wrench, the S-Turns and Cat in the Washing Machine rapids to the vistas of forest, peaks and ice that never stop, the Tatshenshini and Alsek rivers will take your breath away. When you think you've done it all, this trip will make you feel small. And when you are out there on the river, remember to thank all the people who put their energy toward conserving this incredible watershed. It will remain wild if we stay vigilant.

Length: The Trip Notes describe in detail the classic route from Dalton Post, Yukon, to Dry Bay, Alaska, approximately 214 km long. This route can be paddled in a week under optimal conditions. Experiencing optimal conditions is unlikely in the Coast Mountains and this is a once in a lifetime adventure, so plan for lots of extra time. Since the hiking and camping are so good, you will want to spend more time on land than you normally might on a river trip. We took 13 days and that was perfect for us. It was a leisurely pace and we had lots of time to check out places of interest and do some hiking. If you portage the canyon, you will want at least two weeks – more if you haven't had your fill of hiking!

You will definitely want to calculate extra days in your itinerary to deal with any unexpectedly high water. Additionally, rain and low clouds could obscure the spectacular scenery, so you may want to wait for some sun on certain sections. Headwinds can be ferocious and they will slow you down. Your raft support people will be working hard to keep up. (I strongly advise all canoeing parties to have raft support on this route.)

Bad weather as you approach the coast might also put you behind schedule. It is quite likely you will get delayed in Dry Bay. It is not unusual for air charters to be weathered-out in this country. If you plan on flying back to Haines or Whitehorse directly from Dry Bay, this is even more likely. The flight spans extremely mountainous terrain and is very weather dependent.

Theoretically you can shorten the classic Tat/Alsek trip. You could fly out with a floatplane just downstream of Detour Creek on river left, where there is a private cabin in front of which planes can land. If you take hard-shell canoes, you will have to charter with a company from the Yukon or BC. Floatplanes in Alaska are not permitted to carry external loads. This would be a really short trip. You would get to run the whitewater canyon and enjoy Stillwater Canyon, but you will miss the glacier scenery and much, much more.

You could potentially start your trip by putting in at the cabin and there are probably other places farther down on the Tat or Alsek that a floatplane can land where you could put in or take out. A trip starting lower down on the Tatshenshini, below the whitewater canyon, may suit canoeists not wanting a full-on, challenging whitewater experience. But be warned, the rest of the Tat and the Lower Alsek still require advanced whitewater canoeing and rescue skills. Monkey Wrench, the S-Turns and Cat in the Washing Machine rapids can be difficult and there is funky water where creeks flow in all along the route. You simply do not want to swim in this very swift and very cold water.

Call around and talk to the pilots for specifics on these potential shorter trips. As I understand it, you need special permission to land in a national park in Canada and this may be true for the US as well. I'm not even sure – given the permit system for running the route, permits being based on a specific take-out day at Dry Bay – that you can even shorten the trip by taking out upstream of Dry Bay. See the Permits and Fees section of this chapter and the Directory of Services and Organizations at the end of the book to start your research on shorter trip options.

There are really no good options I am familiar with for safely lengthening the canoe route. Running Blanchard River and the upper canyon of the Tat above Dalton Post is a Class 3 and 4 endeavour. The run is 34 km long and the rapids are rocky and continuous in sections. You don't want to wreck the canoe you brought all the way up here or hurt yourself before you even get on the amazing multi-day trip. Save yourself, your equipment and your nerve for the Tat's whitewater canyon below Dalton Post. Raft Blanchard and the Upper Tat on a day trip if you are looking for an early adrenalin fix. Paddling beyond Dry Bay up or down the coast of the Gulf of Alaska is not an option for river canoes or rafts, in my opinion. However, I have heard there is a traditional inland canoe route from Dry Bay to Yakutat, and this may be an option for explorers looking for a longer trip. Start your research on this option by calling the air service in Yakutat. They can refer to you some local residents who may know something.

Dalton Post to cabin near Detour Creek*	44 km
Detour Creek cabin to Dry Bay*	170 km
Dalton Post to Dry Bay*	214 km

* These trips are described in detail in the Trip Notes section of this chapter.

Topographic Maps: NTS 1:50 000-scale maps are recommended for the BC and Yukon sections of the route; and for the Tat canyon, whether you are paddling or portaging it, the 1:50 000-scale 115 A/3 topo is absolutely required. You want to know exactly where you are with regard to the rapids and the rough road on RL, especially if there is trouble and you need to evacuate or if you are portaging. If you want to do some serious hiking and exploring along the river route, you'll also want the larger scale. Because you end up paddling in Alaska you will need USGS maps, and I recommend the 1:63 360s (a similar scale to 1:50 000s where one square inch equals one square mile).

The authors of an excellent rafting guidebook, *The Complete Guide to the Tatshenshini River*, produce a 1:250 000-scale hand-drawn map reduced to fit on one sheet. It gives the paddler an overview of the significant features of the river route and region. With this map or a set of NTS 1:250 000-scale maps of the route, you can gain a much better understanding of the lay of the land you are travelling through and get more out of the guidebook and this chapter with regard to the natural and human history of the rivers. See Cloudburst Productions in the Directory of Services and Organizations in order to purchase the guidebook and map.

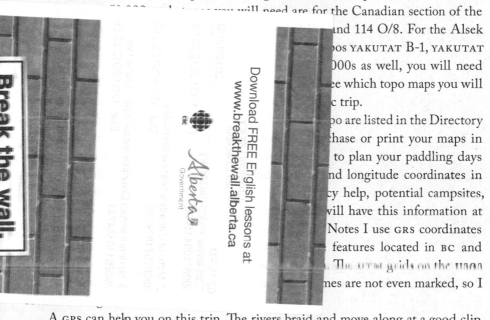

you will need are for the Canadian section of the
and 114 O/8. For the Alsek
os YAKUTAT B-1, YAKUTAT
000s as well, you will need
ee which topo maps you will
c trip.
po are listed in the Directory
hase or print your maps in
to plan your paddling days
nd longitude coordinates in
cy help, potential campsites,
vill have this information at
Notes I use GRS coordinates
features located in BC and
The utm grids on the map
mes are not even marked, so I

A GPS can help you on this trip. The rivers braid and move along at a good clip, making it challenging sometimes to determine exactly where you are. In many places, in order to get to some of the campsites and other areas of interest, you need to make a move far in advance to get over to the correct channel. Make sure your GPS map datum setting is NAD 27 Canada and the position format setting is MGRS (Military Grid Reference System) for the BC and Yukon sections. Change the settings to NAD 27 Alaska and latitude and longitude when you cross the US border. For a discussion of topographic maps and the use of a GPS see the How To Use this Guidebook section.

Permits and Fees: To date, this is the only trip in this guidebook for which you must obtain a permit and pay park fees in order to paddle the route. The Tatshenshini/Alsek is not a cheap or easy trip to plan and execute. You must figure out your dates far in advance, wait to see if you get what you want, do your paperwork and then deal with your logistics.

You will want to get a private trip information packet to help with your planning first. It will outline in detail the procedures for getting a permit and paying fees and will supply general information on a Tat/Alsek trip, such as dealing with customs, required emergency equipment, scheduling of trips, group size (15 per group), type of watercraft, environmental protection and sanitation requirements and a list of equipment and shuttle providers. You get this packet by contacting any of the following:

Glacier Bay National Park & Preserve, Park Headquarters, PO Box 140, Gustavus, AK 99826. Phone (907) 697-2230; fax (907) 697-2654.

Glacier Bay National Park & Preserve, PO Box 137, Yakutat, AK 99689. Phone (907) 784-3295; fax (907) 784-3535. They have a special phone line with river information: (907) 784-3370.

Tatshenshini–Alsek Provincial Park, BC Parks, Postal Bag 5000, Smithers, BC V0J 2N0. Phone (250) 847-7320; fax (250) 847-7659.

The Tatshenshini–Alsek Park website, www.env.gov.bc.ca/bcparks/explore/parkpgs/tatshens, has maps for campsites along the route. These maps show camping locations in the park and rate them as high, medium or low for the likelihood of encountering bears. The report the maps were derived from can be found at www.env.gov.bc.ca/bcparks/explore/parkpgs/tatshens/tat_report.pdf.

The process for applying for a private (non-commercial) permit is pretty straightforward and explained in the trip packet you will be sent. An application for a permit comes as part of the package. The private permit system is basically a waiting list, organized on a first-come, first-served basis. Trips from Dalton Post to Dry Bay are scheduled and managed under a one-party-a-day take-out rule, so you want to apply for a permit to take out at Dry Bay on a day near the end of August (I seriously recommend you only run the Tat canyon at lower water). It took us two years to get a date we could work with. The cost for a permit is currently US$100.

You get on the list for private trip permits by sending your name, address, home and work telephone numbers, email address and payment of US$25 to cover administrative charges to: National Park Service, Yakutat Ranger Station, River Permits, PO Box 137, Yakutat, AK 99869. Payment of the $25 administrative fee may be made by money order, international money order, Visa or MasterCard. To pay by credit card, you need to provide your credit card information (cardholder name, card number, expiration date) and indicate that you would like US$25 to be charged to that card. Note that the National Park Service cannot accept cash or cheques. If you have any questions, contact the Yakutat Ranger Station at (907) 784-3295.

Once you have obtained a permit from the National Park Service, then you must pay the BC Parks fee of $125 per person. The fee includes GST (Goods & Services Tax). For more information on when and how to pay this fee, go to www.env.gov.bc.ca/bcparks/explore/parkpgs/tatshens/parkinfo.html#river_fee or call the Ministry of Environment in Victoria at (250) 952-0932, or toll free in BC 1-866-433-7272 (1-866-433-PASB) or outside BC at (250) 952-0932.

You must pass through customs at some point, maybe even twice, depending on your logistics. A passport is required for entering the US. Remember, there is also a time difference of one hour between the Yukon/BC and Alaska. If it's 1:00 p.m. in BC or the Yukon, it's noon in Alaska.

Getting There and Away: This is normally a drive-in and fly-out trip, unless you figure out a way to shorten it. Haines, Alaska, and Whitehorse, Yukon, are the usual staging places for the Tat/Alsek route. Both can be reached by airline or by driving, or by some combination of flying, driving and ferry. It is about 170 km from Haines to the Dalton Post put-in (a two-hour drive) and from Whitehorse to Dalton Post is around 260 km (a 3½-hour drive).

Coming from Haines north up the Haines Highway (Alaska Route 7, which becomes Yukon Hwy. 3), the Dalton Post access road is on the left, 2.1 km after the Tatshenshini viewpoint pullout. There was no signage for the Dalton Post road as of 2007, but there was a highway rest area sign facing the other way about 100 m before the left turn for the access road.

Coming from Whitehorse, you start off heading west on Hwy. 1 to Haines Junction and then turn south onto Hwy. 3 to Klukshu Village. The turnoff to Dalton Post is about 23 km from the village and on your right. The dirt road to Dalton is about 100 m before the "Rest Area 2 km" sign on the right. If you pass the sign, you have gone too far. You need to keep your eyes peeled.

The dirt road to Dalton is about 5 km long and can be very dusty or muddy and slippery, depending on the weather. It drops gradually at first and then enters a section called the "drop of doom." The road is very steep here. Make sure your brakes are good! The road crosses Klukshu Creek and a salmon weir before reaching the floodplain of the Tat. You will see remnants of old cabins, a new outhouse (as of 2007) and probably some fishing activity here. Continue straight ahead until you almost reach the riverbank. To the left are some good spots to rig and put in, as they are out of the way of any fishing traffic.

For taking out you have the option of flying from Dry Bay to Whitehorse, Haines or Yakutat and onward. Your logistics will depend on the kind of canoes you take and the number of people in your party, what aircraft on wheels are available and how urgent it is that you get back home on the day you planned.

There a couple of options if you are paddling hard-shell canoes. One is to fly to Whitehorse via a DC3, Sky Van or Twin Otter charter. These planes will carry nested canoes, rafts, people and gear and can usually fly in worse weather than a single-engine aircraft. You could get a shuttle to Dalton Post with one of the numerous canoe-outfitting companies in Whitehorse, making for convenient vehicle logistics but a costly trip if you don't have a large group. Flying to Haines or Yakutat wasn't an option in 2004, as there was no wheeled aircraft big enough to carry a hard-shell canoe inside. There may eventually be an aircraft in either of these places large enough to take canoes inside. Call around to see what's out there when you plan to do your trip.

The other option is to sell, trade or store your hard-shell canoe(s) at Dry Bay. Someone I know traded their canoe for 24 beer and some salmon. They figured it was a better deal than flying it out for some big bucks. They could buy another one back home for less or the same amount. You could also arrange to leave your canoes in Dry

Bay until a larger plane chartered by someone else could take them. You may be able to make the arrangement at a shared cost, working this out with the other group via the air service. You would need to find storage at Dry Bay or you could always stash your canoes in the bush by the gravel runway and hope for the best. Canoe free, you can fly with your rafts and gear to Whitehorse, Haines or Yakutat and beyond.

If you have a PakCanoe or some other variation of a folding/inflatable canoe that is very good in whitewater, you have more options. Canoe(s) and raft(s) can go in a chartered wheel plane to Whitehorse, Haines or Yakutat. You just need to find an aircraft that can take your group, gear and collapsed boats. You may need to make two trips or more depending on the planes available, as weight is always an issue when flying, especially in Alaska.

If you are on a tight schedule, flying to Yakutat on a charter and then to Juneau via the scheduled Alaska Airlines flights is your best bet. You fly along the coast rather than through the mountains, so you're less likely to get stuck in Dry Bay. From Juneau you can get anywhere by aircraft and down or up the coast via the excellent Alaska Marine Highway ferry system. Baggage restrictions are going to be your main concern with this option. You may have to pay extra to get all your boats and gear on board. You will also be lugging a lot of stuff around from terminal to terminal.

One way of solving this problem is to have your party split up after Dry Bay. Some people fly away to Yakutat and beyond without anything but their personal gear. The others get the boats and equipment out via a charter to Haines or Whitehorse and pick up the vehicles. There are outfitters in both Haines and Whitehorse that will rent you all the rafts and other equipment you will need and provide you with a shuttle service. Note that renting inflatable or good folding canoes is more likely out of Whitehorse. The outfitters in both places will even pack food for you.

You could also take out just below Alsek Lake at Gary Gray's Alsek River Lodge if you wanted to end your trip a little early and in luxury. Dry Bay can be pretty miserable in wet, cold weather. Gary will provide you with ground transportation to Dry Bay for a fee. You must take out there officially, checking in with the park ranger. If the access channel to the take-out by the airstrip doesn't have enough water to float a boat or you end up missing it (it happens all the time), you can hire Pat Pellet from Dry Bay to haul your load with his ATV and trailer to the airstrip from wherever you end up. You'll need a satellite phone to call him, however. Or you can hike to Dry Bay and find him.

The logistics of the Tat/Alsek trip are all about cost versus convenience. Be creative, call around and make a plan that works best for you. Look in the Directory of Services and Organizations and your Parks trip information packet for contact information for the businesses and information sources that can help you make this amazing trip happen. A number of these are listed on the Glacier Bay National Park & Preserve website, at www.nps.gov/glba/planyourvisit/upload/Services.pdf. Most of these operators have been around a long time and can make suggestions that will help you come up with the best plan for your group.

You must go through US Customs if you drive to Dalton Post from Haines or fly back to there or Yakutat. You will need to have a valid passport to enter the US and you must have it in your possession! Do I hear double Ziploc or Pelly case? Here is a bureaucracy-nightmare story for you. A party of American paddlers hired a driver from a Canadian company to help them with their shuttle. When they re-entered Canada the agent informed them the Canadian driver would not be able to return to Whitehorse with the van unless an American was with him in the vehicle. Big complication making for very long day! Make sure you have all the information you need about your shuttle logistics.

Currently you can camp at the Dalton Post put-in and the Dry Bay take-out for free (in Dry Bay you also have the option of camping at Pat Pellet's Brabazon Expeditions home base) and in Whitehorse, Haines and Juneau at private and municipal campgrounds. Look in the Directory of Services and Organizations for contact information for customs and tourist services in the communities mentioned in this section.

When To Go: August to early September. With canoes, the Tatshenshini canyon is best run at lower water. The lowest levels on the Upper Tat usually come at the end of August and into September; but you don't want to paddle this route too late in the season. Fall comes early in this region and the chances of good weather on the coast will decrease significantly come the end of August. It's a fine balance. If you are going to portage the whitewater canyon on the Tat, you can plan on paddling the route earlier in the season. But the route involves difficult paddling below the canyon as well, so don't go too early.

Below is a table showing average flows for the summer months for the Upper Tat and the Lower Alsek derived from archived hydrometric data. Flows are shown in cubic metres per second and cubic feet per second. The water survey station just downstream of Dalton Post (station number 15129000) measures the Tatshenshini's flow in cubic metres per second, as seen on the Environment Canada Water Survey website. The USGS website shows the Alsek's flow at the station across from Walker Glacier (though it says Alsek River near Yakutat) in cubic feet per second. Having both measures will allow you to work with both websites' real-time data and compare that with historical data.

	Tatshenshini at Dalton Post (1989–2005)		Alsek at Walker Glacier (1991–2005)	
	m³/s	ft³/s	m³/s	ft³/s
May	42.2	1490	773.0	27,300
June	94.8	3348	1987.8	70,200
July	70.1	2476	2486.2	87,800
August	44.3	1564	2211.5	78,100
September	31.5	1112	1359.2	48,000

Sources: Water Survey of Canada Archived Hydrometric Data; USGS Surface-Water Monthly Statistics, October 2007

It is evident why you do not want to be anywhere near the Tat canyon in a canoe in June when the spring snowmelt brings peak flows. After the freshet, Upper Tat water levels drop fairly uniformly and significantly over the summer, with September usually having the lowest. The Lower Alsek does not peak until July normally, but it can peak in August as well. Another reason to go later in August.

The Upper Tatshenshini River acts more or less like any other boreal river on the east side of the St. Elias Mountains. If it rains heavily in the Upper Tat valley the Upper Tat will rise, and that is something to consider when you are setting off to run the canyon. If it has been quite wet, you may want to delay your canyon run until the flow comes down. If it has been dry, you should be good to go in August. You can check the real-time flows on the Tatshenshini just downstream of Dalton Post on the Environment Canada hydrometric website, at http://scitech.pyr.ec.gc.ca/waterweb/fullgraph.asp.

The Lower Tatshenshini and the Alsek flow to a different rhythm. The Lower Tat, from around the Tkope River confluence down to the confluence with the Alsek, and the Alsek itself, are fed by the largest non-polar ice cap in the world. In July, runoff peaks, with snowmelt filling the rivers and feeder creeks and streams as on any boreal river. However, glacier-fed rivers stay up into August as the warmer weather melts the snow and ice of the glaciers. Glacial melt has a major effect on the summer water levels of the Lower Tat and Alsek rivers, particularly under certain weather conditions. Water levels will rise in midsummer during periods of hot, sunny weather (the opposite of boreal rivers) and drop with cool weather. If a warm front comes through with associated heavy precipitation, glacier-fed rivers will rise significantly and very quickly.

To elaborate, if the weather is sunny and hot, the river will rise slowly and stay up. If you have cold, wet weather, the river will rise steadily from the rain and then drop if the rain stops and the temperatures stay down. However, if you have warm, wet weather, the rain runs off and the snow and ice of the glaciers start to melt, so you have lots of water flowing in from all the feeder streams, making for abrupt rises in levels and possibly flood conditions. This is called a "coastal bomb," and it can happen in any month of the paddling season. You can only predict these weather-related water-level fluctuations as well as you can predict the weather in Alaska, and that is not easy. You just have to be prepared for jumps in flows at any time on the Lower Tat and Alsek.

To put the flows in the table in context, we paddled the Tatshenshini canyon on August 21, 2004, and the discharge was 37 m³/s (1307 ft³/s). It was a great technical run at that level. There were lots of eddies to catch. Rocks and holes were our main concern, but there were also some big waves to avoid. The weather was actually hot to start with and it had been dry for most of July and August. The average August flow over 17 years is 44.3 m³/s (1564 ft³/s), so we made the run at a fairly normal water level for that week of August.

Another group of canoeists with raft support ran the Tat/Alsek August 9 to 19, 2007. When they paddled the canyon, the Tat near Dalton Post was flowing at around 74 m³/s (2613 ft³/s). This high water level for August (more like a July flow) was fine for these properly outfitted, exceptional whitewater canoeists. They were able to boat-scout all the rapids from eddies as we had, with one boat swamping in the canyon. M & M Falls and Cat in the Washing Machine Rapid were actually easier at this water level. You can view all archived hydrometric data for the Tat near Dalton Post at www.wsc.ec.gc.ca/hydat/H2O/WEBfrmMeanReport_e.cfm.

Unlike the Upper Tatshenshini, the Alsek was running high when we paddled it in 2004. The high flows were a result of the extended period of hot weather (just like the relatively normal flows we had for the Upper Tat). The day we took out at Dry Bay, September 2, 2004, the river was flowing at 58,600 ft³/s (1659 m³/s) – a July flow, not a September one. The average for the August monthly flow in 2004 was 89,440. It would normally be 78,100, according to historical hydrometric statistics.

You can check the daily real-time flows and the monthly mean statistics over the years for the Alsek at Walker Glacier at http://waterdata.usgs.gov/ak/nwis. Click "Real-time data," set "Predefined displays" to "Daily streamflow" and "Group table" to "-- no grouping --" and then click "go" to get a list of stations.

The Alsek station is number 15129000, about a fifth of the way down the list. Click on the station number, and when the resulting page comes up, set the "Available data for this site" slot to "Time series: Real-time data." Beneath that, in the outlined box, in the second column, under "Output format," select "Graph w/ stats" and click "go." Scroll down the page for the resulting graphs and stats.

To get monthly mean stats for all the years of this station's operation, change the "Available data for this site" slot to "Time-series: Monthly statistics," and in the resulting box below that, tick the box beside "Parameter Code" for the parameter "Discharge, cubic feet per second." Beneath that, under "Choose Output Format," leave everything else blank but choose "Table of monthly mean" and then click "Submit."

When we were paddling the Tat below the Tkope River confluence we could already tell we were in high flows, and when we got to the Tat and Alsek confluence the water was in the trees that were turning colour already. The hydraulics on the Lower Tat and Alsek were quite strong. Boily water and standing waves were of the most concern. My PakCanoe is great in that kind of big-volume, squirrelly water, so all was well. But it was interesting paddling, especially at Monkey Wrench, the S-Turns and Cat in the Washing Machine rapids. The good weather deserted us for a couple of days as we approached Walker Glacier, but then our day down to Alsek Lake and the couple of days we spent there were absolutely fantastic. It was sunny and warm. A storm pounded us the last day as we paddled to Dry Bay, though!

You want to avoid as much wet weather as possible on a canoe trip in Alaska, Wet weather and low cloud make it difficult to see the glaciers and that is what you came for! It will rain no matter the month, but August is the best month for walking the line between summer weather and low water in the canyon and fall weather and lower water in the canyon. And, as I have explained ad nauseam already, the Lower Tat and Alsek are so affected by glacier melt that avoiding flow fluctuations is impossible. For example, the Alsek went into full flood in the second week of August 1997. The river rose from 95,000 to 165,000 in 48 hours! It was high already from torrential rains from a warm front and then there was thought to be a glacial lake outburst on the Upper Alsek. Campsites downriver were completely flooded out! That would just be bad luck and a chance you take on a glacier river trip.

Normally, the gravel bars are more exposed in August, making for good camping. The insect populations have started to die down with the cooler nights, and the berries come out. Life is generally as good as it gets on the river in this usually drier month. One thing to note is that headwinds can be fierce on this route. Plan on paddling in the morning and perhaps again in the evening if this becomes an issue. Be sure to secure your tents and boats, especially as you near the coast. The end of August will be chilly, especially if it's wet. Once you get into the glaciers, you will really feel the cold. They call the sweeping bend before Walker Glacier "Weather Corner." You abruptly experience the change in climate from the boreal interior to the icy coastal. Be prepared.

You will normally have the lowest water flows of the canoeing season in September. You may also have some really good weather early in the month or it could be really wet, cold and windy. It will be chilly in the mornings if it's clear, and snow is also possible. You will need to pack for any weather; expect the worst and enjoy what you get! The joys of a fall trip are the changing colours of the willows, alders and cottonwoods. And the bugs are pretty much dead and gone, except that the blackflies can flare up again if it's warm and dry. I love a late-season trip – when the weather is good. Frankly, that far north, I think you should expect bad weather in September (it is one of the rainiest months of the year) and end your trip in this month, not start it.

Difficulty of the River: ✳ ✳ ✳ ✳ This route is the most difficult in this guidebook. The four-star rating is mostly due to the whitewater in the Tat canyon, the significant rapids lower down on the Tat, the potential danger in the Channel of Death, and because the water is glacial in temperature. It's all about consequences. The chances of capsizing and being in the frigid water too long are greater on this route than for any other trip found in either volume. Rafters say the Tatshenshini/Alsek is a "Class 3 float with Class 5 consequences" because the water temperature approaches freezing even in midsummer. Nothing Class 3 is a float for canoeists, but the consequences of being in the water in a glacial river as opposed to in a boat of any kind are the same. Finally, the rivers run through a remote land and there are no sources of help once you leave Dalton Post until after you paddle Alsek Lake.

The other glacial rivers in this guide, the Taku (covered in volume one) and the Lower Stikine run do not have the whitewater of the Tat/Alsek route. The Rabbit River's whitewater canyons are difficult and you are in a very remote area, but the water is not glacial. (The Netson Creek/Rabbit River route is covered in volume one and rated 3½ stars for difficulty.) I can't stress enough that the Tatshenshini/Alsek route is only for exceptional, very experienced whitewater and tripping canoeists with strong self-rescue skills and support from experienced rafters familiar with assisted whitewater rescues and possessing advanced river rescue skills. At least one canoeist has died as a result of capsizing in the canyon. Another single-boat canoeing party that prudently portaged the Tat canyon flipped around Tkope Creek and decided not to go on. They called for a helicopter and ended their journey there.

The whitewater of the canyon on the Tatshenshini is rated Class 3 to 4. It is Class 4 at peak water levels. The major whitewater occurs in a stretch about 8 km long where the gradient is 11 m/km, or 58 ft./mi. The hazards are boulders, sharp rocks, holes, headwalls, stoppers and large waves. Wood hazards were minimal when we paddled it in 2004, but you must always be on the lookout for these killers. An added dimension of difficulty exists for paddlers who have not run rapids on a silty glacier river. You have to read the river features without the benefit of colour differential. There is only a subtle difference between white and grey and you often have to decide what is ahead of you — wave, rock or log just below the surface — by the shape and nature of the associated hydraulics. You get used to it and then the subtle differences seem almost obvious.

Most of the significant and difficult rapids are steep and relatively long and there are numerous, continuous, less "in your face" rapids. Assisted rescue from other canoes is difficult for most of the canyon. That is why I say don't run this route without dry suits and raft support on top of your normal safety equipment, like PFDs, helmets, proper footwear, throw bags, pin/wrap kit etc. Rafters can get people out of the water and chase and tow canoes much better than other canoes can in this section. They can also carry some of your food and gear, so your canoe will not be too heavily loaded. You may want some significant weight in your canoe, though. It depends on how it paddles empty. A PakCanoe, for instance, needs lots of weight in the middle to have enough rocker for difficult whitewater.

A spray cover for your canoe will keep you warmer and avoid taking on excessive water in the rapids, but it does limit your rescue options. Self-rescues aren't as quick, a canoe-over-canoe assisted rescue is virtually impossible and a canoe-over-raft one very difficult, but your canoe can be towed to shore by the raft. You may decide to go with full flotation instead, tucking and tying in waterproofed gear bags under the middle and bow and stern flotation bags. The rapids are rocky at lower water (when you want to be canoeing the canyon) and there is definite potential for wrapping or pinning your canoe. You will also want the flotation for making righting and re-entering self-rescues easier. I discuss rafts, canoes and rescue and safety equipment and their use in more detail in the special equipment section of this chapter. (I do realize that if you are an exceptional canoeist you already know what I have said already – and what I am going to say – about gear, safety equipment and running rapids, but I need to say it anyway for less-experienced readers.)

Here is a brief rundown on the difficult bits of the route, from the Tat canyon to Dry Bay. The Trip Notes at the end of the chapter will give you more information. In general, the canyon at low water is technical – technical in the sense that the current is really fast, the gradient steep, and the only possible lines require precise manoeuvring in significant-sized and irregular-shaped waves. There are good eddies, especially on river right, to regroup and get out and scout. With the relatively small volume of the Tat, and the steepness and rockiness of the run, you are creeking about as much as most people do in loaded or semi-loaded tandem canoes!

You ease into the more difficult rapids, which is nice, and the canyon also ends with a fun read-and-run section. The larger rapids of note you will encounter as you go down the canyon are (I use the names given by Lyman, Ordóñez and Speaks in their guidebook): Wall #1, Wall #2, Black Bear Rapids, Thread the Needle, and M & M Falls. The first two rapids are not difficult, but the last three are strong Class 3 at lower water levels, pushing Class 3+.

If you have trouble in the canyon, there are two options for getting back to Dalton Post on foot. Your party should have a plan for evacuation prior to setting off, and you should leave a note with any gear left on the side of the river so any parties after you will know what you are doing. The best route back upriver by land is via the rough "road" on river left that provides access to mining claims on Squaw and Dollis creeks (this track is shown on the 1:50 000 topo map, but note that the portage route is not wholly represented. The road actually splits south of Pirate Creek to head to the mouth of Squaw Creek). The track is in quite good condition. You will end up on a gravel bar across the river from the put-in at Dalton Post. You will have to ford the Tat here, but the river is narrow, and getting across it is probably the least of your worries at this point. See the Portaging the Canyon section in the Trip Notes for more information on this route. You will follow it in reverse.

If you end up on river right and need to get back to the put-in, you will have to bushwhack until you reach the road that connects Nesketahin with Dalton Post. There was a rough "road" running all the way along the river to Dalton on this side of the canyon at some point, which you can see on the 1:50 000-scale topo map. The track is reported to be overgrown and hard to find, but if you are on that side of the river already with no way across, then it will have to do.

Lower down on the Tat, where Alkie Creek comes in on river right, there can be some strong hydraulics. After Alkie Creek, where the gradient steepens again and the river begins to braid significantly, there are some fast sections with standing waves. Monkey Wrench Rapid follows with some funky water and large standing waves throughout, as well as pour-over ledges on river left. This rapid is pushing Class 3, depending on water level. You can portage around Money Wrench on river right by clambering over the debris pile.

From the O'Connor River confluence to past Towagh Creek there are holes on the outside of corners and strong hydraulics made by rock outcropping. The current is fast through the braided channels, 13–16 km/h, and there are strong hydraulics at the mouths of the larger tributaries. Where the gravel cutbanks are eroding there may be sweepers and strainers. This section, with all the shallows and wind, is one of the trickiest to navigate in a raft. Stopping and regrouping if you get spread out can be a challenge because it is difficult to get across the river due to the braiding, and the shoreline is often cutbanks with no eddies.

The S-Turns are your next concern. They occur where the Tat narrows down to one channel again. There are Class 2/2+ standing-wave trains around the corners, and there are the occasional stoppers and holes to avoid.

After the confluence of the Tatshenshini and Alsek the river is three times the flow and much, much wider than it was when you started. You will need to use your large-volume paddling skills. As you come around sharp corners and where channels merge there will be boily water and strong cross-currents. After the US border there are some strong hydraulics at "Weather Corner," the last big sweeping turn before Walker Glacier.

After Walker, the current gets even stronger and faster and you must be prepared for Cat in the Washing Machine Rapid (also known as Confused Sea). This rapid approaches Class 3 in difficulty at some water levels and is aptly named (except at moderate levels, when it is more of a kitty cat). There can be some really funky water, with violent cross-currents, large irregular standing waves and a few large rocks and holes for good measure.

The most dangerous section of moving water on the Alsek is the Channel of Death, where the river flows into Alsek Lake. The hazard is icebergs jammed like a big ice strainer across the moving water in the channel. Even if the bergs are not blocking the channel completely, they could shift or roll as you try to squeak past them into the lake. You have three route options and may need to do a complete scout to pick the safest entry to the lake. One of the three options is to avoid the Channel of Death completely by paddling the river right, or western, passage past Gateway Knob, but this is only possible if the water is up. There is also the chance you may not be able to get in to the lake at all when you want to. If you get stuck on The Peninsula, a Cessna on wheels can potentially land there. Apparently people have been flown out from there before. In this case you have to pick the flattest gravel bar around and make your own runway. You will need at least 360 m of straightaway on flat ground devoid of large rocks and other debris.

In a normal scenario, you want to quickly paddle past the bergs and to a camp on the lake where you are in a good position to exit it before things change on you. The ice moves constantly with the wind and current. We were able to enter Alsek Lake through the Channel of Death fairly easily, but we could not get to the Knob or the river exit the same day. The whole lake was blocked by a line of icebergs, from Gateway Knob to the south shore. We spent hours paddling around looking for some way through, along with a commercial rafting group, but no go. We finally had to camp for the night at a random spot on the south shore of the lake.

The next day we found a skinny passage that got us to the eastern shore of Gateway Knob but not the camping area. We had to line and drag our canoe and raft over and around blocks of ice to reach that. Then, to get to the west side of the gravel bar and put back into the lake, we had to portage our gear and boats. We decided not to stay at the Knob in case we couldn't move again the next day. So we hiked up the Knob, took some awesome pictures and eventually camped at The Dunes near the river's exit. The next day we were able to tour the lake because the wind had moved the ice pack to the north a bit and opened up a couple routes.

While paddling Alsek Lake you do not want to paddle close to any of the icebergs if you can possibly help it. They could shift and roll at any time without any warning. The wind is not your friend as you try to navigate the shifting bergs. Leaving Alsek Lake you will enter the current again and need to avoid floating – thus, moving – bergs and chunks of ice as well as ones grounded on sandbars. The grounded ones too can move at any time. How do you class a stretch of river where you avoid moving icebergs instead of stationary boulders?

The last two named rapids on your run to Dry Bay, Constriction and First rapids, have some interesting aspects. The ice should be gone from the river by the time you reach them, which is good. Constriction Rapid is like a smaller version of Cat in the Washing Machine. The river flow is squeezed as the banks narrow, so you get strong cross-currents and even whirlpools along with irregular standing waves. There are also ledges to avoid. First Rapids (which I think is improperly marked on the map – see the Trip Notes) consists of a ledge of rock outcropping on river right that can be a huge hole at some water levels. It is easily avoided, however.

In conclusion, this is not a river trip for a canoeist without a high degree of comfort in continuous Class 3 water, strong self- and assisted-rescue skills and experience and many years of tripping on remote rivers. This is not a trip to do with a single boat, and raft support is highly recommended. If you *think* you are ready for the Tat/Alsek route, then practise canoeing continuous Class 3 water for at least another season and paddle some glacier-fed and large volume rivers. Then apply for a permit for the Tat/Alsek trip when you *know* you are ready.

The gradient of the entire route from Dalton Post to Dry Bay is about 3 m/km (16 ft./mi.). The canyon on the Upper Tatshenshini has a gradient of 11 m/km (58 ft./mi.), while the Tatshenshini River as a whole has a gradient of about 5 m/km (26.4 ft./mi.). This is a steep gradient for a multi-day canoe route. Only the Tuchodi, of all the other rivers in this book, has a gradient steeper than that. It drops an average of 5.6 m/km but doesn't have the canyon whitewater of the Tat. The Tuchodi is a significantly easier paddle in a number of ways, though there are many wood hazards and you are manoeuvring in close quarters.

Character of the River and Region: The only river system to penetrate the St. Elias Mountains (the highest coastal mountains on earth), the Alsek and its major tributary the Tatshenshini carve a corridor of life from the boreal interior in the rain shadow of the Alsek Ranges through massive icefields to the Gulf of Alaska. From Alsek Lake you can see the highest peak in BC, Mount Fairweather. Neither river is overly long, but the Tat/Alsek watershed pumps a lot of water into the north Pacific. This is because it drains the largest non-polar icecap in the world, which hosts some of the biggest valley glaciers in Canada. The combination of the Pacific influence on temperatures, the glaciers and the glacial history of the area have produced an exceptionally diverse range of biophysical conditions, with ecosystems ranging from sea level to over 4500 m ASL and from coastal to subtundra. The region contains habitats not found anywhere else in Canada.

From Dalton Post in the Yukon the Tatshenshini turns south-southwest, running through a narrow boreal valley that widens to a deep U-shaped one as it flows into BC's northwest corner. The Tat flows almost straight south from the Yukon boundary through the St. Elias Mountains, then makes a sharp turn to the west to join the Alsek. Jogging its way southwest, the Lower Alsek flows through a wide valley full of snow and ice before entering the Gulf of Alaska at Dry Bay, a small fishing village south of Yakutat.

Ecologically speaking, the Tatshenshini River lies in the Northern Boreal Mountains ecoprovince and flows through two of its ecoregions. The Upper Tatshenshini lies in the Yukon–Stikine Highlands ecoregion, an area of climatic transition from boreal interior to northern coastal. It falls within the rain shadow of the Coast Mountains (called the Coast Range in Alaska) and encompasses the mountainous area leeward of the St. Elias Mountains. Subdued mountains, plateau-like uplands and wide, low-relief valleys characterize the ecoregion. In the Tatshenshini Basin there are widespread glacio-fluvial features, including kames, kettles, alluvial fans, floodplain deposits, braided channels and outwash terraces, plus wind-deposited materials (loess) in the southwest. The Tatshenshini bisects the Beaton Batholith, thus the canyon and its rapids. The batholith is an igneous (plutonic) rock, solidified magma.

The alpine tundra is low-growing heather, dwarf birch, willow, grass and lichen. Willow/slide alder or scrub birch/willow shrub lands predominate in the subalpine, along with subalpine forests of subalpine fir and white spruce. Aspen and lodgepole pine are common in areas where the forest has burned. Unfortunately, the mountain pine beetle has killed most of the Upper Tat's lodgepole pine forest, so the upper stretch of river is not as scenic as it once was. At lower elevations, old-growth forests of black and white spruce prevail. Balsam poplar, black cottonwood and slide, or Sitka, alder grow along the floodplain with patches of white spruce. The merging of interior and coastal boreal and alpine biomes makes for extremely diverse vegetation communities that support a number of rare plants and animals.

Temperatures in the Yukon–Stikine Highlands are moderated throughout the year by the influence of maritime air masses, but the Tatshenshini Basin itself has a subarctic climate. The basin is relatively hot in summer, cold in winter and comparatively dry for the region. You can expect July and August temperatures to range from 14–18°c and the mean annual precipitation is only 500–600 mm. Precipitation increases as you approach the Pacific Ocean.

Leaving the Yukon–Stikine Highlands, the Tatshenshini then cuts it way south, deep into the St. Elias Mountains and the ecoregion of the same name. The Lower Tat down to its confluence with the Alsek falls in this ecoregion, as does most of the Upper Alsek. The St. Elias Mountains ecoregion contains some of the most rugged, mountainous terrain in North America and the glaciers of the St. Elias Mountains make up the world's largest non-polar icefield. Both the Alsek and the Tatshenshini rivers transect these mountain ranges and this river system is the only one that penetrates the mountains to the ocean. It is the one corridor in this region for plants and animals (and humans) to pass from the Pacific to the interior or the other way around.

The Icefield, Alsek and Fairweather ranges are characteristic of the mountains in the St. Elias Mountains ecoregion. Peaks are serrated with pinnacles and they stand in isolated blocks separated by broad icefields. Mount Fairweather straddles the border of BC and Alaska and is 4663 m ASL in height. Bedrock consists of folded and faulted sedimentary and volcanic rock, intruded by granitic rock. Much of the alpine tundra zone is glacier-covered. The surface materials are mostly some combination of permanent ice and snowfields. The Tatshenshini and Alsek river valley bottoms host boreal forests of birch, willow and black and white spruce. Non-forested alder and willow shrublands, with scattered stands of white spruce and black cottonwood, dominate the floodplains of both river valleys.

Temperature and precipitation vary with elevation. The mean annual temperature for this high elevation area is approximately –0.5°c with means of 10° in summer and

–11.5° in winter. The western icefields average more than 1000 mm of precipitation each year, and the icefields of the Fairweather Ranges receive an astounding 2400 mm.

The Lower Alsek River flows through the Northern Coastal Mountains ecoregion of the Coast and Mountains ecoprovince, dropping south and west to spill into the Gulf of Alaska. Mountain summits in this ecoregion range from 2100–3050 m ASL and are capped by several large icefields. Composed of crystalline gneisses and granitic rocks, these ranges are cut into several segments by large, steep-sided transverse valleys. Relief along sides of the valleys reaches 2745 m ASL in places. Large glaciers move down tributaries to about 150 m ASL in many cases, with several reaching sea level. Isolated patches of permafrost occur in mountain summits over 2500 m ASL. Surface materials are colluvium and glacial deposits, and avalanche tracks are common.

Alpine tundra vegetation is dominated by low-growing heather, dwarf birch, willow, grass and lichen at elevations above treeline. Subalpine forests consist of alpine fir, mountain hemlock and some Sitka spruce at middle elevations. At warmer, more humid lower elevations there are closed-canopied forests of western hemlock, along with some Sitka spruce and devil's club. The broad floodplains of the open river valleys in the region, including the Lower Alsek, are covered with extensive stands of black cottonwood and Sitka spruce forest, mixed with dense shrublands of willows and alder.

The climate of the region is moderate and very humid due to its proximity to the Pacific. In this coastal ecoregion summer temperatures average 10–15°c. Winter temperatures rarely drop into the single digits, with average nighttime lows of -2° to 5°. Rain is the norm in southeast Alaska. April, May and June are usually the driest months of the year. September and October tend to be the wettest. This coastal belt experiences heavy precipitation in winter from snow. Yakutat, not too far north of Dry Bay, gets an astounding annual rainfall of 2900 mm and snowfall of 4818 mm!

The geology of the Tatshenshini/Alsek watershed is extremely complex. The rivers bisect six of the major terranes that formed Alaska over 200 million years ago and cross five major fault lines. Evidence of plate tectonics is all around you on this route. The terranes are made up of different combinations of rock, and you can actually see where they meld in places. The forces generated by the collision of the earth's plates are still at work and this area is an area of intense seismic activity. Earthquakes are common: 26 quakes of 6.0 or greater on the Richter scale occurred between 1899 and 1988.

From a canoeist's perspective, the Upper Tatshenshini near Dalton Post is a fast, small-volume stream, hardly rating river designation in late summer. It braids into narrow, shallow channels running over sand and gravel. Riffles abound and the current can reach 15 km/h at average August water levels. The water is somewhat silty at Dalton Post and quickly gets much more so. As mentioned, when you are running the canyon, you often have to navigate by the look of the water and shapes of the features. The rocks in the canyon are often large and pointy, making scouting from the shore a careful exercise.

After the canyon the river is fed by many large creeks and grows in size rapidly. The Tat braids again through gravel banks and the valley opens up after Silver Creek. Dry boreal forest slopes and mountains without icecaps come into view. The river slows and sediment cutbanks dotted with cliff swallow nests slide by. Hard-rock outcrops again as you enter Stillwater Canyon (also called Quiet Canyon). This is a beautiful section to float. There are no rapids so you can look up and admire the igneous intrusions in the canyon walls. The white rock was once molten and filled in the cracks in the older black rock.

You carry on through the now more open valley with floodplains lined with poplar, catching a glimpse of the Alsek Ranges to come. Near "Bear Bite" Creek, a large tributary flowing down off the Alsek Ranges on river right, the gradient picks up and there is a section of fast water and small waves. Sediments Creek is next on river right, where there is hiking up the creek's floodplain and through the aspen and poplar forest to the alpine meadows.

After Sediments Creek the Tatshenshini braids again, with one section where the river narrows to one channel. The bank is a huge talus slope from the Alsek Ranges. The valley heads south and then braids again. Alkie Creek trying to push its way into the Tat creates some interesting water and paddlers should be careful there. All along this stretch the channels are shallow and there is lots of debris making navigation a bit tricky. The debris accumulations make for small drops of fast water and waves through the braided channels and there is tricky water where flows converge.

At Monkey Wrench this phenomenon is obvious. The river narrows to one channel because of a debris slide on river right and there is a significant drop and large waves. The rocks on river left indicate the river was actually dammed at one point, apparently sometime before the beginning of the 1990 river-running season. This narrow section of river was to be the site of the road bridge to the Windy Craggy mine; the name of the rapid is said to come from regular efforts by persons unknown to ".throw a monkey wrench" into the surveying for the bridge. You can portage around Monkey Wrench on river right by clambering over the debris pile.

As you approach the O'Connor River confluence the river and landscape change. Once both the O'Connor and Tkope rivers join the Tat, it doubles in volume (it has now tripled since Dalton Post). The river bends to the southwest and you are in the heart of the St. Elias Mountains. It can be difficult to navigate here. The river valley is much bigger, with the Tat braiding into wide, shallow channels, and the wind can be a huge factor.

This section can be a slog, especially for rafts. Wind is really a factor in this stretch, as the valley becomes a corridor for the winds that are created when the cold air over the icefields downstream fills the gap beneath the rising air in the warm interior. Dust storms of glacial flour can make for a grey day, though the limestone and plutonic mountains and cliffs of metamorphic bedrock outcropping will catch your watering eyes. The water is very silty now, the riverbed made up of silt, gravel and small rocks. If you listen carefully you can hear the hiss of silt sliding along your hull and near outwashes. You may hear fist-sized rocks rolling with the flow along the riverbed underneath you. No wonder there are rocks strewn all over the floodplain of the Lower Tat!

You will see more exposed bedrock as you paddle down to Henshi Creek, which lies on river right in a huge alluvial deposit of its own making. The tallest mountains of the Alsek Ranges can be viewed here and you soon leave their rain shadow. Once on the windward, or ocean, side of these mountains you will notice the change in vegetation. Interior flora gives way to coastal flora here, indicating the transition to a more moderate, Pacific-influenced climate. The geology is also different beyond Henshi Creek, the obvious differences in the composition of the mountains being one of the most unique features of the Tat.

The geology is what brought about the park you are enjoying. It was up Tats Creek, downstream from Henshi, where the Windy Craggy mine was to be developed to exploit one of the world's largest copper deposits. Instead of a road being built through this amazing wild land, with trucks rumbling out of the mine site every eight minutes, there is only the sound of a mighty creek tumbling down the mountains within the world's largest international park complex. Imagine the dangers of mining and shipping toxic materials so close to the river in such an active seismic zone.

Past Towagh Creek's large outwash you soon leave the white spruce zone and enter the Sitka spruce one. Alder becomes common and will eventually become the most dominant shoreline shrub as you approach the Pacific. Cottonwoods replace the balsam poplar and they hide the mountain scenery for a while as you approach the Alsek confluence.

Once you're through the S-Turns, the Tat spreads one last time, into its delta. The current is very fast as you near the confluence with the Alsek, averaging 15 km/h in 2004. Melt Creek adds its milky flow to the river, nearly doubling its flow. Be cautious when you cross its mouth. There is some funky water there, especially if the creek is up from hot weather or warm and extremely wet weather.

The campsite just downstream of Melt Creek is a fine spot to contemplate the magnitude of the Tatshenshini and Alsek confluence. It is a place you will never forget, a spectacle of natural beauty. You have two very wide river valleys converging, with 360-degree views of mountains, forest and water. The hanging glaciers of the Fairweather Ranges are a focal point for your already strained but appreciative eyes.

Once you are on the Alsek the glaciers become even more remarkable, a more obvious sign of the maritime and ice world than of vegetation, though the mountainsides along the Alsek are soon covered with thick coastal flora. The Icefield Ranges dominate the views on your right and the Fairweather Ranges your left. Upstream winds in the glacial valley can be a concern, and paddling the Lower Alsek is definitely a humid maritime climate experience. Rain and fog are far more likely. This could be a very wet trip from now on, so be prepared for it.

The Alsek is a very large river – the volume of the Tat you left behind times three! The Alsek can also be 1.6 km (1 mile) across in places and it spreads over a wide valley. You will have to adjust your perception of distance. With a silt and gravel riverbed and many glacial streams entering it, the colour of the water is milkier than that of the Tat. The speed of the current averages 15 km/h, and you have to know where you want to be and start to head there early, more so than on the Tat. Again, stay together and with the raft(s). If you end up in different channels you can easily lose each other and accidentally miss sites of interest and good camping spots.

Once past the terminal moraine of Netland Glacier you will see the cutline that marks the border of BC and Alaska. Once across the border, you are in Glacier Bay National Park. The Nose hike provides access to the alpine, a great view of the Tat–Alsek confluence spread, and mountain views that will hurt your teeth!

Braiding goes hog wild approaching Kodak, or Weather, Corner. It's called Kodak Corner because once you pass the screen of cottonwoods along the riverbank you can see Walker Glacier and people scramble for their cameras. It is also called Weather Corner because coastal fronts are often stuck here and rain and wind will often greet you as you make the turn. Have your camera and bad-weather gear handy!

Walker Glacier sits on river left, a massive tongue of a glacier lapping at a small glacial outwash lake. Your jaw will drop here, guaranteed. You can hike up and walk on the glacier. There are a number of campsites at Walker and you may want to camp here so you will have more time to explore. Tie everything down at night, including your canoes and tents. It can be very windy from here to the Gulf, and the water level can fluctuate extremely due to the many active glaciers around.

As you carry on downstream the glacier views are just as good. Sapphire Glacier, next to Walker, is stunning. And if there wasn't already enough eye candy around, you have a pretty little waterfall on river right at Dipper Creek. The 35 or so kilometres to Novatak Glacier are probably the most beautiful section of the trip, other than the confluence and Alsek Lake, mind you. If the weather is clear it is possible to see up to 20 major glaciers at one time along this stretch!

Approaching another major bend in the Alsek, where the river turns south again just upstream of Novatak Glacier, you encounter Cat in the Washing Machine/ Confused Sea Rapid. Put your cameras away and be prepared for some splash. The drop can have good-sized waves at some water levels.

From Novatak, a stunningly huge, striped tongue of ice flowing out of a major valley, there is a long, straight stretch of river with the Brabazon Ranges dripping with hanging glaciers on your right. After the outflow of Novatak Glacier you are on the widest section of the Alsek, and to stop at The Peninsula (also called The Spit) to scout the Channel of Death you need to stay left.

The Peninsula is a sandy spit of land made up of the terminal moraine of the gigantic Alsek Glacier's last great surge, some several hundred years ago. You can camp here, but don't stop too far down the spit, because you will then only have one route to navigate the Channel of Death. This door may close overnight if the wind changes and ice comes in, leaving you without an entrance to the lake. You may see evidence of runways made by icebound travellers desperate to fly away in small planes with tundra tires! You can do a partial scout of the Channel of Death as well as walk the flats of wildflowers to the north bay of Alsek Lake to see the icebergs that often get jammed in there.

Alsek Lake is a relatively new feature of the Alsek River. Historical accounts indicate there was a glacial face and a scree slope here before the lake. The lake, now about 8 by 3 km in extent, was made by the retreat and meltwaters of Alsek Glacier and Grand Plateau Glacier. If you are able to take the shortest route to Gateway Knob and out onto the river again, you will paddle less than three kilometres of it. That's not likely, though, given that iceberg jams are common; and since you do not want to get too close to the bergs, you will likely be zigzagging here and there. The wind can change your route quickly and drastically, so don't gawk too much until you reach camp. Set up as far away from the water as far as possible. If a large amount of ice calves into the lake, you can experience a tsunami generated from the displacement of the water by the ice. This happened to Bill, the brother of John Noble, our raft captain, while he was camped at the Knob.

Camping on the lake is a sensory experience not to be missed. The sound of calving ice and rolling icebergs can keep you up at night! Apparently the freshwater icebergs in Alsek Lake are said to be some of the largest in Glacier Bay National Park & Preserve. At The Dunes you can watch ice float by in the current on its way to the Gulf of Alaska. It's not far, and all too soon you will be on your way downriver and at the take-out. It is a bittersweet place to spend your last night in the wild. Alsek Lake in the sunshine with the water lapping the glaciers and all the blue and black ice and the towering Mount Fairweather in view is magical. This lake is the last of the really special places, a grand finale.

The short run of 22 km or so down to Dry Bay is anti-climactic considering what you've just experienced. You head pretty much straight west through Constriction Rapid, past the hunting lodge on river left and through First Rapids. The wind-lashed coastal vegetation gets sparser and more stunted as you get closer to the Pacific Ocean.

The Alsek River out of Alsek Lake becomes the border of Glacier Bay National Park to the south and Tongass National Forest Reserve to the north. The river borders Tongass National Forest all the way to the coast. At 17 million acres (69,000 km²), Tongass, in southeastern Alaska, is the largest national forest in the US. It is a northern temperate rain forest remote enough to be the home of many species of flora and fauna considered endangered or rare elsewhere.

After First Rapids keep a sharp eye on river left for the small brown park sign and the high cutbank that indicate the entrance to The Slough, the side channel hosting the take-out by the landing strip at Dry Bay. Be warned it is very easy to miss, and it will be a long slog back up from the other end of it.

For more information on the ecology and natural history of the Northern Boreal Mountains and Northern Coast Mountains, consult the Ecoregions of British Columbia website, at www.env.gov.bc.ca/ecology/ecoregions/province.html. Environment Canada's Ecological Framework document, at http://atlas.nrcan.gc.ca/site/english/maps/environment/ecology/framework/1, provides more detail about BC's ecological classifications. A good book for general information is *British Columbia: A Natural History*, by Cannings and Cannings. The BC Parks report on bear activity near campsites, at www.env.gov.bc.ca/bcparks/explore/parkpgs/tatshens/tat_report.pdf, and the Glacier Bay National Park & Preserve nature and science pages at www.nps.gov/glba/naturescience/index.htm both have loads of information on the ecosystems of the Tat and Alsek rivers. Particularly, there is an amazing amount on the natural history of the National Park in the archives at www.nps.gov/glba/historyculture/index.htm. The natural history and geology notes in *The Complete Guide to the Tatshenshini River*, by Lyman, Ordóñez and Speaks, are great, and I highly recommend you bring this book with you on your trip.

A good article on how glaciers move is at www.taiga.net/yourYukon/col130.html. The Tongass National Forest also has a good page on icefields, at www.fs.fed.us/r10/tongass/forest_facts/resources/geology/icefields.htm

And if you really want to learn more about glaciers, bring along John Muir's *Travels in Alaska*. He explains their creation and nature with great enthusiasm. Rapture pretty much sums up how Muir feels about glaciers and the outdoors in general. Additionally, *Do Glaciers Listen: Local Knowledge, Colonial Encounters and Social Imagination*, by Julie Cruikshank, is an amazing book to read on the river. It investigates the relationship between First Nations cultural histories and the glaciers of the St. Elias Mountains. There are stories from First Nations elders, historical accounts and tales of early explorations and descriptions of the work of modern scientists and environmentalists.

A coffee-table book that has some great shots of the Tatshenshini and Alsek rivers and good information is *Alaska to Nunavut: The Great Rivers*, by Neil Hartling of Nahanni River Adventures. He runs numerous rafting trips on these rivers each season.

Local History: ✳ ✳ ✳ The first people known to paddle the Tatshenshini and Alsek rivers were the ancestors of the Yukon's Southern Tutchone and the Tlingit from the Alaskan coast. They used the waterways for trading and subsistence, and these rivers have a special place in their cultural and spiritual heritage. The petroglyphs carved into rock at the confluence of the Tat and Alsek indicate the importance of the river for the First Nations. This area was one of the last to be explored and mapped by Euro-Americans and its history is closely linked to the Klondike Gold Rush. The Tat was once one of the most endangered rivers in the world but is now part of the world's largest international park complex. The Tatshenshini/Alsek watershed is a World Heritage Site and the cornerstone of the largest transboundary global biodiversity preserve on the planet.

According to Canadian Heritage River System (CHRS) management plan documents, Shäwshe Chù is the Southern Tutchone name for the Tatshenshini River. Shäwshe, the Southern Tutchone name for Dalton Post, refers to "the meadows by the river," according to Lyman, et al. A Tlingit chief, Kohklux, indicated on a map he drew for George Davidson of the US Coast & Geodetic Survey (USC & GS) in 1869 that the Tlingit in the area called the Tatshenshini River "Allsegh" and it was considered part what we now call the Alsek River. The name Tatshenshini also appears on the map Davidson eventually made from the information he collected in 1869, but it refers to what is now called Blanchard River, a tributary of the Tatshenshini flowing in above Dalton Post.

After I'd made a long fruitless search for the meaning of the name Tatshenshini, this entry eventually appeared in Wikipedia. It gives an etymology that also appears to support the idea that the Blanchard was originally known to the Tlingit as the Tatshenshini:

Prior to 1891, the name Tatshenshini did not refer to the present-day Tatshenshini River. Instead, the name referred to the present-day Blanchard River, which is a tributary of the present-day Tatshenshini, located about 10 miles upstream from Dalton's trading post. In 1891, or shortly thereafter, the Canadian government reassigned the name Tatshenshini from the present-day Blanchard River to the present-day Tatshenshini River. Apparently, the government did this without knowledge of the English translation of "tatshenshini."

The name Tatshenshini is derived from a Tlingit phrase, the meaning of which was not recorded. However, the original phrase appears to have been t'áchán shahéeni, a compound Tlingit noun meaning "river with stinking chinook (king) salmon at its headwaters" (t'á [chinook or king salmon] + chán [stink] + sha [head of] + héen [river] + i [possessed noun suffix]).

The Tlingit phrase t'áchán shahéeni describes the present-day Blanchard River (pre-1891 Tatshenshini River). Chinook (king) salmon run up the present-day Tatshenshini River to the Blanchard and thence up the Blanchard River. At the headwaters (shahéen) of the Blanchard, the salmon (t'á) die, and their carcasses stink (chán).

I also read in the CHRS notes that Tatshenshini meant Raven's River and that the Southern Tutchone dispute that meaning. No doubt when the Blanchard is full of dead salmon there will be a lot of ravens around, however!

Yukon Places and Names also indicates the name Alsek came from the native name for the river, Alsekh, as reported by the Russian ship's captain Tebenkov in 1825. The preferred Southern Tutchone spelling is Aʔséxh´, a possessive name meaning "the river belonging to Aʔséxh´." The BC Geographical Names Information System

(BCGNIS) website lists other names once given to the Alsek River, including: "Rivière du Behring," bestowed by French explorer le Comte de la Pérouse in 1786; "Jones River," originated by an 1886 *New York Times* expedition, after one of the sponsors; and "Harrison River," so named by the USC & GS in 1890 in honour of a US president. In 1891, the river was officially given back its original native name in the form of "Alsek" by the US and Canadian governments, meaning "place where people rest" river, according to the Yukon Geographical Names Program.

Sometime prior to the 19th century, the Tutchone, an Athapaskan-speaking people, arrived from the interior to fish the rich salmon runs of the Tatshenshini and the Tlingit moved into the Alsek watershed from farther south along the coast. The Tatshenshini and Alsek rivers eventually became the basis of a major travel and trading route, a "grease trail," between the Southern Tutchone and the Chilkat River-based Tlingit. The phrase "grease trail" comes from the fact that a prized trading item, fish oil (usually hooligan, or eulachon, or oolichan oil), was transported in wooden boxes and it dripped on the ground en route. Most trading routes in northern BC had sections of overland travel due to the rough water of many of the rivers.

Hooligan and other fish oils were consumed with dried foods and were used as a preserving medium, ceremonial item and medicine. Trade in these oils among coastal groups and to inland groups was tightly controlled along established routes. In the case of the Tatshenshini/Alsek inter-native trading network, it was the Chilkat Tlingit who brought hooligan oil and other maritime products upriver and overland to trade with the Southern Tutchone in the interior.

The Chilkat were particularly known for their harvesting of hooligan in the Chilkat River. The Chilkat Tlingit lived in communities near present-day Haines on Lynn Canal, of which Klukwan was the farthest north and most significant and was considered by some sources to be the most important Tlingit village in southeast Alaska. Klukwan's location and the access its residents had to great salmon and hooligan runs made for a rich and powerful culture. At some point, the Chilkat expanded their coastal trade inland, travelling up the Alsek and Tatshenshini rivers and overland via the Chilkat Pass and O'Connor River Valley. They would travel overland in the winter and by dugout canoe in the summer. They portaged the Tatshenshini's whitewater canyon.

Besides the hooligan oil, dried hooligan and fine woven blankets they produced themselves, the Chilkat Tlingit traded goods they obtained from other coastal First Nations. For example, from southern coastal groups the Chilkat obtained red cedar canoes, baskets, dentalium, mother-of-pearl and shark's teeth.

The Southern Tutchone traded furs, hides, babiche, clothing, lichens for dye and copper for hooligan oil and other coastal goods. They also acted as middlemen for some trade items, having obtained trade goods from interior nations from farther east and north. The groups of Tutchone in the Tatshenshini and Alsek watersheds had strong trading and social ties with neighbouring southern Tutchone First Nations, the Kluane First Nation to the northwest and the Ta'an First Nation to the east.

Nesketahin, located three miles north of Dalton Post, was the main Southern Tutchone village on the Tatshenshini. It was a seasonal fish camp for many and a home base for some of the region's Tutchone, as well as a focal point for inter-native trade. Elders have related stories about 300–400 Tutchone gathering there to fish for sockeye salmon by gaffing and in traps. The other important village for the Southern Tutchone in this region was Klukshu, just off the Haines Highway not far from Dalton Post. Shäwshe, or Dalton Post, became a very important trading site later in the 19th century.

The Southern Tutchone fished the Tat all the way between Nesketahin and the confluence of the Tat and Alsek, and their camps dotted the river when explorers came through in the 1800s. Oral history and archival sources indicate there may have been ten or more fishing villages in the Tatshenshini watershed in the 19th century.

The Southern Tutchone pursued a subsistence hunting and fishing lifestyle and travelled seasonal rounds, moving to their fishing and hunting areas in response to the local resources available during the year. The annual runs up the Tatshenshini of sockeye, coho and chinook were a time of feasting and celebrating with their relations and neighbours. The gatherings associated with salmon runs would bring people from as far away as Aishihik.

Resident fish species in the lakes and rivers were also an important food source and were taken throughout the year. Caribou, moose, Dall sheep, mountain goat, gophers and small mammals were hunted and trapped for food and clothing. Villages were normally situated on lakes, but the Tutchone were very mobile and often moved their "headquarters" in order to take advantage of new economic opportunities.

In the summer, the Tutchone preferred to walk overland, a safer way to travel given that their territory had large, windy lakes and rivers with strong rapids. They occasionally used log rafts, cottonwood dugout canoes, frame boats covered with moose hide or small canoes made of spruce or birch bark.

The Chilkat used their dugout canoes for more than fishing and travel. They were used as cauldrons to cook the hooligan as part of the rendering process. The canoe builders would fall cottonwood trees in early spring in time to have canoes sufficiently ready for oil processing. As the fish cooked in the hollow of the canoe, its oil saturated the wood, enhancing the waterproof quality of the canoe. These canoes were usually medium-sized, built to carry up to three persons, and used for hunting and fishing. The Chilkat also used skin boats when travelling by water in the interior.

Trade was very profitable for both the Chilkat and the Southern Tutchone and was culturally significant. The present-day Champagne and Aishihik First Nations (CAFN) are descendants of these two distinct peoples, brought into contact via the Tatshenshini/Alsek travel corridor through the St. Elias Mountains. Many cultural exchanges and intermarriages took place between the two cultures, and in former days most people in the southern section of Tutchone territory were bilingual, speaking both Southern Tutchone and Tlingit. According to CAFN at www.cafn.ca/history. html, only a few local elders speak Tlingit today.

The Tlingit also settled at Dry Bay and Yakutat, just up the coast from the mouth of the Alsek. Prior to their arrival, the majority of the population of Dry Bay was of Tutchone ancestry. Both groups travelled up the Alsek to its confluence with the Tat to visit with their relations upriver and at Nesketahin. In 1852 a group of Tlingit from Dry Bay met a tragic end when they were camped at the confluence of the Tatshenshini and Alsek. Lowell Glacier surged and dammed the Alsek River to a height of 200 m and when the glacier dam burst the river flooded the confluence and the Tlingit gathered there were drowned. Additionally, a wall of water 7 m high and 15 m wide swept an entire Tutchone village into the sea at Dry Bay.

The Tat/Alsek watershed and the grease trails became even more important for trade once the Coastal Tlingit and European fur traders made contact. On July 16, 1741, Vitus Bering, a Dane in Russian service, was the first European to sight Mount St. Elias. The mountain was named for the saint's day he sighted it on. Later in the 1700s, the French explorer le Comte de la Pérouse and the English explorer George Dixon visited Yakutat.

Spanish explorers also came, looking for gold and furs. In 1778 Captain James Cook became the first British explorer to reach the north coast using maps from the first two Spanish Bucareli expeditions. (The third and final Bucareli expedition made contact with the Tlingit at what is now called Bucareli Bay in 1779.) These maps inspired Cooke to investigate the coast of America on his third voyage in search of the Northwest Passage. What resulted from this voyage was a demand for sea otter pelts in China. Once word got out, European and American fur traders flocked to the area, hoping to get rich on the sea otter fur trade.

By the end of the 1700s most expeditions focused on finding more sources of sea otter pelts rather than surveying or exploring. The traders made contact with the Tlingit up and down the coast. It was the Russians who were the major trading partners of the Tlingit in the early days of the fur trade. By 1775 Russian fur traders had begun to settle in Tlingit territory and in 1799 the Russian American Company was granted full trading privileges along the north coast. Furs were generally traded for firearms, blankets, beads, gunpowder and shot, steel traps, tobacco and cloth.

Following the extirpation of the sea otter populations along the north coast, the fur trade went inland up the Taku and the Stikine in search of furs from interior species. The Chilkat Tlingit protected their virtual monopoly on the trade of European goods in the Tatshenshini watershed through their control of the Alsek River mouth and the overland Chilkat Pass route to the Tatshenshini and the interior. Even though some Tutchone in the Alsek drainage were related to Dry Bay or Yakutat Tlingit, during the 19th century it was the Chilkat Tlingit that supplied them with western trade goods and native coastal products. Apparently, though trade among coastal peoples was done on an individual basis, trade with peoples from the interior was a hereditary right given to certain Tlingit clan chiefs, such as Kohklux, who made the map for Davidson.

In the 1800s, European activity in northern BC and Alaska was mostly centred on trading and gold seeking. The HBC was working the BC coast, the Stikine region and inland in the Yukon. By 1840, the Russian Coast Strip, now known as the Alaska Panhandle, was leased to the company. HBC wool blankets were the medium of exchange, the value of trade items being denominated in numbers of blankets. The HBC's lease agreement with the Russians lasted until 1867, when Russia sold Alaska to the United States for $7.2-million.

As trade in interior furs intensified, the Tlingit increased their trading journeys upriver and to the interior to two or three times a year in order to get as many fine land furs to trade as possible. The Chilkat Tlingit had the best of the trade with their coastal monopoly, but the Tutchone also did well trading the western goods they got from the Chilkat to their northern interior neighbours who didn't have access to goods from the Alaskan coast.

At the height of the inter-native trading activity in the first half of the 19th century, Chilkat members of the clans of Klukwan maintained a special trading and fishing village, called Nuqwái'ik' in Tlingit, far up the Tatshenshini, about 50 km below Nesketahin and near the confluence of the O'Connor River. The O'Connor River Valley provided easy access to the Chilkat Pass. This may be the village indicated on the map Davidson produced in 1901, which was based on the map Chief Kohklux had drawn for him 1869, and from information he obtained from early explorers in the area. The village did not prosper long. The Tlingit found life in the interior ecosystem harsh, and after a smallpox epidemic in the mid-19th century most of the survivors returned to the coast, with a few joining the Southern Tutchone at Nesketahin.

Obviously, trading came with a price, including increasing conflict between nations. In the mid-1800s, nearly 100 of the Southern Tutchone associated with Nesketahin were killed in a raid resulting from a trading relationship gone sour. They were at their spring fishing camp near an outlet of Dezadeash Lake when they were attacked. This was the culmination of several smaller raids and it greatly reduced the population around the Tatshenshini River. You can read more about this story in the CAFN-produced book *From Trail to Highway*, an account of the First Nations history of the area.

The Tutchone's dependence on the Tlingit for trade goods lessened as the Euro-American traders swept into the Upper Yukon drainage. In 1852 the Chilkat tried to retain their control of the interior trade by ransacking HBC's Fort Selkirk on the Yukon River near the Pelly River confluence, which had been established by Robert Campbell in 1848. The Chilkat were careful not to hurt anyone. The attack was meant to stop the outsiders' interference with their trading network in the interior by taking or destroying the goods and supplies at the fort. Fort Selkirk was not reopened for many years, as the Chilkat forbade foreign traders to travel into the interior through their territory, although according to some sources a few prospectors may have crossed the Chilkat Pass as early as 1875.

One of the first scientists to meet with the Tlingit was professor George Davidson while he was surveying for the USC & GS in 1869. Aurel Krause, a German geographer, reached the Chilkat summit in 1882 and was the first European known to have entered the interior by the Chilkat trading route. The first Americans in the interior were probably a party from the US Army, led by Lt. Frederick Schwatka. In 1883, he and six other men travelled the Chilkat's trail to eventually raft down the Yukon River on a reconnaissance mission. This is thought to be first party to have reached Tutchone country via the southeastern coast of Alaska.

Another early exploration in the area was sponsored by *Leslie's Illustrated Newspaper* from the US and led by Edward James Glave. Glave wanted "to be the first white man to erase from the map the hypothetical and fill up the blank area with the mountains, lakes and rivers which belong to it." In 1890, Glave, along with an Alaskan scout named Jack Dalton and a Tlingit interpreter called Shank, travelled from Kusawa Lake in the Yukon to Nesketahin and then paddled down the Tatshenshini and Alsek rivers in a 20-foot dugout to Dry Bay. At the end of the trip Glave was quoted as saying the Tatshenshini had "such an incessant display of scenic wild grandeur that it became tiresome."

Glave and Dalton came back the next year to explore the grease trail through Tatshenshini country to the Yukon, apparently bringing the first horses to the area. Jack Dalton was so impressed by the country that he stayed at what was to become Dalton Post, establishing the first trading post in the Tatshenshini watershed. By 1895 he had laid out the "Dalton Trail," basically following the Chilkat's trail to the interior. The Dalton Trail eventually connected Lynn Canal on the Alaskan Coast to Carmacks on the Yukon River via the Tutchone villages of Nesketahin, Hushi and Aishihik. The trail began at Pyramid Harbour on the banks of the Chilkat River, headed up the Chilkat Valley following the Klehini River, then through the Chilkat Pass over the summit and down the O'Connor River Valley and up along the Tatshenshini to Nesketahin and on to the other villages.

Dalton set up trading posts along the trail, one near Nesketahin in 1893 (or 1894) and another at Champagne (at the junction of the Dalton Trail and the Dezadeash River) by 1902. He advertised "his" trail to the Yukon as a horse and cattle trail. The trail became a major route to the Klondike, and Dalton charged a toll for its use. He also traded for furs, packed in and sold supplies, offered a "pony express" service for travellers for a short period, and did some prospecting. Shäwshe/Dalton Post or House on the banks of the Tatshenshini became the major southern Yukon trading centre of the 19th century. An account of Dalton's setting up the post and his time living there can be found in *Life Lived like a Story: Life Stories of Three Yukon Native Elders*, by Julie Cruikshank. Dalton left in the 1920s to go back to the States.

Apparently Dalton got permission from the Chilkat to use their trade route, but they wouldn't have given it had their lands not already been overrun by the first wave of prospectors before the Klondike Gold Rush really got going. The influx of Klondikers and traders following in their wake eventually completely destroyed the Coastal Tlingit's blockade and monopoly on trading routes to the interior. The Dalton Trail was mapped in 1897, and the same year, a NWMP post was built at Dalton Post, which closed in 1904.

In 1879, 1880 and 1890, John Muir, the famous American naturalist, made trips to Alaska to research the natural wonders of that land. Muir sought understanding, while others searched for gold. He was especially interested in the glaciers. He visited Walker Glacier on the Alsek and "discovered" Glacier Bay. An account of his expeditions in Alaska and northern BC are found in his book *Travels in Alaska*. His passages are full of awe for this land of trees, rock, water and ice and should be read on the river for full appreciation. The book is useful for understanding the natural history of the northern Pacific Coast and for getting a sense of the human history of the region before and during that time.

Muir's raves about the glaciers in Alaska had caught the public's imagination, and there was a demand for increased access to and protection for them. In 1902, President Theodore Roosevelt established the Tongass National Forest of Alaska, and in 1925 the forerunner of Glacier Bay National Park & Preserve was established. See www.fs.fed.us/r10/tongass/forest_facts/resources/heritage/heritage.shtml and www.nps.gov/glba/historyculture/index.htm for more on the history of these protected areas.

In the early 1900s there were several expeditions in the Tatshenshini/Alsek watershed. A.J. Brabazon carried out a boundary survey in 1906, and the westernmost range of the Coast Mountains is named after him. He surveyed the US and Canadian border, having travelled upstream on the Alsek. There were also a few mountaineering expeditions to the region, one of which included the first ascent of Mount Fairweather in 1931.

The First Nations in Tatshenshini/Alsek watershed experienced massive population losses and shifts in settlement patterns as a result of the establishment of the Euro-American fur trade, the influx of foreigners during Klondike Gold rush and the associated epidemics. Despite the hardships, traditional culture persisted, and the Southern Tutchone and the Tlingit began a long period of activism in response to the loss of their rights and lands under the political climate that resulted from the sale of Alaska to the US and establishment of BC as a province and the Yukon as a territory.

The long-standing controversy concerning the boundary between the Alaska Panhandle and BC was aggravated by the large number of miners travelling to the goldfields. The boundary was finally decided in 1903 by a six-man tribunal composed of American, Canadian and British representatives. The decision was generally favourable to the US, giving the river mouths along the coast to Alaska and the rivers to BC, an action that has made for continued international discord over salmon fishing rights, especially along the Stikine.

The boundary decision also resulted in the Coastal Tlingit becoming US citizens while the majority of Inland Tlingit became Canadian citizens. This did nothing for either group – their territories were not considered in the decision. The boundary between BC and the Yukon was finally fixed in 1908, and though some Southern Tutchone occupied parts of the Tatshenshini River watershed in northern BC, their claim to traditional territory in BC was not recognized. Their claim to homelands in the Dry Bay area in Alaska was also put aside and the area was later claimed by the Yakutat Tlingit.

More change was to come for the Chilkat and Southern Tutchone with the building of transportation infrastructure. The Haines Highway was built during the Second World War by the US Army to provide tidewater access to the Alaska Highway. The road to Haines closely followed the Dalton Trail. By the late 19th century, Klukwan, at 22-Mile on the Chilkat River, was the last remaining Chilkat Tlingit village. After the 1920s and '30s, the Chilkat lived primarily in Klukwan and Haines, but once the road was built they resided permanently in or near Haines. The Tutchone also settled permanently in communities connected to the new roads. Ironically, the completion of the Alaska and Haines highways once again increased interaction between coastal and interior groups in the 1940s. This increased interaction was the impetus for increased political activism associated with land claims in both Alaska and the Yukon.

The Coastal Tlingit fought to retain their political rights and control over their subsistence resources by organizing the Alaska Native Brotherhood/Alaska Native Sisterhood in 1912. In 1929 the Tlingit in Alaska began a struggle to regain more control of their natural resources, which ultimately resulted in the Alaska Native Claims Settlement Act of 1971. The act gave roughly 44 million acres (17.8 million hectares, or 10 per cent of the state) and almost $1-billion to Alaskan native peoples in exchange for renunciation of all aboriginal claims to land in the state. Now the Katalla–Chilkat Tlingit Provisional Government and the Central Council of the Tlingit and Haida Indian Tribes of Alaska formally represent the Alaskan Tlingit.

In 1993, after more than 20 years of negotiations, CAFN's rights to the Yukon portion of its traditional lands and resources were finally confirmed with the signing of a final agreement between the Champagne and Aishihik First Nations, the Government of Canada and the territorial government of the Yukon. Land claim negotiations concerning the portion of CAFN territory within BC are not yet complete, but in the interim the BC government and CAFN have reached an innovative and precedent-setting agreement that provides joint management authority of the Tatshenshini–Alsek Provincial Park. CAFN also jointly oversees the Canadian Heritage River System (CHRS) management plan for the Yukon section of the Tatshenshini. The river was in great need of protection.

Paddy Duncan, a native of Nesketahin, made a gold discovery at Dollis/Squaw Creek on the Tatshenshini River in 1927 that caused some excitement, but after the 1930s, mineral exploration occurred only sporadically in the region. However, intensive exploration in the 1980s led to the discovery of a large copper deposit at the head of Tats Creek, a tributary of the Tatshenshini River. Shortly thereafter, a major mineral exploration project began in the headwaters of Tats Creek, on Windy Craggy Mountain. Development of the $430-million Windy Craggy project would have resulted in the northern hemisphere's largest open-pit copper and gold mine. Environmental hearings were begun as part of the process of obtaining a mining permit. It quickly became apparent that the project would seriously jeopardize the Tatshenshini and Alsek ecosystems.

Luckily, many more adventurous nature lovers had experienced the beauty of the Tatshenshini and Alsek rivers since John Muir's time. The river-running history of the Tat/Alsek river system includes the first descent of Turnback Canyon in 1971 by Walt Blackadar, the first person to ever travel the entire length of the Alsek River, and Sobek Expeditions' first commercial rafting trip down the Tatshenshini/Alsek route in 1976. The fact that the rivers were world-class paddling destinations by the time the threat of the Windy Craggy mine loomed helped the conservation movement. Paddlers were at the forefront of the fight to protect the Tatshenshini.

In the late 1980s and early 1990s, river users and environmentalists rallied in an unprecedented fashion. Tatshenshini Wild, an umbrella organization representing over 50 major environmental groups in the US and Canada, spearheaded a high-profile international campaign aimed at securing protection for the area. In 1993, the BC government officially established a Class A provincial park to protect the Tatshenshini and Alsek watershed. The park status prevented any further mineral exploration or development and resulted in all mineral claims being extinguished. The Champagne and Aishihik First Nations supported the protection and the concept of a UNESCO World Heritage Site for the area. They successfully negotiated a state-of-the-art co-management agreement with the BC government for the park, and as a result of their added support, the World Heritage Site designation was granted in December 1994. The result of the conservation movement and the subsequent creation of the BC provincial park adjoining other parks and reserves in the Yukon and Alaska was the establishment of the world's largest transboundary global biodiversity preserve. In 2004, the Tatshenshini was designated a Canadian Heritage River.

In 1999, three teachers out sheep hunting in the mountains near the Tatshenshini River found a human body that had been preserved in a glacier for something like 550 years. The glacier was melting, exposing the body still with clothing intact and even tools and food in a pouch. Though a cool discovery by all accounts, what struck me after reading this story in a magazine was that while doing research for this book I kept finding references to glaciers melting in this area. Muir explored Walker Glacier in the later 1800s and it was much larger then, rimming the Alsek's shore. Commercial rafters note that since the 1990s one has to hike an additional kilometre from the campsites along the river to reach the Walker. Unfortunately, changes to the glaciers of northern BC, the Yukon and Alaska may soon become exponential as ice mass disappears from icefields all over the world with increased global warming. The impact of the disappearing glaciers is global in terms of climate and specific with regard to rivers.

For example, in a report published on the web, a Department of Fisheries & Oceans habitat biologist interested in the impact of receding glaciers on fish, Al von Finster, notes that when he first visited the Tatshenshini River about 12 years ago he noticed that a number of small unnamed streams near the confluence of the Tatshenshini and the Alsek were loaded with silt from melting glaciers. When he returned a few years later, he noticed that the water in some streams had cleared and salmon had moved into them. Von Finster surmised that this change was probably due to the fact that the streams' feeder glaciers had melted back from the river and were no longer a source of silt.

Von Finster speculates that as the icecaps and glaciers in the Coast Range continue to melt, more water will flow into lakes such as Atlin, Bennett and Tagish. The higher water levels in the lakes will last longer through the summer, affecting habitats along the shorelines. As the meltwaters from glacial ice decrease in flow as a result of the decreasing mass of the glaciers, the lake levels will change again. The list of possible effects on fish habitat is a long one because fish live in so many different environments. There could be winners and losers among fish species as a result of climate change. The rivers are certain to lose volume in the end.

There are First Nations accounts of passing under ice bridges on the Alsek, Stikine and Taku, and these experiences will likely never occur again. The Taku Glacier bridged the Taku River for the last time in the 1950s, and though it was one glacier that was actually building mass, it too is now showing signs of receding. The Tatshenshini and Alsek rivers are now protected from development in the region, but we need to start working on the larger picture so that they will continue to run through a magical land of ice, and in fact continue to run at all. The glaciers are the reason the rivers flow as they do.

To end this section on a positive note, there are some very good books to read while on a journey down these magnificent glacial streams. For a great source of information on the prehistory and history of the Tatshenshini and Alsek rivers, try Julie Cruikshank's *Life Lived like a Story*. It contains stories told by three women First Nations elders from southern Yukon and northern BC. These women were born in the heart of the St. Elias Mountains and though they and their families experienced the cultural dislocations of the past century, they still keep the oral tradition alive. The book includes an account of the Lowell Glacier's glacial burst on the Alsek that washed away villages and changed the landscape forever.

Do Glaciers Listen? Local Knowledge, Colonial Encounters and Social Imagination, also by Cruikshank, is another amazing book to read while on the river. It investigates the relationship between First Nations cultural histories and the glaciers of the St. Elias Mountains. The book questions the concept of "wilderness." It is often forgotten that likely anywhere you go in northern BC (or nearly anywhere in the world, for that matter), you are in some First Nation's front or back yard. The land is wild, yes, but it is not without a human history. For this reason, in 1996 the First Nations involved in management of the Tatshenshini–Alsek Wilderness Provincial Park asked that the park be renamed simply Tatshenshini–Alsek Provincial Park.

An online search will bring you a plethora of sources for more information on Southern Tutchone culture and these First Nations' current activities. A couple of sites of interest are www.north-land.com/ypa/JimmyKane.html; CAFN, at www.cafn .ca/index.html; and the Yukon's 14 First Nations, at www.yfnta.org.

For reading about the Tlingit try Aurel Krause's *The Tlingit Indians – The Results of a Trip to the Northwest Coast of America and the Bering Strait*, Frederica de Laguna's article "Tlingit" in *The Handbook of North American Indians, Volume 7, Northwest Coast* and her magisterial *Under Mount Saint Elias: The History and Culture of the Yakutat Tlingit*. Also of interest are "Traditional Tlingit Country," a map and complete listing of the Tlingit tribes, clans and clan houses, at www.ankn.uaf.edu/ANCR/Southeast/ TlingitMap/TlingitMap.pdf; and an overview of Alaskan Tlingit history and culture at www.everyculture.com/multi/Sr-Z/Tlingit.html.

To Save the Wild Earth: Field Notes from the Environmental Frontline, by Ric Careless, has a chapter on the campaign to stop the Windy Craggy mine. In *Tatshenshini: River Wild*, Ken Budd and some three dozen of the continent's best outdoor photographers and over a dozen political and environmental leaders donated words and images to this beautiful pictorial celebration of the Tat to help with the campaign to protect the river. *Tatshenshini Wilderness Quest and Other River Adventures*, by Ken Madsen, also gives a good sense of the river and the efforts to protect it. *Wild Rivers, Wild Lands*, by the same author, also has a chapter about running the Tatshenshini and Alsek rivers. Other publications by Madsen with information on the Tatshenshini and Alsek rivers are listed in the references section of this guidebook.

Level of Solitude: ✳ ✳ ½ You will likely see at least one rafting party on the river. You may bump into one every day, the same one or another one, but you also might go for several days and see no one. Groups tend to bunch up at special places and then quickly spread out again. The permit system of regulating the number of users on the route by take-outs rather than put-ins per day and regulating how long you can camp at certain spots seems to be working. Currently, 1,000 people per year travel the Tatshenshini and Alsek rivers via commercial rafting companies, but you wouldn't know it.

Other than the occasional raft, the physical evidence of human activities between Dalton Post and Dry Bay is an old dock near Village Creek, the cable at the water survey station before the canyon, the junk at Squaw Creek, the hunting cabin just below Detour Creek, the border cutline, the water survey station at Walker and the hunting lodge after Alsek Lake. Apart from the odd plane overhead or boat as you approach Dry Bay, you can really appreciate the solitude this immense protected wild land can provide.

Wildlife: ✱✱✱ The protection provided the Tatshenshini and Alsek rivers by all the interconnected parks and protected areas makes for a watershed that contains some of the richest habitat for wildlife in North America. Large predators, such as grizzly bears, which need a lot of room to roam and feed undisturbed, do well in this land. Black bears do too. Tatshenshini–Alsek Provincial Park is also home to the glacier bear, an extremely rare blue-grey colour phase of the black bear, found only within the protected areas in Canada and just over the border into Alaska.

Large mammals, including moose, Dall sheep and mountain goat, can be seen on this route. Wolf, lynx, wolverine, fox and beaver are also common to the region. I have to say my party did not see much for wildlife on our trip in late August 2004. Lyse and Brad saw a couple of bears when they were ahead in the canoe (John made me row the raft for that flat stretch!). I think it may have been because we were quite often just behind a rafting party and their presence scared the animals away. Another party of canoeists, who ran the river in 2007 a couple of weeks earlier in August than we did in 2004, saw 20 grizzly in 10 days. The salmon were likely running!

You may see seals fishing in the river as you approach Dry Bay. Given all the salmon around in August, you can expect to see many, many bald eagles. Golden eagles also live in the region, especially in the Upper Tatshenshini's narrow valley. There are also huge numbers of migratory birds that make their way south in the fall across this region. You may see swans along the river or resting near Dry Bay.

For a complete list of birds and mammals you could see on your Tat/Alsek trip, see *The Complete Guide to the Tatshenshini River*, by Lyman et al. See also the BC Parks wildlife-viewing and "wilderness" ethics materials at www.env.gov.bc.ca/bcparks/explore/gen_info/wild_gen.html.

Fishing: ✱✱ The Tat hosts runs of all five species of salmon: king (chinook), chum, sockeye, coho and pink. However, fishing for salmon below Dalton Post with regular tackle is likely to leave you empty handed. You need the right tackle, lures and know-how. If you have never fished a river for salmon, particularly a silty river, and want to try it, you'll need to do your research. It is beyond the scope of this book and my expertise to explain the intricacies of catching salmon in this kind of environment and time of year.

You may be able to catch bull trout (known locally as Dolly Varden trout) at the mouth of clear streams flowing into the Tat. They tend to lurk in the mix of silty and clear water waiting for something shiny to grab. A spin caster rigged with small spoons or spinners will do fine or you can fly fish.

Camping, Hiking and Other Activities: ✱✱½ Camping is good on the large gravel bars and tributaries' outwash plains. These flat areas are often covered with yellow dryas and you usually can't complain about the views from your kitchen! The river braids so much it's not likely you won't find somewhere to set up camp on most sections. However, when you get to the Lower Alsek there are not as many spots. You will need to plan your days a little more carefully.

You can definitely do some alpine hiking, some shorter treks up creekbeds, even walk on Walker Glacier! The views are amazing from The Nose and Gateway Knob. Finally, you can hike to the ocean and back from Dry Bay. These day hikes and other suggestions for stretching your legs are described in the Trip Notes.

If you are looking for a little break from camping and cooking in the outdoors, Gary Gray's hunting lodge, just below Alsek Lake, has pretty nice accommodations and a dining room. It also has a sauna. Gary offers bear viewing, fishing and photography tours if you arrange them in advance.

Dry Bay only has one tourist outfit: Pat Pellet's Brabazon Expeditions, which offers transportation, communication services, camping platforms, showers, meals etc. Even where I come from, this is not even a hamlet. There are no opportunities for doing anything but more camping, exploring, hiking, socializing etc. as though you were still on your river trip. But the scenery is not as intense by any means. At least you can stop at the park ranger station for a chat with someone new when you deregister. Or you can head down to Pat's for some great hospitality.

The weather usually isn't great in Dry Bay. Bring cards and books in case you have to hunker down and wait a couple days until your plane can pick you up. There may be another group with you if you are weathered in, and you can trade leftover snacks. My last point in regard to this tiny seasonal fishing village: bring extra food in case you are stuck there for a while.

Special Equipment: This is the only route for which you must carry a "boom box" or "groover" to carry your waste (poop!) with you. You can dump your waste in Dry Bay before flying out. See the park permit application package you receive for more information.

You absolutely need your passport. Rain gear that is 100 per cent waterproof and for heavy-duty use is also a must. You will get rained on, unless you are unusually lucky with your weather. I also recommend rubber boots for around camp (but not for paddling).

The rivers are glacial and very, very cold. You absolutely must paddle in a dry suit with thermal insulation underneath or a wetsuit with a dry jacket and insulation at the very least. You will have to be able to withstand a long swim should you capsize. Thick neoprene footwear with a good sole is the best footwear for a glacial water trip like this. Helmets are also a must for the very rocky rapids.

Rescue and safety gear and a repair kit are required, as on any canoe trip, but with a few added items. Two spare paddles per boat, one in your canoe and one in the raft in case one gets lost in a flip, is a good idea. Spray skirts/and or flotation for the canoes are mandatory. A heavy-duty pin/wrap kit is necessary for setting up a z-drag system in case a raft flips or you wrap a canoe. Minimum equipment includes two pulleys, two locking carabiners, two prusiks and a 6-m piece of tubular webbing. You can use your throw bags for ropes. If you don't know how to set up a z-drag, you should not be paddling the Tat/Alsek route. For the rafts, include in your repair kit an extra-long strip of floor patch and lots of adhesive. For the canoes, bring extra seat parts, wire and assorted nuts and bolts. And bring duct tape, lots of duct tape.

Because so many people float this route, bring a firebox for fires along with your cooking stove and fuel. These metal boxes with grates make a great BBQ and cooking unit, use far less wood than a campfire and can be taken apart to take up little room. There is no visual impact on the environment if you set them up on gravel or sand. Once the fire burns out, crush the ashes in the box and then spread them over a wide area or dump them in the river.

Bring extra-heavy-duty tent pegs and stakes to secure the rafts. Wind can be a problem and rapid changes in water level are always possible. It's a good idea to bring straps for gathering firewood into bundles and securing them on a raft. There is minimal firewood at popular campsites.

You will want binoculars for mountainside mammal viewing and for scouting the Channel of Death from afar. They can also help you look downstream and navigate the braids in the river, as well as add to your glacier-viewing experience.

A water filter is also important on this trip. If you run out of clear water from streams you can get rid of the silt in the river water by letting it stand in a pot for a while, but the possibility of "beaver fever" needs to be dealt with. Take extra water bags for filling up at the clear streams to save your filter some hard work.

This far north the bug population will be active in most summer months, though it usually dies down by mid-August. On my trips on the coastal rivers in this book, the Taku, Lower Stikine and Tatshenshini/Alsek, the bugs have never been that bad. Still, I would never travel anywhere up north without bug repellent, just in case. You are in the boreal mountains to start with, and that is likely where the mosquitoes and blackflies will be the worst.

You may seriously want to consider carrying pepper spray and/or an air horn to deal with possible bear encounters.

Trip Notes:

MAP NO.	GRID REF.	FEATURE	DESCRIPTION
115 A/3	865660	Dalton Post; Put-in; Camping	At the end of the road and off to the left you will find yourself on RR of the Tatshenshini, where there is a beach to rig out on. The whole area is flat floodplain, so camping is good. There is a new outhouse about 50 m back up the road, at the edge of the large clearing. However, Dalton Post can be a really busy place. Fishing parties and bears frequent the area. You are better off to head downriver for your first night. **Note:** Dalton Post is managed by the CAFN. This is their traditional territory, and you should get permission to camp here.
	862665	Camping	Just under 1 km from the put-in is a marked gravel bar on RR that will make do for a camp. There is a larger and better one on RL downstream, however.
	851666	Camping	On RL on the large, marked gravel bar there is a good place to camp. There is a small beach to land on, small trees for cover, and flat spots to put up tents. The river continues to be fast, with narrow, braided channels all the way to the start of the canyon. There are some sharp corners. Follow the main current and be vigilant for wood hazards. There are riffles and **Class 1/1+** waves in many spots.
	837657	Cable	A water-gauging station is here on RR, with an associated cable crossing the river.
	836656	Cabin	On RR there is a cabin (in 2004 there was also a dock). This is the last human-made landmark before the canyon. It starts in around 1.5 km where you see the first orange cliffs appear on RL. The river is still shallow and fast through the preliminary **Class 1+** rapids.

Portaging the Canyon: This is a Tatshenshini adventure for the really hardy and those with folding/inflatable canoes that can be carried in a proper backpack or light whitewater canoes with a very comfortable yoke. The **portage is going to be about 18 km one way** if you paddle down from Dalton Post to the access point where the west fork of the road ends at the river – just about 1.5 km downstream. The carry will take you two days minimum if you do two trips. The trail is the rough road that services old mining claims at Dollis and Squaw creeks (Dollis Creek is the one that joins Squaw Creek and crosses the marked road at GR 814565). The majority of the road portage is marked on topo map 115 A/3, except where you want to turn right to head down an-other track to get to the Tat via the mouth of Squaw Creek. You miss all canyon rapids if you put in at Squaw Creek. The first access point for the rough road begins about 600 m down and across the Tat from the Dalton Post put in. Access is on RL at GR 860665. The "last chance" access point is at GR 671857 on RL, across the river from Nesketahin. Since you will likely not be portaging your raft(s), you will need to work out a plan for meeting up with your support crew after the canyon. Silver Creek is the campsite of choice, not far downstream from the Squaw Creek put-in. Make sure you have what you need for your portage camp but don't overload the raft(s), paring down your outfit for the carry.

Having never portaged the canyon myself, but based on information from Dan Rabinkin, who has done it, I recommend that after you cross Pirate Creek at GR 822598 you start keeping a careful eye out for the track that will branch off to the right and take you down to the Tat. The fork is around 700 m south of the Pirate Creek crossing. (Remember, this spur of trail down to the Tatshenshini is not shown on the topo. If you cross Pirate Creek and eventually start going sharply uphill, you've missed your turn to the right.) The sandy beach put-in on the Tat is just upstream of the Squaw Creek confluence, at GR 795571. There is a camping spot used by locals there and an old boat.

Running the Canyon: The canyon begins with the first orange cliffs on RL at around GR 838642. The first rapids are easy Class 1+/2− S-bends with waves on the outside of the bends and shallow riffles on the inside. The last of the whitewater is a final S-bend of Class 2/2+ rapids at GR 803578. The following notes describe the meat of the whitewater of the Tat canyon in between these points. We boat-scouted every-thing, but you may want to get out and scout the larger, named rapids from shore. The rapids are quite continuous, and there are long sections of Class 2+ rapids in between the named rapids that you can just read and run (not described in detail). There are no coordinates attached to the named rapids in the Trip Notes. You will find them! The only one I am quite sure you can locate on your map easily beforehand is M & M Falls. Expect your canyon run to take about three hours if you don't have any trouble and you boat-scout everything. My advice is to camp on the big gravel bar on RL down-stream of Village Creek for your first night and run the canyon the next day. You will be fresh in the morning for this adventure.

Wall #1	This **Class 2/2+** corner rapid has a wall on RL. Stay RR on the inside of the bend to miss the biggest waves. Read-and-run rock dodging continues downstream.
Wall #2	This **Class 2+/3−** rapid has a wall on RL as well, but it also has pour-overs and rocks on RR so be wary of running too far RR on the inside of the bend. Catch the eddy on RR to scout Black Bear Rapids, which you can see downstream. Be careful when clambering over the sharp rocks along the shore.

	Black Bear Rapids	This **Class 3/3+** rapid is one of the three really meaty rapids of the canyon. It is about 1 km long and you can scout it from RR. The rapid really gets going just after the small creek on RR. There are numerous boulders and stoppers to avoid, and the waves are large and irregular. After this first minefield you need to navigate two holes at the bottom of the straightaway before the wall on RR.

Following Black Bear there is a 1.8-km read-and-run section of continuous rapids averaging **Class 2+**. There are rocks and stoppers to avoid and good-sized waves.

Next up is Thread the Needle. Look for another creek on river right as a landmark. There are good eddies on RR to get out and scout from.

	Thread the Needle	Here there is a bedrock outcropping on RL, an eddy on RR and two big boulders in the middle of the channel downstream. Expect to take some water running this **Class 3/3+** rapid. The waves are large below the boulders.

Following Thread the Needle is a 1.5-km read-and-run section of **Class 2+** rapids, a snaking boulder garden with some sharp corners.

The final large rapid, M & M Falls, is on the corner where the river bends sharply to the right and Pirate Creek flows in on RL. Be cautious on your approach. There could be wood on the left (the outside of the bend) on a knob of rock outcropping. Then there is either a big hole, pour-over or boulder with a big wave drop beside it sitting midriver waiting for you!

810596	**M & M Falls**	The meat of M & M is a **Class 3/3+** drop as you round the corner by Pirate Creek. Eddy out to scout on RL before you get too close to the corner. At low water the gigantic boulder midriver becomes a pour-over and a green tongue flows by it on RL that you can run. You drop into a large stopper or curling wave, depending on the water level. Expect to get a lot of water in your boat, but you can regroup and bail below. M & M is easier at more moderate water levels.

This is the last of the meaty whitewater of the Tat canyon, but after M & M Falls you still have a long section of fun **Class 2/2+** read-and-run boulder-garden rapids with sharp bends. The canyon rapids end after the set of standing waves following a cliff on RR.

795572	Camping; Evac route	There is an established campsite used by locals on RL at Squaw Creek. There's a bunch of junk around, so it's not a spot of choice, but if you had trouble in the canyon you can stop here. To get help via Dalton Post, go up the track by the creek to the old mining road shown on the map. The route (described in the other direction) is outlined in the Portaging the Canyon section of the Trip Notes.
780564	Camping; Clear water	The floodplain of Silver Creek on RR makes for a great camp. There are two spots of note, one just above and one just below the creek mouth. I like the downstream one better. Silver Creek provides clear water and you can hike along it after dinner. You might even take a day off and try and reach Wade Lakes via the track shown on the map.

Watch for sweepers and wood in the next section of river down to Stillwater Canyon.

114 P/14	768513	Camping	If Silver Creek is occupied you may want to try this smaller camping area on the RR gravel bar. There is a good landing spot but no source of clear water. Fill up on your way.

About 2 km downstream from this camp (GR 763500 approximately), be alert for wood hazards. In 2004 the river had changed its course and we had to stay in the RR channel to avoid the trees that had come down the bank from erosion.

754494 744474	Stillwater Canyon	This canyon has slow water and scenic cliffs. It's about 3.5 km long in total. **Note:** some rafting guides call this "Quiet Canyon."
	Potential camping	You could possibly make a small camp in the canyon if the water is very low and one of the exposed gravel bars is big enough for your group. There are some potential campsites on RL after the cabin below Detour Creek, but the next prime campsite is at "Bear Bite" Creek, about 23 km downstream from the beginning of Stillwater Canyon.

The river slows from the canyon to Detour Creek (GR 717424), with the current ranging from 4–5.5 km/h. Good for enjoying the views of the upcoming Alsek Ranges.

721423	**Cabin;** **Potential** **put-in/** **take-out**	A hunting cabin sits high on RL. Floatplanes can land on the river here. It is a point to note in case you need an evac arranged. It may also work as a put-in or take-out for a "custom" trip. The cabin is about 500 m downstream from the mouth of Detour Creek, which comes in on RR. We saw trumpeter swans on the floodplain of the creek.

After Detour Creek the current really slows and the river goes through a marshy area with alders lining its banks. Then the flow picks up again just before "Bear Bite" Creek.

727335	**Camping;** **Clear water**	"Bear Bite" Creek's floodplain on RR provides a flat area for a large camp. There is a beach landing on the upstream side of the creek. Don't put your tent near the game trail, however. There was a report of a bear incident here, thus the rafters' name for the creek!
728333	**Rapids**	About 200 m down from Bear Bite the river gets squeezed by outwash, making rapids with **Class 2** waves. Keep to RR, away from the main current and the RL wall to stay dry.

The river continues to be peppy up to Sediments Creek with some tight turns to navigate. Watch for a logjam on the head of the gravel bar island at GR 731324.

723304	**Camping;** **Hiking;** **Clear water**	Sediments Creek is a popular place to camp and hike. There are three campsites on RR upstream of the creek mouth and one on the downstream side of Sediments. The three upstream sites are up along the slough formed by the clear little stream just north of Sediments. It's best to camp at one of these if you are going to do the hikes, as the southern camp is on the wrong side of Sediments Creek.

There are two hiking options with great views: a short one (about two hours round trip) and a long one (six or more hours round trip). The short hike is to an outlook point at an open meadow; the long hike gets you up to the alpine. The trail for both starts about 250 m up the floodplain of Sediments Creek, where you will find a well-used path up through the aspen forest. After reaching the outlook point at the meadow, the destination of the short hike, the trail carries on into an old cottonwood forest and then gets harder to follow as you reach rock and a scree traverse. Head up the cleft on a steep final climb to the top of the ridge. You can hike anywhere from there; just make sure you can find your way back to the trail! See Lyman et al. for some great natural history notes and more details on these hikes.

114
P/11

After the Sediments Creek camp the river braids and braids, with one narrow spot where the channels converge. The narrows is the home of the notorious Monkey Wrench Rapid. The current is fast for most of this stretch, all the way to the O'Connor River confluence. There are sections with good-sized standing waves, some approaching **Class 2+**. It's read-and-run fun but be vigilant for funky hydraulics at creek mouths and for wood hazards in the braided channels.

755198 **Rapids**

Approaching Alkie Creek coming in on RR, the standing waves begin in earnest. There are sets of **Class 2−** up to a big rock on RL.

755182 **Camping; Clear water**

The best camping area at Alkie Creek is on the downstream side of its main outlet. Stay RR to get to the landing eddy in time. You might want to stop on the upstream side to scout the rapids that follow (see notes below).

Rapids

There are some funky hydraulics that bump the difficulty of these rapids to **Class 2/2+**. The tricky section includes the narrows and on past the mouth of the main outflow of Alkie Creek. At the creek mouth, watch for boils and cross-currents while preparing to eddy out RR to reach the camping site at Alkie.

Up to **Class 2** wave sets continue to shortly before Monkey Wrench Rapid, where the river narrows to one channel.

759153 **Monkey Wrench Rapid**

This **Class 3−/3** rapid is created by the debris/ outwash flow of a glacial creek. You will see a large pile of white and grey boulders on RR. The river is pushed to the left around this debris and then back right again by hard rock on RL. From your boat you can't see where the creek comes in on RR, but you can scout the whole rapid if you get out on RR before the ridge of debris and climb up. You could also portage over the debris pile, but be careful of your ankles!

The rapid has some large boulders on RL and lots of large and pointy haystacks in the main flow. Staying RR on the inside of the turn is the most conservative line, but don't stay so far right that you end up in the funky shore-and creek-induced hydraulics. After the creek mouth the rapids continue as **Class 2** wave sets to around GR 761146.

The next section of river to the O'Connor confluence is braided and fast, with a standing-wave train of note at GR 763133.

748102 Camping; Clear water

On RR and the downstream side of the O'Connor River mouth there are camping spots – probably pretty old ones, considering that the Chilkat trading route came through here. There was also a fishing village located near this confluence. The camping area is difficult to get working left, with the point where the thick willows come down to the river's edge as your heading. There are pools of clear water around to replenish your drinking water.

Wind can really be an issue from here on down to Towagh Creek (and all the way to Dry Bay, but this stretch can be bad!). The headwinds can be fierce and the glacial grit in your eyes makes navigating the many shallow, braided channels with fast current even more of a challenge. Always be looking ahead for the channel with the most flow. You raft will find grounding out easy, but stopping on purpose is difficult, as the river's edge is often cutbanks of gravel. The flow of the Tat nearly doubles with the O'Connor River joining it and there are many channels in this very wide section of river. Stick together and plan ahead to reach stopping/camping spots at Henshi, Tats and Towagh creeks. Getting to them requires making your moves early.

Be alert for funky water at the mouth of the major creek outlets and where the river flows by rock outcropping and cliffs.

693047 Rapid

There is a **Class 2/2+** rapid around a rock island here. Stay RR for the most conservative line, cheating the inside of the turn. Watch for funky hydraulics from Henshi Creek's outlet on RR, however.

| | 691044 | Camping; Clear water | There is a nice camping site in the trees on RL on the marked gravel bar across the river from Henshi Creek's floodplain. The spot is out of the wind and there are lots of trees for tarp rigging. It's not a large site but it makes for better camping than a large windswept floodplain. |

The river continues to braid until just upstream of Tomahnous Creek, where it suddenly narrows, squeezed by this glacial creek's outwash on RL and a rock outcrop on RR. There is squirrelly water here, so be alert.

Just downstream from that funky spot is another hydraulic hot spot. Directly upstream of Tats Creek's outflow is a large ledge of bedrock on RR poking out into the river's main flow. It creates strong cross-currents and boils. Stay loose through this churning fast-water stretch that continues on past Tats Creek.

| | 635993 | Camping; Clear water | Downstream of Tats Creek's outflow there is floodplain camping on the RR marked gravel bar. A copper mine was going to be located up Tats Creek at the base of Windy Craggy Mountain. You can go explore after dinner to stretch your legs. |

| | 620954 | Camping; Hiking; Clear water | Downstream of Towagh Creek's RL outlet there are a couple good camping spots on the floodplain, with some cover from the willows. Back in the alders there is a spring flowing in the silt to replenish your drinking water supply. This is your last source of clear water before the Alsek confluence. There is also an opportunity here to hike up the creek floodplain. |

The current continues to be strong and fast through the next braided section to Basement Creek and the S-Turns. Where the river narrows the whitewater action picks up. Be prepared.

| 114 P/5 | 560943 | S-Turns; Rapids | The S-Turns, **Class 2 and 2+**, are a long section of snaking bends where standing waves and holes lace the outside of the corners. You can read and run the sets of waves quite easily, staying to the insides of the bends to avoid the largest waves and features. Watch out for wood near the islands and on the outside of the bends. Most of the major action is over by GR 525925 and then the Tat widens out and braids again. |

493943	**Camping**	You can camp upstream of the mouth of Ninetyeighter Creek (hard to discern, as it can be dry) but the better spot to enjoy the Alsek confluence is at the Melt Creek camping site on RL downstream. However, you will not easily be able to visit Petroglyph Island from the Melt Creek camp, especially if the flow is up on the Lower Tat. Your other option is to forgo camping on RL altogether and camp on Petroglyph Island itself.

The river is remarkably wide here, so be sure to start making your way far RL early if you plan on stopping at Melt Creek. You can camp on the upstream floodplain (GR 466944) but there is more cover on the downstream side a ways, just before the point.

Note: The hydraulics at the mouth of Melt Creek can be really gnarly: big whirlpools and cross-currents in higher water. We upstream ferried across the outflow rather than trying to sneak by. |
| **461945** | **Camping; Hiking** | Downstream of Melt Creek there is a vast floodplain camping area with amazing views. If you head down to where the willows and alders are, you can set up tarps. I love this camp. You can hike up Melt Creek for a bit to stretch your legs. However, you will only reach the glacier up the creek with great effort. The confluence of the Tat and Alsek is truly a magical place. Many people have camped here before you, and there used to be a seasonal village site here until the drowning deaths occurred as a result of the glacial outburst on the Alsek in 1852. |

453959	Petroglyphs	Petroglyph Island is the largest of the wooded islands on RR of the Tat where the delta begins to spread out. The topo map shows it as the only forest island – the white one marked with an "F." It will be tricky to get there no matter where you come from. Plan your route and navigate carefully. Be warned, you may not be able to reach the island from Melt Creek at all depending on water levels. The best landing spot is on the western tip where the map dots indicate gravel. The coordinates represent the campsite, and the trailhead to the petroglyphs starts there. The trail goes up to a large, flat rock at the high point of the island. Look carefully at the rocks where the trail ends for the two circles. The CAFN asks visitors not to take rubbings of the petroglyphs.
427956	Clear water	This is an approximate GR coordinate for some clear pools of settled river water at the base of the larger delta island right where the Tat meets the Alsek. I haven't been here, so I'm referring you to information in the Lyman et al. guidebook.
	Camping	Some other second-hand information (from BC Parks maps) indicates there are three camping spots on the Alsek in this area: GR 401946 on RL, and GR 387959 and GR 378957 on RR (all coordinates approximate). I suspect these camps are not often used and may be more subject to flooding given their low locations.
	Confluence	The Alsek is a glacial light grey, scooping up the clearer water of the Tat. The Alsek here is three times the size of the Tatshenshini you've left behind. Now you must really concentrate on staying together as a group.

You are entering the land of ice. Glaciers hang all around you. Hope for sun so you can really see them, but expect more wet, coastal-type weather, along with some wind as you approach Weather Corner upstream of Walker Glacier.

You will notice the vegetation is changing to coastal species. You will also see the cutline in the forest on the mountainsides, indicating you are heading into Alaska and Glacier Bay National Park & Preserve.

Note: All coordinates are now given in approximate latitude and longitude, NAD 27 Alaska.

Yakutat	59° 25' 51"	Hiking;
B-1	138° 02' 00"	Clear
		water

The Nose hike may be your first US attraction. The views are incredible from the destination alpine ridge, but it is not a hike for everyone. It's a steep, rugged endeavour, wading creeks, bushwhacking and traversing a rocky slope. To get to the "trailhead" – there is no real trail – make your way to the far RL channel at the US border. Paddle close to the shore of the steep alluvial fan at the base of the Matterhorn-shaped peak (The Nose is a shoulder of this mountain and is marked on the USGS map at 2410 ft. ASL). Keep an eye on the alders lining the river's edge until you see a clear stream coming down from a waterfall farther up the mountain. There is a small eddy to pull into at the stream's mouth. Wade up the stream until you are directly under the hanging ice face and then bushwhack to your right through the alders to another stream. Go up this next stream to where you can see a flat route to traverse across above the waterfalls. This natural "road bed" will take you to the alpine ridge of The Nose. Be careful as you make your way above the large waterfall. There is a good drawing of this hike and some natural history background in Lyman et al. You will need good boots for this hike. You can collect water from the stream at the "trailhead."

Now you are about to round Weather, or Kodak, Corner. Be prepared with rain gear or a windbreaker and your camera. Walker Glacier (and possibly a coastal onslaught of precipitation or icy wind) is coming up after the 90° bend in the Alsek after The Nose. There can also be some strong hydraulics where the channels converge.

	59° 24' 12"	Camping;
	138° 03' 24"	Hiking;
		Clear
		water

Stay RL after The Nose to reach the base of Walker Glacier, but not too far left, as there are shallows and gravel bars. You can easily get hung up if you head left out of the main current too early, but you need to get over to RL as soon as possible in order to reach the camping spots and/or hike on the glacier. You will have to work your way up the eddy to reach the upper campsites.

There are three main camping spots at Walker. The farthest upstream is the highest, most protected site and the raft(s) can be parked out of the current. The middle camp is below a moraine ridge of the glacier. The berm protects you from the cold wind coming down off Walker. The farthest downstream camp is by a clump of alders that affords some wind protection and a place to tie the raft(s) off. Park your boats to start with so you can go up and see which site you like best given the weather and whether you actually have a choice of sites. Remember, the river can rise abruptly and even flood you out here, so don't camp too close to the shore. Tie your boats down really well, for wind reasons if not water-level reasons.

Walker is a busy camping spot, as everyone wants to get up close and personal with a glacier. You may want to hike for the day and move on downstream to camp for the night if the place looks too much like Banff when you arrive or you are concerned about keeping to higher ground.

To get to the clear water source, you will have to paddle up along the shore from the farthest upstream camp until the water begins to turn clear. You will reach a tiny lake fed by a spring and can fill your containers by dipping them in right from the boat.

The standard hike from the meltwater lake to the ice-pinnacled crevasse field takes 2–3 hours round trip, depending on how long you spend taking pictures and enjoying the scenery

There is a trail along the moraine on the left side of the lake (left if you are facing the glacier). It is steep where you approach Walker and then you have to scramble to get up on the ice. Be cautious walking on the glacier. Do not walk on patches of snow – they could be bridging a crevasse and collapse under your weight. You may want an ice axe for cutting steps in gnarly spots. Bring some flares and a throw bag; they are handy items in case of trouble. Also, it will be cold on the ice, so take extra warm clothing and a hat and gloves or mitts with you.

The next section of river, from Walker Glacier down to Alsek Lake, is probably the most beautiful of all – if you can imagine the scenery getting any more amazing. The Alsek is fast, averaging 13 km/h, so relax and enjoy — until Cat in the Washing Machine Rapid!

59° 23' 42" 138° 05' 00"	Water gauge	On RR about a mile down from the Walker Glacier campsites is the active water-survey station.
59° 23' 30" 138° 06' 42"	Clear water	On RR is a lovely little creek to collect clear water from. It's known as Dipper Creek and there is a pretty waterfall up high. Landing is best on the little beach upstream of the creek mouth.
59° 22' 24" 138° 15' 00"	Rapid	**Cat in the Washing Machine** is a **Class 3–** 800-m-long mess of whitewater. Also known as "Confused Sea," this rapid lies where the river is squeezed on the sweeping bend to the left before Novatak Glacier. You can see the whole rapid from the boat as you approach. You can also stop and scout from the RL shore wherever you can find a shore eddy that will work for your flotilla. A raft may have difficulty stopping, so you could send them down first and then pull over to scout. The standing waves are large and irregular, and there are rocks and holes here and there. Just stay loose and away from boily eddy lines. I like to run these kinds of rapids to the inside of the turn and out of the main flow. The waves are often more predictable if you paddle a line angling off of river centre but not messing with the eddy line. This rapid is easier at more moderate water levels.
59° 21' 48" 138° 15' 30"	Camping	There are three possible camping sites near Novatak Glacier. Fireweed Point or "Purple Haze" is on RL on the corner where the river bends to the south. It gets its name from the mass of flowers found there in summer, though it won't be as colourful when you are running the route later in the season. This is a good spot to camp, the only one I have stopped at of the three I note.
59° 22' 06" 138° 15' 54"	Camping	On RR on the outwash peninsula is a camping spot indicated on the BC Parks map.
59° 21' 36" 138° 17' 00"	Camping	The Parks map also shows another spot to camp about 1 mile downstream of the previously noted one. It's on the marked gravel/outwash area on RR with the number 36 on it.

The current is very strong down to Alsek Lake from Novatak Glacier. If you want to visit The Peninsula, stay RL as you approach Alsek Lake.

| Yakutat A-1 | 59° 14' 00" 138° 12' 30" | The Peninsula; Hiking; Clear water; Scouting | From this long spit of land you can hike pretty much straight across The Peninsula to the northwestern bay of Alsek Lake through a vast area of wildflowers. From the bay you can see the icebergs on the lake and the glaciers fringing it. |

To land, stay tight to RL to find a sandy beach in a harbour of large boulders. This is the first good spot to land that you will see. You can walk back upstream to get clear water from the creek marked on the map.

You can also scout the Channel of Death (CoD) from the tip of The Peninsula or from "Bear Island" (the large island at the end of The Peninsula) if water levels allow you to cross to it on foot. In higher water you can paddle between the tip of the spit and Bear Island.

You can also stop farther downstream to scout CoD from the top of the ridge of glacial deposits on The Peninsula. See the Channel of Death section below for more on scouting options. A full scout may be in your best interest, depending on ice conditions and water level.

The Peninsula provides a number of good sites to camp. The first is at the sandy beach among the boulders at **59° 14' 00" / 138° 12' 30"** – the "trailhead" for the hike across the spit to the bay. The mid-Peninsula camp is below a ridge of moraine at **59° 12' 42" / 138° 12' 00"**. The ridge is another scouting spot, discussed in more detail below. The southernmost spot lies just around the tip of The Peninsula, on Alsek Lake at **59° 12' 24" / 138° 11' 42"**. Camping here commits you to entering the lake through the CoD's Door #1. Check ice conditions at the ridge scouting spot first before making the decision to camp here, and remember that wind and iceberg movement could close this door at any time. You may have to lay over for some time before getting across the lake if you camp here and the ice blows in; or if you can't wait, you may have to fly out. See the Difficulty of the River section in this chapter for specifics on preparing a runway.

The Channel of Death: Here is the lowdown on the **three potential routes** to enter **Alsek Lake.** Take this entrance very seriously. The dangers the mix of icebergs, wind and moving water present where the Alsek River enters the lake are real and dynamic. Lyman et al. supply a good map of the scouting options and three possible routes for entering Alsek Lake. The first two routes take you through the Channel of Death, while the third bypasses it completely. **Door #1** is the far RL route, where you pass just to the right of the tip of The Peninsula and the islands south and east of it to turn left into the lake. For **Door #2** you also begin far RL, but instead of turning left to enter the lake, you carry on straight ahead, paddling the potentially ice-free channel along the eastern shore of the long, skinny island pointing south–southeast toward Gateway Knob. **Door #3** is the bypass option. You stay far RR, paddling past all the islands and Gateway Knob to the right. Note that this western channel into Alsek Lake is only open when the water is higher. It is the best option when it has water and the icebergs are jammed in on RL of the islands.

    To scout the routes there are three choices. **Option A** is to hike out to the tip of The Peninsula and Bear Island, as mentioned in the table above. The drawback is you want to stop at the beach with the boulders so you can still have the option of scouting from RR, and thus the hike all the way to the end of the spit of land and the islands to scout will take a long time. To top things off, ice and wind conditions can change on you quickly. **Option B** is to do a partial scout by stopping farther down The Peninsula and hiking up the ridge of glacial deposits. From the ridge you can't see whether Door #3 is clear, but you can see enough of #1 and #2 to decide whether you can paddle through either of them. **Option C** is to do a full scout from the RR scree slope below the Brabazon Range (at approximately 59° 12' 30" / 138° 12' 12"). You can still stop and hike across The Peninsula and then make your way far river right to the base of the Brabazons, just downstream of the last RR creek marked on the map before Alsek Lake. Land on the rocky shore just below the protruding hump of rock and scree. You will have to climb up the slope of loose rock to get a view of the channels. Make sure you are not climbing above your boats! Using binoculars you can see if there is enough water to bypass the Channel of Death routes (Door #1 and #2) and take Door #3. If not, look to see if there is enough room to get through the icebergs into the lake via one of the other two doors. If the two doors to the left are not safe or open and the water is too low to paddle Door #3, you may decide to portage or drag its shallows to enter the lake. At least from this scouting spot you can make that decision and still camp at the tip of The Peninsula in case you have to wait for the ice to move.

    If you do enter Alsek Lake and can't get to Gateway Knob or the river outlet because ice is blocking you from crossing the lake, you will have to find a camp along the lakeshore like we did and then hope things change! It is not difficult to find a camping spot on the lake, especially for smaller groups. Note that you don't want to camp too close to the shoreline if you can help it – the possibility of calving ice making waves that will wash your camp away is always there.

59° 11' 18" **138° 10' 30"**	**Gateway** **Knob;** **Hiking**	This sentinel island has a great view from the top and is well worth hiking up. The trailhead is at the base of the steep slope on the southeast side of the Knob and the rough path goes up through the alder thickets and boulders. Once you reach the top of the bluff via the south side, you can follow another trail through the alders to the north side for another view.
	Camping	There are three usual campsites on the island. One is on the southeast side closest to the trailhead for the Knob hike, at **59° 11' 18" /** **138° 10' 30"**. The other is just south on the gravel flats at **59° 11' 12" / 138° 10´ 30"**. If you come through Door #3, you can camp on the back, or southwest, side of the gravel bar at the tip of the island at **59° 11' 12" /** **138° 11' 00"**. Camping on the island can be pretty bleak in bad weather because it is so exposed, but there is usually driftwood for fires. Do note that by camping here you run the risk of being trapped if ice blows in. We didn't chance it, given we had already spent the night on the lakeshore at a make-do camp. When we finally got through the iceberg jam blocking us from getting to Gateway Knob, there was no gate at the Knob to get through the next ice jam, so we had to portage across the large gravel bar of the island to get across to the riveroutlet side of the lake. Portaging a raft is not as easy as portaging a canoe . . .
59° 10' 06" **138° 12' 42"**	**Camping**	The Dunes camp on the southwest shore of the lake just before the river outlet is a great camp. It is one of the nicest on the route (actually one of my favourite camps of all time!), though it is a bit more out of the way for exploring the lake. It is much more protected than the Knob sites, and there is lots of driftwood for fires. Icebergs float by in the current and you can hike around the sandy topography there. You can also get an early start for the final leg of the river to Dry Bay.
59° 10' 48" **138° 11' 42"**	**Camping**	The Flowers camp is on the northwestern shore of Alsek Lake, RR at the outlet of the river. It is the last camp you can make on RR, as you need a special permit to camp in Tongass National Forest, which

borders the lower reaches of the Alsek. This camp is exposed and low but more protected from weather than the Knob camps. It is especially accessible from Door #3 and also makes for a quick getaway to Dry Bay. It is nowhere near as nice or as large as The Dunes camp, and exploring the lake can be difficult if the current is up.

59° 11' 12" 138° 17' 00"	Rapid	**Constriction Rapid**, at **Class 2/2+**, is made up of irregular compression waves and funky water that follows a midriver rock reef. The river gets squeezed as it makes a turn to the left. You will have to decide whether to take the inside of the turn, cutting far RL to sneak the waves, or go RR and ride the waves. The RL option leads you into some whirlpools at the run-out.
59° 11' 30" 138° 18' 12"	Clear water	A creek on RR about half a mile down from Constriction Rapid will allow you to collect some clear water for your stay at Dry Bay, which could end up being longer than you may wish!
59° 11' 30" 138° 20' 12"	Lodge	Gary Gray's Alsek River Lodge sits on RL. You could take out here or just stay for a night or two in luxury. Gary can arrange ground transportation to Dry Bay, as well as bear viewing, fishing and photography tours if you book ahead.
59° 11' 24" 138° 21' 00"	Rapid	Just below the hunting lodge there is a rapid created by a bedrock outcropping on RR. You want to stay RL here to avoid the hydraulics created by the outcrop. This rapid is not marked on the map and may really be First Rapids. See the notes below.
Yakutat A-2	59° 11' 24" 138° 25' 06"	First Rapids	There was nothing here for rapids in 2004. I think the mapmaker misplaced it. It may be the rapid back upstream or the river has changed dramatically at these two points since the 1940s. Not likely given the rapid upstream was created by the river eroding down to bedrock – that takes awhile! Make sure you stay RL after the island on the left so as not to miss the side channel into Dry Bay and the landing strip take-out. It will come sooner than you think. The current is fast.

59° 11' 18" 138° 28' 06"	**High water take-out**	You really need to be on your toes to get into the side channel to take out at Dry Bay, called The Slough. Once you spy a fairly significant gravel cutbank on RL, start looking for the small brown national park sign on a post up on the top of the bank. It's easy to miss. You want to take the first left after the sign. Be ready!

Once in The Slough channel you will see a few buildings on RL. First up is the fish plant and associated buildings and then about 300 m downstream is a small brown building with a green roof. Just past this park ranger cabin is the take-out area, where there is another brown park sign (about 1 m^2) up on the bank. Yes, you have to lug everything up to the landing strip. This is Dry Bay central and the whole hamlet really just consists of this central area and scattered seasonal fishing cabins.

59° 11' 06" 138° 28' 30"	**Camping**	You can camp anywhere in the take-out area but don't take up too much room. If the weather is bad, other groups will be there or coming in behind you. A park ranger or an assistant will usually come along to check your papers. If they don't, go to their cabin or just leave your paperwork in the stand by the sanitation dump station. Yes, you can get rid of your waste here before flying out. The dump station is located in the northeast corner of the clearing and there is an outhouse behind it.

59° 11' 00" 138° 29' 00"	**Alternative take-out route**	If the upper channel of The Slough is too dry to float or you miss the turnoff to the head of it, you will have to carry on down the Alsek to channel's outlet and then paddle The Slough upstream to the take-out. From a rafter's perspective, it will take about 45 minutes or less to float the Alsek to this downstream entrance and then an hour and a half to row up The Slough to the take-out, near the landing strip. **Note:** there is an old, dry channel mouth about halfway downstream from the channel you want. It has a high cutbank entrance, whereas the one you want has low land around its larger entrance.

If you miss both the take-out channel entrances and get stranded somewhere downstream, you can call Pat Pellet of Brabazon Expeditions in Dry Bay via satellite phone at (254) 381-3030 to help you out. If you don't have a phone you will have to hike to Dry Bay and find him.

Pat will also arrange for transportation out to the ocean if you don't want to do the flat, easy 10-mile (16-km) hike round trip from Dry Bay to the Gulf of Alaska and back. The track to the ocean veers off the one running along The Slough to the south and passes by the downstream end of the airstrip.

*** Don't forget to call Customs when you arrive in Haines or Juneau!

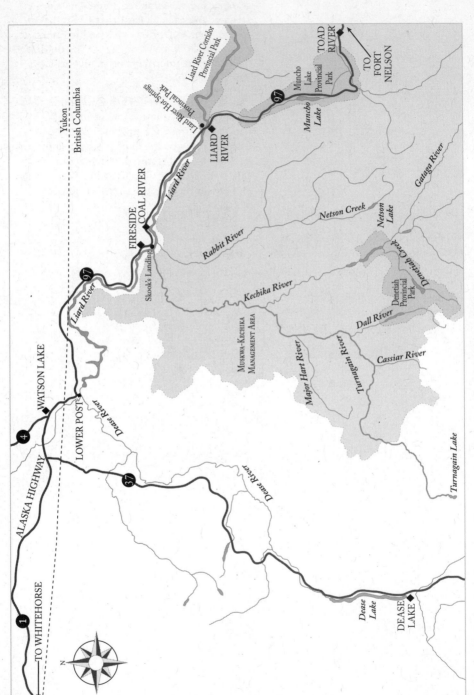

Turnagain/Kechika Rivers

CHAPTER FIVE:

TURNAGAIN/KECHIKA RIVERS

People often ask me what my favourite river trip in northern BC is. It's an impossible question for me to answer. There are too many great trips to choose from. However, the Turnagain River does come to mind, along with a couple others. I really like long, remote routes with lots of whitewater, particularly ones running through a diversity of landscapes, from alpine headwaters to a floodplain confluence with a mother river. The Turnagain is all that and more.

The headwaters of the Turnagain are a short distance from the divide between waterways flowing west to the Pacific Ocean and those flowing north to the Arctic Ocean. The Turnagain's flow is taken up by the Kechika River to eventually end up in the Beaufort Sea, compliments of the Liard and Mackenzie rivers. This is hard to believe when you begin in a beaver pond, move on to moose puddles lined with eskers, pass through the rugged, mountainous heart of jade country and portage a three-tiered waterfall in an amazing mountain goat canyon. The Barren Lands seem a long way away!

Arctic grayling and rainbow trout fishing are awesome on the clear Turnagain and its tributaries. On top of the great fishing to be had, there is some really fun whitewater on this mountain river. You can also explore the sandy Kechika and even paddle for a short ways on the mother river of this Arctic watershed, the mighty Liard. You get three very different river experiences in one canoe trip!

The route has a long history of First Nations travel and sustenance, particularly below the falls on the Turnagain and along the Kechika and Liard rivers. The Turnagain watershed also boasts a good tale about Samuel Black, a blackguard explorer of the fur-trade era who didn't find what he was looking for, and another about Alice and Vern Shea, a prospecting couple who did. They literally stumbled onto the fifth-largest gold nugget ever found in BC.

You will rarely find a more interesting and fun river to run than the Turnagain, but there is some work to be done on this route. This truly magnificent canoe trip hosts the longest mandatory portage described in this book: the carry around Turnagain Falls. Depending on where you start, the portage is over 6 km one way! If that strenuous challenge doesn't appeal to you and you have the cash, why not splurge on a heli-portage – if you can handle your rafting friends laughing at your turncoat expense!

Length: The trip from Turnagain Lake to Skook's Landing on the Liard River is approximately 310 km long. The length of the Turnagain is about 215 km, then you paddle about 93 km on the Kechika and down the Liard for a scant 1.5 km.

If you run the majority of the rapids and do not hike much, you can do the whole route in a minimum of 12 days, including carrying the long portage. The current is good on both rivers, but the sheer number of rapids on the Turnagain will slow you down considerably. Plan on paddling only 20–25 km a day on the Upper Turnagain and 13 km the day you paddle The Big Three. You need time to scout and line. You also need two days for portaging Turnagain Falls. You don't want to have to rush that either! After the falls, though, you can really make time on this route.

If you plan on lining or portaging lots of the rapids, you will need extra days. A heli-portage of the falls will save you at least one day if the weather cooperates. I encourage you to plan for at least one layover day, because there are lots of activities other than paddling to enjoy on this route.

One final note about planning an itinerary is that you cannot count on being able to fly from Dease Lake or Muncho Lake to the put-in whenever you wish. Given the topography involved, the flight to the put-in is weather dependent. Have extra time to deal with that contingency.

You can shorten this trip by taking out on the Lower Turnagain, forsaking the Kechika section of the route. You will have to check with the air charter companies and the outfitters on the river to see if you can charter a floatplane or jet boat to pick you up at one of the two lodges. If you take out at Turnagain River Lodge, that would make for a trip of 136 km. Turnagain River Adventures' camp is 191 km down the Turnagain. You could also charter a jet boat to pick you up below the falls, making for a short trip of 117 km with all the best whitewater. If you want to avoid the major whitewater component of the route and the portage around Turnagain Falls, you could put in either below the falls or at one of the lodges and just paddle the Lower Turnagain and the Kechika. This would make for a much easier trip of 193, 184 or 119 km respectively.

You cannot lengthen the Turnagain/Kechika rivers route unless you have the skill and stamina to continue to paddle and portage down the Liard River. This is a major undertaking only possible in low water and by exceptional whitewater canoeists with many years of experience. Frankly, I know a lot of canoeists, but very few that could do it and even fewer that would want to! Enough said.

Turnagain Lake to below Turnagain Falls*	117 km
Turnagain River Adventures to Skook's Landing*	119 km
Turnagain Lake to Turnagain River Lodge*	136 km
Turnagain River Lodge to Skook's Landing*	184 km
Turnagain Lake to Turnagain River Adventures*	191 km
Turnagain Falls to Skook's Landing*	193 km

* These routes are described in detail in the Trip Notes section of this chapter.

Topographic Maps: Maps at a scale of 1:50 000 are required for at least the Turnagain River portion of this route. The Grid Reference System (GRS) coordinates I use in the Trip Notes are much more user-friendly with NTS topos of this scale and you will need to know where you are with regard to the rapids and the portage around the falls on the Turnagain.

The NTS 1:50 000-scale maps you will need for the run to the confluence of the Turnagain with the Kechika are 104 I/6, 104 I/7, 104 I/10, 104 I/9, 94 L/12, 94 L/13 and 94 M/4. For the rest of the trip, from the Turnagain–Kechika confluence to Skook's Landing on the Liard, you will need 94 M/5, 94 M/12 and 94 M/11. The three 1:250 000-scale NTS topos covering the route are 104 I, 94 L and 94 M. I like to carry this scale of topos for identifying the larger features of a region and planning extended hiking expeditions. If you are doing a shorter, customized trip, see the Trip Notes for the maps you will need.

I suggest you purchase or print your topo maps in advance. Not only will you be able to plan your paddling days, but using the coordinates in the Trip Notes you can mark the locations of sources of emergency help, known hazards, rapids, portages and potential campsites (there are some sections where good campsites are scarce), fishing holes and other sites of interest, so you have the information at hand when navigating the river. Remember that river features can change with each freshet and flood, especially wood hazards. You are responsible for always being on the lookout for these and being able to deal with them safely.

When paddling the Upper Turnagain, don't be alarmed if you don't know exactly where you are. The twisty creek section is confusing. But don't spend too much time looking down at your map; you should be looking ahead for logjams and strainers! This is true all of the time for the whole route. Note that my GPS often gave me strange readings on this trip. If you use one on this route, be aware that I relied mostly on the topo maps and Grid Reference System for creating the Trip Notes. I could not figure out the discrepancies between some GRS coordinates for features that were correctly represented on the topos, and the GPS readings I got on the ground. They did not match up. My advice is to follow your maps instead of your GPS and we will all be on the same page, so to speak – the one based on the topo maps and Trip Notes. If you do use a GPS with the 1:50 000s, make sure the map datum setting is NAD 27 Canada and the position format setting MGRS (Military Grid Reference System). For a discussion on topographic maps and the use of a GPS see the How To Use this Guidebook section.

Getting There and Away: This is normally a fly-in and drive-out trip. If you customize it due to time constraints or other limitations, you will have to fly or boat in or out from one of the lodges on the Turnagain or charter a jet boat out from below Turnagain Falls. There is a possibility of a drive-in trip, taking on the challenge of four-wheeling the track to the Boulder City Lake mine. We researched this option, but decided it was too much for loaded vehicles. It would be a long, difficult shuttle. I think you could get to the river near Three Kettle Lake (see the maps and Trip Notes) and leave your vehicle there. The "road" goes all the way to the mine at Boulder City Lake, a good place to start your trip, but where the track crosses the Turnagain, there is no bridge. If the river is up you would have difficulty getting across it without a really big truck. The mine uses buggies to haul out ore and jade and we were seriously discouraged from making an attempt on the road. Talk to the officers at the BC Parks office in Dease Lake for more information.

To paddle the whole route you must charter a floatplane to either the put-in at the north end of Turnagain Lake or the dock at Turnagain Lake Lodge on the eastern shore. Your pilot may choose for you, as the landing for the north-end put-in by the campsite is tricky. You should get permission to land at the dock of the lodge. The common take-out is Skook's Landing on the Liard, where you can easily access the Alaska Highway. The logistics for the classic Turnagain canoe trip are simple compared to many in this book.

Dease Lake is a convenient community to stage your trip from. BC–Yukon Air and Northern Thunderbird Air have floatplane bases there and the flight to Turnagain Lake is short and cheap. Northern Thunderbird Air also offers scheduled flights from Smithers to Dease Lake. The shuttle to and from Skook's Landing is long, however. It's about 400 km one way from Dease Lake to Skook's (around 5½ hours of driving), but the route is scenic and easy and you don't need four-wheel drive.

From Dease Lake, drive north on the Stewart–Cassiar Highway (Hwy. 37) to its junction with the Alaska Highway. Turn right, east, and drive through Watson Lake and on to Fireside. Carry on eastward down the Alaska Highway past Fireside for about 5 km until you spot a not so obvious turnoff on your right. There is a big rock in the ditch by the access road of the highway. This little gravel road leads to Skook's Landing on the Liard. Once you have turned right onto the access road to Skook's, there may or may not be a Muskwa–Kechika Management Area sign on your left as you drive the 500 m or so down to the river.

The turnoff to the Skook's access road off the Alaska Highway is not easy to see. You will know you have missed the turnoff if you reach the Whirlpool Canyon Recreation Site (the rapids you see from here are actually Mountain Portage Rapids; Whirlpool Canyon is downstream). Turn around using that access road and drive back west for 1.5 km to the Skook's Landing access road. There is parking right by the river at Skook's, and in my experience it is safe to leave your vehicle there. You can also camp at Skook's.

The canoe outfitter at Dease River Crossing and Stikine RiverSong at Telegraph Creek offer shuttle services and canoe rentals. Bruce at BC–Yukon Air may also be able to help you with your shuttle if you only have one vehicle. There are no car rentals in the region. Smithers, Whitehorse or Fort Nelson are your closest options.

For other sources of help with your shuttle, try the canoe outfitters mentioned in the Spatsizi and Stikine chapters, as most provide shuttle services. If you do arrange for a shuttle with them, it may be more convenient to fly from Tatogga Lake with North Pacific Seaplanes (formerly Harbour Air). You can also rent canoes, skirts and other equipment from Red Goat Lodge near Iskut.

Muncho Lake is another good staging place for this route. Northern Rockies Lodge, on the eastern shore of Muncho, can provide you with everything you need. You can charter your flight right from Muncho Lake. Liard Air and Northern Rockies Lodge are both owned and operated by the Schildknecht family. The flight to Turnagain Lake will cost you more but the shuttle will be much shorter. You can also rent good canoes, skirts and other equipment from Northern Rockies Lodge.

Chartering a plane from Liard Air comes with free safe parking. For a fee they will also pick you up at Skook's, so you don't even have to do a shuttle if you choose not to. But if you have two vehicles, doing the shuttle from Muncho Lake is quick and easy. The distance between Northern Rockies Lodge and the Skook's Landing turnoff is approximately 125 km on the Alaska Highway, about a 1½-hour drive one way.

Coming from Muncho Lake, when you get about 8 km west of Coal River you will see a turnoff to the left for Whirlpool Canyon Recreation Site. Carry on west down the Alaska Highway past this turnoff for about 1.5 km to another turnoff on your left. This gravel road leads to Skook's Landing on the Liard. There is no sign for the turn, but there may be a Muskwa–Kechika Management Area sign on your left as you drive the 500 m or so down the track to the river.

You can camp at Skook's if you arrive too late to finish your shuttle or to camp at one of the provincial parks near Muncho Lake. I believe the park campsites close their gates at 11:00 p.m. If you decide not to camp, you have a choice of accommodations at Northern Rockies Lodge. They have rustic cabins on the property and luxurious rooms in the main building. The dining room is very good, making this a great all-in-one option for those coming from afar and those that like their creature comforts before and/or after a great adventure.

If you wish to travel without vehicles or canoes, you have a number of options. Smithers, Terrace or Fort Nelson or Whitehorse are destinations with scheduled flights from southern cities. You can also fly from Smithers to Dease Lake on a scheduled flight with Northern Thunderbird Air. Alternatively, from any of the major northern BC communities and from Whitehorse you could rent a car and drive to Tatogga Lake, Dease Lake or Muncho Lake or charter a wheel plane to either Dease Lake or Northern Rockies Lodge at Muncho Lake. Both places have landing strips and you can easily arrange for canoe rentals and shuttles to stage your trip from either location. Turnagain Lake Lodge may be willing to rent you canoes, as they offer guided canoe trips on the Turnagain.

If you are interested in the heli-portage option around Turnagain Falls, Pacific Western Helicopters of Dease Lake has experience with this. Before flying out from Dease Lake to the Turnagain we met with Jim, the chief pilot, nailing down a date, time and location for pickup. We called him via satellite phone when we arrived at the appointed place on the river to confirm our pickup time the next day. It all worked out very well and was sinfully fun and easy. I got some great aerial shots of the falls.

For a shorter trip that avoids the significant whitewater of the Upper Turnagain river and the long portage around Turnagain Falls, you could charter a jet boat to get you to the bottom of the falls. There are also the options of cutting out the upper or lower reaches of the trip by flying to or from the lodges or chartering a jet boat. See the Directory of Services and Organizations for contact information for jet boat, floatplane and helicopter services and canoe outfitters and the lodges, as well as other tourist services in the region.

When To Go: Mid-July to September. You do not want to run the Turnagain in a canoe during peak runoff, which usually happens in June to early July. There are too many pushy rapids, tight corners and wood hazards on the river. If you go too late in the season, ice on the small lakes may be an issue. This is a challenging river and best run by most canoeists at lower water, usually August and September flows unless it's been an unusually rainy summer and fall. Flows on the Kechika and Liard rivers will also be significantly less in late summer and early fall. You will not be sorry you waited for lower water when you come to ferry across the Liard.

Only parties of advanced and exceptional moving-water paddlers should consider a trip in July. At high water, excellent moving-water skills and extra vigilance are required to navigate the boat-wrecking rapids and dangerous wood hazards. The bonus of high flows is you will make good time on the route, especially if the Kechika is up, leaving you more hours to relax, hike and take in the sights on the Turnagain. The insect population will be out in full force in July as the heat turns on in the long hours of daylight, but so will the wildflowers in the alpine and forest and all over the floodplains.

July daily highs at Dease Lake and Fireside average around 22°c; nights are cool, and expect lower temperatures in the higher elevations day and night. Frost is possible at night in any month in the region. You will likely have some sun, but July can also be a rainy month. Annual rainfall amounts are relatively low in the Cassiars compared to the Coast Mountains, so it doesn't usually pour for days on end in this region. Afternoon thunderstorms and associated heavy rain showers are common in July and August, though, and I've been hammered by hail on the Kechika a couple of times!

On boreal rivers in northern BC, water levels usually drop come the end of July. August is normally a lower-water month for this route, the preferred time for most parties to paddle the Turnagain. Waiting until later in August would be a prudent choice for some, noting that heavy rains can cause water levels to rise in any month.

Gravel bars are more exposed in August, making for good camping. The insects start to disappear with the cooler nights, and the berries come out. Life is generally as good as it gets on the river in this usually drier month. The only drawback to an August trip is that hunters in jet boats will be on these rivers already. Stone sheep season starts August 1 and you will meet up with at least one boat of hunters on the Kechika from the August long weekend on into the fall. You will see even more boats after moose season opens.

You will likely have even lower flows in early September. But with a rainy fall water levels may actually rise on the Turnagain. It will often be frosty in the mornings, and snow is definitely possible. On the other hand, you could get very warm sunny days throughout your journey. You will need to pack for any weather; expect the worst and enjoy what you get! The joys of a fall trip are the changing colours of the many deciduous trees and shrubs in this region, and you will often see more wildlife than you normally would if you are hiking away from the river. The hunters will have spooked or shot anything near the water. The bugs will have really died down, making camping and hiking even more pleasant.

I love an autumn trip. But if you are not experienced fall canoe trippers, consider a late August trip so you don't have to deal with more significant weather challenges while paddling a difficult route. The other drawback of a late-season trip to that hunters will be out in full force when moose season starts. There will be a number of jet boats of hunting parties on the Kechika in September but most don't go up the Turnagain any great distance.

There are no active water-gauging stations on the Turnagain or the Kechika anymore, due to federal budget cuts in the mid-1990s, but there is still one on the Liard that is helpful for determining water levels on this route. Using real time flow data from this station, at Lower Crossing, you can monitor water levels on the Liard and get a general idea of levels on both the Turnagain and the Kechika as well.

Archived hydrometric data for the Turnagain's flow just upstream of the mouth of Sandpile Creek (Sandpile Creek flows into the Lower Turnagain right by Turnagain River Adventures' camp) indicate that the volume of the Liard at Lower Crossing is normally around 12 times the flow of the Turnagain at this location during the prime canoeing months. From a similar comparison of archived data available from the R-ArcticNET (www.r-arcticnet.sr.unh.edu) and Environment Canada websites, it appears there is a ratio of about 4:1 between the Liard's flow at Lower Crossing and the Kechika's at its mouth during the canoeing season.

Average Monthly Mean Flows, m³/s

	Turnagain above Sandpile Creek (1967–1994)	Liard at Lower Crossing (1944–2005)	Kechika at mouth (1963–1994)
July	195	2470	595
August	115	1460	371
September	107	1200	294

Sources: Environment Canada, Archived Hydrometric Data Report, June 2007; R-ArcticNET

So, through obtaining a real-time reading for the Liard River at Lower Crossing and dividing it by 12, you can broadly estimate the flow of the Turnagain. You can also surmise the Kechika's levels near its mouth by dividing the reading by four. That said, it is important to understand that the Turnagain is a much smaller river with a large catchment basin, so levels will fluctuate significantly more quickly with heavy rain than on the Kechika or the Liard. Before you even leave home, call Bruce at BC–Yukon Air or one of the lodges to see how precipitation has been in the Turnagain watershed specifically.

To access real-time flow data for the Liard at Lower Crossing, go to the Environment Canada hydrometric website, at http://scitech.pyr.ec.gc.ca/waterweb/formnav.asp?lang=0. Set the "Find Station By" slot to read "Province," and in the "View all Real Time Stations within" slot, choose "British Columbia." In the resulting alphabetical list of station names, scroll down to "Liard River at Lower Crossing" and click the "Go to Station" button. In the resulting "Disclaimer" screen, go to the bottom and press the "I accept" button. In the resulting page, at the top left, make sure the "Data Category" slot is set to "Real Time," and just beneath that, change "Parameter Type" to "Discharge." The graph will show actual flows, in cubic metres per second, for the past week up to the current date. You can change the date span of the readout to anytime since January 1, 2007, by resetting the date controls just beneath the graph and hitting the "Redraw" button.

You can also compare the real-time readings to more specific historical flow data on the website. The table I've provided only gives you average monthly mean flows, whereas the website graph will give you a more detailed picture of the changes throughout a given month. To change to historical mode, choose the "Historic" option in the box near the top and hit "Go." The server is crunching a lot of data, so the screen may take a moment to change. Use any year for your search. What you really want is the baseline information to compare your real-time reading with. So, be sure to click the "Max," "Min" and "Mean" buttons on the lower left side of the page. "Upper quartile" and "Lower quartile" flows are of interest too. They can tell you if the real-time flows are in the top or bottom 25 per cent of all recorded flows. Once you have your options selected, click on Go to get a graph with different lines representing all the statistics. Ignore the line that represents the data from the random year you used; look instead for where your real-time reading fits in. If you were to plot your reading of, say, 1500 m^3/s on this graph, would it sit above or below the mean line? Keep repeating this process every week or so until you leave for your trip. By then you will know whether the Liard is fluctuating normally or not. Do the math to figure out what the Turnagain and Kechika are running at and then make your decision as to whether the water levels are going to be low enough to paddle the route. Have a backup route already researched, so if the Turnagain is just too high, you can paddle your second choice instead.

Some context for the data in the table is in order. When I was on the Turnagain and Kechika rivers in late July to August 9, 2005, the Turnagain was quite a bit higher than when my friend Tony Shaw and his group ran it in the last two weeks of August 1999. The historical data showed, however, that 2005 was generally normal for river flows in the region, while 1999 was slightly lower than normal throughout the canoeing season.

I estimate (using the 1:12 ratio with the Liard and the archived data from the Lower Crossing station) that we ran the Turnagain at around 150 m^3/sec or more and that Tony's group ran it at about 100 m^3/s. According to available historical data and my rough ratio for estimating the level of the Turnagain, both trips took place at about normal levels for the times each of our parties were paddling the river. In lower water in later August, Tony lined the first part of the first of The Big Three rapids, but we were able to run it. The only route through was difficult and required precise manoeuvring. We were nearly swamped in the second of The Big Three, where Tony was not. We both ended up lining the final rapid of The Big Three, though Tony actually ran the top of it with some serious difficulties ensuing. The water levels both our parties experienced were suitable to our skills, a mix of intermediate to advanced and exceptional moving-water paddlers. The Trip Notes reflect average water levels for the Turnagain, as neither of our groups had heavy rains before or during our trip.

You can be more sure of the Kechika's water levels throughout the season in a relatively normal year. Its flows will not change as drastically or as quickly as that of the Turnagain. The Turnagain is a small-volume river for much of its length, similar to the Upper Gataga (covered in volume one) and Toad rivers, but the Kechika is a medium-volume river at its confluence with the Turnagain. Average July, August and September flows near the confluence are 361, 235 and 166 m^3/s respectively (this data, from the archives of R-ArcticNET, was collected from a gauge near Boya Creek on the Kechika that is no longer active). By the time the Kechika reaches the Liard, it is flowing almost double again and at its mouth is more of a medium- to large-volume river compared to many in this book. Its volume is similar to the Dease River's (covered in volume one) where it flows into the Liard.

To give you some context for Kechika water levels, in the third week of July 2004 the Kechika at its mouth was flowing at about 300 m^3/s, according to my calculations.

This was low for that time of year and it was a fine paddle for my party coming down the Gataga. In 2005, when I was on the Kechika in the first week of August, flows were much higher, more like 410 m³/s. This nearly average water level for August presented more of a challenge, though it was not overly pushy for the party of more advanced paddlers with me. Of note is that the ferry across the Liard was more challenging in the higher water of 2005, though both the Kechika's and Liard's levels were almost average for that time of year. As such, the Trip Notes for the Kechika reflect the river's features at both low and average water levels for August.

In conclusion, water levels and your party's skills should determine when you run this route. If you are skilled enough to paddle the Turnagain, the Kechika will not be a problem. All but the most-skilled whitewater canoeists will want to avoid the higher flows of July. In August when the water levels have gone down, intermediate moving-water canoeists paddling with advanced and exceptional ones will enjoy and be challenged by this route. If the Turnagain is high or likely to be high and you are not advanced or exceptional paddlers, consider moving your trip to a later date or pick a different trip or put in below Turnagain Falls. This is not a river trip for novice canoeists at any time. See the difficulty section below for more specific details on the skill requirements for this route.

Difficulty of the River: ✳ ✳ ✳ The three-star difficulty rating for the Turnagain/Kechika route is mostly based on the challenging rapids of the Turnagain, their length and nature, the lack of portages around them, and the long, strenuous portage around the falls. However, at normal August water levels, you can line The Big Three and heli-portage around the falls. Getting around Kechika Spit – the last big rapid on the route, where the Kechika drops into the Liard – would be a bit of an epic to portage, but it could be done. That said, you would still be required to run up to Class 2+ whitewater on the fly. You could line some of these Class 2 or more rapids, but if you lined or bushwhack portaged all of the whitewater on the route, it might take you a month or more to do the trip. That's not a bad thing, but it would be strenuous and you would need excellent lining and portaging skills! There are no large open-water crossings, and though the three rivers on the route are cold in summer, none of them are glacially cold. Still, the Turnagain and Kechika are remote rivers and the route is long with few sources of help.

The Turnagain has long sections of continuous whitewater. The rapids on the route average Class 2, with the exception of the named rapids discussed below. The majority of the significant rapids, especially the long ones, are boat-wreckers. There are also tricky currents where channels converge and at sharp bends. Set the Tone, The Big Three, Shadow of Big Three (dubbed so because it was unexpectedly challenging at our water level) and Entrance Rapids are the crux of the whitewater on the Turnagain, but there are other tricky boulder gardens. You can't line or easily portage Set the Tone. You can line The Big Three in lower water, as well as Shadow of Big Three. Entrance Rapids, a long, tricky stretch of rapids ending just before Turnagain Falls, and the falls can be portaged via horse trails.

The Kechika has a couple of named rapids, Flowerpot and Kechika Spit. They are runnable by intermediate canoeists after scouting. Flower Pot Rapids can be cheated, but Kechika Spit, the most difficult rapid on the Kechika, cannot be and does not have a portage trail or good lining options. Some canoeists may decide after scouting that they would rather do a mountain goat carry over the very steep river left bank to put in on the Liard, which is flowing on the other side of the spit of land. It would be strenuous and scratchy to portage this Class 2+/3– rapid, to say the least, but it is possible. There are a number of smaller rapids on the Kechika that are easily run.

Excellent lining and portaging skills are needed on this route, especially if you don't have excellent whitewater skills and are also carrying the falls. A swim in the bumpy Turnagain is not going to be pleasant. Even if you line much of the tough whitewater, you must be prepared to rescue canoes quickly if a canoe gets away on you. For these reasons you need strong self-rescue and assisted rescue skills, have swift-water rescue training and know how to set up and use a z-drag in the case of a wrap or pin. Ideally, you want to have three boats in your party, so one canoe can look after the people and the other can go after gear and equipment.

Crossing the Liard to its northern, or river left, bank is more challenging at higher water and is a must-make move at any flow. It is about 400 m across the Liard, but given that Mountain Portage Rapids starts less than 2 km downstream, you will want to upstream (front) ferry. This will get you across in control and you will lose the least ground. Flipping is not an option.

You can start your ferry from an eddy along the Liard's southern bank just upstream of the Kechika's mouth and end it over at the lovely sand beach on the north side of the Liard. Then, heading downstream on the Liard, keep tight river left until you see the point that makes a good-sized eddy in front of Skook's Landing. Scoot into the eddy as high as possible. It's obvious, but you don't want to miss it!

In conclusion, intermediates paddling with advanced or exceptional whitewater canoeists will enjoy this route. Even advanced whitewater enthusiasts will be challenged if the water is up. Intermediate whitewater canoeists should go later in August for lower water and have at least one more advanced paddler in their party or take a qualified guide. Paddlers should have excellent lining, portaging and river rescue skills and a high level of bushcraft and should run the route in a party of three canoes or more.

The gradient of the Turnagain is about 2.3 m/km, and taking into consideration the small lakes and large falls, this is a good gradient for a fun mountain river trip. The Kispiox (covered in volume one) has a similar gradient but a different nature on the whole. The Kechika drops at around 1.1 m/km. The current is good all along the route, never less than 5 km/h and probably averaging 7 km/h or more, with the exception of the headwater and small lakes of the Upper Turnagain. The current on the Lower Kechika is particularly fast. My GPS measured our speed without paddling at 12 km/h and more on short sections in 2004. In 2005 I clocked over 14 km/h in the same stretch.

Character of the River and Region: Ecologically speaking, the Turnagain/Kechika route lies wholly within the Northern Boreal Mountains ecoprovince. The Turnagain River is characteristic of the Boreal Mountains and Plateaus ecoregion, while the Lower Kechika and the short stretch of the Liard are representative of the Liard Basin ecoregion (also called the Liard Plain). As you descend the route you can see the landscape changing and the trip has incredibly diverse scenery.

The upper headwaters of the Turnagain are found on the Spatsizi Plateau, which is part of the larger Stikine Plateau. (See the Spatsizi and Upper Stikine chapters for more on the plateau environment). The river begins as a series of beaver ponds at the north end of Turnagain Lake, and then flows languidly through more wetlands until it becomes a creek. The water is as clear as it gets. The headwaters are shallow throughout and often have a sandy bottom, often with underwater vegetation that moose thrive on. You will likely see lots of moose in your first few days on the river.

A quick creek, the Turnagain drops east through the spectacular Stikine Ranges of the Cassiar Mountains, then dallies here and there at small, pretty lakes with eskers. Three Kettle and Boulder City lakes were obviously named by prospectors.

The forest along the lakeshores and upper river is often spruce and with a moss understorey, though on the sandy eskers there are often lodgepole pine and understorey plants that like drier climes. Crowberry, lichen, strawberries, larkspur, broadleaf willow herb, cow parsnip, cinquefoil and yarrow can be found in the valley floor forest and along the riverbanks and gravel bars.

Above 1000 m ASL, willow and birch shrubs are dominant. Subalpine fir and white spruce make up the open subalpine forest. There is bare bedrock at elevations above treeline and alpine vegetation consists of heath and tundra, along with willow and birch and other dwarf shrubs, alpine grasses, sedges and mountain avens. Typical of the Stikine Ranges of the Cassiar Mountains, the peaks you see on the Upper Turnagain are comprised of Cassiar batholith, granitic rocks folded into volcanic and sedimentary rocks, with a significant component of limestone/dolomite in some places. The highest peaks in the Cassiars reach 2500 m ASL. Ridges and summits are rounded below 1800 m and sharply scalloped above that elevation due to glaciation. The rugged mountains are dissected by widely flaring valleys mantled with glacial drift.

The climate of the Cassiar Mountains is influenced by Pacific weather systems. Considered northern continental, it is somewhat warmer and wetter than the Spatsizi Plateau, and noticeably so on this river trip. To give you an idea of temperature, at Dease Lake average July daytime temperatures reach 20°C. You will be at a higher elevation, so expect daytime temperatures averaging around 15°–17° in good weather.

Mean annual precipitation can be up to 700 mm in the alpine, but as you descend to close to the Liard Plain, it's more like 400 mm. The weather changes constantly and quickly in these mountains. Convective thundershowers are common at the higher elevations on warm afternoons. You can also have cold, wet weather for days when a system comes down from the north. Compared to the rivers in the Coast Mountains, though, this is a dry place to be.

Heading northeast off the Spatsizi Plateau the Turnagain gains volume from small creeks and the gradient increases. Pushed north by the Stikine Ranges at Kutcho Creek, the river really picks up steam. When it turns to head east-southeast the Turnagain crashes through a narrow valley hosting the trickiest rapids, and then, after a short respite in between, the river drops in thunderous sets of unrunnable cataracts through a slit of a canyon, home of Turnagain Falls. In fact, there are three main parts to the falls, with continuous rapids in between, all funnelled between vertical walls.

On the Upper Turnagain the rapids are predominantly boulder and rock gardens. The boulders in the Turnagain's rapids and along its shores can be very large. You will encounter rocks the size of Volkswagens to small rocks making up beaches. There are some huge rounded ones in The Big Three. The Big Three and Shadow of Big Three are boat-wrecking boulder gardens and there are many more smaller ones. Ledges, holes, deepwater chutes and wave trains are also present in some of the significant rapids Set the Tone, the second of The Big Three rapids and Entrance Rapids particularly. Turnagain Falls displays all the kinds of hydraulics you have likely ever seen.

After the three-tiered falls, the river is unexpectedly quiet as it swings back northeast and out of the Stikine Ranges. The Turnagain flows placidly into 360-degree panorama views at the confluence of the Dall River down to an unnamed creek in a valley to the northwest. The river is shallow and steadily growing wider. It doesn't braid that much except for the low section near the Dall River confluence, where there are many significant wood hazards caused by bank erosion.

The river comes into the Kechika Ranges like a lamb and the ridges are a pastoral green. These mountains form the eastern edge of the Cassiars and are not as high as those in the Stikine Ranges. They sit in the rain shadow of the western Cassiars and have shallow, wide valleys. Glacial/fluvial deposits and outwash plains are common. The forest composition is the same as in the rest of the Cassiars, but there are extensive patches of grassland. Prescribed fires to enhance ungulate habitat have converted vast areas of forest to early successional stages.

Meandering its way, the Turnagain flows north through the Kechika Ranges toward its confluence with the Kechika River. The wide valley is characteristic of the Cassiar Mountains. At these lower, warmer elevations lodgepole pine and white and black spruce make up the majority of the boreal forest and the understorey is lichen and moss. Gravel bars are covered with mountain avens, northern grass-of-parnassus and Canadian butterweed. In areas of cold-air ponding in the valley bottom, the forest gives way to subalpine shrub and grassland shrub vegetation.

Nearing the Kechika confluence, the Turnagain quickens again as it drops northeast through a number of small canyons with differing natures but without rapids of note. The Lower Turnagain's gorges host sedimentary rock walls as well as pretty outcrops of bedrock. Sage shows up growing on rock outcropping around the Major Hart River confluence. Stabilized and now forested sand dunes are located near the confluence of the Turnagain with the Kechika. Both rivers host erosion formations, or what are known as hoodoos.

The Turnagain flows out of the Cassiars and joins the Kechika at the very northern end of the Rocky Mountain Trench. At the confluence a great view can be had from a high point of land between the two rivers' flows. The living seam between the Turnagain's clear waters and the Kechika's silty-grey flow stretches north, framed by mountains against a wide sky. Once the Turnagain River flows out of the Cassiars and joins it, the Kechika then begins to snake north along the western side of the Rabbit Plateau, heading east-northeast across the Liard Plain to join the Liard River.

As the Kechika snakes north and then northeast across the sandy Liard Plain, you begin to see the rolling green grassland slopes – similar to the area around the Dall River confluence and Hidden Valley – that so characterize the Kechika for me. This is Skook Davidson ranching country. There are wide valley views, and camping is really good on gravel bars and islands. Erosion formations occur, making for some scenic corners.

The Liard Plain is a broad, rolling, low-lying intermountain area covered with sandy glacial deposits (eskers, kames, kettles and outwash plains) and Tertiary sediments. There are many small lakes, streams and wetlands. Bedrock is limestone and shale, and the boreal forest is mostly composed of lodgepole pine, white spruce, aspen, poplar and some birch. In moist sites there are black spruce and larch with Labrador Tea and horsetail. Moss dominates the understorey. Raspberries, blueberries, high-bush cranberries, soapberries and kinnikinnick are common in the forests of the Liard Plain.

One source on the natural history of the area claims a glacier tongue blocked the Kechika River somewhere below the Turnagain confluence, temporarily diverting the Kechika's flow eastward through Graveyard Lake and into the Lower Rabbit River. If you have ever paddled the low-volume Rabbit River (covered in volume one), the slippery-smooth rock walls in the Grand Canyon make a lot more sense given that information.

From 4 km downstream of Kitza Creek to the Kechika's confluence with the Liard, you encounter the liveliest water on what is by now a medium- to large-volume river. Where bedrock outcrops you get ledge rapids. All are easily runnable or can be cheated, that is, until the last one, where the Kechika drops into the Liard. Kechika Spit, so called by my good friend Tony Shaw for the fact that you are literally shot out of the Kechika's mouth, is by far the most difficult rapid on the Kechika. The rapid is made up of two channels formed by the river flowing around an island of stones. Where the wave trains converge there is a nasty reef of the cheese-grater black rock so characteristic of the Liard.

The Liard looks big and blue when you reach it. The shorelines are sandy with pointy, ragged black outcropping in places, and groves of balsam poplar. Balsam poplar predominates on the floodplains of rivers in the Liard Basin. They look like black cottonwoods, also a species of poplar, but the balsam poplar is smaller on average and is only found in BC above 56° north latitude. Balsam poplar replaces or mixes with cottonwood forests along riverbanks from the Upper Stikine River north to Atlin and east of the Rockies. The Liard River – the Rivière aux Liards, or River of Poplars – was named by the voyageurs for the many balsam poplar and cottonwood trees growing along its length.

Down on the Liard Plain the climate is subarctic. Temperatures vary extremely from summer to winter and the mean annual precipitation is 350–450 mm. The average July daytime temperature in Fireside is 22°C and this area generally has an extended summer. Clear, sunny weather makes for very warm days, but when the weather socks in you can find yourself in a cold three-day rain. Wind can be a factor when paddling in this region, especially during thunder and hailstorms. Perhaps there is a reason the Kechika was called "big windy" by the Sekani, or maybe they meant windey, as in all the twists and turns this river makes as it loops its winding way onto the Liard Plain!

For more on the ecology and natural history of the Cassiars and Liard Basin, consult The Ecoregions of British Columbia, at www.env.gov.bc.ca/ecology/ecoregions/province.html. Environment Canada's Ecological Framework at http://atlas.nrcan.gc.ca/site/english/maps/environment/ecology/framework/1, provides more detail about BC's ecological classifications. A good book about the earth's processes that created and are still working on these landscapes is British Columbia: A Natural History, by Cannings and Cannings.

Local History: ✳ ✳ ✳ The Turnagain/Kechika route lies primarily in Kaska territory, and according to the BC Geographical Names Information System (BCGNIS), their name for the Turnagain River is Guzagi K'úgé or Gacho. The meaning of the name is not given, but from what I understand, Gacho is an anglicized version of the Kaska word meaning "big." Kechika is said to mean "big windy or windy valley" in Sekani, indicating their presence in the area. The Sekani have been said to refer to the Liard as Itzehadzue, meaning "great current river," and the Kaska call the Liard Nêt'i Tué, meaning "river flowing from where the sheep are snared."

The Sekani of northeastern BC were pushed west with the coming of the fur trade and the associated Cree and Dene-thah (Slavey) migrations from the east. The Kaska claim that all of the Turnagain and Kechika rivers lie in their traditional territory, and sources indicate they didn't mind the Sekani coming into their territory after their fur-trade-related displacement. There was room for them. The Kaska are also associated with much of the length of the Kechika River. From the upper reaches of the Liard downstream of the mouth of the Kechika to at least the Toad River confluence is also traditional Kaska territory.

The Upper Turnagain and Upper Kechika seem to be the grey areas with regard to traditional First Nations territory. There is some evidence that Tahltan frequented the Turnagain's headwaters and the area around the Dall River confluence. It was likely the Tahltan and the roaming Sekani of the Cassiars that Samuel Black, the first European to travel the region, encountered on his 1824 explorations. For more information on the Tahltan and the Sekani in the area, see the Spatsizi and Upper Stikine chapters; and for further reading on the Sekani, see the Toad/Liard and Tuchodi/Muskwa Rivers chapter. (The history of the Sekani exoduses from their homelands is covered in more depth in the Omineca, Kispiox and Fort Nelson/Liard chapters in volume one of this guidebook series.)

The name Turnagain River originated with Samuel Black, an explorer and fur trader for the NWC and later the HBC after the two rival companies amalgamated. In 1824 Black was appointed to search for a fur-trade route that could connect the voyageur routes radiating from Rocky Mountain Portage House (also known as Peace River Portage House) on the Peace River to the yet untapped northwest of BC. The HBC, under the direction of George Simpson, hoped to expand the fur trade of New Caledonia north and west to block the Russians from moving inland from their base at Wrangell on the Pacific Coast near the mouth of the Stikine. Simpson instructed Black to search for the sources of Finlay's Branch (River) of the Peace River watershed and to explore the western side of the Rocky Mountains north of Fort St. James. In addition to finding the source of the Finlay, Black was directed to locate a waterway (possibly the Stikine) on which to base a fur-trade route from New Caledonia to the northwest.

There has been speculation the name Turnagain comes from the fact that upon reaching the river, Black wished the Turnagain would turn to the west and join the Stikine, and not what he began to believe, that it would keep heading north and east to join with the Liard and flow into the Mackenzie. Until Black's journals were recovered and consolidated, it was thought the river was called Turnagain because it was winding, or, as R.M. Patterson notes, because some First Nations group was thought to regard it with superstitious dread and turned back when they came to it.

Black travelled 2400 kilometres, or 1500 miles, in mostly uncharted territory via the Finlay and then overland, finally reaching the Turnagain late in the season. He turned back from the river without ever finding a west-flowing route suitable for travel and never concretely made the connection between the Turnagain and the Liard watershed. So the story that rings truest is that Black called the river Turnagain (also spelled Turn-again River according to some sources), influenced by reading about Captain Cook's experience in Alaska. On his final voyage in search of the Northwest Passage, in 1778, Cook admitted defeat and turned back south from an unknown river. Black's similar experience and his reading of Cook's journals are likely the reason the Turnagain got its English name.

It is said the fact that Black did not discover any suitable route for travelling to northwest BC from Fort St. James was a result of following Simpson's instructions too closely instead of following his own instincts. This, ironically, was against his nature. It is difficult to know how far he travelled on the Turnagain once he reached it, but had he carried on down the Turnagain Valley he would have ended up on the Kechika and perhaps connected the Liard with the Finlay via the Kechika River, Fox River and Sifton Pass, following basically the same route as the Altse Dene Tunna and Davie trails; or, had he been lucky enough to find the Kaska trail from the Turnagain over to McDame to make his way up the Dease River and over the height of land to the Stikine, he would have found his own northwest passage.

Despite his dreams, Black did not become a famous explorer like Simon Fraser, Alexander Mackenzie or David Thompson. His journals were lost for over 40 years, so he didn't even get credit for exploring the Finlay River. An NWC man by the name of John Finlay retained that honour, though he had only explored the mouth and turned back at the first difficult whitewater. For Samuel Black the Turnagain was like the Mackenzie River had been for Alexander, a "River of Disappointments."

Ironically, due to some mapping and historical errors, the Kechika, the river Samuel Black did not "discover," became known as Black's River. Then, to add to the comedy of errors, the apostrophe in the name got dropped and the Kechika became the Black River. Black even lost this incorrect namesake in the end.

Another historical and local name for the Kechika is "Muddy River." The Kaska IR across from the mouth of the Kechika carries the same name and was once home to the HBC's Mud Post. Fur traders also called the Turnagain "Little Muddy River," a common convention for naming tributaries, the Turnagain being a major tributary of the Kechika.

On the 1890 map created by R.G. McConnell, the man who officially surveyed the Liard for the Geological Survey of Canada, the whole of the Kechika is marked as Mud, Black or Turnagain River. Note that an early map even applies the name Turnagain to various portions of the Liard River. According to the BCGNIS website, on H.S. Tanner's map of North America from 1839, the section of the Liard River from the Kechika confluence downstream to its mouth at the Mackenzie is labelled "R. Turnagain or R. of the Mountains." On 1832–1852 editions of John Arrowsmith's map of British North America, that same stretch is labelled "R. au Liards or Mountain River," and a single watercourse above Finlay River, combining portions of today's Liard, Kechika and Turnagain rivers, is labelled "R. Turnagain, Itzehadzue, Great Current or Liard River." On the 1854 edition of Arrowsmith's map, the Turnagain and Kechika are labelled "Turnagain or Black River" and are shown as tributaries to the Liard.

To add to the already murky waters of original names, an 1888 map detailing the surveys of George Mercer Dawson labels the Kechika as "Mud or Black River."

Then, Inspector J.D. Moodie, of the NWMP who led an expedition to cut a trail to the Yukon, referred to the Turnagain as the "west branch of the Turnagain or Black River" in his 1897 report. On his subsequent 1898 map the Turnagain is labelled "Turnagain River," with the east branch of the Liard identified as "Kachika River" [sic]. Confusing!

Regardless of the confusion about names, it is agreed that Samuel Black was the first European to explore the source of the Finlay and to reach the banks of the Turnagain. The Sekani that Black met on the Stikine Plateau near the headwaters of the Chuckachida, a west-flowing tributary of the Upper Stikine River, had had little contact with Europeans prior to 1824, except for sporadic trading to the east at Rocky Mountain Portage House on the Peace River or at McLeod Lake. The Tahltan and Tlingit First Nations would not allow them to trade in the Pacific Basin, guarding their monopoly on trade with the interior tribes.

Some of the Sekani that Black met went with him as far as the Chuckachida River but then turned back. This was unfortunate for Black, considering they may have been able to help him find the Stikine from there, the Chuckachida being the first major tributary of the Stikine he had encountered. Perhaps they also could have told him upon reaching the Turnagain that it was a tributary of the Liard via the Kechika. It is possible that after Black's party carelessly caused a large forest fire in the region the Sekani were not so given to helping his expedition reach its goals. When Black met the Sekani again on his return trip to Fort St. James, he found they did seem particularly anxious to have a trading post established in their territory.

In his journal Black writes with praise about the contributions his First Nations guides and their wives made to his 1824 expedition. This was not all that common during the early fur-trade exploration days. He also points out that the First Nations people already knew the land he explored. Black's account of his exploration, *A Journal of a Voyage from Rocky Mountain Portage in Peace River to the Sources of Finlay's Branch and North West Ward in Summer 1824*, makes for very good on-the-river reading. R.M. Patterson also recounts Black's exploits in the region as well as Swannell's and his own in his book *Finlay's River*. See www.calverley.ca/Part 02 - Fur Trade/2–015.html for an article on Samuel Black. There is another good biographical sketch in *Thompson's Highway: British Columbia's Fur Trade, 1800–1850*, by Alan Twigg. Tony Shaw's article on his Turnagain River trip, "Doing the Turnagain: Samuel Black's Enigma," is a good read for paddlers wanting to get a sense of the river and an introduction to its place in history.

One of the first written accounts noting the Kechika River's existence came seven years after Black's journey. The location of the mouth of the river is documented in the 1831 journal of John M. McLeod, chief trader for the Hudson's Bay Company. McLeod started up the Liard River from Fort Simpson on the Mackenzie with eight other men and his dog. He was in search of the source of the Liard. On August 14, McLeod's group reached the mouth of the Dease, having passed the Kechika's mouth en route some days before. McLeod marked the Kechika down as being Black's River on his map. This would seem to be the cause of the confusion about exactly which river Black reached in his explorations and the subsequent years of multiple and interchangeable names for the Kechika and Turnagain rivers as well as the Liard. Apparently McLeod knew Black had reached the Kechika watershed because he had heard it from a local First Nations guide.

Most of the prehistoric and post-Contact evidence of the Kaska residing in the Kechika River region has been found along the river and at Graveyard Lake, lying between the Kechika and Rabbit rivers, with another significant site at Aeroplane Lake, just west of the Kechika. The Kaska often travelled overland and had an extensive array of trails in their territory. Certainly the Upper Turnagain would not be attractive to people using bark, spruce or birch and skin-covered canoes.

The archaeological record suggests small Kaska groups travelled to hunting, fishing and trapping camps in a seasonal pattern via a trail network across the Liard Plain and the uplands to the south. The east/west trails cut across the drainage grain parallel to the Liard about midway between the river and the mountains. Along with trails on both sides of the Liard, these midway trails linked the Liard Basin with the upland lakes and passes from one headwater of the northerly draining tributaries of the Liard River to the next. Confluences were key sites in the annual round and the trails along rivers and streams dissecting the region were used for hunting and to pursue beaver trapping. Camping and cache sites are recorded at the confluences of the Turnagain with the Kechika and the Kechika with the Liard.

Fort Halkett, founded in 1829, became the first fur-trading post for the Kaska in the region. Though first located at the confluence of the Trout River with the Liard, the second and more important Fort Halkett, established by John M. McLeod in 1832, was built at the confluence of the Smith and Liard rivers.

Trading was brisk at Fort Halkett in the first few seasons and Kaska culture underwent extensive changes in a short period of time in order to maximize this economic opportunity. It is thought that once the fur trade became established the Kaska moved from spending most of their time subsistence living from their upland and mid-elevation camps, where there was better access to big game other than moose, to using lakeside central base camps in lower elevations. Beaver and other fur-bearing animals were far more abundant there and moving to the lakes of the Liard Basin put the Kaska closer to Fort Halkett.

The Kaska began to spend most of the winter and spring trapping and preparing furs for trade with the HBC. Fishing lakes became more important, as the Kaska no longer frequented the highlands for hunting like they used to. Only later, when they began using dogs and horses (introduced later in the 1800s), were the Kaska able to access the higher elevations again for meat. They could bring it back to the lower-elevation base camps more efficiently and still have the time to participate in the fur trade.

HBC records show a decline in both the quality and quantity of furs coming in to Fort Halkett after about five years of trading. Subsequently, the fort was kept open only sporadically after 1850. The HBC eventually abandoned the middle Liard River as a trade artery in 1865, owing to changes in policy and not in small part to the difficulties encountered in persuading guides and employees to navigate the dangerous waters of the river. Few if any voyageurs ever signed on for another two-year contract on the middle Liard, mainly because of the horrendous portages and cataracts and great current of its Grand Canyon section. For more information and reading on the Kaska in northern BC and the history of the Liard River, see the Toad/Liard Rivers chapter and the References section.

The Kaska, whose annual rounds included the Turnagain and Kechika drainage, eventually did most of their trading at Lower Post, which was connected via the Dease and Stikine rivers to the coast and also to Fort Ware on the Finlay River via the Altse Dene Tunna and Davie trails. However, for a short period there was a trading post on the Turnagain just upstream of its confluence with the Kechika. It was established in 1886 by none other than Rufus Sylvester, who had already built two posts in the Cassiar, one at McDame and another at Lower Post. Eventually selling both the latter posts to the HBC, he also sold the post on the Turnagain to the HBC in 1888.

The confluence of the Turnagain is littered with archaeological sites showing the Kaska's use of this area. The Kechika is an easy river to navigate compared to others in the northern Rockies. But as the Kaska normally chose to walk rather than line or pole a canoe or moosehide boat upstream, there was a trail that ascended the Kechika from near its mouth on the Liard and then up the Turnagain. We found evidence of an old summer campsite (no stumps indicating snow camping) with teepee or tent poles on the Lower Kechika on river right and a trail running along the river. The campsite is not on the Davie Trail according to the map, so it is likely on the trail to the Upper Kechika and Turnagain. Inspector Moodie, on his 1897 trail-blazing expedition to the Yukon, followed a Kaska trail up the Kechika and then up the Turnagain and over to McDame. This trail connected the Kaska of the Dease River area to the Kaska of the Turnagain watershed.

The Kaska of Lower Post and the McDame/Good Hope Lake area belong to the Kaska Dena Council of BC, as does the Kwadacha band at Fort Ware on Williston Lake. Long before the existence of the Davie Trail, a route mainly travelled by parties on horses, there was a foot trail connecting the Kaska in the Liard River Valley and Dease River regions to the Kwadacha Kaska and Sekani groups living in the Finlay River area. The name of the trail in Kaska is Altse Dene Tunna. Eventually, after the Kaska began to settle at Lower Post, the main trail ended there, connecting the Kaska north and south.

The BC Parks website history notes on the Kechika mention that the Davie Trail got its European name in the 1800s from "Old Davie," a highly regarded

First Nations prophet. Davie is said to have been able to understand and translate the Europeans' language when they first arrived. This is not so surprising given an ethnography by Jenness which notes that Davie was the son of a French-Canadian trapper and a Sekani woman from Finlay River area. He married a Sekani woman from the Upper Fox and Kechika rivers region and thus Davie obtained the hunting rights to the area, inherited from a recently dissolved kindred band. His band was called Otzane and eventually some Kaska from Lower Post also became part of the band. The connections between the prophet called Davie, the Davie Trail and this material recorded in 1937 are intriguing, especially given the Davie Trail's location. It suggests that Old Davie was likely the namesake of the horse trail and that indeed the Sekani were resident in the upper and middle Kechika River Valley after the fur-trade-induced migrations.

The Altse Dene Tunna, before the creation of Williston Lake, followed the Finlay River Valley, then went north up the Fox River Valley to Sifton Pass. The Davie Trail now starts at Fort Ware and from Sifton Pass it reaches the Gataga River and then follows the Kechika for a significant stretch. The trail crosses the Gataga and Kechika canoe route in a number of places as indicated on the topo maps. Note, however, that the summer trail is actually much higher up along the ridges of the valleys than is shown on the map. The maps show the winter route, too low and swampy for easily travel in the summer. At present it is mostly hunting outfitters using the trail and mainly the section that runs along the Gataga and Kechika rivers to Lower Post. Apparently the Kaska First Nations are interested in developing the entire length of the Davie Trail for tourism.

After the fur trade was diverted in 1865, the middle Liard country was quiet again until gold was found in the Klondike. Ferdi Wenger's book about his travels on the Liard River, *Wild Liard Waters*, is a must read for your journey. Wenger integrates historical accounts of the hardships of the explorers John McLeod, Robert Campbell and R.G. McConnell and the voyageurs and Klondikers to compare and contrast his parties' experience of the Liard in the 1970s. Robert Campbell, one of the first Europeans to ascend the Liard, may also have explored up the Kechika some ways. Kitza Creek is named after one of his two Iroquois guides from the east.

On a tough day on the river I often reflect how difficult such travel was in the past, especially on such a river as the Liard. The Liard was also known as the Great Current River in the early exploration days and after you ferry across from the mouth of the Kechika to where Mud Post used to be, you will understand what an accomplishment it was to travel the Liard. Imagine paddling upstream from Fort Simpson to Fort Halkett through the Grand Canyon (Liard)! Many voyageurs and prospectors lost their lives.

On my Turnagain trip in 2005, I paddled with five friends, Liana Nolan, Greg Harling, Blair Richardson, Sheila Achilles and Bruce Reeder. I was astonished to find out that Bruce's great-grandfather, William McAusland, had been one of the

Klondikers that made his way up the all-Canadian route to the Yukon via the Liard River and survived to tell the tale.

The Altse Dene Tunna/Davie Trail was also a route to the Klondike. A number of prospectors still looking for gold in the Omineca used the trail to get to the Yukon goldfields. I've read that, of the main "all-Canadian" routes, this one was the easiest to travel.

Another "all-Canadian" route that involves the rivers in this chapter was the Police Trail, later referred to as the Old Moodie Trail. Running from the Peace River to the goldfields, it followed the southern part of the Davie Trail and then branched off to go north via the trail up the Turnagain and over to McDame, then to Teslin Lake via other First Nations trails. The project began in 1897 and was undertaken by the North-West Mounted Police (NWMP) with the goal of making it easier to police the vast lands of northern BC and the Yukon during the Klondike. Inspector Moodie led the first attempt to cut and blaze the trail, but it was never completed.

In 1900, a drive of 500–600 head of cattle was undertaken from Vanderhoof (near Fort St. James) to the Klondike via the Davie Trail. Following that epic journey there was a renewed attempt in 1905 to develop a decent overland trail to the Yukon. This second Police Trail followed a different route, joining up with the Telegraph Trail. After 1200 kilometres, or 750 miles, of trail were cut and blazed, the BC government decided in 1907 that it didn't want to share the cost of the project anymore and this trail too sank into oblivion.

The Stikine, Omineca, Cassiar and Klondike gold rushes brought many prospectors and changes to northwestern BC, but significant gold discoveries did not occur along the Turnagain until 1932. Then, in 1936 and 1937, Alice and Vern Shea found the motherlode creek: Alice Shea Creek, a tributary of Wheaton Creek, the south-flowing tributary of the Turnagain that comes in just downstream of Boulder City Lake. While prospecting this small stream with her husband in 1936, Alice stumbled across the first of a number of large gold nuggets. This initial find weighed in at 15 ounces. Three weeks later Vern Shea found nuggets of ten ounces and two ounces. Though reports differ, the BCGNIS website indicates that in the summer of 1937 it was Vern Shea, not his wife as other sources state, who picked up the largest nugget ever found in Alice Shea Creek, weighing 52¾ ounces and about 20 cm long. The gold nugget, the fifth largest ever found in BC, was purchased that year by the British Columbia government for $1,500, or about $22,000 today. The story goes that all the gold nuggets were found in plain sight and within a mile of each other on the creek.

After the Kaska population became more centralized during the heyday of the fur trade and the gold rushes, the next massive change to their lives came with the building of the Alaska Highway in 1942. The northern Rocky Mountain Trench, home of the Kechika River, was one of the routes considered for the highway. The road brought even more contact with Euro-American culture and further concentrated families in places like Lower Post and Watson Lake. The Kaska Tribal Council today is working to deal with the consequences of these cultural changes and of industrial development in their homelands.

In the fall of 2004, a letter of understanding was signed by the Kaska and the Yukon and BC chapters of the Canadian Parks & Wilderness Society to formalize their long-standing relationship with regard to conservation in Kaska traditional territory. This historic document is the beginning of a protocol agreement to ensure that special environmental and cultural values of the Kaska's traditional territory are respected, protected, preserved and maintained and that conservation priorities are supported during upcoming resource planning, among other goals. Hopefully, the Turnagain and Kechika rivers will benefit from this initiative in the future.

At present there are no parks protecting the Turnagain River proper, but one of its tributaries, the Dall River from Dall Lake, is one of the highlights of Denetiah Provincial Park. This park and one other, Dune Za Keyih Provincial Park, protects a stretch of the Kechika upstream of its confluence with the Turnagain. That's it for park protection for this canoe route. These parks are part of the Muskwa–Kechika Management Area (MKMA), but the MKMA itself remains the only avenue for conserving the Turnagain and Lower Kechika rivers. However, much of MKMA is open for resource development, including roadbuilding and hydroelectric projects. Only park status prohibits these kinds of activities.

The creation of MKMA began as a result of a meeting between George Smith (CPAWS) and Wayne Sawchuk (Chetwynd Environmental Society), both of whom had been working independently within their organizations to protect the Northern Rockies. The meeting led to an alliance among some 20 groups from all over the northern region. The alliance brought their ideas to the land-use planning tables for the Fort Nelson, Fort St. John and Mackenzie land districts, along with the usual stakeholders representing tourism, First Nations, local and provincial governments, communities and resource interests. The result was the 1998 establishment of the MKMA, a vast, 6.4-million-hectare area that includes over one million hectares of provincial parks.

This new conservation model features core parks and protected areas within large buffer zones of legislated special management areas. The Special Management Zones (SNZS) are open to development but the development is supposed to be done in a way that is sensitive to environmental qualities, including wildlife and their habitats.

Interestingly, information about access routes into the MKMA is limited by the BC government decision to promote only 13 access routes, to be shared by motorized and non-motorized visitors alike; other "routes, trails, campsite and airstrips will be unmapped and unadvertised." According to Larry Pynn in his 2002 article on the High Trail, the official argument is that concentrating vehicles along certain routes and minimizing use of other trails helps keep the northern Rockies wild. I have often wondered why the BC government has not promoted the many canoe routes in northern BC and I am not the only one coming to the conclusion that someone wants backcountry users to stay on the beaten paths in BC. Why? In whose interest might that be?

The MKMA is funded by the provincial government. The funds are directed toward research, monitoring and promotion and support for the Muskwa–Kechika Advisory Board. The board has representatives from various stakeholders in the MKMA who advise on natural resource management with regard to upholding the purpose of the MKMA. The legislated mandate of the MKMA is "to maintain in perpetuity the wilderness quality, and the diversity and abundance of wildlife and the ecosystems on which it depends, while allowing resource development and use in the parts of the Muskwa–Kechika Management Area designated for those purposes."

Unfortunately, although the MKMA is a creature of legislation, it is still subject to the whim of the government of the day for its funding and direction. Funding has been reduced significantly over the years since the creation of the MKMA. Timelines for planning and implementing agreed-upon goals have also been reduced. Wayne Sawchuk, CPAWS and their partners continue to push for full implementation of the management plan, and the struggle for conservation of this area is far from over. For more information on the MKMA, see www.Muskwa-Kechika.com; www.spacesfornature.org/greatspaces/muskwa.html; and www.roundriver.org (click on Where We Work, then Canada/Muskwa Kechika/Reports & Publications).

Sawchuk has also produced a great coffee-table book featuring the Muskwa–Kechika Protected Area's history, structure and goals and its amazing scenery. *Muskwa–Kechika: The Wild Heart of Canada's Northern Rockies* is a must-read for canoeists wanting to paddle rivers in the MKMA. Another good book that's sure to get your conservation juices flowing is Karsten Heuer's *Walking the Big Wild: From Yellowstone to the Yukon on the Grizzly Bears' Trail*. Heuer hiked through the Muskwa–Kechika on his way from Yellowstone National Park to the Yukon and the book highlights the marvel that is this area. Information on the Y2Y initiative promoted by Heuer's hike, a cross-border conservation project that complements the work of the MKMA, can be found at www.y2y.net.

Hikers considering making a long journey in the MKMA should be well prepared. In August 2008 a hiker went missing and is presumed to have drowned. According to an article by reporter Larry Pynn of the *Vancouver Sun*, a 43-year-old German hiker attempted a 40-day solo trek from the Tuchodi Lakes to Frog Lake, 150 km to the west. He was not carrying a communications device, and when he didn't make his rendezvous with his charter floatplane pickup, searchers were sent out. His last camp was found at the confluence of the South Gataga River with the Gataga River. A small dry bag with his wallet, maps and passport was found on the Gataga and his backpack was found 90 km downstream near the lodge at Terminus Mountain on the Kechika River. It is likely the hiker drowned crossing the Gataga River, but no one will know for sure.

The MKMA does not include the headwaters of the Turnagain, as its boundary lies downstream of Boulder City Lake. This is not surprising given the mining exploration activity along the Upper Turnagain and the placer gold and copper mine at the lake. Jade is king in the region, being extracted from the Greenrock and Polar Jade mines to the north of the Turnagain and from Provencher Lake, King Mountain and Letain, Wheaton and Kutcho creeks to the south. There is a large concentration of jade mines along and around Kutcho Creek's headwaters, but the area was also extensively explored in the 1980s for copper, zinc, silver and gold. Mining is definitely one of the present and future concerns for the watershed.

The Kechika is the largest remaining undisturbed watershed in the province of BC, but it hardly has any protection. In 1996 it was designated a BC Heritage River for its outstanding ecological and "wilderness" recreation values, but essentially this does little to protect a river from development. To date there is not even a management plan in place.

Though there has been relatively little forestry activity in the Liard Basin so far, there is likely to be more in the future. In fact, I've heard rumours that there is some push from the forestry industry associated with Mackenzie, a community at the south end of Williston Lake, for a road from Fort Ware north to the Alaska Highway, 325 km up the northern Rocky Mountain Trench. It would likely follow the Davie Trail route. There is a significant history of mineral exploration based on extensive documented mineralization, including lead and zinc deposits on the west slope of the Rockies that may become more attractive to develop should a road be in the works. The headwaters of the Kechika are not protected in any way, except perhaps under the provincial heritage river designation, but that remains to be seen.

In the 1980s the Liard River was in danger of being dammed for hydroelectric power. Studies were already in the works by the 1970s. The plans included damming the Liard at Devil's Gorge, which would have flooded the Kechika's lower reaches, perhaps impacting the river as far up as the Turnagain confluence. This catastrophe was averted by a decision in 1986 to forgo the project for at least a 20-year period. This period ended in 2006 and the Liard may again be being considered for hydro development as you read this, although I have heard nothing along this vein as yet. Likely it won't happen in the Grand Canyon of the Liard, as the canyon and a significant portion of the river are protected by the large Liard River Corridor Provincial Park & Protected Area, designated in 1997. Ferdi Wenger's book *Wild Liard Waters*, beyond being an excellent read and source of history about the Liard, points out the damage a dam would cause on this amazing waterway.

Besides Wenger's book, Samuel Black's journals and Patterson's *Finlay's River*, you might consider the following books for some on-the-river reading. Jack Boudreau's *Wild & Free: The Story of Frank Cooke and Skook Davidson* is about two outfitters in the Turnagain/Kechika drainage. Skook's Landing is named for John Ogilvie "Skookum" Davidson and it was the staging point for his ranch/outfitting camps at Terminus Mountain and Scoop Lake. Skook Davidson was a legendary packer, surveyor and eventually big-game outfitter in the Kechika River Valley, with his headquarters at a lodge at the base of Terminus Mountain. He started his camp there in 1939 and cabins from that era still stand. Cooke bought his guiding area from Skook and had his main camp at Scoop Lake. *Wild & Free* has lots of stories about events in the Kechika region, including accounts of numerous UFO sightings.

Edward Hoagland's *Notes from the Century Before* also recounts Skook's life and times in the Kechika River Valley. *The Headless Valley*, by Sir Ranulph Fiennes, describes a river-based exploration of the Rocky Mountain Trench, including the Kechika, as part of a 1970s north/south traverse of the province.

Level of Solitude: * * * on the Turnagain and *** *** below the falls and on the Kechika. The Turnagain/Kechika is a remote river trip, but it does not have quite the level of solitude you would expect in such a wild land. There are modern distractions along it such as mining activity, lodges, cabins and jet boats. That said, the route won't be crowded with canoeing or rafting parties by any means!

The mining on the upper reaches of the Turnagain will make the biggest impact on the canoeist's sensibility. You will see exploration activity along the river near Three Kettle Lake, where the Boulder City mine road follows the river left bank. Then the mine is very obvious on Boulder City Lake. There are three lodges (the first you encounter is on Turnagain Lake) and a significant number of cabins along the route, but these are just minor blips in the "out there" experience. Jet boats, seen mainly on the Kechika section of the trip during hunting season, are harder to ignore.

We didn't see any other canoeing parties on either the Turnagain or the Kechika in 2005 and neither did Tony Shaw in 1999. We did see a fishing party below Turnagain Falls. A couple of commercial rafting companies have run the Turnagain since 1996, but I think only one is still advertising it. Rafters often run the river earlier in the season rather than later to have enough water to run their big boats through the rocky rapids, and they usually take out at Turnagain Falls. There are a number of relatively established campsites along the way, indicating that hunters and paddlers travel these rivers with some consistency. The Kechika is well travelled compared to the Turnagain, and you may even bump into a canoeing or rafting party coming down from running the Gataga. All in all, though, this route provides the solitude and "back to nature" experience most canoeists are looking for.

Wildlife: * * * for the Turnagain and *** *** for the Kechika. You are likely to see many of the large mammal species characteristic of the Cassiars and the Liard Plain on this route, including grizzly and black bear, moose, woodland caribou, mountain goat, Stone sheep, mule deer, wolf, lynx and wolverine. The Upper Turnagain's lodgepole forest with lichen understorey provides excellent habitat for caribou in the winter. They can paw and nuzzle through the snow to get at the lichen. You can also see many smaller fur-bearing creatures. These species include beaver, marten, fisher, muskrat, mink, otter, red fox, coyote, hoary marmot, Arctic ground squirrel and snowshoe hare.

We saw lots of moose on the Upper Turnagain and heard wolves howling on our second night on the river. Our most exciting mammal sighting was a mountain goat in the canyon while we were exploring the portage trails. It was standing looking at us from across the deep chasm filled with churning Class 5+ whitewater. It was on the very lip of a crumbly rock cliff and looking very cool about it! We saw a grizzly on the Kechika in 2004 and Tony saw elk in 1999. Note that the elk you may see along the Kechika section of the route are transplants and not Rocky Mountain elk. They are actually Manitoba elk, introduced into the Kechika River Valley in 1984. We also saw otters, beavers and a couple of minks.

Notable bird species in the Cassiars include gyrfalcon and peregrine falcon, bald and golden eagle, raven, willow ptarmigan, least sandpiper, red-necked phalarope, snow bunting and Smith's longspur. There are many boreal songbirds in the forest, and osprey, kingfishers, swallows, gulls and Arctic terns wheel over the river. Both the Turnagain and Kechika rivers host large waterfowl populations. I enjoyed seeing the harlequin ducks and mergansers bobbing around in the rapids! Canada geese can be seen grazing on the riverbanks. Loons are common on the small lakes. On the Kechika we saw a great horned owl and many hawks.

The Rocky Mountain Trench is an important migration corridor for many bird species, especially waterfowl, and the Liard River Valley functions as a migration corridor for many raptors and passerines. As you approach the Liard River, you may also see tundra swans, trumpeter swans and sandhill cranes on their way south for the winter.

Don't be too disappointed if you don't see lots of wildlife on the trip. You'll still have an opportunity on your travels. The section of the Alaska Highway between Fireside and the eastern border of Stone Mountain Provincial Park provides the best wildlife-viewing potential in Canada, in my experience! Stone sheep, caribou, bears and moose are often just standing beside the highway, or even on it – particularly the bison that hang out near the Liard Hot Springs!

Fishing: ✳ ✳ ✳ ½ for the Turnagain and ✳ ✳ ½ for the Kechika. The Turnagain is the best fishing river in this volume of the guidebook series. It can't be beat for rainbow trout and Arctic grayling fishing. Angling for bull trout (known locally as Dolly Varden trout) can also be fast-paced. And the fish are big! The fishing party we met at the bottom of Turnagain Falls said they caught a lake trout just downriver from our camp, so you may be able to sample quite a variety of finned treats on this route. On the Kechika there are also Arctic grayling and bull trout to be had.

Rainbow trout and grayling can be caught with flies or tiny spinners in clear creeks. They are found where there is fast water, eddies, deep pools with debris in them to hide in and where tributaries flow into the rivers. Bull and lake trout like spinners and spoons and they are often caught in eddies and deep pools, striking at anything moving and shiny. They also hang around the mouths of creeks and larger tributaries where clearer water mixes with the main flow of the rivers. Always be conservative with your catch. Grayling and bull trout stocks are declining in many watersheds in northern BC.

Camping, Hiking and Other Activities: ✱ ✱ ✱ Camping spots are generally good and plentiful on this route, except on a few stretches on the Turnagain and then on the lower reaches of the Kechika. They are pointed out in the Trip Notes. Plan your days carefully for the first part of your trip, especially in regard to where you are going to camp before and after The Big Three. I suggest you only take on 13 km the day you run and line these. Camp at the last site before The Big Three, at GR 239079, a nice island camp, and then end your day at the forest campsite we called Rainbow Camp at the mouth of "Sam's Creek," GR 338030. On the latter part of the river and on the Kechika there are plenty of large gravel bars to camp on and even some nice sites in the forest. There are a significant number of "established" campsites, including a rudimentary one at the put-in at the north end of Turnagain Lake, at Kutcho Creek and "Sam's Creek," but on the Kechika most of them are hunter's campsites. You may want to give them a miss because of potential bear activity. Driftwood is plentiful on the gravel bars, and dead, dry lodgepole pine is all around in the forest.

Alpine or ridge hiking is possible at points along the route. Paddlers have hiked to the alpine from Turnagain Lake. There is a horse trail at the put-in, but I don't know where it leads. If you plan on exploring it and heading up into the alpine, you will have to have some extra time – along with 1:50 000-scale maps, a compass and the ability to use them. You can also access the alpine from the camping spot at the mouth of "Sam's Creek."

The effort to get to the alpine from the Turnagain may be more than many paddlers are willing to take on, considering they are likely faced with a heck of a hike on the falls portage! However, hiking the grassy slopes and ridges along the Kechika is not difficult. The Davie Trail also provides a less strenuous option for stretching your legs. It crosses the Kechika for the last time just down from the confluence of the Turnagain with the Kechika, striking off northwest to Lower Post. The Davie Trail is marked on both scales of NTS topo maps.

If you are interested in travelling the alpine or Davie Trail more extensively, consider a horse trek with an outfitter in the area. Look in the Directory of Services and Organizations for contact information.

Swimming at the put-in on Turnagain Lake is pleasant in August and the Kechika on a hot afternoon is okay. You must soak in the Liard Hot Springs after your trip. It is only about 70 km east of Skook's Landing and on your way back to Muncho Lake. You will feel like a million dollars in those pools, I guarantee it!

Special Equipment: The Turnagain has many boat-wrecking rapids. You will need a plastic canoe suitable for running Class 2+ whitewater and carrying enough food and gear for a long, remote trip. I would take longer painters than you might normally, as you will likely be lining around large boulders. You will want a spray deck for your canoe as well, particularly if the water is up. You will wish you had one in The Big Three (you may really need one for #2 if the water is up!), the rapid below "Sam's Creek" (a.k.a. Shadow of Big Three) and Kechika Spit. Flotation bags in the bow and stern are recommended.

A comfortable, padded yoke is necessary for the portage around the falls. You will also want to be parsimonious with how much gear you bring, the kinds of food you pack and what you pack it in. You will want to do the carry in two trips maximum.

A pin/wrap kit is compulsory on this kind of river. The basic equipment for the kit should include two pulleys, two locking carabiners, two prusiks, a 6-m piece of tubular webbing for an anchor, and a throw bag (one for each boat is required). If you don't know how to set up a z-drag, you should reconsider paddling the Turnagain. Strong river rescue skills are required.

You will want a water filter because "beaver fever" is always a possibility. Additionally, the Lower Kechika is so silty you will want to bring water containers for collecting clear water from the many creeks that flow into the river. This will save you cleaning your water filter every couple of litres!

You will need a compass and to know how to use it if you plan on some major hiking. A GPS is great, but always have a backup for electronic technology.

The blackflies and mosquitoes can be ferocious in the plateau headwaters. The portage will be a nightmare if you are not prepared. You will likely be camping in the forest at some point and the Liard Plain too is notorious for insect activity. Take a hooded bug jacket with a face net and insect repellent with loads of DEET.

You may want to consider carrying pepper spray and/or an air horn to deal with possible bear encounters.

Trip Notes:

MAP NO.	GRID REF.	FEATURE	DESCRIPTION
104 1/6	906603	Put-in option; Lodge	Turnagain Lake Lodge sits on the eastern shore of Turnagain Lake. You should get permission to unload at their dock.
	903628	Put-in; Camping; Hiking	Bruce of BC–Yukon Air will drop you at the very north end of Turnagain Lake. It's a pretty tight spot, but this guy is good!
			There is a small spot to camp by the horse trail on the hill. The site has been used before and is not great, but the view is.

You can hike around the plateau from here on the horse trails or bushwhack straight up to the alpine on the west side of the lake.

904627	**Beaver dam**	The Turnagain is a creek at the outlet of the lake. You will have to pull over a beaver dam to start your river trip and then a number more before you are out of the headwater puddles. We pulled over at least seven dams in 2005.
906646	**Camping**	It looks like you could make camp up on the treed bank at the very northeast end of the small, unnamed lake.

Now you are on a creek run. Expect constant, technical riffles and be especially vigilant about logjams and other wood hazards.

903665	**Camping**	On RL, on the inside of the turn, there is a small gravel bar to camp on.
898678	**Camping**	On RR there is another small gravel bar for camping.
897680	**Logjam**	**Caution**: in 2005 there was a river-wide logjam here we had to pull over. Approach carefully!
898681	**Camping**	On RL after the logjam there is a gravel bar you can camp on.
897682	**Logjam**	**Caution**: in 2005 there was another bad logjam here that was basically river-wide. We lined it on RL. Be cautious on your approach.

After the riffle at the corner you can go either way around the island.

You will see the mining road to Boulder City Lake in places from here to where it crosses the Turnagain.

904725	**Camping**	On RL there is a gravel bar to camp on by the mouth of the creek coming from the tiny lake.
906725	**Camping**	Just downstream at the mouth of Little Greenrock Creek is another gravel bar camping site.
912728	**Riffles**	**Class 1+** riffles and chutes take you into Three Kettle Lake.
922732	**Campsite**	There is a hunting campsite at the northeast end of Three Kettle Lake. We saw tent poles there. You may want to give it a miss if you are concerned about bear activity.
923725	**Camping**	Try this spot on the spit to the south for an esker camp.
924728	**Riffles**	**Class 1+** riffles take you downriver from Three Kettle Lake past Greenrock Creek and into an S-bend rapid. The riffles continue to just before the cabin on RL.

	944736	Cabin	There's a trapper's cabin on RL.
	953735	Road access	This is where the road to the Boulder City Lake mine crosses the river. If you put in here it takes 20-some km off your trip but adds many hours to your shuttle!
	954735	Riffles	There are **Class 1/1+** riffles for 200 m after the road crossing.
	980737	Mine	Nothing like a big mine to ruin a very pretty little lake. The mine is on the south shore of Boulder City Lake.
	990743	Campsite	There is a hunting campsite on RR as you leave the lake. I'd say bears are likely here, and given the mine is right down the way, this is not a site of choice. There is a nice natural site downriver about 500 m.
	993744	Cabin	Up on the bank on RR is a cabin that looks well used.
	998749	Camping	Up on the RL esker there is a nice spot to camp. You will see a trail up to the top of the bank. Access up to the site is steep, but there is a great view of Mount Shea, likely named for Vern and/or Alice Shea, the prospecting couple who found a huge gold nugget up a feeder stream of Wheaton Creek.
			We could hear the mine generator until 6:00 p.m. here and then all that broke the silence was a pack of wolves howling! We thought it a great place to spend the night.
104 1/7	008750	Camping	On RR there is a small camping spot on a gravel bar at the mouth of Bobner Creek.
	009751	Riffles	**Class 1/1+** riffles take you through a recently burned area and into the unnamed lake. Moose were thick here in 2005.
	053770	Rapids	Now the Turnagain is more of a river than a creek. However, this set is a shallow **Class 1+** technical rock garden, similar to what you've already encountered – just with a bit more volume.
			After the island there are similar Class 1+ stretches up to the Hard Creek outlet on RR, where you will again see evidence of mining activity along the Upper Turnagain. There was even a sign by the river in 2005 announcing that this was an active mineral exploration area.
	074788	Riffles	After the exploration sign there are more easy riffles to run around the islands up to GR 075789.

087805	**Exploration camp**	In 2005 there was an exploration camp on RL. Following the camp there are easy riffles that flow into an S-bend rapid.
094813	**Rapid**	Where the elevation line crosses the river on the map there is a fun **Class 1+** s-bend rapid. It ends near the rock outcrop on RL.
102815	**Rapids**	These rapids begin with a **Class 1+** set as you approach the dogleg turn to the left. The next set at the sharp corner rapid is **Class 2** with a big rock on RR. Stay RL to the inside of the turn. You can eddy out RL after the Class 1+ set to scout the Class 2 dogleg chute.
		Following the dogleg rapid you will encounter riffles up to Class 1+ rapids on and off all the way to Set the Tone Rapids, the first significant drop on the Turnagain.
108829	**Camping**	A nice little camp can be made on the foot of the island.
110834	**Rapid**	**Set the Tone**, aptly named by Tony Shaw's group, as it is the first of the significant rapids and previews the fun to come, is **Class 2+/3−**. It is probably a harder run at lower water, as the line would be tighter.
		You will want to scout from RR. As you approach the bend in the river to the left, where you can see the river is narrowing and dropping, eddy out on RR on the gravel shore against the high bank. Eddying out sooner is better than later!
		There is a rough trail traversing the steep bank. Follow it until you can see the whole rapid. Set the Tone is a short drop with boulders up top,
		standing waves and a stopper wave of note near the end to avoid. The line is RR of RC moving to RL to miss the stopper.

104
1/10

There is a gorgeous waterfall, Evelyn Falls, set back on RL about 200 m downstream of Set the Tone. Following it is a pretty gorge with calm water, which is surprising given the topography.

Note: If you want to run the rapids marked on this 1:50 000 topo when you are fresh, camp at Kutcho Creek. There is only one good spot a few kilometres down from it, and then not another one for about 24 km. There are lots of rapids in between Kutcho and there. Kutcho Creek adds significantly to the volume of the Turnagain.

145859	**Camping;** **Fishing;** **Hiking**	There is a good spot to camp on the upstream side of Kutcho Creek, which flows in on RR. The campsite is in the forest and not obvious from the river. Land at the forested bank upstream of the creek mouth. You pull your boats up into the trees here and head up the short path to the kitchen area by the creek. There is fishing potential along Kutcho and at its outflow. You can also stretch your legs after dinner up the mining track.
146867	**Rapids**	The four sets of hatch marks on the topo quite accurately represent the location and length of the rapids to come. All four sets are **Class 1+ to Class 2** rock gardens. The last major set ends at GR 136884, but riffles up to Class 1+ continue sporadically all the way to the next rapids of note, at GR 154996.
133905	**Camping**	A small camp can be made on RL on the downstream gravel bar at the mouth of the unnamed creek. **Note:** This is the last good spot to camp, that I am aware of, for about 24 km.
154995	**Rapid**	There is a **Class 2** rapid with large boulders on RR to avoid.
160020	**Rapids**	There is a **Class 1+/2−** boulder garden for about 200 m. There are riffles on pretty much every corner to follow, right up to the next significant rapid.
193068	**Camping**	On RL on the gravel bar just downstream of the unnamed creek is a small camping spot.
195071	**Camping**	There is another camping spot about 400 m downstream on RL. There is a beach to land on and we found evidence of previous occupancy. I think some rafters built a sauna here.
196073	**Rapid**	Just after the camping spot is a short, **Class 1+** rock garden, and then there are riffles around the islands.
211073	**Rapid**	There is a **Class 1+** ledge on RR easily avoided by staying RL. The Turnagain River Valley begins to narrow here and the peaks get higher. You are now paddling through the last of the Stikine Ranges. The Big Three are coming up! Your last chance to camp before them is 3 km downstream, just after the **Class 1+** riffle around the island.

| 239079 | Camping; Rapids | On the foot of the long, narrow island in the bend in the river is a nice camping site that has obviously been used in the past. The landing is best approached from the RL channel. You run through a **Class 1+** wavy riffle to pull up on the sandy gravel bar. There are nice views of the cliff on RL and the mountains downstream. |

This is your last chance to camp before running The Big Three. There are no good sites before or in between these significant rapids, that I am aware of. It will take you a good day of scouting, paddling and lining to go the next 13 km. Don't rush this stretch of river.

| 246067 | Rapids | For a warm-up run, there is 400 m of **Class 2–/2** rock dodging. |

| 248066 257055 | Rapids | **Big Three #1** starts just before the first of four hatch marks on the topo. In the next 1500 m or so there are several sets of boat-wrecking rapids, the first being the most challenging. |

The rapids start as a steep boulder garden that is very busy at the beginning. You must get out on RL before the start of the rapids to scout. The boulders are all different sizes (some are very large!) and often rounded. The chutes between them do not line up well, making the top of the drop a **Class 3/3+**. You can line this top section from RL, as Tony's group did. If the water is up, there is a really tight line on far RL that we ran. Do not attempt to run the first

part of Big Three #1 if you are at all unsure about the line or being able to paddle it. The consequences to your boat and body are too great. You need both for the rest of this long, challenging trip!

After running this first set, we made a move off to RR and stopped to scout the next set from the RR shore. The rapids get easier farther down, averaging **Class 2+ and ending as Class 2–**.

From start to finish, you need to pick your way down this long stretch of rapids by eddy-hopping. Get out and scout when you come to the bends.

270050	**Rapids**	**Big Three #2** has a different nature than #1 or #3. It is not marked on the map at all, but there are two distinct sets of rapids, a **Class 2-/2** and a **Class 3**. Where the river widens before the creek coming in on RR you will encounter a rocky, shallow **Class 2-/2** rapid about 150 m upstream of a shoal in RC (there may be a channel around it on both sides or only on RR, depending on water levels). Ahead of you the horizon line drops away and you know there is something big down there!

Once through the first set, get out as soon as you can on RL to scout the second, much meatier set at GR 272050. If you decide to run it you will likely have to run the RR channel around the shoal in RC. It has the most water and you will want to be able to get over there. Landing on RR did not look possible, however.

The RR channel swoops in front of a rock face before the big drop. You will need to get set up to run the inside of that turn, staying as far to the left as possible. Then, as soon as you can, you must get over even farther left to run the final part of the big drop down or just on the edge of the wave train on RL. It's a biggie and you'll be happy you have a skirt.

The big drop has some huge boulders and big holes on RR and large, swamping waves on RL. Lines RR of RC have more consequences if you miss them than those RL. The line we ran was the **Class 3** RL wave train. You may be able to miss some of the wave train by staying farther RC; it depends on the water levels. Success for us depended on getting over to RL to head straight down the wave train. That was not easy, as there was not much water in the RR channel around the shoal above. The current was really fast, too. I think you may be able to line along the rocky RL shore and then only run the wave train. If you decide to carry around this drop, your best option is a bushwhack portage on RL. A creek comes in mid-channel on RR, making it appear to not be as good an option.

277047	**Rapids**	About 550 m downstream from Big Three #2 is a **Class 2+** rapid on the bend to the right. It is a 125 m rock/boulder dodge with some good-sized waves.

Note: Riffles continue from the end of this set to the start of Big Three #3. Be ready to eddy out on RR at the top of this last, steep boulder garden.

104 1/9	302040	Rapids

Big Three #3 starts just upstream of the ten hash marks indicating its location on the topo. Like #1, this is a real **Class 3/3+** boat wrecker of an S-bend, boulder-garden run. It even has a headwall at the bottom. In my opinion, like the top of BT #1, this is stretching the upper limits of what a canoe tripper on a remote river should run in a loaded tandem canoe, even with a plastic boat and spray cover. There is just too great a chance of injury and your boat wrapping should you flip.

I suggest you **line this rapid on RR** from the top. Eddy out RR as soon as you see the beginning of the rapid. There is not a great eddy to land that I can point you to. Just stay tight RR and hop out at your first opportunity. Note that there is a creek mouth on RR just down from the top of the rapid. Lining the creek mouth is not a big problem, but the lining is tricky on the whole. Go slowly and carefully. The boulders on shore are large and can be slippery.

Fast water and riffles continue from the ledgey runout below the headwall to the long island. See the description of the rapids around the island below.

	314039	Rapids

Around the long island there are **Class 2−** waves with a few rocks to avoid. The rapids end after the foot of the island at GR 322038.

	332034	Riffles

There are some **Class 1+** riffles around the island as the river bends to the right.

	338030	Campsite; Fishing hole; Hiking

On RR on the downstream side of the large but unnamed creek is a somewhat established campsite in the forest. This is a nice spot and there is really good fishing. We called this campsite Rainbow Camp because we caught so many fine rainbow trout (and grayling) in the creek. Its water is a wonderful colour. Tony refers to this bouncy creek as "Sam's Creek," as he figures you are at the spot where Samuel Black reached the Turnagain on his exploration of northern BC in 1824. Tony pointed out to me that there are blazes on the trees about 4'6" off the ground which indicate the stature of the men in Black's party. Being small is an asset when canoeing, eh Tony?!

You can hike up the creekbed on game trails (surely the ones Black followed) to look for blazes or to go all the way to the alpine ridge. Rainbow Camp is a great place to spend a day off if you have time.

340029 346029	**Rapids**	We called this rapid "Shadow of Big Three," because we were somewhat surprised by it. We thought the big rapids were over, but this one is significant. It **starts and ends as Class 2**, but has a short **Class 3−/3 section**.

The rapid is marked on the topo and is a 600-m-long boulder garden with a chute that has a large stopper wave near the end. Eddy-hop down the Class 2 boulder-garden section. When you see the chute and wave train, quickly eddy out RL above it to scout. Missing the stopper is the challenge of this short tricky section. The rapid gets easier after the wave train, but this is a wrap rapid so be careful and conservative throughout.

A pretty section of the river and "Sam's Gap," as Tony calls it, is coming up.

354043 356044	**Riffles**	After the midriver island a small canyon begins. There are shallow gravel shoals to avoid at the beginning, followed by small **Class 1+** waves and then boils as the river is squeezed between the rock walls. There is a hatch mark on the topo after the creek coming in on RL, but there is no significant drop there in reality.
360044 362043	**Rapids**	Following the canyon is a marked rapid, which is a **Class 2** rock garden about 250 m long.

An old burn shows up in the landscape, as well as a surprise around the corner!

367044	**Caterpillar**	Yup, as in machinery. There is an old bulldozer on the RL shore. Stop and get some great shots of paddling this bucket of bolts!
373047 378050	**Rapids**	Fast water follows the dozer and then you encounter shallow **Class 1+** rapids for about 600 m. The hatch marks on the map do not represent any significant drops great than Class 1+.
416035	**Riffle**	A **Class 1** riffle takes you into a fast stretch of water down to the two possible heli-pad/camp spots. The current averages 9−10 km/h here.

447023	Heli-pad #1; Camping; Hiking	On RR is a huge gravel bar split by the mouth of the creek. The downstream gravel bar is on a large bend in the river and is the biggest and flattest. This is your first heli-pad option. Note that when the helicopter lands you must have all your loose gear packed away so it doesn't blow around. Wear your sunglasses to avoid eye injury from the sand and dirt that will be kicked up.
		Camping is great here in good weather. The views are excellent and you can hike along the game trail that goes all the way downriver to the falls. You could also ferry across the river to do some alpine hiking on the ridge to the north.
462020	Riffles	There are a few **Class 1+** riffles up to and then around the large midriver island, which rafters call Portage Island.
470025	Heli-pad #2; Camping; Hiking	On the downstream side, or foot, of the island is a marked gravel bar that makes another great natural heli-pad and camping site. Take the RL channel to the site.
		You can also do some hiking from here, ferrying to either side of the river. On RR you can follow the game/horse trail to view the falls.
		Note: You can also walk the portage trails and explore the falls after your heli-portage from the landing gravel bar/campsite. See the notes on the campsite/put-in after the falls.
474024	Trailhead; Long portage	The long portage option that takes you around the rapids before the falls and the canyon hosting the falls is about **6.2 km**. What appears to be a game trail on RR eventually becomes a horse trail.
		Eddy out on RR just after the foot of the island and before the first set of Entrance Rapids. The game trail runs along the RR bank and then into open forest with a mossy understorey. You will cross two small creeks and eventually reach a trail off to the river's shore where there is a **small, established campsite at 506017**, about 250 m from the brink of the falls. There, or at a spot down the canyon portage trail, you can camp to split up your portage into two reasonable chunks. See the short portage option description for more information on the rest of the trail and other camping sites.

475025 510017	**Rapids**	Entrance Rapids is an approximately 3.4-km stretch of nearly continuous chutes, S-bends and boulder/rock gardens with a few ledges thrown in. The **stretch is graded Class 3**. Making a mistake is not an option. The **consequences are Class 6** if you mess up near the falls. I have not run these rapids, only seen them from the air and parts of them from the portage trail. I do know they have been run, and I believe that if you are a party of advanced and exceptional whitewater paddlers, the stretch can likely be navigated in some combination of paddling, lining, wading etc.

Given that skill level, you will figure out how to do it safely. Be aware that the last S-bend rapid (note the rock outcrop cliff on RL) takes you right up to a midriver rocky, gravel-bar shoal near the brink of the first drop of the falls. Stay RR of the shoal and pull out where it feels comfortable. When you scout, you will see a fairly large eddy on RR about 10 m above the falls. This is an option for pulling out, but a must-make eddy if I ever saw one! Having taken out above the falls, you will have a real hump up the very steep ridge to the portage trail.

506017	**Camping**	There is a small, not very nice campsite just off the portage trail about 250 m above the first drop of the falls. The camping site is just downstream of the second creek you cross and off the horse trail toward the river. Attractive tent sites are at a premium, but there is a kitchen clearing and a fire ring. There are two much prettier sites overlooking the canyon's falls and rapids. See the descriptions of these campsites following the description of the second part of the portage trail.
506017	**Trailhead; Short portage**	There is a trail that takes you along the canyon wall to view the falls and you can carry on portaging using it. In my exploration of the area, I found at least two trails you could portage on. They both end up at the Cassiar River, where you can put back in. The northern trail goes along the canyon for a ways before coming down the ridge to the Cassiar River, while the southern route takes you through the forest and then down the ridge to come out by the river. I can recommend the camping and views on the canyon option, but I don't know the difference it makes in length. Both the trails have their pros and cons. There is a low,

swampy area that is difficult to navigate on the southern trail at GR 510015, but that trail has less topography than the canyon one.

But not the views! Once down the ridge you will see flagging and blazes and there are trails all over the place. If you get off track and reach the Cassiar River farther upstream than intended, just head north down its bank to the Turnagain.

Once you reach the Turnagain, load your gear and paddle around the corner to choose from a couple good camping spots; there is one where the heli-portage ends and an established site just past the side channel. You can camp at the end of the portage in the forest, but it is very, very buggy and there are no views!

510017	Campsite	There is a lovely, established campsite down the canyon wall trail. You have a view of the largest falls in the canyon. You will have to carry water for cooking etc. from above the falls if you camp here.
514023	Viewpoint; Camping	Another amazing camp can be made at this viewpoint, but it is a long way to haul water.
532017	Heli-pad; Camping	This large, flat gravel bar on RL is the spot your helicopter portage ends. A nice camp can be made back up by the trees.

We camped here for a couple days to explore the canyon and portage trails. To get to the Cassiar River to hike the trails, line up the shore and then ferry over to the river mouth.

531017	Campsite	On RL, just across the side channel from the heli-pad camp, is an established campsite in the trees. It has furniture and has seen a lot of use. It's a nice location, however.

Across the river on RR is an old, decrepit cabin, probably used for trapping.

530021	Riffle	There is a shallow riffle at the corner downstream of the camping sites.
536030	Rapids	There are **Class 1+** rapids with boulders to avoid, including one in RC and more on RL.
563073 573082	Riffles	There are riffles and waves at the corners in this 1.4 km stretch.

The valley really opens up after the falls and the unmistakable scenery of the Kechika Ranges comes into its own.

94 L/12	582087	Rapid	A **Class 2** ledge here is easily avoided.

581097	**Camping**	There is a big gravel bar on RL with a treed bench for shelter. This is a good camping site.
583102	**Hoodoos**	On RL are some attractive erosion formations.
589097	**Hunting camp**	On RL at the old side channel opening is a hunting camp. There is evidence of lots of ungulates around, especially as you approach the Dall River confluence.
590097	**Camping**	On RR the marked gravel bar is a nice spot to camp.
625120	**Cabin**	On RL after the corral fencing you will see a cabin.
626119	**Rapids**	Expect some **Class 1+** waves on the coming bend at higher water levels.
632120	**Lodge; Potential put-in/ take-out**	Turnagain River Lodge sits on the RL bank. It looks like it has a lawn! Just some fine Kechika country wild grass, I hope.

The next section of river, flowing by Deeh Ridge on RL and the Dall River Valley on RR, is slow. The views are great, but there are wood hazards to watch for in this moose lowland area.

675153	**Camping**	The elevated stretch of the marked gravel bar on RL makes a nice camp with panorama views and wildlife-viewing potential.

The Turnagain River Valley is really spectacular from the Dall River confluence down to where Major Hart River flows into the Turnagain. Steep mountain ridges in the distance ring the wide valley bottom.

685162	**Camping**	There is a camping spot with mountain views on the marked gravel bar on RL.
693210	**Camping**	The marked gravel bar on RR has excellent views down the valley and of Deeh Ridge.
692216	**Logjams**	**Caution:** In 2005 there were two logjams on RR, one in the side channel at the head of the island and one at the foot. Be careful on your approach to this section and stay RL. The second logjam was potentially the more dangerous one when we paddled the river.
670254	**Cabins**	As marked on the topo, there are some cabins on RR.
654290	**Hazards**	**Caution:** There may be wood hazards in the riffle in the RR channel around the midstream gravel bar island.
655314	**Hunting camp**	There is a hunting campsite on RL. There is a better spot to camp coming up on RR after the minor rapids.

654318	**Rapids**	There are **Class 1+** rapids for 300 m at the S-bend.
655321	**Camping**	Just after the rapids on the foot of the marked gravel bar on RR is a good camping spot. There is a sandy beach landing and forested bench in behind.
667363	**Cabin**	Up on the high bank on RR just before the bend in the river is a hunting cabin with a guestbook. It shows a number of canoeing parties have stopped here over the years. We had lunch on the "porch" during a huge deluge of rain.
		The scenery of the Turnagain River Valley changes in this stretch and is very diverse right up to the river's confluence with the Kechika. There are interesting gorges and mini-canyons that are all different.

94 M/4

664414	**Campsite**	In the heart of "Surprise Canyon," a pretty gorge that comes out of nowhere and reminds me of the Toad River, there is an established campsite on RL at the north end of the marked gravel bar. Unfortunately there was garbage there when we came by, so we decided against camping.
657421	**Camping; Fishing**	On RL, just on the downstream side of the Major Hart River confluence, is a small gravel bar. It provides a landing site and kitchen area. There are sites for tents back in the grassy areas and the forest. The scenery is interesting and you can explore up the Major Hart. The fishing for bull trout was good in the eddies at the mouth of the river, too.
657429	**Camping**	On the foot of the marked gravel bar on RR there is a camping spot.
652448	**Camping**	On RR there is another spot to camp just before the outlet of the small side channel around the gravel bar "island."
655460	**Riffle**	In higher water there are **Class 1+** riffles around the midriver island. The RL channel is the best choice.
655461	**Camping**	There is a good camping spot on the island. Land on the gravel bar on RL. There are trees for shelter in behind.
668492	**Lodge; Potential put-in/ take-out**	On RL you will see Turnagain River Adventures' lodge and associated cabins.
678505	**Campsite**	There is an established campsite higher up on the marked gravel bar on RR. A good spot to camp if it is clean.

693511	**Rapids**	Where the + marks are, near the creek mouth on RL, there is a 200-m **Class 2–** boulder garden. There is an easy line to run down RR.
		The current really picks up in this section as you descend into the Rocky Mountain Trench.
718515	**Rapid**	This **Class 2–** rapid has a huge boulder in RC. There is a good line to run on RL.
736525	**Rapids**	There are **Class 1/1+** riffles for about 650 m. Following the riffles, where the dashes are marked in midriver (GR 747525), are a set of **Class 2** waves.
		Minor riffles and wave sets follow at most of the bends all the way down to the Turnagain and Kechika confluence. The most significant fast water is in the last "coal" canyon of the Turnagain, which ends with hoodoos a couple kilometres from the confluence.
803577	**Confluence; Campsite**	At the confluence of the Kechika and the Turnagain is a small, not so nice, established campsite. It's probably used by jet-boating hunters. In 2005, we had lunch there to enjoy the view of the confluence and do a little fishing. On RL of the Kechika, right at the point where the clear Turnagain flows by, is a path up to the site through the spruce. Fishing is very good at the confluence. If you are at all worried about bears and have a small party, try the potential camp spot on the island 1 km downstream.
		You are now at the very northern end of the Rocky Mountain Trench and heading out onto the sandy Liard Plain! The Kechika is really moving as it descends onto Liard Plain, flowing from 7–9 km/h at average August water levels.
803585	**Camping; Fishing hole**	On the head of the island (southern tip), just down on the east side, there is a small sandy spot to camp. The sandbar changes from year to year, so don't count on this spot to camp. But there is an eddy to pull into to land and we had great grayling fishing here!
794617	**Riffle**	At some water levels there is a **Class 1** riffle in the RL channel around the long gravel-bar island.
784649	**Hiking**	The Davie Trail crosses the Kechika here. You can get out and stretch your legs for as long as you want.
809673	**Riffles**	There are riffles and **Class 1/1+** waves around the island here, and after the channels converge, the boils and cross-currents continue to GR 814674.

	815678	**Hoodoos**	There are pretty erosion formations on RR at the corner.
			You are now getting into a very sandy section of the Kechika with good camping.
94 M/5	791690	**Cabin**	Up on the north end of the marked RR gravel/sandbar is a trapper's cabin. Nice location!
	797697	**Camping**	On RR there is a very old campsite used by long-ago travellers. Back in the trees by the game trail you can see evidence of what I believe are poles for teepees but they may have been used for a tent. This camping spot is treed and large. Look for it back from the gravel bar you land on.
	794707	**Camping**	On RR there is a high, sandy gravel bar to camp on in good weather.
	789714	**Camping**	On RR, just at the south tip of the marked gravel bar, there is a more protected camping area. It has a sandy beach landing and tent and tarp spots back in the trees.
	800732	**Camping**	On RL, just at the sharp turn where a gravel bar is marked, there is an open-forested bench for tents and tarps back of a sandy landing spot. This is a nice camping site.
	787755	**Camping**	There is a huge area for camping on the marked RL sand/gravel bar.
			You are now approaching a long section where the Kechika is deeply incised into the Liard Plain and you really feel like you are in a mature river valley. We saw a great horned owl and a grizzly on this stretch in 2004.
	759865	**Camping**	Another large camp can be made on the north end of the marked gravel bar on RL. It has a sandy landing and open bench in the back with trees for shelter and tarps. There is lots of firewood and you can do some walking. I found evidence of an old campsite away from the river near the trees.
	753925	**Camping**	If you want a camp near clear water and with potential bull trout and grayling fishing as well, try this RL spot on the downstream side of the creek mouth.
94 M/12			The number of good choices for camping spots decreases on the Lower Kechika, but the current increases. The stretch of river from 4 km downstream of Kitza Creek to the confluence of the Kechika with the Liard is the most exciting in terms of rapids. There are erosion formations on several of the RL corners to admire as well.

	819040	Rapids	Around the sweeping bend there are **Class 1+** waves with a few rocks to dodge for about 300 m at lower water.
	836038	Rapids	Just above where the river jogs to the right there are **Class 1+** waves for 150 m.
	839036	Rapids	On the next jog to the right there are **Class 2−/2** waves with two big boulders to avoid and logjams on RR and then RL, making for a tricky spot in higher water.
94 M/11	859058	Riffle	There is a line of rocks here that makes some **Class 1/1+** waves in higher water.
	872062	Campsite	There is a great established campsite on the southeastern tip of the large island. Take the RR channel to spot it. The RL channel has a rapid in it that looks like it might be up to Class 2− in difficulty, but I have never run it or seen it up close enough to say for sure. Watch for wood, as the channel is narrow and has a significant bend in it.
	883056 886055	**Flowerpot Rapids**	This is a pretty spot on the river. You will first see a sweeping turn to the right with bedrock outcropping on RL. The **Class 2/2+ and 1+** rapids are at the end of this right turn, just before the river makes a hard turn to the left.

There is a flowerpot rock island RR of RC. The RR channel around it is a cheat route at certain water levels, and is only **Class 1+.** The main flow goes to the left of the Flowerpot, and there is a **Class 2/2+** rapid, depending on water levels. There is a ledge just off the left side of the flowerpot island, and in RC there is a big V with good-sized standing waves at higher flows. For a dry line, take the cheat channel on RR if there is enough water in it. For more excitement, but to still stay dry, take the RL channel and cut off the ledge to the left and miss the wave train to the right.

Following the hard turn to the left are some **Class 1+/2−** standing waves, which are bigger on RR. There is a beach to bail at if necessary, on RR near the end of the rapids.

	894061	Riffle; Camping	On RL there is a bedrock ledge making a **Class 1/1+** riffle. In the eddy behind it you can land to make a small camp up on shore.
	906057	Rapid	Just after the bend in the river to the left there is a **Class 1+/2− ledge** sticking out from the RR shore that goes two-thirds to three-quarters of

the way across the river, depending on water level. If you stay far RL you will stay dry.

| 914066 | Rapids | The river is split by a bedrock reef in RC. Both the RL and RR channels have easy **Class 1+** rapids. |

| 916077 | Rapid | There is a **Class 1+** ledge sticking out from the RL shore on the bend in the river to the right. The drop and associated boily water is easy to avoid by heading RR to the inside of the turn. |

| 916077 | Camping | You can camp on RR across from the ledge. There is a beach landing and the trees up behind provide shelter in inclement weather. |

| 929079 | Rapid | There is a **Class 1+** ledge on RR that is easily avoided by staying RL. |

| 937090 | Riffle | There is another ledge, **Class 1/1+**, on RR which is also easily avoided by staying RL. |

You will eventually observe an old burn on RL. The current is flying along at about 10 km/h here! Once you reach the gravel bar islands around GR 023110 it gets even faster. You are approaching the Liard quickly and the navigation can be confusing. You want to be sure to know where you are so you can stop and scout the last set of rapids before the Kechika dumps into the Liard: Kechika Spit. You are going to be spat out of the Kechika's mouth!

| 025111 | Caution | There is a **logjam** in the RL channel around the gravel bar island. Take the main flow that goes RR. |

| 032110 | Rapids | Around the bedrock island in the middle of the river are riffles and then there is a set of rapids with a few rocks and **Class 1+** waves that run up to the relatively sharp right turn at GR 037113. Here the waves at some water levels can reach **Class 2−** and may carry on almost to where Kechika Spit Rapids begin, depending on water levels. Be on your toes (knees!), and ready to eddy out on RL to scout. This section is fast! |

| 046109 048110 | Kechika Spit; Rapids | This last set of rapids on the Kechika are **Class 2+/3−**, depending on water levels. You want to approach these rapids with caution. Stick to RL after the last waves of the previous rapids, and eddy out in the shore eddy of the high cutbank on RL. Get into the eddy as soon as possible. From there you can scramble up the steep gravel ridge and out to the point to scout. It is not an easy scout, but well worth it. There is no portage trail, but there is evidence |

of parties bushwhacking over the ridge to the Liard, where there is a nice, sloping sand beach to regroup. Carrying here would not be fun. It would be very strenuous and scratchy!

Kechika Spit has two parts. The first is a drop split by a gravel bar island. The RR channel has the most flow and can have some impressive standing waves. The RL channel can have a big stopper in it and can be rocky at lower water levels.

It's the second part of the rapids that makes the run tricky. Following the two channels' convergence there is a jagged bedrock reef (extending from RR to RC) that you really want to avoid, and of course the majority of the water is flowing toward it, especially at higher flows.

The line I like is to run the standing waves in the RR channel tight to the gravel island (backpaddling will keep you drier). Then, using the small patch of slower water behind the island, change your angle and upstream (front) ferry across the flow coming out of the RL channel to avoid the reef.

Once past the reef you ride a few small waves into the Liard!

Fishing hole

The eddy on RL after the reef is a good place to fish. You can also paddle up the RR eddy of the Liard to clean your fish or have lunch on the sloping beach there. It is a beautiful place.

Note: I suggest crossing the Liard's blue waters from the RR eddy of the Liard, accessed by paddling out of the Kechika's mouth via the fishing eddy on RL. Then you are set up for an upstream (front) ferry over to the shore of the Muddy River IR. This is a long, intimidating ferry for some, the Liard being big and fast moving, but it is not a difficult manoeuvre. If you are more comfortable with S-turns, make a wide, carving turn out of the Liard's RR eddy and then cross to make another turn into a shore eddy on RL of the Liard. You have time. Mountain Portage Rapids, the first of the Liard's rapids you could possibly encounter, is still 2 km downstream. It is not a rapid you would be able to run blind (and only very exceptional canoeists in the right conditions could run it successfully, even if they knew the line) and you certainly don't want to swim it.

I hate to say it, but you cannot afford to flip when crossing the Liard. Be relaxed and Zen about this crossing. If something does happen, your first priority is to get people to shore. Have a rescue plan already made based on the number of boats you have and people's swimming abilities.

Once on the RL side of the Liard, pick your way down close to the RL shore to Skook's Landing.

The sandy beach of the Muddy River IR is enticing across the Liard, but permission from the Band is required to stop there.

060115   Camping   A sandy bank with trees in behind makes a nice option for a last camp, your first on the lovely Liard. The spot is on RL just upstream of the take-out at Skook's Landing.

062115   Take-out   **Skook's Landing** is on the RL shore of the Liard. There is a large eddy out front. Look for it after the point following the camping spot described above. You will likely see trucks and trailers parked back up by the trees.

CHAPTER SIX

TOAD/LIARD RIVERS

The Toad River highlights the stunning landscape of the far northeastern Rocky Mountains and foothills. The geology and topography of the Toad watershed make for a very scenic journey. Fossils literally fall from sedimentary rock faces in deep, steep-sided gorges. Glacial blue-green water, fast current and many rapids, including some big, bouncy drops between vertical canyon walls, make for some exciting paddling.

Wildlife abounds. The Toad River Hot Springs are a major mineral lick in the region, providing canoeists with a great opportunity to see some big mammals up close. Grizzlies, Stone sheep, elk and moose frequent this legendary "tropical valley." The fishing is good and camping sites are plentiful along the Toad.

The Toad flows into the Liard, the mother river of BC's far northern reaches. The confluence of the rivers is downstream of the Liard's Grand Canyon, a fearsome series of cataracts, but the paddling on the Lower Liard is relaxing. Ending at historic Fort Liard, this canoe trip has a great cultural component. Visions of First Nations gatherings, fur-trade forts and voyageur feats of endurance and skill will be conjured up under the big sky of the Taiga Plain.

This two-for-the-price-of-one river route snakes through two of the remotest regions of northeastern BC, yet access and egress are easy. Unfortunately, the Northern Rockies Foothills and the Taiga Plain are also two of the most threatened ecosystems in the province with regard to oil and gas development.

Length: The Toad/Liard route is approximately 308 km long. Putting in at "The Springs" just off the Alaska Highway, you paddle approximately 92 km on the Toad, and then about 216 km on the Liard to Fort Liard. Canoeists can comfortably do the entire river trip described here in 9 or 10 days. The Toad is so pretty you'll want to take four days to paddle it. If you don't have to fight strong headwinds on the Liard, five days is a good amount of time to paddle to Fort Liard. Take some extra time if you want to do some hiking or more exploring on land.

For those paddlers with more money and skill than time, you can paddle the whole Toad River section to pretty much anywhere you want on the Liard, arranging for a floatplane or jet boat charter to pick you up. Most parties could run the Toad in three days, doing 31 km a day. Then, you can do about 45–50 km a day on the Liard because it has good current and the paddling is easy (that is, if you don't get brutal headwinds).

TO FORT SIMPSON

Petitot River

7

71

LIARD HIGHWAY

Kiwigana River

FORT NELSON

97

Prophet River

TO FORT ST. JOHN

Muskwa River

Northwest Territories
British Columbia

FORT LIARD

Nelson Forks

Fort Nelson River

Liard River

Yukon

Dunedin River

ALASKA HIGHWAY

Tetsa River

Beaver River

Scatter River
Old Growth
Provincial Park

Liard River Corridor
Provincial Park

Liard River

Toad River

TOAD RIVER

Summit Lake

Stone Mountain
Provincial Park

Scatter River

Toad River
Hot Springs

Racing River

Crow River

Muncho
Lake
Provincial Park

Liard River
Hot Springs
Provincial Park

Muncho
Lake

Trout River

Muskwa–Kechika
Management Area

TO WATSON LAKE

97

LIARD RIVER

N

For canoeists not skilled enough to tackle the Toad just yet, you can paddle just the Liard portion of this trip. It is one nice stretch of river. You would need to charter a jet boat or floatplane to drop you below the Toad River confluence. You can't put in much farther upstream of there because of the dangerous rapids of the Grand Canyon of the Liard. They are not for the average canoeist and that is a serious understatement!

To extend your trip, you may want to put in farther upstream on the Toad, adding a day of whitewater. For a major expedition, consider paddling on to Fort Simpson at the confluence of the Liard with the Mackenzie, another 300 km or so. Those with a whole lot of time could head on down the Mackenzie from there to where it flows into the Beaufort Sea of the Arctic Ocean!

The Springs put-in on the Toad to the Toad–Liard confluence*	92 km
The Toad–Liard confluence to Fort Liard*	216 km
The Springs put-in on the Toad to Fort Liard*	308 km

* These trips are described in detail in the Trip Notes section of this chapter.

Topographic Maps: Maps at a scale of 1:50 000 are required for the Toad River section of the route. You want to know where you are with regard to the canyons, especially if there is a problem and you need to evacuate. The 1:250 000 topos are fine for paddling the Liard, but the Grid Reference System (GRS) coordinates in the Trip Notes will not be as user friendly. If you a less experienced canoeist wanting to upgrade your river-tripping skills by only paddling the Liard section of this route, it is an excellent opportunity to practise navigating a river using the GRS and 1:50 000 topos. This is also a good trip to practise with a GPS. For use with the GRS coordinates in the Trip Notes and the 1:50 000-scale topos, make sure the map datum is set to NAD 27 Canada and the position format to MGRS (Military Grid Reference System). See a further discussion on topographic maps and the use of a GPS in the How To Use this Guidebook chapter.

For the Toad River, the 1:50 000s you will need are 94 K/14, 94 K/15, 94 N/2 and 94 N/7. If you want to carry on using 1:50 000s on the Liard, you will need 94 N/10, 94 N/9, 94 O/12w, 94 O/13w, 95 B/4 and 95 B/3 (this topo covers the last 2 km to Fort Liard and is not really necessary). The 1:250 000s for the Toad are 94 K and 94 N, and for the Liard you will want 94 O and 95 B (as well as 94 N). I like to carry both scales of topos, the 1:50 000s for navigating the river and the 1:250 000s for identifying the large features in a region, including peaks, mountain ranges and plateaus, and for planning longer hikes. When actually hiking I use the 1:50 000s as well.

The BC Forest Service publishes a recreation map, *The Fort Nelson Forest District*, which gives you a good overview of the main features of the region such as the winter and logging roads and water bodies. It also lists some recreational opportunities in the area if you plan on doing some touring. It does not show contours and is not a substitute for the topo maps, but it is a useful planning tool and guide for some "road" hiking on the Liard. I recommend getting the map of Fort Liard available from the Visitor Information Centre at Fort Liard. It will help you make a take-out and parking plan that fits your logistics. See the Directory of Services and Organizations for contact information for ordering these two optional maps.

I suggest you purchase or print your topo maps in advance. Not only will you be able to plan your paddling days, but by using the coordinates in the Trip Notes you can mark the locations of sources of emergency help, known hazards, rapids, portages and potential campsites (there are some sections where good campsites are scarce) and other sites of interest so you have the information at hand when navigating the river. Remember that river features change with each freshet and flood, especially with regard to wood hazards, and you are responsible for always being on the lookout for them and being able to deal with them safely. The Scatter Ass Flats of the Toad is a case in point.

Getting There and Away: If you do the whole Toad/Liard route, you can drive in and drive out. The Alaska Highway follows the Toad River for a stretch, and Fort Liard is just off the Liard Highway to Fort Simpson. If you decide to do a "custom" trip, such as just paddling the Liard River section of the route, you will need to use other modes of transportation.

To get to the most convenient put-in for the Toad/Liard route the locals call "The Springs," drive west past the community of Toad River. On the left-hand side of the Alaska Highway, about 1.5 km past the Toad River Lodge, you will see a garbage-can pullout. Just past that on the right is a gravel road. Turn right onto the gravel road, which becomes a track down to the river. Keep right at the forks, going about 600 m to arrive at the put-in, a nice little beach on the river-right bank of the Toad. The Springs is just to your right, a very cold freshwater source bubbling up in the black sand. You can camp just off the track and there is a fire pit at the turnaround by the river.

There are numerous possible put-ins west along the Alaska Highway should you decide to extend your trip and paddle more of the Toad. The put-in at The Springs is convenient because you can easily leave one of your vehicles close by at the Toad River Lodge and walk back to the put-in.

Which take-out you choose to use in Fort Liard will depend on the shuttle logistics you set up. Coming from Fort Nelson on Hwy. 97, the Alaska Highway, drive approximately 28 km west and then turn right and head north on Hwy. 77, the Liard Highway. If you are coming from the other direction, west from Toad River, turn left onto Hwy. 77 at 28 km before Fort Nelson. Highway 77 is a good gravel highway that can be travelled by the average car. It becomes Hwy. 7 once you cross into the NWT. Keep going north on Hwy. 7 until you see the sign indicating the access road to Fort Liard. Turn left and drive west toward the village and river. Distances useful for figuring out your shuttle for the drive-in/drive-out trip are Fort Nelson to Toad River, about 195 km one way; Toad River to Fort Liard, about 345 km; and Fort Nelson to Fort Liard, about 205 km.

If you have more than one vehicle, this shuttle is easy, though long. You can leave your canoes and gear and some people at the Toad put-in and then drive two vehicles or more up to Fort Liard. Drive back with one vehicle, park it at the Toad River Lodge and then walk to the put-in. Or you can leave all your vehicles at Fort Liard and take the bus back to Fort Nelson and on to Toad River. The other option is to charter a plane from Fort Nelson to take you right to Toad River. There is a fine little airstrip there. The flight would not be overly expensive if you have a larger party.

For safe parking in Fort Liard, there is the ferry/barge landing and the Fort Liard airport. I am a big fan of parking at airports. It doesn't cost much if there is pay parking, and at most small places it's free. It's safe too, given that oil and gas workers and hunters leave their vehicles there and you don't mess with those guys. The walk to the airport from the boat launch is about 10 minutes. Fort Liard is a small place, so you will have no difficulty getting to where you want to go. People are friendly and will direct you. You can also pick up a great map of Fort Liard from the Visitor Information Centre at the centre of town or have them send you one by snail mail ahead of time.

Things get more interesting if you don't have a second vehicle or the numbers in your party make the regular shuttle set up impossible. If your party has one vehicle and two drivers, you can rent a car in Fort Nelson and do the shuttle with it. You'd have to drive your canoe and gear to the put-in with your vehicle, as they usually don't have canoe racks on rentals. Then drive both vehicles up to Fort Liard, leave yours there and drive the rental car back to Fort Nelson. From there you can take the bus to Toad River. Finally, as this will take a long time, you are set to paddle to Fort Liard.

The quickest shuttle possible is if you have one vehicle and a PakCanoe or some other folding/inflatable canoe that is good in whitewater. You can drive straight to Toad River to put in at The Springs, leave your vehicle at the Toad River Lodge and paddle to Fort Liard. Charter a wheel plane to get you and all your gear and canoe in a bag back to your vehicle. The lodge is across the highway from the airstrip. At risk of repeating myself, a PakCanoe is a great craft and will save you time and money when paddling in northern BC!

Another option, good for two-boat parties with only one vehicle, is to use Ernie McLeod's scheduled shuttle service to Fort Nelson. His large van takes mail and local passengers between Fort Liard and Fort Nelson. This way you can again go straight to the put-in, paddle to Fort Liard and use McLeod's service to shuttle your party, two canoes and gear to Fort Nelson. From there you can send a driver up to Toad River to get your vehicle either by bus or air charter. If there are more than four people in your party and more than two canoes, call Ernie and see what he can do. He had two vans going in 2005.

At the time of printing, the shuttle service was running three times a week: Mondays, Wednesdays and Fridays at around 9:30 a.m. – remember, you are in the NWT, so you have to set your watch an hour ahead coming from BC – and things change all the time up north! Check the shuttle schedule before setting off, and book ahead.

Ernie's place is right on the Liard, just down from the boat launch. You can paddle up to the bank in front of the office, pull up your canoes and leave them there for loading in the morning. The driver will drop you and your stuff wherever you wish in Fort Nelson. The Fort Nelson Information Centre and the airport are two good possibilities.

There are no canoe outfitters in Fort Nelson. You can, however, rent canoes, spray covers, paddles and safety equipment in Fort Liard from Deh Cho Air. Depending on your group size and shuttle plans, this may be an option for your trip. Otherwise, you will have to have your own canoes or rent them from somewhere down south or from Northern Rockies Lodge at Muncho Lake. If you want to travel without canoes and vehicles, there are scheduled flights with Air Canada and Central Mountain Air to Fort Nelson and vehicle rentals available from the airport. See the Directory of Services and Organizations for contact information for the services you will need to arrange the logistics that work best for your party.

You can camp for free at The Springs put-in and there is a free municipal campsite, Hay Lake Campground, with 12 sites, on the small lake just outside Fort Liard, off the access road from Hwy. 7. It has firewood, fresh water and a cooking shelter. Ernie McLeod may also allow you to camp on his property if you are using his taxi service. Tourist accommodations and services are limited in Toad River and Fort Liard. Check the websites listed in the Directory of Services and Organizations to find out what is available in these communities or who to email or call to find out more.

When To Go: August and September. You do not want to run the Toad at higher water. The canyon rapids will be pushy for canoes and there are too many tight corners and wood hazards to navigate on the river.

In a normal year, the river peaks from late June to early July. It stays up with hot sunny weather and warm weather with rain in July because it is also fed by glacier melt, like the Gataga and Tuchodi rivers. By August and September the water has usually dropped significantly. The later you go in August the more likely it will be that you will have lower levels for First Canyon. That said, warm temperatures with heavy rain in any month will affect the Toad's flow in a big way. The Toad can rise and drop quickly. You may have to wait a few days for water levels to drop to run the canyon if you head out in or after heavy rains.

Normally, the gravel bars are more exposed in August, making for good camping. Days are warm, the insects are fewer and the berries come out. Life is generally as good as it gets on the river in this usually drier month.

You will usually have even lower water in September. It can be frosty in the mornings if it is clear, and snow is definitely possible. Cold northern headwinds and rain may occur, particularly on the Liard, but you also may have very warm, sunny days throughout your trip. The dry Liard Plain is known for its extended summer. You will need to pack for any weather; expect the worst and enjoy what you get! The joys of a fall trip are the changing colours of the many deciduous trees and shrubs in this region. The bugs will have really calmed down, making camping and hiking even more pleasant.

Unfortunately, being that water levels are key to having an enjoyable and safe trip on the Toad, there is no longer an active water-gauging station on the Toad. You do have some resources to consult about water levels, however. One is to ask the locals, perhaps contacting someone at Toad River Lodge or Urs at Northern Rockies Lodge/ Liard Air at Muncho Lake. He will have been flying around the Northern Rockies all summer. You want to know how much rain they've had lately and whether water levels are normal for that time of year or not. The other way to gather information on the Toad's flow is by checking out what the Lower Liard is running at using the Environment Canada hydrometric data website, which you want to know anyway. The bonus of obtaining real-time flow data for the Lower Liard is that from it you can extrapolate what is generally happening on the Toad. Using the table below and the historical data for the Liard on the website, you will be able to tell if water levels are high, average or low on the Liard and the Toad for that time of year.

The table below summarizes the historical flow data for the Toad found online at www.r-arcticnet.sr.unh.edu. The table compares average monthly mean flows for the Toad with those of the Lower Liard. The times when you don't want to be running the Toad in a canoe are obvious. Note that the Liard usually peaks earlier than the Toad. The Toad is fed by glacier and snowmelt and lies at much higher elevations, so runoff is later. Most useful for river runners is that a comparison of average August and September flows between the two waterways shows there is a ratio you can use to estimate the Toad's flow from the Liard's at Lower Crossing. The Lower Liard's volume will normally be around 7 times greater than the Toad's in August and 8½ times greater in September.

Average Monthly Mean Flows, m³/s

	Toad River near Mouth (1983–1994)	Liard River at Lower Crossing (1944–2005)
May	100	1660
June	288	3670
July	308	2470
August	208	1460
September	140	1200
October	86	960

Sources: Archived Hydrometric Data Report, Environment Canada, June 2007; R-ArcticNET

To access real-time and more specific historical flow data for the Liard at Lower Crossing, go to the Environment Canada hydrometric website, at http://scitech. pyr.ec.gc.ca/waterweb/formnav.asp?lang=0. Set the "Find Station By" slot to read "Province," and in the "View all Real Time Stations within" slot, choose "British Columbia." In the resulting alphabetical list of station names, scroll down to "Liard River at Lower Crossing" and click the "Go to Station" button. In the resulting "Disclaimer" screen, go to the bottom and press the "I accept" button. When the next page comes up, look to the top left and make sure the "Data Category" slot is set to "Real Time." Just beneath that, change "Parameter Type" to "Discharge." The graph will show actual flows, in cubic metres per second, for the past week up to the current date. You can change the date span of the readout to anytime since January 1, 2007, by resetting the controls just beneath the graph and hitting the "Redraw" button.

You can also compare the real-time readings to more specific historical flow data on the website. The table I've provided only gives you average monthly mean flows, whereas the website graph will give you a more detailed picture of the changes in flow throughout a given month. To change to historical mode, choose the "Historic" option in the box near the top and hit "Go." The server is crunching a lot of data, so the screen may take a moment to change. Use any year for your search. What you really want is the baseline information to compare your real-time reading with. So, be sure to click the "Max," "Min" and "Mean" buttons on the lower left side of the page. "Upper quartile" and "Lower quartile" flows are of interest too. They can tell you if the real-time flows are in the top or bottom 25 per cent of all recorded flows. Once you have your options selected, click on Go to get a graph with different lines representing all the statistics. Ignore the line that represents the data from the random year you used; look instead for where your real-time reading fits in. If you were to plot your reading of, say, 500 m3/s on this graph, would it sit above or below the mean line? Keep repeating this process every week or so until you leave for your trip. You will know by then if the Liard is fluctuating normally or not. Do the math to figure out what the Toad is running at and then make your decision as to whether the water levels are going to be low enough to paddle the route. Have a backup route already researched, so if the Toad is just too high, you can paddle your second choice instead. You have lots of routes in the region to choose from, and a number of good options are covered in the two volumes of this guide.

To put this discussion of flows in context, when Karlene and I ran the Toad and Liard rivers from August 9 to 18, 2004, the Liard at Lower Crossing dropped from 1090 to 894 m³/s. August 2004 was quite a low-water month (in the bottom 25 per cent of all recorded flows). The mean for Lower Liard flows in August over 60 years is 1460 m³/s. It didn't rain really at all from mid-July to nearly the end of August. Given the ratios I've come up with, I am pretty sure we ran the Toad at water that was low even for August. The flow was probably around 145 m³/s when we hit First Canyon, more like what you would expect in the beginning of a normal September. This water level was excellent for running the rapids of the Toad, especially Crux Rapids in First Canyon, the most intimidating of all the drops.

If you are into planning for your trip early, you can also check how any given year's water levels are shaping up by watching the snowpack on the Environment Canada River Forecast & Snow Survey website, at www.env.gov.bc.ca/rfc. On the website is a snow survey (snowpack and water supply outlook) bulletin, published starting in January and updated eight times per year. The publication includes data gathered from snow and hydrometric measuring stations. The regional snowpack and water supply forecasts basically tell you whether water levels are expected to be lower or higher than normal in a region come the summer and how much of the snow has melted and how fast. This is good general information, useful in deciding when to schedule your trip. If there is lots of snow in any given year, like 2007, you may want to delay your trip to even later in the season. In a year with a huge snowpack and a late, cold spring followed by a cool start to July, you could have high flows into August. Once the heat turns on, the flows will skyrocket and stay up for some time.

In conclusion, only parties of advanced and exceptional moving-water paddlers should plan for a trip earlier in August. If you have less experienced paddlers in your group, plan your Toad/Liard trip for late August or September, monitor the flows carefully and have a well-researched backup route to paddle.

Difficulty of the River: ✳ ✳ ✳ for the Toad and ✳ ½ for the Liard. The Toad River section of this route gets a three-star rating for difficulty. This is due to the sheer number of rapids, the significant drops in First Canyon that you must run and the large number of wood hazards on the river. The Toad is not a river for basic moving-water paddlers. Strong intermediate whitewater paddlers should only run the river in low-water conditions in late August and September and with three boats in their party. Advanced and exceptional whitewater canoeists will enjoy the challenge of the whitewater of the Toad earlier in August, especially the rapids of First Canyon.

The river always runs swiftly, and there are numerous sections of continuous Class 1+ to Class 2- rapids. There are short Class 2 and 2+ drops along the way as well. The water of the Toad is cold, glacially cold, making long swims dangerous. Strong self-rescue and assisted rescue skills are required in the event of capsizes. The Class 3 Crux Rapids of First Canyon must be run. There are no portage trails on the Toad and there is no way around the canyon, except a nightmare, mountain-goat, super-long bushwhack carry that I'm not sure where you would start or finish.

There are many wood hazards on the Toad. Logjams, sweepers, strainers and deadheads abound where the river braids, especially in a long section where the river slows significantly. In this approximately 30-km stretch I call the "Scatter Ass Flats of the Toad," there are many midstream gravel bar islands making for places where wood can gather to create dangerous logjam hazards. Like Scatter Ass Flats on the Stikine, this section will be more difficult and dangerous if the water is up. In the flats and all along the route, there are often wood hazards at tight bends with strong current. You must have the river-running skills to be able to avoid midstream hazards and to avoid trees that have come down due to the erosion of the banks.

The Toad section of this canoe route is not strenuous, as there are no portages, but your ability to focus will be tested by the continuous riffles and Scatter Ass Flats. The Toad is medium volume after the Racing River joins it and the water can be boily with small whirlpools where currents converge or the flow is squeezed, as in the canyons. There are no large crossings of open water to be made, but given the water temperature and the fast nature of the river, if you capsize you are likely in for very cold and long swim. This is a very remote trip and you are a long ways from any source of help. Until you reach the Liard, a helicopter is your only evacuation option.

The Liard River section gets a 1½-star rating for difficulty. It is large volume and has some very wide stretches. There are no significant rapids (the waves after the Scatter River confluence can be avoided for the most part), just some riffles and fast-water sections with a few boils here and there. There are logjams on the Liard, but they can be seen from a long ways away and avoided. The Liard is not a cold-water route in August and September. There are no portages, but paddling can be strenuous if you encounter headwinds.

In conclusion, the Toad River section of this route is only for strong intermediate whitewater canoeists if they are paddling with advanced canoeists or if they go late in the season at the lowest water and have at least two other canoes in their party. Each canoe should to be able to read and run up to Class 3 rapids loaded. You have to boat-scout much of First Canyon from eddies. Paddlers should be competent in swift-water assisted and self-rescue techniques. Preparations for running First Canyon should include donning immersion paddling gear, delegating responsibilities for rescuing people and boats and a plan for evacuation in a worst-case scenario.

The Liard section of the route is one of the best trip choices in this book for canoeists with minimal moving-water experience who want to undertake a remote river expedition. There is much to be learned on the Liard about river paddling and navigating, and it is a relatively safe environment (given you don't go when the river is in full spring runoff or flood and if you stay fairly close to shore on the very wide Liard) for practising river-tripping skills. Only the Fort Nelson River is a better choice for learning the ropes. The Liard is a great summer solo trip for those inclined to try that or those who enjoy a solitary experience.

The gradient of the Toad River from The Springs to the confluence of the Toad and Liard is 4 m/km, a steep gradient compared to other rivers in this book. Only the Tatshenshini/Alsek route, at 5 m/km, and the Tuchodi River, at 5.6 m/km, are steeper runs. However, the Toad actually drops more than the average gradient reflects, particularly in the upper stretches and in First Canyon. The 30-km-long slow section of Scatter Ass Flats skews the average. The gradient of the Liard from the confluence of the Toad to Fort Liard is a mere 0.5 m/km. The current of this giant is steady with no large drops or overly slow sections. The Toad/Liard route is a bit of a Dr. Jekyll and Mr. Hyde experience with regard to whitewater: lots and then none! In this way it is similar to the Tuchodi/Muskwa route. The Tuchodi has many continuous rapids, while the Muskwa is pretty much just fast flat water with some sets of standing waves.

Character of the River and Region: Ecologically speaking, the Toad/Liard canoe route lies in both the Northern Boreal Mountains and the Taiga Plain ecoprovinces. The upper section of the Toad flows through the Northern Canadian Rocky Mountains ecoregion of the Northern Boreal Mountains and the Lower Toad, and a section of the Liard after the confluence flows through the Muskwa Plateau ecoregion of the Taiga Plain. The Liard carries on to incise the Northern Alberta Uplands ecoregion of the Taiga Plain all the way to Fort Liard. The landscapes vary, sometimes dramatically, between the two ecoprovinces and three ecoregions, making for a trip with diverse scenery.

The Northern Canadian Rocky Mountains ecoregion's main feature is the rugged Muskwa Ranges. Peaks reach 3000 m ASL and a number of glaciers occur around the higher peaks. The headwaters of the Toad flow out of these mountains of sedimentary rock, mostly limestone and shale up to 1.5 billion years old. To the south and east of the Toad are the peaks of the Stone Range and to the north and west are the mountains of the Sentinel Range. The Muskwa Ranges have been modified as a result of glaciation and erosion, among other natural processes. Glacial drift, colluvium and bedrock outcrops are common surface materials.

The trip begins with the shallow, small-volume Toad (about half the flow you find at the mouth) riffling helter-skelter over a flat gravel bed through a narrow valley. The floodplain of the Toad is debris from glacial outwash, and the river bottom is made up of round rocks of various sizes plus gravel and sand. The Toad is somewhat milky with glacial flour and also cold as result of being fed by glacier melt. The current is fast, flowing from 8–14 km/h.

About 16 km from the put-in at The Springs, the Toad runs by alluvial terraces where the hot springs are found. The pools are hot but extremely muddy with silt. The lower alluvial terrace hosts diverse thermal plant communities and a meadow of shrubs, including honeysuckle, common snowberry, western chokecherry and silverberry. The higher terrace hosts a balsam polar forest with a thick herb understorey.

The Racing River joins the Toad just after the hot springs, increasing the Toad's volume by at least a third. The river valley widens and there are many gravel bars covered with vegetation along the riverbanks. Bedrock outcrops create a few notable rapids. After Ram Creek comes in on river right, the river is fairly wide but remains shallow.

The mountains lining the Upper Toad River Valley host common alpine vegetation consisting of dwarf willow and birch, alpine grasses and sedges. The treeline generally lies somewhere around 1600 m ASL. Subalpine forests are dominated by subalpine fir and white spruce, along with willow and birch shrubs. Forests of lodgepole pine and white and black spruce dominate at lower, warmer elevations. Along the river you will see lots of aspen and poplar. Willow and wildflowers flourish on the sandy gravel bars.

The climate of the far eastern Rocky Mountain ranges and foothills is influenced by Pacific weather systems, which often regenerate in northeastern BC, but it is normally dry. To give you an idea of temperature, July daytime highs reach 20°C at Muncho Lake. Mean annual precipitation can be up to 800 mm in the alpine ridges. Rain and convective thundershowers are common at the higher elevations on warm afternoons. The showers can be heavy and flooding can occur. You can also have cold, wet weather for days when a system comes in. Compared to the rivers lying farther west, though, the Toad watershed is a dry place to be!

The river, still steady on its course northeast, drops into the foothills of the Rockies. Skipping quickly through this narrow band of high hills onto the Muskwa Plateau, the Toad cuts down into bedrock and you encounter First Canyon. The river has eroded the vertical rock walls incredibly smooth in the heart of this canyon. The rock is limestone, typical of the northern Rockies. First Canyon reminds me of the Grand Canyon of the Rabbit River, though it doesn't require the same level of skill to paddle. Still, you'll need skill enough to navigate the chutes, big waves and boily water of Crux Rapids!

Second Canyon follows after a wide, shallow section of river. In this second canyon, the Toad drops evenly and gradually through softer rock. There are riffles as opposed to rapids between its towering walls. You can see the layers of sediments in the hard sandstone and shale. In places, you can see what appears to be oil seeping from the strata. Those with an interest in natural history and fossils could spend a lot of time here!

After Second Canyon there is a long stretch of braided river littered with wood hazards. This graveyard of trees, mostly balsam poplar, reminds me of the notorious Scatter Ass Flats of the Lower Stikine route. In this section the Toad's banks are often actively slumping cliffs. This bank erosion dumps trees into the river, and they end up as wood hazards. It's not a very pretty stretch of river, and this is the most difficult and potentially dangerous section to navigate on the route. First Canyon's Crux Rapids are intimidating but the consequences of a swim if you are properly geared up are not deadly, unlike getting pinned under a wood hazard. Like Scatter Ass Flats on the Stikine, this section will be more difficult and dangerous if the water is up.

Eventually you will see more coniferous forest along the banks and the flats get easier to paddle. Once they end for good, you come upon some cool cliffs dripping with fossils. Then you are in the third and last canyon of the Toad. The canyon walls are vertical for a stretch and the stratification of the sedimentary rock is pure art. This is a very pretty section of river that takes you to the wonderful confluence of the Toad and the Liard.

The Muskwa Plateau ecoregion of the Taiga Plain is a drier region than the Northern Rockies and foothills of the Boreal Cordillera. Annual precipitation ranges between 400 and 500 mm. Bedrock outcroppings and cliffs of Cretaceous shales and sandstones characterize the Lower Toad, with elevations ranging from 760–975 m ASL. The forest is commonly made up of medium to tall stands of lodgepole pine, along with the climactic species of the region, black and white spruce. Wetlands are common, covering 25–50 per cent of the ecoregion.

On the plateau, the grey Liard takes up the aqua waters of the now medium-volume Toad. The Grand Canyon of the Liard, the mightiest and most dangerous section of the river, sits upstream of the Toad confluence, and the Liard River is large-volume and silt-laden by this point. The Liard River Valley has two different natures in the Taiga Plain ecoprovince. The first stretch after the Toad confluence is really beautiful, similar to the Muskwa River Valley just after its muddy waters take up the glacial green-blue waters of the Tuchodi. The Liard is deeply incised after the Toad confluence, unlike lower down on the Liard. The uplands of the Muskwa Plateau rise some 400–500 m and have steep scarps on their eastern sides. The bedrock is composed of sedimentary strata. This makes for very striking scenery on your journey through this ecoregion.

The current is fast on the Liard – 12 km/h or more. However, it slows as the river enters the Northern Alberta Uplands, running around 8 km/h on average in August, depending on water levels. Even then, if you listen carefully you will hear the silt particles hitting your hull and making a hissing noise. The riverbed of the Liard is more sand and gravel than silt, however. The river braids extensively around islands and gravel bars. There are numerous abandoned channels and they make for good wildlife-watching. With these dry channels and large islands, the Liard can be three kilometres across in places. It is often one kilometre wide, even in its straight stretches with only one channel.

At the confluence of the Fort Nelson River and the Liard you can see the two different-coloured waters meeting and running side by side until the brown flow of the Fort Nelson is absorbed by the grey of the mighty Liard. Tannic acid accounts for the brown of the Fort Nelson's waters. After the Fort Nelson River joins the Liard the scenery of the Northern Alberta Uplands ecoregion becomes dominant. The region is drier in terms of precipitation, but 50–70 per cent of the Alberta Uplands ecoregion is covered by wetlands. The surface material in the uplands is moraine, which is often covered with organic deposits supporting open stands of black spruce and some birch. The upland slopes without an organic blanket are covered with loamy glacial till supporting a mix of white spruce, balsam fir and aspen forest.

The rolling and hummocky moraine of the region is really evident at some points along the Liard, such as at La Jolie Butte; but the glacial remains you will most enjoy are the gravel bars along the river. They are often very large and treed, making for great camping. The other obvious feature of the Lower Liard is that its banks are lined with balsam poplar and black cottonwoods. Balsam poplar look like cottonwood trees, also a species of poplar, but the balsam poplar is smaller on average and predominantly found in BC above 56° north latitude. The balsam poplar is dominant along riverbanks from the Upper Stikine north to Atlin to east of the Rockies. As you leave the Muskwa Plateau you are likely to see a mix of cottonwoods and balsam poplar along the Liard.

Eventually you will see the Liard Range of the Mackenzie Mountains to the north and west. There is alpine tundra on the tops of the sedimentary rock peaks, which have been extensively glaciated. Approaching Fort Liard, Pointed Mountain and then Mount Coty dominate the view.

Around Fort Liard, built on a terrace overlooking the river, the Liard River Valley is lush. It has been nicknamed the "Tropics of the Territories" because of its microclimate that makes for hot summer days. It also gets the occasional chinook in the winter. The trees and undergrowth here grow fast and tall with all the daylight in summer. Spruce trees in the area grow large enough to build spruce bark canoes, and birch bark is plentiful from good-sized paper birch trees. The first- (over 6 m tall), second- and third-largest measured aspens in the world grow just outside of Fort Liard! Berries are abundant in the area, including high and low bush cranberries and blueberries, saskatoons, kinnikinnick, bunchberries, raspberries, blackberries, chokecherries, strawberries and bunchberry. Wild rose and twinflower are also common understorey vegetation.

The Lower Liard section of the canoe route sits in a subarctic climate zone. The mean annual precipitation is 350–450 mm. Temperatures vary extremely, with the winter being very cold and the summer quite warm. At Fort Liard the daytime highs in July average 22.7°c. Arctic air often brings long periods of clear, sunny weather to the region. However, when the weather socks in you can find yourself in a cold, three-day rain. Headwinds from the north can be ferocious. But in general, month for month, this is a much warmer, drier trip than many of the ones outlined in this book. This has been my experience, especially in August. Some of the hottest days I've ever had canoeing in northern BC and the NWT have been on the Liard in that month. Afternoon thunderstorms often build up as a result of daytime heating. This area also generally has an extended summer, making the Toad/Liard a good fall trip. Paddling in the fall, expect temperatures in the teens during the day and cooler nights.

During the longest days of summer, sunset is around 10:30 p.m. and sunrise around 4:00 a.m. The long hours of sunlight and long dusks and dawns result in only about an hour of complete darkness, starting around 1:00 a.m. In late August and September, however, you may just be able to stay up for potential northern lights displays!

For more on the ecology and natural history of the northern Rockies and Taiga Plain, consult The Ecoregions of British Columbia, www.env.gov.bc.ca/ecology/ecoregions/province.html. Environment Canada's Ecological Framework, at http://atlas.nrcan.gc.ca/site/english/maps/environment/ecology/framework/1, provides more detail about BC's ecological classifications. A good book to consult is *British Columbia:*

A Natural History, by Cannings and Cannings. For more on the Rocky Mountains in particular, try Ben Gadd's *Handbook of the Canadian Rockies*. *Muskwa–Kechika: The Wild Heart of Canada's Northern Rockies*, by Wayne Sawchuk, has some amazing photos and stories that will make you want to explore all over the area. The Fort Liard community website, www.fortliard.com/location.htm, has some interesting local information on the ecology of that area.

Local History: ✱ ✱ ✱ for the Toad and ✱ ✱ ✱ ✱ for the Liard. The McDonalds, a Kaska family, are the stewards of the Upper Toad River region. Interestingly, near the headwaters of the Toad, by Moose Lake, is a reserve of the Fort Nelson First Nation. This First Nation is based in Fort Nelson and its membership is mostly of Dunne-thah (Slavey Dene) and Cree descent, along with a number of members of Dunne-za (Beaver), Sekani and Kaska ancestry. The Sekani roamed in the Toad River region and have close ties with the Kaska in the northeastern Rockies – the band at Kwadacha near Fort Ware, for example – so it seems possible that the allocation of the Moose Lake IR to the Fort Nelson First Nation stems from the amalgamation of a number of Kaska and/or Sekani families associated with the northeastern Rockies into the Fort Nelson First Nation.

The Lower Toad, closer to the river's confluence with the Liard, is associated with Kaska groups from Lower Post and Fireside. Kaska traditional lands are thought to have extended all the way down from the Upper Liard in the Yukon, past the mouth of the Toad, to Nelson Forks at the confluence of the Fort Nelson and Liard rivers. That said, some sources indicate that the Toad's mouth marked the boundary between the Kaska and Fort Nelson First Nation. It is safe to say that at present, somewhere downstream of the Beaver River confluence, the Lower Liard is associated with the Fort Nelson First Nation and then farther downstream on the Liard their territory overlaps with the territory of the Acho Dene (Slavey Dene, or Dunne-thah) First Nation from Fort Liard. The grey areas with regard to the traditional territories of Kaska, Dunne-za, Sekani and Dunne-thah First Nations are a result of fur-trade expansion from the east and subsequent displacements and amalgamations of these peoples.

The Toad River is marked on Arrowsmith's 1854 map, Jorgensen's 1895 map and the BC Lands map from 1917 and is named as such on all three. This discounts the story of the name's origin adopted on the Toad River Lodge website:

There are many stories of how different places got their names along the highway. We kind of liked this one about Toad so we've adopted it. Back around 1942 when the Canadian and US armies were busy building the Alaska Highway (it was not the super highway you just drove in on) there were problems crossing the river, what with no bridge yet built, so it was par for the course to be 'towed across.' The proprietors of this establishment at that time adopted 'Towed River' as the name of their lodge. Did someone really think they meant 'Toad' or were their language skills lacking? Your guess is as good as ours at this point. So that's our story and we're sticking to it, for now anyway.

In fact, according to a notation from 1952 showing on the BC Geographical Names Information System (BCGNIS), the traditional name for the river is Tsal-eh-chesi. No meaning or language group is given. The current name for the river is noted in John McLeod's journal from his 1831 exploration of the Liard as coming from the great number of toads seen along its banks, many of them very large. McLeod writes:

> Toad River falls into the West Branch [of the Liard] on the left shore, and is at its entrance about 40 Yards across but shallow and Rapidous; it derives its appellation from the number of Toads seen along its banks and some are of immense size; I have seen some which weighed upwards of a pound, and the Indians inform me there are some to be seen of a much larger size.

The Frog River watershed sits just to the west of the Toad, so clearly this part of the Rockies has more frogs and/or toads around than others.

According to the BCGNIS, the Kaska name for the Liard is Nêt´i Tué, meaning "river flowing from the mountains where the sheep are snared." Other First Nations names for the Liard as found in Coutts's *Yukon Places and Names* are Erett-chichi, Thatradesse and Too-Tee. Another I found was Itzehadzue. All the names express the size or force of the river. The Acho Dene Koe of the Fort Liard area refer to the Liard and Mackenzie as one river, Deh Cho, Deh meaning "river" and Cho meaning "big."

The name Liard comes from the descriptive name given the river by the early voyageurs. Rivière aux Liards (there are many renditions of this French name) means River of Poplars or Cottonwoods. Cottonwood is a species of poplar, and cottonwoods and balsam poplar grow along the Liard, with balsam poplar predominating from the Liard's headwaters to east of northern Rockies. In early summer, the white seed clusters of the trees look like large snowflakes and they waft on the wind like cotton.

The Liard had many other names in the historical era. Deloire River and Lizard River are from the Cassiar Gold Rush period and anglicized versions of Rivière des Liards, another rendition of the original voyageur name. Great Current River and Mountain River are two names from the early fur-trade and exploration days, as is Black's River. There was a lot of confusion about what river Black discovered on his 1824 explorations, but it certainly wasn't the Liard. The Liard was also referred to as the South or West Branch of the Mackenzie River in early HBC documents. There were many documents and maps that used the name Liard for other rivers – the Dease, Fort Nelson and Kechika among others – making things quite confusing.

My personal favourite name for the Liard in history is River of Malediction, bestowed by Robert Campbell, the first HBC fur trader and explorer to reach its headwaters. He and his party paddled and portaged up the Liard in canoes when it was in flood in June, so no wonder the name. Walking would likely have been easier!

In fact, the Toad River watershed and upper and middle Liard were at one time laced with foot trails radiating north, south, east and west from the river valley. The archeological record of these trails suggests small Kaska groups travelled to hunting, fishing and trapping camps in a seasonal pattern via a trail network across the Liard Plain and particularly the southern uplands that cut across the drainage grain parallel to the Liard about midway between the river and the Rocky Mountains. Along with trails on both sides of the Liard, these midway trails linked the Liard with the upland lakes and passes from one headwater of the Liard tributaries to the next.

Confluences were key sites in the annual round, and old trails along rivers and streams that dissected the area were used for hunting and beaver trapping. There is a cemetery at the Toad and Racing River confluence and it was apparently a gathering site for trade between the Kaska and a northern group of Sekani. The ethnography suggesting this also surmises from the archeological record that wood bison were native to the grassy area around this confluence and were hunted by the First Nations there. The McDonalds, a Kaska family grouping, still live, hunt and trap in the region, and just a few generations ago this family-based group was still travelling down the Liard in boats to trade at Fort Nelson. The BGGNIS indicates that Mc Donald Creek, which flows into the Racing River not far from its confluence with the Toad, was named after Charlie MacDonald (the current family name spelling is McDonald and the creek's name was changed in 2002 to reflect this), "the patriarch of the Grand Lake Indians who was living near this creek in 1944 when topographic surveys were completed."

The confluence of the Toad and the Liard was also a seasonal gathering place for trading and socializing for the Kaska of the Middle Liard region and their relatives by marriage. At some point a fur-trade post also operated at the mouth of the Toad and a group of Sekani lived near the Toad confluence sometime after 1825, according to ethnographic sources. Apparently, by the 1890s there were three trading posts operating in the Kaska territory associated with the Toad River.

The Beaver River was an important travel route for Kaska coming from the north. The confluence of the Beaver and the Liard was also the site for gatherings and trading between the Kaska and the Fort Nelson First Nation. A fur-trade post was built there and operated for some period of time. The Kaska from the Yukon and the Toad River Valley would also travel down the Liard in canoes and skin boats to trade at Fort Nelson and Fort Liard.

Before the fur trade really got rolling in BC, the lands around Fort Nelson were populated exclusively with Athapaskan-speaking (Dene-na) First Nations. According to Gerri Young's *The Fort Nelson Story*, a local publication, the original inhabitants of the Fort Nelson watershed were the Beaver (Dunne-za), Sikanni (Sekani), Nahanni, Grand Lakers and Dogrib people. From my research I have noted that the names Nahanni and Grand Lakers have often been used to refer to Kaska groups in the past.

The historical record indicates that with the expansion of the fur trade from eastern Canada to the north and west, the First Nations territories in the Fort Nelson River region changed. Groups of Dene (Dene is a compound of two words: De, meaning "flow," and Ne, meaning "Mother Earth," which has been translated to mean "the people" as in "of the earth") migrated north and west, pushed by an influx of Plains Cree well equipped with guns from the fur trade that was booming to the east. As the Cree spread into the NWT and northern BC with the expansion of the fur trade, groups of Dunne-thah (Slavey Dene), Dunne-za, Sekani and possibly Kaska were pushed farther west. Apparently, by 1775 these changes in territories were already taking place, and by the time the fur traders came to the Fort Nelson and Lower Liard rivers and set up their posts in the early 1800s, things had settled down.

In the Fort Nelson area, the Cree and Dunne-thah ended up amalgamating. The Fort Nelson First Nation, based on a reserve near the community of Fort Nelson, was formerly called the Fort Nelson Slavey Indian Band. However, they changed their name to recognize the Cree and diverse Dene-na ancestry of their population. Though many of the people of the Fort Nelson First Nation are of Dunne-thah and Cree ancestry, some members are also of Dunne-za (Beaver), Sekani and Kaska ancestry. And although some groups of these three Dene-na or Athapaskan-speaking nations likely had been displaced from the Fort Nelson region, they still travelled from the south, east and north to gather and trade at Fort Nelson and other posts in the area. Treaty 8 documents indicate the Dunne-za, Sekani and Kaska had a history in the region, and for years after the Fort Nelson First Nation signed the Treaty 8 adhesion in August 1910 there was still the question of reserves for the small roaming bands of Sekani and Kaska in the area. The Dunne-za Beaver people were allocated small reserves on the southern tributaries of the Fort Nelson. See the Tuchodi/Muskwa Rivers chapter for more on the Dunne-za and Sekani First Nations prehistory and history in the northern Rocky Mountain and Foothills region.

The First Nations territories in the Liard River Valley and region also changed with the coming of the fur trade. The lands along the Lower Liard in far northeastern BC and the NWT, including the Fort Liard area, are the historical and current lands of the Acho Dene Koe First Nation. Acho Dene Koe members call themselves Slavey and they are closely related to the Dehcho First Nations of the Mackenzie River and Great Slave Lake areas, possibly having originally been more closely associated with those areas before the fur trade and subsequent migrations. They have a close relationship with the Fort Nelson First Nation, the new Nation their Dunne-thah cousins helped form. From around the Beaver River confluence downstream to below Nelson Forks, the Lower Liard is associated with the Fort Nelson First Nation and then farther downstream on the Liard their territory overlaps with that of the Acho Dene Koe First Nation from Fort Liard. An Acho Dene Koe territorial map shows the border of their traditional lands as being the spot where the Liard crosses the BC boundary into NWT.

With so many groups of First Nations moving west, the eastern homelands of the Kaska may well have become an area frequented by a number of First Nations. There is overlap on the Lower Liard between the Fort Nelson First Nation and the Kaska. Kaska traditional lands are thought to have at some time extended all the way down from the Upper Liard, past the mouth of the Toad, to Nelson Forks at the confluence of the Fort Nelson and Liard rivers. That said, sources also indicate that the Toad's mouth marked the boundary between the Kaska and Fort Nelson First Nation. It is certain that the Kaska used the Beaver River to travel south and north to trade and socialize, and the Beaver confluence is a good distance downstream of the Toad confluence. The Lower Liard from the Toad to Nelson Forks is a grey area with regard to First Nations territories and was well travelled in prehistory and the fur trade.

The first written account noting the Toad River's existence is the 1831 journal of John McLeod of the HBC. McLeod started up the Liard River from Fort Simpson on the Mackenzie in NWT with eight other men and his pet dog. He was in search of the source of the Liard. On July 19, McLeod's group reached the mouth of the Toad, and this is when he notes in his journal the nature of the river's mouth and that its name came from the many and large toads found on its banks. He did not explore the Toad, but carried on up the Liard.

The first fur trading post the Kaska in the region frequented was Fort Halkett. Founded in 1829 by John Hutchinson, Fort Halkett was the HBC's first trading post in the middle Liard region. The first post was established at the mouth of the Trout River, but this site was abandoned for some reason. Fort Halkett was re-established at the mouth of the Smith River in 1832 by John McLeod Senior. Trading was brisk in the first few seasons and Kaska culture underwent extensive changes in a short period of time in order to maximize this economic opportunity.

It is thought that once the fur trade became established, the Kaska moved from spending most of their time subsistence living at their upland and mid-elevation camps, where there was better access to big game other than moose, to using lakeside central base camps in lower elevations. Beaver and other fur-bearing animals were far more abundant there. Moving to the Liard Plain also put the Kaska closer to Fort Halkett.

The Kaska began to spend most of the winter and spring trapping and preparing furs for trade with the HBC. That being so, fishing lakes became more important because the Kaska didn't travel to the highlands for hunting as they once did. Only later, when they began using dogs and horses, did they travel to the higher elevations again more frequently for meat. They could bring it back to the lower-elevation base camps more efficiently and still have the time to participate in the fur trade.

Before horses were introduced in the 1800s, travel in summer was mostly by foot and boat. Traditional canoes were one- or two-person craft made of spruce bark: a single sheet of bark sewn with spruce root fore and aft, with holes plugged with moss and spruce gum and with ribs and gunwales of spruce. Spruce-bark canoes were use for river travel, but according to sportsman and explorer Warburton Pike, these hastily made craft were only used to ship goods downstream and were left at the traveller's destination, the Kaska preferring to pack heavy loads on trails rather than work a canoe upstream. Small birchbark canoes were crafted for lake travel. After contact with the fur traders, larger birchbark canoes were constructed.

Small moosehide boats were traditionally used on rivers for hunting and fishing. The largest ones could take up to 20 hides to construct, and they were reserved for long-distance travel. The hides could be traded on arrival at a trading site. Later, moosehide and spruce-framed boats modelled on the HBC's York boats were crafted. In the 1940s, river scows with motors became the craft of choice, and these sleek wooden boats are still used today. You will see them skimming along the Liard and moored at Fort Liard. Now jet boats are the rage on the Muskwa, Fort Nelson and Liard rivers. Pun intended for canoeists who are not big fans of jet boats on wild rivers, including myself in most cases.

HBC records show a decline in both the quality and quantity of furs coming in to Fort Halkett after about five years of trading and only sporadically kept the post open from 1850 on. The company eventually abandoned the Liard as a trade artery in 1865, owing to changes in policy and not in small part to the difficulties encountered in persuading guides and employees to navigate the dangerous waters of the river. The Kaska, whose annual rounds included the Toad River drainage, eventually did most of their trading at Lower Post, which was connected via the Dease and Stikine rivers to the coast and to Fort Ware on the Finlay River by an ancient foot trail called the Altse Dene Tunna, which became the basis for the Davie Trail, used predominantly by travellers on horseback. See the Turnagain/Kechika Rivers chapter for more on the trails associated with the Kechika River watershed.

After the fur trade was diverted, the middle Liard country was quiet again – until gold was found in the Klondike. Ferdi Wenger's book about his canoe trips on the river, *Wild Liard Waters*, is a must read for your Toad/Liard journey. Wenger integrates historical accounts of the hardships of the explorers John McLeod, Robert Campbell and R.G. McConnell and the voyageurs and Klondikers to compare and contrast his parties' experience of the Liard in the 1970s. Reading the accounts Wenger supplies, you can hardly believe people could survive such hardships (many didn't).

I actually met Ferdi Wenger when we were both racing in the Yukon River Quest in 2006. He was racing at 70-some years young, with his son as his partner. I had a quick moment at the Kirkman Creek checkpoint to tell him how much I admired the fact that he had paddled the Liard, one of the most difficult rivers to canoe that can actually be paddled in northern BC, and that I loved his book about his adventures. He was very gracious. I didn't have time to tell him I had paddled the Toad. He and his party had considered paddling it when they realized on their first journey down the Liard that they wouldn't have time to paddle the Grand Canyon. They were looking for another way to Fort Simpson that would take less time. They were told there was a canyon in the Toad that was pretty bad, so they chose to paddle the Fort

Nelson to the Liard instead. I wanted to tell him the canyon wasn't so bad and that I was glad I hadn't read his book before I actually ran the Toad! Maybe I wouldn't have, either, given that information. Timing was on my side.

When Wenger paddled into Fort Liard on that first journey in the 1970s, he arrived at a small community still not connected to the world by road. Fort Liard is still a small community with a big history. The area is traditionally known by the Acho Dene Koe as the "place of the land of the giants" and they are "the people" of this place. There is a tale about a giant lying down to rest and forming the mountain range to the west as seen from Fort Liard. After the fur trade began, Fort Liard was called Fort Rivière-du-Liard, from the voyageurs' name for the river. The fort was established by the NWC in 1804 as the traders made their exploration and initial trading journeys into the region. Fort Liard, at the confluence of the Petitot and the Liard, was traditionally an annual summer gathering place, so it was a likely spot for the traders to set up shop. Archeological digs at Fisherman's Lake, across the river from Fort Liard, show evidence of 9,000 years of Slavey Dene occupation.

According to the community website, in the old days so many people came to Fort Liard in early summer for the gathering that all the canoes, laid side by side, would stretch across the Liard River, nearly a half a kilometre wide at this location. The original camping place appears to have included or been on the top of the cliff you will see on the river left side of the Petitot. There is a legend about a battle on the cliff, and all the bloodshed caused the rocks and soil to turn red, thus the colour of the cliff. Also, some elders say that when a rock falls off the cliff face it is a bad omen.

Confluences like that of the Petitot and Liard were key in First Nations annual rounds before the fur trade came and even more so after it became firmly established. The HBC came to Fort Liard in 1824 under the leadership of Murdoch McPherson. Robert Campbell and R.G. McConnell were other noteworthy explorers to visit Fort Liard on their exploratory journeys. Campbell was later also the chief factor there, as well as being one of the first European explorers in northern BC and on the Liard. Clifford Wilson's *Campbell of the Yukon* is a good book to read on a canoe trip down the Liard.

There was another HBC trading post on the section of the Liard you will paddle, called François, just downstream of the mouth of Sandy Creek. Apparently Nelson Forks, at the confluence of the Fort Nelson and Liard rivers, was used only as a cache and not a fur-trading fort as such. But it must have been of some importance as a settlement of some type, given that it is marked on the NTS maps. According to *The Fort Nelson Story*, Nelson Forks was supposed to have been a pretty place, built against a hill, with long steps up from the river to the HBC building, the houses and the mission. When you go there now it is hard to believe such a community existed.

The Métis population in northern BC grew with the establishment of the fur-trade posts. There were Métis from the East employed in the fur trade, often with French-Canadian coureur de bois fathers and Cree or Ojibwa mothers, but many of the northern Métis were offspring of Athapaskan-speaking mothers and fathers of northern European backgrounds (Scottish, Scandinavian, English, Irish, German etc.). Fort Nelson apart, with its significant Cree and French Métis populations, after 1850 many Métis in the Mackenzie District were of Scottish and Dene ancestry, as at that point the HBC had been primarily hiring Orkneymen to run the Canadian fur trade. Many of the northern Métis were affiliated with the Anglican or other Protestant churches, although there was a large Roman Catholic minority. For a comprehensive history of the Métis in the Northwest, see www.telusplanet.net/public/dgarneau/metis.htm. A history of the Métis in the Liard and Mackenzie river valleys can be found at www.dehcho.org/members/fort_simpson_metis.htm.

Missions began as early as 1858, at Fort Liard. An Anglican mission arrived that year and a Catholic one was established the next. The two denominations competed for converts through the rest of the 19th century. Father Petitot, OMI, travelled extensively through Canada's western Subarctic from 1862 to 1878. Apparently, during that time, he was the first European to travel the Petitot River from its headwaters to Fort Liard. The Petitot River, once known as the Black River for its dark, tea-coloured waters, was named in his honour.

Once the local families began spending most of the winter and spring trapping and preparing furs for trade with the HBC, their culture began to change more quickly. The HBC had abandoned the middle Liard River as a trade artery in 1865, but they didn't give up on the Fort Nelson River or the Lower Liard. Fort Nelson was re-established by the company in 1865 and was a busy river for shipping furs and goods long after the Alaska Highway was built and the road to Fort Simpson came through, apparently built as an alternative route to the Alaska Highway in case of Japanese bombing. In the 1960s the fur trade finally collapsed but the legacy of the HBC continues in commercial operations in both Fort Liard and Fort Nelson today, though Northern Stores are now the proprietors.

Charles Camsell, geologist, surveyor and eventually the founder of the Canadian Geographic Society, was born in Fort Liard, the son of the factor at the HBC trading post there. Charles became a Klondiker in 1897, along with his brother Fred, though they never made it to the goldfields in the Yukon. Instead, they chose to look around northern BC for awhile and Camsell became enamoured of geology. His autobiography, *Son of the North*, recounts some of his travels on the Liard and other northern rivers and is a good on-the-river read.

The number of people travelling on the Fort Nelson and especially the Liard exploded when gold was found in the Klondike. The Fort Nelson River, via Fort St. John and the Peace River, was one of the feeder routes to the Liard and the all-Canadian route to the goldfields. In 1898, joining the men with gold fever, Andrew Jackson Stone of the American Museum of Natural History went in search of his own type of discoveries. He went up the Stikine, down the Dease, then down the Liard River to Fort Liard and eventually the Mackenzie River to Fort McPherson, collecting northern specimens of plants and animals. He was the man that differentiated Dall from Stone sheep.

Both the Fort Nelson and the Acho Dene Koe First Nations signed treaties with the Canadian government in the early 1900s, but it did not radically change their lifestyle at the time. The government was far away and communications were sparse, given the available technology and the great distance. In 1922, 12 years after the Fort Nelson First Nation and the Métis in the area signed an addition to Treaty 8, the Acho Dene Koe and Métis in the Fort Liard area signed an addition to Treaty 11.

The First Nations in northeastern BC and southern NWT continued to be fairly autonomous until about the First World War. Subsistence hunting and trapping were the norm, because that was what fed the First Nations and the fur traders alike. This changed with a huge rise in prices for furs. The money that could be made from trapping made it a far more attractive economic enterprise than it had been in the past, and more store-bought food was available in the North.

It was after the Second World War and the building of the Alaska Highway and the beginning of oil and gas exploration that the peoples' lives in this area were changed radically. R.M. Patterson and his cousin Christopher travelled in the Fort Nelson area in 1954, and Patterson recounts his adventures on the Sikanni Chief and Fort Nelson rivers in a story in *Far Pastures*. The story illustrates some of the changes that were taking place in that era. Some people were still living close to the land, but by the 1960s most communities had lost their traditional economies for good. With government monetary assistance and compulsory education, many of the First Nations people in the area became more sedentary and more reliant on the purchase of food from stores. With the building of the Liard Highway in the 1970s, oil and gas exploration and resource development became the basis of the economy, and those activities along with forestry are now the major industries in the Fort Nelson and Fort Liard regions.

Fort Nelson is home to one of the largest gas-processing plants in Canada and also one of the largest wood products plants in BC. With all the exploration and helicopter activity you will see as you travel the Liard by canoe you will realize just how much resource extraction is in the works. The Pointed Mountain operation was being decommissioned when I was in Fort Liard in 2006, but upstream from there I noticed a new road reaching the river and new drilling equipment nearby. There was much more activity even since I had last been there in 2004.

Though the Liard is once again a busy waterway, there are far few people residing or travelling in the Toad watershed today than was ever the case before. Two travellers of note in the area in 1931 were Mary Henry and Knox Freeman McCusker. Henry was an American amateur botanist who travelled extensively in northern BC looking for unique species of plants. She hired McCusker, a land surveyor in the Peace River district, as her guide for her 80-day expedition to find the mysterious "tropical valley" in the northern Rockies.

The Henry party travelled from the Peace to the Liard by horse and foot. Their route from Halfway River near Fort St. John to the Toad River Hot Springs was along the High Trail, a major First Nations trail in the northeastern Rockies. Mary was somewhat disappointed with the Toad River Hot Springs, which is certainly not as impressive as the Liard River Hot Springs, the "tropical" place she sought, but she absolutely loved the adventure and the land. She made other long journeys in the years that followed and McCusker continued to guide her parties, collecting enough information to map the Alaska Highway. See the Tuchodi/Muskwa Rivers chapter and Larry Pynn's magazine article "Lost on the High Trail," listed in the References section, for more information on Henry, McCusker, the High Trail and the mapping of the Alaska Highway.

McCusker's map from the 1931 Henry expedition shows McDonald Creek, a tributary of the Racing River, as "McDonnell River." The creek flows into the Racing River 6 km south of where it joins with the Toad. According to BCGNIS the creek was named after Charlie MacDonald, the patriarch of the Grand Lake (Kaska) Indians, who was living near this creek in 1944 when topographic surveys were completed. Likely McCusker was referring to the same person. The creek's name changed in 2002 to McDonald to reflect the current spelling of the Kaska family still living in the area. Larry Pynn, in his article "The Last Mountain People," suggests the renditions of McDonald are corrupted versions of the Kaska families' real name in Kaska:

> They are the last of their kind, six Kaska Dena . . . the McDonalds (an incongruous surname, thought to be corrupted from their native language) . . . live primarily in two bush encampments . . . alongside the Toad River . . . All six are descendants of Charlie McDonald, a Kaska chief and prominent hunter and guide who died in 1975, having been married twice, to Kaska sisters of the Stone family.

In 2004 when I ran the Toad, the McDonalds were still in residence on the Upper Toad. The Kaska population became more centralized during the peak of the fur trade in the interior and with the building of the Alaska Highway. The highway further concentrated families still living seasonally in the middle Liard region in places like Lower Post and Watson Lake. In the 1960s children were required to go to school and the semi-nomadic nature of traditional Kaska life was changed forever. Families living off reserve on their traditional lands, like the McDonalds, became few and far between. Big-game hunting and resource extraction exploration are the main activities in the Toad watershed now.

The Kaska Tribal Council is working to deal with the consequences of culture change and questions surrounding sustainable development in their homelands. In the fall of 2004, a letter of understanding was signed by the Kaska First Nations and the Yukon and BC chapters of the Canadian Parks & Wilderness Society to formalize their long-standing relationship with regard to conservation in Kaska traditional territory. This historic document is the beginning of a protocol agreement to ensure that special environmental and cultural values of the Kaska's traditional territory are respected, protected, preserved and maintained and that conservation priorities are supported during upcoming resource planning, among other goals.

Hopefully, the Toad and Liard rivers will benefit from this initiative in the future. Though the Liard Plain has so far seen relatively little forestry activity, there is likely to be more in the area in the future. Past resource extraction activities include two copper mines operating in the Racing River watershed from 1966 to 1975 and a gas rig on the Toad River near Mile 40 of the Alaska Highway, abandoned long ago. However, now it is oil and gas development that is the greatest threat to the Toad and Liard ecosystems. Exploration on the Toad and the lower reaches of the Liard has taken off in the past few years and it is an issue that has some residents very concerned.

I've heard there are plans for a road following the Toad River Valley all the way from the Alaska Highway to the Liard. As well as hearing local Toad River residents' accounts of issues tabled at Muskwa–Kechika Management Area (MKMA) committee meetings they've attended, I've seen with my own eyes the intensive exploration activity along the Toad and Liard. If they find enough "black gold," there will be a road along the Toad. See the Turnagain/Kechika Rivers chapter for more on the history and issues facing the MKMA.

The MKMA is full of areas ·where development can take place, including roadbuilding, and a 2007 BC government bulletin confirms that the upper and middle Toad is being targeted for more exploration and resource development. It notes that in the summer of 2005, ARKEX Ltd. and JEBCO Seismic Canada began acquiring an airborne geophysical survey of the Muskwa–Kechika, covering 3,000 km^3 of the northern Rocky Mountain Foothills. The survey was completed in 2006 and the data acquired provides previously unattainable, detailed information of geological structures over this large area.

The Lower Toad is not even in the MKMA, so it is completely open for business. Only about the last 7 km of the Toad to its confluence with the Liard is protected from resource development, as that stretch is within the Liard River Corridor Provincial Park. A second park, tiny as it is, protects the Toad River Hot Springs.

The Toad River Hot Springs on the Upper Toad was first made an ecological reserve in 1974 and then a protected area in 1997 under the Fort Nelson Land & Resource Management Plan. In 1999, the hot springs area was designated a provincial park. The status was conferred due to the "regionally significant hot springs for wildlife viewing, hiking and First Nations values" as well as the diverse ecology associated with the hot springs. The springs are an important mineral lick for moose, Stone sheep and other ungulates, and the area is also heavily utilized by their common predators: wolves and black and grizzly bears.

The Liard River Corridor, a provincial park, protects the Liard from around the

Liard River Hot Springs to the Scatter River confluence, including the very lower reaches and mouth of the Toad. It is a large park of 88,989 hectares. The park's eastern quarter includes the last seven or so kilometres of the Toad and its mouth. This large section of the Liard was designated a park because it provides representation of the Hyland Highland to the west and the Muskwa (Northern Rocky Mountain) Foothills and Muskwa Plateau, which are home to a diverse variety of wildlife species. Its designation was meant to establish a large, distinct, relatively undeveloped corridor to protect the Liard River Valley as an intact ecosystem. The historical and recreational values were also considered high and important to protect.

The Liard River is also protected by the Scatter River Old Growth Provincial Park, a small park adjacent to the Liard River Corridor Park to the east. The primary role of the Scatter River park is to conserve an example of floodplain old-growth white and black spruce forest. The park contains a diversity of landscapes and ecosystems associated with forest succession from the series of large fires that have swept through the Liard River Valley. The secondary role of the park is to provide recreational opportunities, including camping, fishing, hiking, horseback riding, canoeing, river boating, wildlife viewing, hunting and photography. The park, at 1140 ha, is zoned Nature Recreation to provide for backcountry recreation opportunities in a largely undisturbed natural environment.

By the 1970s studies were already in the works for damming the Liard for hydroelectric power. In the 1980s plans were made to dam the Liard upstream of the Beaver River confluence. The dam was to supply power for a large pulp mill planned for Nelson Forks. A railhead was also to be built to ship the wood products out. A second proposed dam at Damsite X, or better known as La Jolie Butte or Cap Jolie, would have flooded the area to the 1,000-foot contour line. Such a catastrophe was averted by a decision in 1986 to forgo the project for at least 20 years. That period ended in 2006, of course, and the Liard may be being considered for hydro development again as you read this, although I have heard nothing along this line as yet. The provincial park status afforded the middle Liard means it will likely not take place in the Liard River Corridor, i.e., upstream of the Fort Nelson confluence, but it still could happen anywhere else along the Lower Liard. There are no parks protecting any sections of it, nor do I know of any government plans for conservation in the area.

For more information on boreal forest and other conservation activities in northern BC, and to find out what you can do to support them, contact CPAWS BC at www.cpawsbc.org and see www.spacesfornature.org/greatspaces/muskwa.html, www.muskwa-kechika.com and www.roundriver.org (click on Where We Work, then Canada/Muskwa Kechika/Reports & Publications).

Level of Solitude: ✱ ✱ ✱ for the Toad and ✱ ✱ ½ for the Liard. The Toad is a good river for finding solitude. Once you leave the Alaska Highway behind, there are no roads crossing the river and no settlements or hunting or fishing lodges along its banks, just a few cabins here and there. The river is not a regular jet boat run and it is only lightly rafted by a BC company. Neither the rafters I've talked to nor I myself know of any other canoeing parties that have ever paddled the river, so it is not going to be a crowded route. We did meet a private rafting party on our first paddling day, friends of Kelly Knight, the co-owner/operator of Main Current Rafting Expeditions.

The main activity I observed along the river was helicopters flying around supporting oil and gas exploration. This was intrusive and worrisome to me, given what I'd already heard about the possible road through the Toad River Valley.

The upper section of the Liard from the Toad confluence to the Beaver River confluence is very quiet, though the Scatter River confluence is under a jet flyway. After the Fort Nelson confluence there is more boat traffic and you will see a lot more evidence of oil and gas exploration, staging areas, helicopters and jet boats. There are also barges on the Lower Liard. Stay well, well away from them. They are huge and make a big wake and they cannot manoeuvre easily or quickly like you can.

For sure you will see local people out on the river hunting and fishing with their boats. I enjoy when they stop and chat. Their cabins dot the Lower Liard, particularly as you approach Fort Liard. Several families enjoying being out on their traditional lands invited me in for tea when I was on a solo trip in 2006.

Wildlife: ✷ ✷ ✷ The Toad/Liard route has good wildlife-viewing potential. The Toad River Hot Springs are a major mineral lick for moose and other ungulates, like Stone sheep and woodland caribou. Rocky Mountain elk and white tail and mule deer are also found in the watershed. Karlene and I saw a number of moose on the Toad in 2004, two at the hot springs alone. Wolves and black and grizzly bears frequent the hot springs area, given all the food around!

We saw a grizzly on shore our first day on the Liard after running the Toad. I have seen many black bears along the banks of the Liard over the years, including two young ones breaking into a cabin and a number swimming across the river. A long swim on this wide river should make canoeists reconsider the idea that island camps are not likely to be visited by bears! Evidence of wolves, black and grizzly bears and ungulates is abundant on the silty shorelines down the length of the Liard. Looking at all the tracks and trying to identify which animals made them is something most canoeists will enjoy on this river.

You can almost be sure to see bison on the Lower Liard from the Beaver River confluence to Fort Liard. I have seen many on my trips down this river, solitary animals and in small herds of up to five. The first time I saw them I was totally bewildered. Being from Saskatchewan, had I come all this way to see vestiges of home? I had no idea bison roamed in far northeastern BC. Apparently, the bison were reintroduced near Nahanni Butte, NWT, in the 1980s and have dispersed into BC. They have been seen as far south as Fort Nelson.

The bison are thriving, perhaps too much so according to some locals in the Fort Liard area. Moose, a traditional source of meat, browse the same vegetation bison do. The bison are competing for the moose population's food source. I was told that many residents of Fort Liard don't consider bison a desirable food and that even though the community can take a bison a year, they don't.

Beaver are also characteristic of the Liard. Other fur-bearing animals include marten, lynx, muskrat, mink, red squirrel and snowshoe hare. Also found in the area are porcupines, whose quills the Dene traditionally used to decorate hide products and bark baskets.

Bald eagles are certainly plentiful with all the fish around, and golden eagles are not uncommon. We saw a golden eagle on the Toad just before we entered First Canyon. It was a good omen for some nervous paddlers attempting to run a canyon that in the past had been run only by rafters, according to local knowledge. You may also be treated to a glimpse of a less commonly seen fish-eating raptor, the peregrine falcon. Other potential raptor sightings include hawks and osprey.

Mergansers and Canada geese are commonly seen on the river Liard. You may get lucky and see tundra and trumpeter swans, sandhill cranes and ducks on the way south for the winter. The Liard River Valley functions as a major migration corridor for waterfowl. Grey jays, various songbirds and woodpeckers, ravens and grouse are also characteristic of the region.

Fishing: ✻ ✻ The Toad's clear waters host grayling and bull trout (known locally as Dolly Varden trout). These populations are susceptible to overfishing, and according to locals, access to the Toad via the Alaska Highway has impacted both grayling and bull trout populations over the years. Consider your use of this resource in light of that. Grayling bite on flies or tiny spinners in fast water. Bull trout often can be found lurking in the pools near the fast water, striking at anything moving and shiny.

Fishing is not the greatest in the silt-laden waters of the Liard, though it hosts a great diversity of species. You will likely catch a northern pike or two if you try at the outflow of creeks and tributaries where clearer water mixes with the murky river flow. You may also catch bull trout at the mouths of clear tributaries, large and small. You can use the same tackle for both pike and bull trout. I've had lots of success with mid-sized spoons.

Walleye, or what I've always known as pickerel in Saskatchewan, are native to the Petitot River, and I've seen people standing on the shore at the river's confluence with the Liard fishing for them. Casting with small spoons can be successful, but jigging with lead heads and bait from a boat positioned in the eddy is often best. These fish like the eddy lines of fast-moving water and generally feed deep, just off the bottom.

Camping, Hiking and Other Activities: ✻ ✻ ½ for the Toad and **✻ ✻** for the Liard. You can camp for free at The Springs put-in on the Toad if you arrive too late in the day to get on the river. There is a fire pit already in existence by the turnaround, but camping is unorganized. It's a nice spot and the spring has cold, cold, clear water.

Once on the river, most groups will choose to camp on gravel bars, and there are normally many good ones to choose from. However, do plan your days with regard to the possible camping spots described in the Trip Notes when paddling Scatter Ass Flats and as you approach Fort Liard. Good campsites are scarce on these long stretches. Once on the Liard, great camps can be made on islands with poplar trees, as well as on sandy pine benches along the shore.

Nearly all the gravel-bar campsites mentioned in the notes will be pristine, the spring floods having washed them clean. Do not rely on them to clean up after you, however. No-trace your campsite as much as humanly possible. I'm sure the canoeing party behind you (in the unlikely event there is one, but it's the point, really) will appreciate not seeing evidence of you. See Appendix B for information about camping with minimal impact on the environment.

Hay Lake Campground provides the canoeist with free camping at a small lake just outside Fort Liard. It is a free municipal campsite with 12 sites, firewood, fresh water and a cooking shelter. You can find it off the access road from Hwy. 7.

There is some hiking to be done along the Toad. You can bushwhack fairly easily up some of the ridges, and you can hike in the hot springs area, walking back toward the highway on an 8 km trail used by ATVs to access the area. There is also a hike up the floodplain of Ram Creek, a tributary of the Toad. Serious hikers may want to plan some multi-day hikes in the region before heading downriver. *Northern Rockies Hiking and Motorized Trail Guide: From Mild to Wild*, by Heather MacRae, is a local guide available at the Fort Nelson Visitor Information Centre.

The Muskwa and Stone ranges are amazing and there are trails between the Toad and Gataga watersheds that will take you to the heart of the northern Rockies. It would be well worth adding a horse-trek adventure to your itinerary if you have the time and inclination. You could book a trail ride with Stone Mountain Safaris, a ranch/lodge in the Toad River Valley. This is a smart outfit not too far west on the Alaska Highway from the Toad River Lodge. The legendary Wayne Sawchuk also guides horse treks through the region and his tours are highly recommended. See the Directory of Services and Organizations for contact information for outfitters in the area.

On the Liard section of the route, you can stretch your legs by hiking up the floodplain of the Scatter River. There are also winter roads to walk along. Look at the topos and Forest Service map for these and consult the Trip Notes for "trailheads." There are also some hikes around Fort Liard if you want to end your trip with a hike. For instance, you can get a great view of the country from hiking up Mount Coty. Locals call it the fire tower hike. You can get all the information you need on local hikes at the Visitor Information Centre–Acho Dene Native Crafts in Fort Liard.

One of the highlights of my visits to Fort Liard is stopping at this information centre and craft store. The staff are so welcoming and willing to share local information and there are so many beautiful crafts by local artists. You have to go with your wallet in hand. Shopping and canoeing sometimes do go together!

Special Equipment: For the Toad River section of this route you will need a proper whitewater/tripping canoe that you are comfortable running up to Class 3 rapids in. Though the rapids on the Toad are not the boulder-garden boat wreckers you find on rivers like the Turnagain, I am a fan of plastic canoes on remote rivers like this one. There are no portage trails and help is a long way away. Canoes should have spray skirts, especially for First Canyon. If you are only running the Liard section of the route, any proper tripping canoe that can easily carry your load of gear will do.

Mandatory rescue equipment that you should have for any trip, but particularly the Toad River, includes one throw bag per canoe. The bag should be set up to tow, with a quick-release system in place. The Toad's current is always swift and there are fairly continuous rapids and riffles along its length, so you need to be prepared to chase and tow boats at any time. If you get into trouble towing, you must be able to disengage immediately. That being said, the water of the Toad is very cold, so getting people to shore quickly is your first priority.

I highly recommend wearing immersion paddling gear for First Canyon, such as a dry suit or a wet suit and dry top over insulation layers. This is mandatory if you are a one-boat party running the river (a three-boat party is recommended, unless you are exceptional moving-water canoeists). You will have to rescue the boat yourself and that means you will be in the water for a longer period of time, unless you are proficient at righting and re-entering your canoe in moving water. I'd still want immersion gear for this. In Crux Rapids there is nowhere for swimmers to get out on shore or to swim or tow canoes to until the gravel bar at the mouth of Scaffold Creek.

On the wide Liard, you should be prepared to tow a canoe and people for a long distance. It could take a long while to cross the river to shore; so, as on the Toad, my first choice is to have paddlers self-rescue by flipping the canoe right side up, climbing back in and then paddling the swamped canoe to shore. If they can't self-rescue, they should stay with the canoe for an assisted rescue. A canoe-over-canoe rescue is best, but very difficult with skirts and loaded canoes, so you usually must tow. Paddlers should hang on to their canoe so you can be sure they are okay and the party does not get separated. The Liard is actually not that cold in August. However, the paddlers should keep as much of their upper bodies out of the water as possible by clambering up on the canoe and kicking to help you make progress.

A satellite phone in case of trouble is highly recommended. There are very few potential sources of help on this route. If you lose a canoe or someone is badly injured, it's going to be a very, very long walk out for help. You could call for a helicopter on the Toad section or a floatplane on the Liard at certain spots, but you can't rely on any technology to work for sure. For that reason, always take a compass on this and any of your river trips in case you have to walk out for help.

A water filter is a good idea – as my own case of "beaver fever" attests to. The Liard is silty, so you may also want to take water containers to collect fresh water from clear creeks and give your water filter a break.

The Liard also has quite an active bug population in the summer months, though it usually dies down by September. You will want to take a head net, bug jacket, repellent or some combination of the three. I never go anywhere up north in the interior without my hooded bug jacket with a face net and repellent with a percentage of DEET. In 2006 on the Liard I used my bug jacket and a lot of repellent.

I would carry pepper spray and/or an air horn to deal with potential bear encounters. There are a lot of bears along the whole route and as you near Fort Liard the ones you may encounter are likely habituated to humans.

Trip Notes:

MAP NO.	GRID REF.	FEATURE	DESCRIPTION
94 K/14	699257	The Springs; Put-in; Camping	This is a good place to put in. The name comes from the very cold, clear stream that bubbles up here. The put in is a small sandy beach on RR of the Toad. The beach is reached by driving 1.5 km past the Toad River Lodge going west on the Alaska Highway. On the left you will see a garbage can pullout and then across on the right just down the highway is another pullout with a gravel road leading to the river. Turn right onto the gravel road (watch for big potholes), which becomes a track that goes down to the river. Keeping right, go about 600 m to arrive at the small beach. There is lots of room to camp on the treed bench where the track ends, and there is a fire pit at the turnaround by the river.
			The Toad here is a swift, narrow and shallow river. Riffles will be your constant companions and they are usually more significant at the bends in the river. The only rapids noted in the Trip Notes are Class 1+ or greater in difficulty.
	701261	Rapid	You are right into the riffles, and at the first bend of note there is a **Class 1+** wave train.
	704265	Rapid	Another **Class 1+** wave train.
	713264	Camping	A camp can be on the marked gravel bar on RR. There is a good, sandy landing spot.
	720272	Camping	The marked gravel/sandbar on RL makes a good camp.

728274	Camping	Another camping spot can be found on the marked gravel bar on RR.
730281	Logjam	Caution here at this corner, as there may be a wood hazard. In 2004 there was a logjam just after the creek coming in on RL.
750284	Camping	There is an unmarked gravel bar on RL with a great view of Toad Mountain that makes a good camping spot.
751286	Rapid	There are **Class 2−** standing waves around the corner where the river runs close to the mountain on RL. More sets of waves to come at the bends in the river.
773299	Rapid	An approximately 250-m set of **Class 1+** waves takes you into a straighter section of the river. There are some midstream boulders you will need to avoid.
775304	Camping	The gravel bar island on RR is a potential camping site.
782312	Rapid	Bedrock outcropping here makes for a **Class 2+/3−** drop that should be scouted. Stop on the gravel shore on RL above the drop and walk carefully over the rock to scout. There is a large wave or hole, depending on water level, near the top of the drop. The waves that follow down and around the corner from the chute are good-sized. You can line on RL if you wish. Following this first significant rapid are numerous **Class 1+** sets that are not described in detail.
806333	Hot Springs	The Toad River Hot Springs are over 1 km upstream of where they are marked on the topo map. After the river starts to swing to the right, look for a grassy open area up a stony bank on RL. The pools are a great place to view wildlife. They are a mineral lick and not good for soaking unless you really like mud baths. There is one pool with a rock ring built around it, but it is very shallow and muddy. You could camp here, but I would think you will have a lot of four-legged visitors keeping you up at night! This is a provincial park, believe it or not.
817328	Confluence	The Racing River is a startling colour of blue and its flow about doubles the volume of the Toad. The confluence is very beautiful and worth stopping for a look around. Do not disturb anything you may find associated with the old cemetery.

Now the Toad is really moving fast and you will need to vigilant, as **Class 1+ and 2– waves** are your constant companions for a long stretch.

The river valley widens and there are many gravel bars covered with vegetation along the riverbanks.

	835346	**Cabin**	There is an old cabin up on RL in an area that looks like it was burned at some point.
94 K/15	869369	**Camping**	There is a marked gravel bar on RR that provides camping and pretty views of the cliff on RL.
	869370	**Rapid**	Just after the cliff is a set of **Class 2** standing waves that carry on around the bend.
	880375	**Rapid**	At the next rock cliff outcrop there is a **Class 2/2+** drop with big waves and a large rock/hole on RL to avoid.
	885380	**Hiking**	You can hike up the floodplain of Ram Creek a ways to stretch your legs and look for wildlife.

After Ram Creek comes in on RR, the river flattens out again.

94 O/2	972451	**Rapid**	There are **Class 2/2+** waves in the channels around the gravel bar island.
	970457	**Rapid**	An approximately 400-m **Class 2+** rapid sweeps around the braided bend to the right. There are big waves and a few rocks to avoid. Where the channels converge you can run RR to cheat the big stuff at the bottom.
	977467 990473	**Camping**	The river really braids again and camping opportunities are plentiful throughout this section to GR 990473. The first island on RL is an especially nice spot.
	005487	**Rapid**	There is a **Class 2** rapid in the narrow squeeze here. There are a few rocks to avoid and some good-sized waves. We ran RL to RR.
	040507	**Rapid**	At the sharp corner with the gravel bar island (marked on the topo), there is a **Class 2** set of waves with some rocks to avoid.

You are now coming up to First Canyon, home of the most difficult stretch of whitewater on the Toad. Batten down the hatches, don immersion gear if you haven't already and make your rescue plans in the event of a swim. You will paddle some riffles, and then the walls of the canyon will close in as you approach the end of the canyon where the two significant drops are. There are two blind corners you

Toad/Liard Rivers

299

will not be able to scout from shore, only from your boat in the eddies. Pick your way slowly, hopping from one eddy to the next. The river is squeezed, so expect big waves, eddy fences, boily water and tricky cross-currents.

019529	**Crux Rapids**	Where the river narrows to one line on the topo is the beginning of Crux Rapids of First Canyon. There are two major drops, the first is **Class 2+** and the second approaches **Class 3**. They are very close together – it's really a series of chutes in a very narrow and smooth-walled canyon. Imagine my trepidation the first time I ran this stretch of river. A rafter told me it was Class 3, and I only had that to go on!

The first significant chute has a large boulder on RL, large waves at the bottom and then very swirly water with cross-currents made by the squeeze. Eddy out on RR as soon as possible. The first drop is followed directly by the second significant drop, a steep chute that sluices into a large wave just above a blind corner. There is a short wave train after the large wave, with swirly, boily water at the run-out. There is nothing of note below this last drop, though, and the last sharp corner of First Canyon hosts nothing but fast water.

The end of the canyon is around the blind corner and then Scaffold Creek comes in on RL. This spot on the Toad is absolutely beautiful.

There are some exposed sand/gravel bars that would do for a camp after First Canyon, but nothing with shelter. There is a camping spot coming up in a few kilometres.

030552	**Tricky water**	At the corner there is some really boily and swirly water.
031559	**Camping**	On RR is a gravel-bar camping spot with a beach to land on at its north end.

There are more deciduous trees now, as you are on the Muskwa Plateau.

014605	**Camping**	On RR there is a flat gravel bar with small trees for your tarp. There is a good landing spot on the north end of this camping spot.

You are now heading into the scenic Second Canyon, which is much different than First Canyon! There are riffles in this short canyon with lovely sedimentary rock walls, but no significant rapids. The cliffs seep something black and slick here. You can see why the Toad is being targeted by oil and gas exploration. There are fossils to be found in this area, but leave them as you find them.

After Second Canyon the river begins to braid again, and does it ever. This is the Scatter Ass Flats of the Toad. You must be very, very careful to avoid wood hazards. This is an approximately 30-km-long, tricky stretch of water where you must be vigilant in sticking to the main deepwater channels to find a clear route through the masses of dead trees. It's not easy.

Gravel bars abound but they don't make for good or nice camping. They are exposed and littered with tree carnage.

Actively slumping cliffs on RL add more trees to the already plentiful wood hazards.

At around 80 km into your Toad River run, the graveyard of wood peters out. The forest has more conifers again and the gradient picks up as you close in on Third Canyon and the confluence of the Toad with the Liard.

984784	**Camping**	On RL there is a sandy bench to camp on at the base of the hill near the trees. Across the river is a fossil hunting spot.
		This is the beginning of Third Canyon, a pretty stretch of river with no rapids of note. However, there is one tricky corner coming up.
975796	**Tricky water**	There are whirlpools created by the rock point on RL. Be prepared for squirrelly water.
947808	**Camping**	A small camp could be made on the gravel bar on RL, a bit rocky but what a spot here at the gate to the Liard. Good fishing may be had downstream at the lovely creek's outflow.
939810	**Camping**	There is good camping on the head of the treed RL gravel bar "island" marked on the topo. This is the last camping spot on the Toad.
909825	**Confluence**	The confluence of the Toad and the Liard is a magical place. It feels steeped in history to me and it was an important place for the Kaska and other First Nations who rendezvoused here before the fur traders came. Apparently there was a small trading post at the confluence at one time. Voyageurs must have loved this place on their downstream run to Fort Liard. They had survived the Grand Canyon one more time and were home free from scary rapids all the way to the fort.

The Liard is fast here, the current clocking at least 12 km/h, but after the first few bends it slows to an average of around 8 in August in a low-water year. You can expect faster current at higher water. The eroded cutbanks and sedimentary buttes of this section of the Liard make for a scenic float.

915840	**Camping**	You can camp on RL of the Liard on the marked gravel bar just downstream of the mouth of Graybank Creek.
937843	**Camping**	There is a sandy bench to camp on RL. A nice spot, but the view is not as good as the last site.
959872	**Camping**	The head of the large island is sand and gravel and provides a spot to camp.
966880	**Camping**	On RR just downstream of the marked gravel bar is a sandy spot to camp.
967903	**Camping**	On RR at the foot of the treed island is a sheltered spot to camp in inclement weather. There is a steep approach up to the spruce forest for cover.
94 N/10 055015	**Camping**	On RR, just downstream of Ruthie Creek, is a pretty spot to camp. There are grassy flats and a sand beach to land and walk along to stretch your legs after supper.
053084	**Camping**	Where the Scatter River joins the Liard is an awesome spot to stop and camp or just spend some time exploring. You can camp anywhere at the mouth of the Scatter River, upstream or downstream, on the sand or in the trees. Just pick your favourite spot or one that suits the weather.
	Hiking	Take a hike up the floodplain of the Scatter River and check out the cool erosion formations, which you can just see from the Liard as you pass the main outflow channel of the Scatter.
		Note: your satellite phone may not work very well here. There is a major jet flyway overhead.
052091	**Cabin**	On RL there is a cabin sporting a large radio antenna. This sight was quite startling for me in 2004. We hadn't seen any sign of any human presence for a number of days except for helicopters doing exploration work.
051098	**Rapid**	There is a **Class 1+/2−** big-volume riffle where the Liard gets squeezed up against (and is eroding) a slumping cliff on RR. There are good-sized rebounding waves on RR as a result

and some big boils and cross-currents at the run-out. Stay RL to miss the funkiest water. This is the most significant rapid on the Liard from the Toad confluence to Fort Liard.

	047113	Camping	On RR there is a small grassy flat in the middle of the beach that would make a decent camping spot.
94 N/9	171235	Cabin	On RR there is a cabin.
	245196	Camping	A sandy bench on the marked gravel bar with trees on RR makes for a good camping spot.
	271182	Confluence	The Beaver River joins the Liard here. There was an HBC trading post here and the clearing is still obvious up the steep bank on RL. The Beaver was an important travel route used by the Kaska in the southern Yukon and northern BC to socialize and trade with each other. You can feel it is an important confluence. I've met local people from Fort Nelson going up hunting and fishing in this area a number of times.
	272157	Camping	There is a good spot to camp on RR on the marked gravel bar. There is some shelter in between the trees and a sandy bench for tents.
	326120	Camping	Another, larger site is on RR at the head of the marked gravel bar. There are big poplars or cottonwoods (I can't tell!) on the bench, so the site is sheltered.
	325095	Camping	There is yet another site on a gravel bar on RR. This is a nice spot. There is a good gravel landing and a flat bench up top with trees for shelter.
	368047	Camping	On the head of the long, narrow island there is a sandy bench with trees that makes for a good site to camp.
	386969	Confluence	The sluggish Dunedin River comes in on RR.
		Side trip	If you are interested in checking out Nelson Forks, a prehistoric trading site and the location of an historic HBC fur-trade cache, one option is to try one of two channels on RR of the Liard that connect it to a side channel of the Fort Nelson (GR 397977 or GR 401984). Both of them may be blocked with logjams, though. If so, you'll have to paddle upstream quite a distance from the confluence of the two rivers (GR 429010). Nelson Forks is on RR of the Fort Nelson River at GR 430954 Map 94 N/8. All that remains of this hub of the busy river of days

gone by are some overgrown ruins of log cabins up in the bush. There is a winter logging road in behind The Forks. Apparently this is the route the railway would have taken if they had dammed the Liard and built a pulp mill here.

94 O/12w	439013	Camping	If you take the RR channel around the large island delta at the mouth of the Fort Nelson, there is a good gravel/sandbar to camp on, on the east side of the island.
94 N/9	430028	Confluence	The Fort Nelson's muddy brown waters flow into the Liard here. The Liard is really moving again, 8–9 km/h in August 2006. That year was a higher-water year, with flooding early in the season. There were lots of freshly downed trees adding to the existing wood hazards. Keep your eyes open. There will be logjams on islands and in side channels, even more than on the upper section you have just paddled. The

current slows a lot as you approach La Jolie Butte, 4–6 km/h depending on water level and time of year.

	430039	Camping	On RL, next to an island, there is a marked gravel bar that makes for a spot to camp.
94 O/12w	460119	Camping	There is a large gravel bar at the foot of the island complex. It is treed and provides sheltered camping.
	466130	Camping	Another good site with trees and a good view of La Jolie Butte.
	475157	Camping	On the east side of the large island, across from the butte, is a gravel bar you can camp on.
	495185	Cabins	There are two cabins on RR by a cutline.
	516217	Camping	A treed gravel bar on the northeast side of the island makes a good camp. There is an easy landing and unloading area in front.
94 O/13w	524280	Camping	There is a treed gravel bar on the head of the island that makes for a camping spot.

There is no short cut to François anymore. Logjams block the first two main RR channels. You can go RR of the last three northern islands, though. This can be a very windy corner, in my experience. Once, on a solo trip, I couldn't make any headway at all so I just stopped on the big island, lay down and had a nap. The silt blowing around on the gravel bar covered me while I was sleeping!

	512313	Cabin	By the old channel exit there is a cabin.

	532353	**Historic site**	François, just downstream of Sandy Creek on RR, was an HBC trading post and is now a private camp with half a dozen cabins. The current picks up a bit to around 7 km/h again after François.
	523374	**Cabin**	There is a cabin downstream of an old side channel.
	527376	**Camping**	A small camp can be made in a tiny, old channel opening. There is a flat gravel area in among the trees lining the sides.
	525390	**Drill camp**	In 2004 there was a camp spot here, but in 2006 it had been transformed into an oil and gas drilling supply camp. There was a helicopter just landing as I paddled by.
			The RL channel that passes the confluence of the La Biche River is slow, and there is nothing much of interest to make the side trip worth it, in my opinion. The RR channel around the island conglomerate is the faster and prettier route.
	547487	**Cabin**	There is a cabin on RL at the beginning of the side channel. In 2004 we saw two black bears trying to break in!
	557508	**Cabin**	Another cabin sits on RR by the tiny creek.
95 B/4	557517	**Border**	Here you cross the BC–NWT boundary, with the Yukon boundary just 500 m to the west. Cool! Someone has actually put a sign up on RR. Funny!
	532544	**Road**	There is a winter road coming down to the river on RL. There was drilling activity here in 2004 and 2006.
	536573	**Cabin**	There is an old cabin on RR.
	534574	**Camping**	On the marked gravel bar at the head of the island on RL, there is an area to camp with a good gravel beach landing and a sandy bench up in the trees for tents.
			Go to the far right channel as soon as possible in this hugely braided section of the river. It is the fastest route.
	564607	**Riffle**	There is some very fast and boily water here when the river is up.
			In 2004 we saw five wood bison on the big island that splits the river.
	577631	**Cabins**	On RR there are a couple of cabins. One has a green tin roof.

574635	**Camping**	Camping is good on the gravel area with trees at the foot of the island on RL. **Note: this is the last good quiet spot to camp before Fort Liard.**
		On the islands on the right at the next bend I saw four wood bison in 2006. I've also seen half a dozen black bears in the area over the years.
		The Kotaneelee River coming in on RL has a very mucky mouth and there is no camping.
633724	**Cabin**	There is a cabin on RL just upstream of another winter road with drilling support activity at the riverbank. The current is 7–8 km/h and really picks up for a short stretch.
677747	**Riffle**	When the river is up there is a set of **Class 1+** standing waves for about 250 m. There can be some funky boils too. More potentially scary is the fact that every time I get near this spot on the river a huge barge comes along squeezing me to the RR shore where there is a huge logjam. Both the barge and wood hazard are daunting! Stay well away from both.
704748	**Cabins**	Two cabins sit on RR.
715753	**Road**	There is an old road coming down to the river on RR where there is a big clearing. You are almost at Fort Liard!
731775	**Confluence**	On RR the Petitot River's red-brown waters flow into the milky Liard here and you are at Fort Liard.
	Fort Liard	You have a choice of a number of take-out spots on RR at Fort Liard. Pick the one that suits your logistics the best. The map the Visitor Centre provides will really help you orient yourself.
	Take-out option #1	There is a public boat launch with cement pads close to the Northern Store and the Visitor Centre. You can just walk up the road to either.
	Take-out option #2	You can also pull up to the steep bank at Ernie McLeod's if he is your transport to Fort Nelson. He will give you directions and landmarks.
	Take-out option #3	You can land at the barge dock at the very northwest end of town. You can't miss it.

CHAPTER SEVEN

TUCHODI/MUSKWA RIVERS

The Tuchodi and Muskwa rivers canoe trip takes you from the stunning Northern Rocky Mountains into the foothills, onto the Muskwa Plateau and finally into the lowlands of the Fort Nelson region. The turquoise twin lakes and topography of the Upper Tuchodi watershed make for a very scenic beginning to your journey. Sharp rampart peaks with steep rock faces tower over the West and East Tuchodi lakes' psychedelic-coloured waters. This route is unique in having such large and beautiful lakes on it. Enjoy them! Hiking, fishing and wildlife-viewing opportunities abound. You will also want to explore the huge alluvial fan creating the lakes.

However, the lure of the fast current and many shallow rapids of the Tuchodi River will soon call. On the river you pass through an area so obviously shaped by a glacial past. The large outwash floodplain of the Upper Tuchodi sits in a wide u-shaped valley with great views of sedimentary alpine ridges. Gorgeous erosion formations line the river and incoming creeks.

Lower down on the Tuchodi the river becomes more intimate and the rapids increase in size. In the green foothills, the forest and valley close in as the Tuchodi descends steeply to join the Muskwa, a waterway of a completely different character. Its murky flow cuts through black sand cliffs under the big sky of the Taiga Plain.

Ending just downstream from the confluence of the Muskwa and the historic Fort Nelson River, this canoe trip also has a cultural component. You can visit Old Fort Nelson, once an HBC fur-trade post of importance and a vibrant community of First Nations and Métis from lands far and near.

This route snakes through two of the most remote regions of northeastern BC. Though the Tuchodi Lakes and Tuchodi River are protected by the Northern Rocky Mountains Provincial Park, much of the foothills area of the Northern Rockies as well as the Taiga Plain through which the Muskwa flows are targeted for oil and gas development.

Length: The trip described in detail is approximately 239 km long. You put in at the southwest end of West Tuchodi Lake, paddle approximately 77 km on the Tuchodi lakes and river and then run the Muskwa River for 160 km. From the confluence of the Muskwa with the Fort Nelson River it is a 2 km and change paddle to the Fort Nelson River Bridge take-out. Canoeists can comfortably do the route in eight days. However, you may want to take more time to explore, hike and fish at the Tuchodi Lakes. They

Tuchodi/Muskwa Rivers

are marvellous and you do not want to miss what they have to offer. They really are a highlight of this canoe trip.

To shorten the route and get the best of the scenery (to be honest, the last stretch of the Muskwa is not a pretty float), paddlers can take out at the Muskwa River Boat Launch, with access to the Alaska Highway. This will cut 92 km off the Muskwa River section of the route.

To extend your trip for another six or seven days, you can paddle the Fort Nelson and Liard rivers to Fort Liard, NWT. Or, for a really long journey, you can carry on to Fort Simpson, at the confluence of the Liard and the Mackenzie, another 315 km or so. Those with a whole lot of time could head on down the Mackenzie to its mouth on the Beaufort Sea of the Arctic Ocean. How cool is that?!

West Tuchodi Lake to Muskwa River Boat Launch*	147 km
West Tuchodi Lake to the Fort Nelson River Bridge*	239 km
West Tuchodi Lake to Fort Liard**	509 km

* These trips are described in detail in the Trip Notes section of this chapter.
** The Fort Nelson to Fort Liard section of this trip is described in detail in the Fort Nelson River chapter of volume one and the Liard section of the route in the Toad/Liard Rivers chapter in this volume.

Topographic Maps: I strongly reccommend the 1:50 000-scale maps for the Tuchodi River section of the route. You will want to know where you are with regard to the rapids and the many wood hazards. The 1:250 000 topos are fine for paddling the Muskwa, but just remember that pinpointing features using the Grid Reference System coordinates in the Trip Notes is more of a challenge on that scale. If you want to do some hiking and exploring at the Tuchodi Lakes and in the surrounding mountains and lower down on the Muskwa, I strongly suggest you use the 1:50 000-scale topos and carry a compass and know how to use it. However, I would also bring the 1:250 000 topos on this trip because the old horse trails that would make for extended hiking adventures are marked on them and they allow you to identify at a glance the larger features of a region, such as mountains and valleys, and plan for longer hikes. I carry both scales when hiking and paddling. To figure out what extra topos you need for any extended hiking trips, consult the index for NTS topographic maps for BC online at www.maptown.com/canadiantopographical/bcntsindex.html.

For paddling the Tuchodi River the 1:50 000s you will need are 94 K/2, 94 K/1 west, 94 K/1 east, 94 K/8 east, 94 J/5 west and 94 J/5 east. For the Muskwa River section to the boat launch the 1:50 000s are 94 J/12, 94 J/11 and 94 J/13. For the paddle all the way to Fort Nelson, add 94 J/14, 94 J/10 and 94 J/15. The 1:250 000s you want for the whole route are 94 K and 94 J. You only need 94 J for the Muskwa

River section. See the Fort Nelson River (covered in volume one) and Toad/Liard Rivers chapters for the maps for an extended trip to Fort Liard.

I suggest you purchase or print your topo maps in advance. Not only will you be able to plan your paddling days, but by using the coordinates in the Trip Notes you can mark the locations of sources of emergency help, known hazards, rapids, portages and potential campsites (there are some sections where good campsites are scarce) and other sites of interest so you have the information at hand when navigating the river. Remember that river features change with each freshet and flood, especially with regard to wood hazards, and you are responsible for always being on the lookout for them and being able to deal with them safely. Note too that it is difficult to know exactly where you are on some sections of this route because the rivers' channels have changed over the years.

This is also a good trip to practise with a GPS. For use with the GRS coordinates in the Trip Notes and the 1:50 000-scale topos, make sure the map datum is set to NAD 27 Canada and the position format to MGRS (Military Grid Reference System). See a further discussion on topographic maps and the use of a GPS in the How To Use this Guidebook chapter.

Getting There and Away: This is normally a fly-in and drive-out trip. The simplest logistics have you flying to West Tuchodi Lake and driving out from either the Muskwa River (also known as Kledo or Kledo Creek) Boat Launch or the Fort Nelson River Bridge take-out. The flight to the Tuchodi Lakes is incredible, worth every penny. The scenery is astounding and wildlife viewing is great from the plane! Lyse, my paddling partner on this route, thought it was the best flight she had ever been on.

If you are taking hard-shell canoes, you will have to fly in via floatplane. The only floatplane charter service in the area is Liard Air at Muncho Lake, about 250 km west of Fort Nelson on the Alaska Highway. Liard Air and the Northern Rockies Lodge are owned and operated by the same family and the lodge makes for a good staging area for the Tuchodi/Muskwa rivers route.

Beyond flying right from the lodge's dock on Muncho Lake, you can rent good canoes from them. There is safe parking, a very good dining room and a choice of accommodations, from rustic cabins to luxurious rooms in the main building. There are also some nice provincial campgrounds around Muncho Lake. Plus, you can see lots of wildlife and amazing mountain scenery on the drive to Muncho Lake through Stone Mountain Provincial Park. There is also some great hiking in the area and you just might want to visit the famous Liard Hot Springs for a soak.

Logistically, you have a number of options for shuttles to and from Muncho Lake. If you have two vehicles or more and your own canoes, you can do a regular shuttle, leaving your take-out vehicles at the Fort Nelson airport, about 500 km round trip and six hours of driving. If you choose to take out at the Muskwa River Boat Launch the shuttle is shorter by about 174 km. The access road to the boat launch is at km 520 of the Alaska Highway.

If you only have one vehicle and rent a canoe(s) from Northern Rockies Lodge, your party can take the bus from Fort Nelson to the Lodge, leaving your vehicle at the Fort Nelson airport's main terminal parking – it's safe and free. Or, you can charter a wheel plane flight to land at the lodge's airstrip, instead of taking the bus. From the lodge, fly in to Tuchodi Lakes and paddle to Fort Nelson and then drive the canoe(s) back to Muncho Lake. Northern Rockies Lodge will also organize a vehicle shuttle for you for a fee.

There are no canoe outfitters in Fort Nelson to rent canoes from or organize a shuttle through. Northern Rockies Lodge is your only source for both of these services. Fort Nelson does have scheduled flights and vehicle rentals. You could fly in to Fort Nelson, take the bus or a charter aircraft to Muncho Lake, rent a canoe from the Northern Rockies Lodge and fly out from there. Then you could paddle the route to Fort Nelson and have the lodge pick up the canoes from Fort Nelson. It may be cheaper to rent a vehicle (with a roof rack or a truck with a long box) and drive the canoe(s) back to Muncho Lake. Then head back to Fort Nelson, drop off the rental and catch your scheduled flight out.

The logistics I put together for my trip were somewhat special because I have a PakCanoe, a great folding/inflatable canoe. It can be transported in a duffle bag, and I can charter wheel planes instead of floatplanes to access some rivers, making for cheaper flights. There is an airstrip at Tuchodi River Outfitters' lodge on the Tuchodi and we chartered a small plane out of Fort Nelson to get there. From the lodge, Larry Warren, the owner/operator, took us up to West Tuchodi Lake in his jet boat. His fee was reasonable and the family hospitality at the lodge was fantastic. Note that you need to contact Tuchodi River Outfitters well in advance of your arrival about use of the airstrip and any other services you wish them to provide.

These logistics worked well. We left my vehicle at the Fort Nelson airport, flew out from there and then paddled back to Fort Nelson. I left Lyse with the boat and gear at the Fort Nelson River Bridge and hiked up the road a few kilometres to the airport to retrieve the vehicle from Villers Air Service. Safe and free parking and no driving shuttle required! You can camp for free at the take-out at the Fort Nelson River Bridge and there are other private campgrounds in Fort Nelson. You can camp near or at Muncho Lake at one of the provincial park campgrounds or stay at Northern Rockies Lodge. The put-in spot described in the Trip Notes at the southwest end of West Tuchodi Lake has a large, established campsite.

For more information on services in Fort Nelson and logistics for paddling all the way to Fort Liard, see the Toad/Liard Rivers chapter. For contact information for transportation, outfitters and other services, see the Directory of Services and Organizations.

When To Go: Late July to September. You do not want to run the Tuchodi or the Muskwa at peak flows in June or July. There are way, way too many wood hazards, particularly on the Tuchodi, and the river runs very fast. Each freshet creates new logjams on this narrow, small-volume river. Less flow means more time to react.

Spring snowmelt, precipitation and glacier melt from the Lloyd George Icefield, feed the Tuchodi and Muskwa rivers. Being partially fed by glaciers, when it's warm and there is rain, the rivers will rise quickly, particularly in the case of the Tuchodi. It is a small, short river with a large surface catchment basin. As on the Rabbit, Gataga, Toad and Taku rivers, water levels will fluctuate significantly with the weather. Flash flooding is possible at any time and you want to be cautious if levels are rising. Archived hydrometric data shows the Muskwa can swell to 20 times its average summer volume in July. Its soft banks are very susceptible to erosion during flood stage, making for new wood hazards.

Near the end of summer, when temperatures drop, the glaciers normally no longer contribute much to the river's flow. Come the end of August levels will usually drop significantly and September normally has the lowest flows of the canoeing season. However, as with any rivers fed even partially by glaciers, water levels can rise dramatically with warm, wet weather and that is possible any time during the paddling season.

Very experienced and skilled parties of moving-water paddlers will enjoy the challenge of the feisty little Tuchodi at mid- to late-July water levels. The river will be up and navigation will require excellent boat-scouting and reading-and-running skills, but there will be fewer jet boating parties on the river and the month is great for wildflowers in the alpine. July can be a rainy month at higher elevations in the northern Rockies. Heavy showers, often associated with thunderstorms, are common. Average daytime temperatures at Muncho Lake reach 20°c.

Parties wanting a less rollicking ride should paddle this route in August. The later you go in the month, the surer you can be that you will have lower water. With less flow, you will have more time to boat-scout or stop and assess rapids and wood hazards. The exposed gravel bars make for good camping and the berries come out in full force in this normally drier month. The insects are not so populous toward the end of the month, making camping and hiking more pleasant. The drawback to running this route in August is that jet boats can be a real nuisance and a navigational hazard. Lots of hunters use them to access the region, and hunting season for Stone sheep begins August 1.

You will usually have even lower water in September. You will likely have to fly with a floatplane to the Tuchodi Lakes, however, as Larry can't get upriver in low water. It will be frosty in the mornings if it is clear. Snow is also possible. You will need to pack for any weather; expect the worst and enjoy what you get! The joys of a fall trip are the changing colours of the deciduous trees in this region, and the bugs will have really calmed down, making camping and hiking even more pleasant. The jet boats will be around, but likely not at the lakes or on the upper stretches of the Tuchodi. Wildlife viewing up there will be great.

Unfortunately, being that water levels are key to having an enjoyable and safe trip on the Tuchodi, there is no active water-gauging station on the river to determine the river's real-time flow. However, you can contact Larry at Tuchodi River Outfitters. He is out on the river all the time and will know what levels are like and how they are fluctuating.

The Muskwa's flow is actively monitored and you can obtain real-time readings from the Environment Canada website. As you can see from the table below, the Muskwa peaks in either June or July, depending on the spring conditions.

Average Monthly Mean Flows in m³/s

Muskwa River near Fort Nelson (1945–2005)	
June	563
July	606
August	388
September	241

Source: Environment Canada, Archived Hydrometric Data Report, June 2006

You can use the table above to compare the real-time readings you get from the website to see if the Muskwa is running at high, average or low flows for each month. To access real-time and specific historical flow data, go to the Environment Canada hydrometric website, at http://scitech.pyr.ec.gc.ca/waterweb/formnav.asp?lang=0. Set the "Find Station By" slot to read "Province," and in the "View all Real Time Stations within" slot, choose "British Columbia." In the resulting alphabetical list of station names, scroll down to "Muskwa River near Fort Nelson" and click the "Go to Station" button. In the resulting "Disclaimer" screen, go to the bottom and press the "I accept" button. In the page that follows, at the top left, make sure the "Data Category" slot is set to "Real Time," and just beneath that, change "Parameter Type" to "Discharge." The resulting graph will show actual flows, in cubic metres per second, for the past week up to the current date. You can change the date span of the readout to anytime since January 1, 2007, by resetting the controls just beneath the graph and hitting the "Redraw" button.

You can also compare the real-time readings to more specific historical flow data on the website. The table I've provided only gives you average monthly mean flows, whereas the website graph will give you a more detailed picture of the changes in flow throughout a given month. To change to historical mode, choose the "Historic" option in the box near the top and hit "Go." The server is crunching a lot of data, so the screen may take a moment to change. Use any year for your search. What you really want is the baseline information to compare your real-time reading with. So, be sure to click the "Max," "Min" and "Mean" buttons on the lower left side of the page. "Upper quartile" and "Lower quartile" flows are of interest too. They can tell you if the real-time flows are in the top or bottom 25 per cent of all recorded flows. Once you have your options selected, click on Go to get a graph with different lines representing all the statistics. Ignore the line that represents the data from the random year you used; look instead for where your real-time reading fits in. If you were to plot your reading of, say, 500 m³/s on this graph, would it sit above or below the mean line? Keep repeating this process every week or so until you leave for your trip. You will know by then if the Muskwa is fluctuating normally or not. Have a backup route already researched so if the Muskwa and likely the Tuchodi are just running too high for your comfort level, you can paddle your second choice instead. You have lots of routes in the region to choose from in the two volumes of this guide.

To put this hydrometric data discussion in some context, when we ran the Tuchodi/Muskwa route the week of August 13–22, 2005, the Tuchodi was definitely low, but basically normal for that time of year, according to Larry. The Muskwa was running at 455, 433, 428, 314, 381, 350, 326, 308, 305 and 309 respectively on those days. The average flow of the Muskwa in August, as noted in the table, is 388, so we were on the river at relatively normal flows for that time of year. It was generally sunny but not overly warm and the river dropped, as one would predict.

Though the Muskwa is a much larger-volume river than the Tuchodi, it also really responds to rainfall and glacier melt and will rise and drop significantly over extended wet and dry periods. Earlier in August 2005, the Muskwa jumped from 345 to 1020 in 24 hours! Then a week later it was 560. When we were paddling the Muskwa it looked like there had just been a large flood. There were lots of fresh trees in the river and hanging from eroded banks. Once I looked at the hydrometric data later, it all made sense.

Arctic air masses often bring long periods of clear, sunny weather to the Fort Nelson region. This makes for warm paddling days and cool nights. This has been my experience, especially in August. Some of the hottest days I've ever had canoeing in northern bc have been on the Muskwa, Fort Nelson and Liard rivers in that month, yet I've had frost at night. That said, headwinds from the north can be ferocious and a three-day rain is possible.

If you are into planning for your trip early you can check how any given year's water levels are shaping up by watching the snowpack on the Environment Canada River Forecast & Snow Survey website, at www.env.gov.bc.ca/rfc. On the site is a snow survey (snowpack and water supply outlook) bulletin that is updated eight times per year starting in January and is based on data gathered from snow and hydrometric measuring stations. The regional snowpack and water supply forecasts basically tell you whether the water levels are expected to be less or more than normal in a region come the summer and how much of the snow has melted and how fast. This is good general information and useful in deciding when to schedule your trip. If there is a lot of snow in any given year, as there was in 2007, you may want to delay your trip to later in August. You could have high flows throughout July and into August in a year with a huge snowpack.

Difficulty of the River: ✷ ✷ ✷ for the Tuchodi and ✷ ½ for the Muskwa. The wood hazards in the many shallow, rocky rapids of the Tuchodi River are the reason the first part of the route gets a three-star difficulty rating. The Muskwa River has no significant rapids, but wood hazards are of concern.

The rapids of the Tuchodi are not large or difficult in themselves, but the continuous nature of many of them, along with the large number of dangerous wood hazards in this narrow, fast-flowing, braided stream make this a tricky run. Canoeists need strong moving-water skills in order to avoid several dangerous logjams and the many sweepers and strainers on the river more than they do for running the rapids. When there are both hazards and rapids, you will have to be able to make quick decisions and precision moves, including stopping in tiny shore eddies or just ramming right up on the gravel bars. Strong intermediate moving-water canoeists will be challenged by the Tuchodi River, and these paddlers should go at lower water and be prepared to stop, scout and line at any point. More time should be allotted for the descent of the Tuchodi section of the trip.

Caution is required when paddling the Tuchodi Lakes. These are large bodies of water without shelter from the wind and you can find yourself in big chop very quickly. Stay close to shore. The water is cold, even in summer.

The Tuchodi River always runs swiftly, and there are numerous sections of continuous, shallow and rocky Class 1+ to Class 2 rapids. There are a few short Class 2+ drops along the way, one in Hoodoo Gorge and another upstream of the mouth of Dead Dog Creek. The Tuchodi is always braiding, and finding the deepwater channel is challenging. That is often the line with the least hazards, but not always. The logjam, strainer and sweeper hazards are always changing and wherever you see trees down or stands of dead trees, eddy or ground out to stop and walk ahead to look for the safest way around the hazards. If you've never run a small-volume stream with wood hazards like those in the Toad River or the Scatter Ass Flats of the Lower Stikine, you should consider another route.

The Tuchodi section of the trip is not strenuous, except for carrying around or pulling over logjams and wood hazards when necessary. Those are the only mandatory portages. Your ability to focus will be tested in the continuous riffles, rapids and hazards. This is a remote area, but given the jet boat traffic, help would probably forthcoming at some point if you wreck your canoe. However, it won't be in time if someone is pinned against or under a logjam. Jet boat traffic itself is a hazard. Eddy out immediately if you hear or see one coming.

The Muskwa is a medium-volume river after the Tuchodi joins it. The water can be boily where currents from different channels converge or the river's flow is squeezed. Rapids consist of a number of easily run Class 1+ to Class 2– standing wave trains and most of these can be cheated. There are logjams and other wood hazards on the Muskwa, but they can be more easily seen and avoided than on the Tuchodi. The river is not particularly cold in the heat of the summer. There are no portages, but paddling can be strenuous if you encounter headwinds.

In conclusion, the Tuchodi/Muskwa route is only for moving-water canoeists able to run up to Class 2+ rapids with precision and in a loaded canoe. Paddlers should have excellent river-reading skills and fully understand the hazard that wood in moving water presents. Stopping in moving water is the key to safety on the Tuchodi. Canoeists must be able to eddy out in micro-eddies along shore. Scouting wood hazards from shore and lining and pulling around them will be required at a moment's notice. Paddlers should be competent in swift-water assisted and self-rescue techniques. Intermediate parties should go later in August and be made up of three canoes so one can assist swimmers while the other goes after the boat and gear. This is not a route for novice moving-water paddlers in any month.

The gradient of the Tuchodi, from its outlet on East Tuchodi Lake to its confluence with the Muskwa (about 60 km), is a whopping 5.6 m/km! This is the shortest and steepest river in this book – only the Tatshenshini whitewater canyon has more gradient. What is great is that the drop is evenly spread out along the river and all the rapids can be run, except when there are dangerous wood hazards in them. The Muskwa River section to Fort Nelson has a gradient of 1.7 m/km and the current is fairly fast and steady.

Character of the River and Region: Ecologically speaking, the Tuchodi/Muskwa canoe route lies in both the Northern Boreal Mountains ecoprovince and the Taiga Plain ecoprovince. The Tuchodi lakes and river lie in the Northern Canadian Rocky Mountains ecoregion of the Northern Boreal Mountains, and the Muskwa flows over the Muskwa Plateau and into the Hay River Lowland (commonly known as the Fort Nelson Lowland), two ecoregions of the Taiga Plain. Paddling in two different ecoprovinces and three different ecoregions en route makes for extremely diverse scenery on this canoe trip.

The very small, shallow and lively Tuchodi River flows northeast from its headwaters in the eastern Muskwa Ranges into the Tuchodi Lakes. From these magnificent aqua lakes ringed by pretty peaks, the Tuchodi rushes off northeast again. Then it quickly turns east to run through the foothills of the Rockies, finally speeding southeast, then northeast to drop onto the Muskwa Plateau of the Taiga Plain to join the Muskwa River. The Muskwa's brown flow wends northwest, then northeast across the plateau to slide eastward down into the Hay River Lowland. It joins the equally brown waters of the Fort Nelson River at Fort Nelson.

The main feature of the Northern Canadian Rocky Mountains ecoregion is the rugged Muskwa Ranges. The Tuchodi Lakes area showcases fine examples of these mountains made up of sedimentary rock up to 1.5 billion years old. Rock of the Muskwa Assemblage, only seen in patches in the northern Rockies, occurs in the mountains around the Tuchodi Lakes, making for more colour variation on their slopes. In other areas of the Northern Rockies the mountains are generally grey, made up mostly of slate, shale and limestone.

The most imposing peak on the north shore of West Tuchodi Lake is 2686 m ASL. The tallest mountains of the eastern Muskwa Ranges are around 3000 m ASL. The mountains have been modified as a result of glaciation and erosion, among other natural processes. Glacial drift, colluvium and bedrock outcrops are common surface materials. Glaciation has resulted in broad u-shaped river valley bottoms, mountain cirques and morainal ridges.

The headwaters of the Tuchodi feed the Tuchodi lakes. The alluvial fan at the mouth of the creek on the north side of the lake was created by glacial outwash, and the debris backs up the flow of the river creating West Tuchodi Lake. The sand and gravel debris at the mouth of Joplin Creek near the far eastern outlet of the Tuchodi River also keeps the Tuchodi's flow backed up, creating East Tuchodi Lake.

After the lakes the Tuchodi River continues on as a small-volume river through-out its journey to the Muskwa, riffling helter-skelter through braided channels. The floodplain of the Tuchodi in gravel from glacial till, and the river bottom is made up of small rocks, gravel and sand. Glacial flour makes for the slightly milky appearance of the aqua-coloured Tuchodi. The current is fast, up to 14 km/h. As you leave the lakes, the river valley is wide for a while with great views of the last of the Muskwa Ranges. Hoodoos also grace its length.

The mountains lining the Upper Tuchodi valley host common alpine vegetation consisting of dwarf willow and birch, alpine grasses, sedges and lichen. The treeline is at about 1600 m ASL. Subalpine forests are dominated by subalpine fir and white spruce, along with willow and birch shrubs. Forests of lodgepole pine and white and black spruce dominate at lower, warmer elevations. Along the river you will see lots of white spruce and aspen, as well as some balsam poplar. Grasslands can be seen on the slopes, especially around Tuchodi River Outfitters. From the Rocky Mountains east into the foothills, large-scale burning to enhance wildlife range has resulted in extensive young aspen stands and grasslands. Even sage can be found in the grassy areas, along with goldenrod. Willow and wildflowers flourish on the sandy gravel bars.

The climate of the eastern Muskwa Ranges and the Rocky Mountain Foothills is influenced by Pacific weather systems, which often regenerate in northeastern BC. Mean annual precipitation can be up to 800 mm on the alpine ridges. You can have cold, wet weather for days when a system comes in, but compared to the rivers flowing through the Coast Mountains, the Tuchodi is a dry place to be! Arctic air masses often bring dry air to the region, making for clear, sunny days. Rain and convective thundershowers are common at the higher elevations on warm afternoons. The showers can be so heavy that flooding can occur.

The Tuchodi River's floodplain shrinks and the valley narrows as you enter the foothills. These lower reaches of the river are more intimate, with small gorges and many shallow rapids. The rock of the high, steep-sided hills is sandstone and shale.

After the narrow band of foothills, the Tuchodi ends its journey on the Muskwa Plateau of the Taiga Plain, dropping into the Muskwa River. The stretch of the Muskwa right after it absorbs the Tuchodi's aqua waters with its muddy brown flow is really beautiful. Towering black sand cliffs make up the riverbank. The scenery is similar to the Liard downstream of the Toad River confluence.

The uplands of the Muskwa Plateau have steep scarps on their eastern sides. Bedrock is composed of sedimentary strata, shale with hard sandstone and conglomerate layers on top. The hard rock resists erosion and forms the escarpments, which can be up to 200 m high. The Muskwa flows through a long shale valley that parallels the Rockies and separates the foothills from the Taiga Plain.

The Muskwa Plateau ecoregion of the Taiga Plain is drier than the northern Rockies and foothills. Annual precipitation ranges between 400 and 500 mm. The forest is commonly made up of medium to tall stands of lodgepole pine, along with the climactic species of the region, black and white spruce. Lowlands are black spruce complexes with intermittent muskeg areas, while escarpments are dominated by aspen and white spruce.

The Muskwa continues as a medium-volume river across the Plateau and the current is fast, averaging 10–14 km/h. There are standing waves here and there as the river steadily and evenly drops toward the Fort Nelson River in the Hay River Lowland (Fort Nelson Lowland). The Muskwa's riverbed gets more mucky and silty as you descend. The river braids in sections, with wood hazards and riffles. You know you are leaving the plateau when the good natural camping spots start to become few and far between.

The Hay River Lowland, or what is more commonly called the Fort Nelson Lowland, has a cold continental climate, making for cold winters and hot summers. It is an area of extremely low relief, with an average elevation of 450 m ASL. The Muskwa and Fort Nelson rivers are deeply incised, as much as 150 m. Elsewhere, streams meander across a surface little changed since the retreat of glacial ice during the Pleistocene. Drainage is poorly organized over much of the region. Wetlands and bogs cover 25–50 per cent of the land. The Muskwa in its lower reaches has oxbows and numerous abandoned channels that make for good wildlife viewing opportunities.

The lowland has a gently sloping terrain with extensive muskeg and black spruce bogs. Fire has been widespread among the forest, making for mixed forests of aspen and poplar, balsam fir, lodgepole pine, white and black spruce, some birch and shrubs. Berries are abundant in the area, including high and low bush cranberries and blueberries, saskatoons, kinnikinnick, bunchberries, raspberries, blackberries, chokecherries, strawberries and wild rose hips.

The lowland is underlain by flat or gently dipping Cretaceous shale and sandstone. Bedrock outcropping is rare, even along the rivers. During the Pleistocene, the continental Keewatin ice sheet covered the Hay River Lowland. Today the lowland is covered with a veneer of glacial drift that is comprised of debris transported from Precambrian areas far to the east.

At the confluence of the Fort Nelson and the Muskwa, you can't tell which stream is which from colour, only from the map. I have to say, the Lower Muskwa around Fort Nelson gives the Fort Nelson River a bad rap. The Fort Nelson downstream of the community of Fort Nelson is actually quite a bit less mucky and chewed-up-looking than the Muskwa, and as it approaches the Liard it gets much more scenic. It is a nice canoe trip and much more enjoyable than the Lower Muskwa with its few good camping spots.

For more information on the ecology and natural history of the Northern Rockies and the Taiga Plain, consult The Ecoregions of British Columbia website, at www.env.gov.bc.ca/ecology/ecoregions/province.html. Environment Canada's Ecological Framework document, at http://atlas.nrcan.gc.ca/site/english/maps/environment/ecology/framework/1, provides more detail about bc's ecological classifications. A good book to consult is *British Columbia: A Natural History* by Cannings and Cannings. For more on the Rocky Mountains in particular, try Ben Gadd's *Handbook of the Canadian Rockies*. It's a great reference book to take with you.

Local History: ✻ ✻ The Tuchodi drainage appears to be a grey area with regard to First Nations traditional territories in northeastern bc. The Kaska claim the Tuchodi river and lakes lie in the far eastern reaches of their traditional territory. Other sources indicate that the entire Tuchodi River to its confluence with the Muskwa is the northwestern border of the territory of the Dunne-za (Dunneza, Dane-zaa, Tasttine or Beaver) First Nations of the Peace River region. Prior to the fur-trade-induced migration of the Cree into northern Alberta and northeastern bc and the subsequent shifts in other First Nations territories, Dunne-za and Sekani territory is said to have extended over the entire Fort Nelson watershed, including the Muskwa, Prophet and Sikanni Chief, all major tributaries of the Fort Nelson River.

It appears that after the displacements and amalgamations resulting from the fur trade, the territory of the Dene-thah and Cree people of the Fort Nelson First Nation overlapped with that of the Dunne-za to the northeast of the Tuchodi River and along the lower reaches of the Muskwa. Sekani and Kaska traditional territory also overlapped in the far northeastern Rockies, and both are associated with the Finlay River region. With different groups moving west, traditional Kaska territory to the east may well have become frequented by a number of First Nations. See the Toad/Liard rivers chapter for more information on the Kaska in northeastern bc.

The Dunne-za and Sekani First Nations are thought to have a common cultural heritage, and their languages belong to the same Athapaskan branch. The Dunne-za and Sekani were pushed west by the fur-trade-related migration of the Cree into northeastern BC. Sometime before 1760, according to Alexander Mackenzie, gun-bearing Cree drove the Dunne-za people out of the Athabasca and Peace regions. Some moved farther west into the eastern slopes of the Rocky Mountains, where they displaced or mixed with the Sekani, who had already retreated to the west. Some Dunne-thah were also on the move sometime around 1775 and along with the Cree migrated into the Fort Nelson area. The result was the Cree and Dene-thah newcomers and some Dunne-za, Sekani and Kaska families still in the region becoming a new First Nation. The fur trade, Cree cultural influence, introduction of horses, arrival of missionaries and eventually the building of the Alaska Highway made significant impacts on the people of the northern Rockies and foothills and Taiga Plain.

According to Akrigg and Akrigg in *British Columbia Place Names*, the name Tuchodi comes from Slavey (Dunne-thah) words meaning "the place of big water," which they propose is in reference to the Tuchodi Lakes. Cho means "big" in Slavey so this meaning for Tuchodi seems likely. I was also told that "Tuchodi" may be a version of a Sekani word referring to the aqua colour of the water.

The Akriggs suggest that the name of the Muskwa River is Cree in origin. Though indeed Muskwa means "black bear" in that language, it is more likely the name of the river is derived from the Slavey name Mah Qua and that that was the name of the hunter with territorial rights to the river. On an 1895 map the Muskwa River was labelled "Sicannie River," but in 1914 the Geographic Board of Canada adopted "Muskwa River." A 1917 BC land map called it the Musqua River. The notes on the BC Geographical Names Information System (BCGNIS) website state: "The only name which the Indians recognize is the Musquah. The custom apparently is for a separate band of the Sikanni Indians to hunt on [one and only one] of these rivers, and the rivers receive the names of the leaders in each band – thus Musquah's River, Prophet's River, Sikanni Chief's River and Fantasque's River." This information was taken from the report of Major E.B. Hart, who participated in 1912 Department of Lands survey of the Liard River. According to George Behn, a past chief of Fort Nelson First Nation, the name Muskwa is derived from the Slavey name Mah qua.

It is possible the Muskwa was also called the Sicannie River as the 1895 map suggests and that the name changed with the shifts in traditional territories of the First Nations resulting from the fur trade spreading northwest. In *The Fort Nelson Story*, Gerri Young writes: "The native name for Fort Nelson was Thikanni Qua, meaning 'People of the Rocky River.'" This name indicates the Dunne-za (Beaver) and Sekani were resident there at some point – Thikanni, as in Sekani, and Qua meaning "river" (the Dunne-za and the Sekani were considered one tribe in the past, as they spoke the same dialect). Sekani is the English version of the Sekani name for themselves and means "people on the rocks." The Fort Nelson was also known as the Sekani River at one time, which may be connected to the fact that its main tributary is the Sikanni

Chief River, as in the river in the Sikanni chief's hunting area. The history of the First Nations and river names in northeastern BC is certainly intriguing!

In the northern Rockies, the First Nations usually travelled by foot and then often by horse after horses were introduced in the 1800s. There is an ancient First Nations trail, now called the High Trail and usually travelled by hunting and horse-trek outfitters, that runs along the eastern side of the northern Rockies. The main section runs 400 km from Hudson's Hope on the Peace River to Summit Lake on the Alaska Highway. It has two branches, one of which crosses the Tuchodi River below the lakes. Larry Pynn's magazine article "Lost on the High Trail" gives a good overview of the route and tells the tale of his great adventure on a horse trek along the trail. From Summit Lake the prehistoric trail heads over to the Toad River, and likely a trail continued north along the Toad to the Liard valley to link up with the network of Kaska trails there.

Most of the rivers in the mountains were just too wild for spruce and birchbark canoes and moosehide boats. But these craft were used to travel the waterways of the foothills and Taiga Plain, including the Muskwa River. Small moosehide boats were traditionally used for hunting and fishing. The largest ones could take up to 20 hides to construct, and they were reserved for long-distance travel. The skins could be traded on arrival at a trading site. Later, moosehide and spruce-framed boats modelled on the HBC York boats were crafted. In the 1940s, river scows with motors became the craft of choice and these sleek wooden boats are still used today along the Fort Nelson/Liard canoe route. Now jet boats are the rage on the Tuchodi and Muskwa rivers and also increasing in number on the Fort Nelson and the Liard. Pun intended for canoeists who are not big fans of jet boats on wild rivers, including myself in most cases.

The first Europeans to travel the far northeastern reaches of the Rockies and the Muskwa River region are thought to have been NWC men. The traders came to the Fort Nelson and Muskwa rivers by way of the Mackenzie River, named so for the first European to travel it, Alexander Mackenzie. From Fort Simpson, established by the NWC in 1804, the fur traders, guided by local First Nations, travelled upstream on the Liard and then, depending on the account you read, up the Fort Nelson River to build the first Fort Nelson. The fort was named after Admiral Horatio Nelson, who had become a British hero with his winning tactics in the Battle of Trafalgar, which took place on October 21, 1805, during the Napoleonic Wars.

The community of Fort Nelson is said to the third oldest non-native settlement in BC because of its birth as a fur-trade post. I've read a number of different accounts as to where the first Fort Nelson was located and have come to no conclusions. Some accounts say the fort was established on the Liard, and it appears from HBC records that indeed the first Fort Nelson could have been on the Liard. Adding to the confusion is that in the early days of the fur trade, as I mentioned, the Fort Nelson River was sometimes called the Liard. Others sources, such as Gerri Young's *The*

Fort Nelson Story, say the first Fort Nelson was established about 50 km north of the confluence of the Fort Nelson and Muskwa rivers. From my calculations, that puts it at the confluence of the Snake River, where there was a seasonal gathering place. All sources agree it was founded by the NWC, but there is some question as to whether the post was built in 1804 or 1805.

Old maps indicate a second Fort Nelson was established farther south on the Fort Nelson River. I'm not sure why the fort was moved or of its exact location, but according to historical accounts this second Fort Nelson was recorded as destroyed by fire in 1812 or 1813 after an attack by a party of Slavey. Eight people were killed, including the factor of the post and his family. The post was abandoned following the incident.

The European trading rights along the northern Pacific Coast passed from Russian to English hands in 1839 and the HBC stepped up its maritime operations, basically abandoning efforts to conduct trade with the west from the interior. The major forts, Fort St. James and Fort McLeod, continued to collect furs and send them back east but the push to develop new routes to the interior was no longer a priority.

Then, in 1865, looking again at the interior of northern BC, the HBC established the third Fort Nelson on the west bank of the Fort Nelson River near where the Muskwa joins it. St. Paul's, the first Roman Catholic mission in Fort Nelson, was founded here in 1868. In 1890, the fort settlement and the mission were destroyed in a huge flood. It is said that a resident of Fort Nelson at the time heard the steeple bell ringing as the church was swept away, rocking on the raging river.

The next Fort Nelson, the fourth by that name, was moved to higher ground across the river on the east bank, where your topo map indicates "Old Fort Nelson." St. Paul's Mission was also relocated there. Soon after being rebuilt, Fort Nelson became part of what was known as the Edmonton Trail, a route to the Klondike in the late 19th century.

With modern technology changing the nature of trade and travel in the region, Fort Nelson eventually became a summer barge landing. Goods were shipped from the south via Fort St. John, then down the Peace and Slave rivers to Great Slave Lake, down the Mackenzie and then up the Liard and Fort Nelson rivers. It was called "The Long Way Around" – you don't say! Apparently the first motorized barge of goods reached Fort Nelson on July 6, 1933. It had travelled 1,500 miles in five to six weeks. The horse-packing trail from Fort St. John brought goods in three weeks.

The building of the Alaska Highway in 1942 changed the direction of trade and travel and eventually caused the abandonment of the fourth Fort Nelson (Old Fort Nelson) in favour of the settlement then called Muskwa, which was growing up around the highway on the bank of the Muskwa River near the confluence with the Fort Nelson. In 1958, the post office was relocated to Muskwa and the name Muskwa was changed to Fort Nelson.

Old Fort Nelson was never designated as reserve land, and beginning in 1959 the treaty members of Old Fort Nelson were strongly encouraged to move onto the reserve farther east and away from the river but nearer to the highway. The school, the HBC store and the mission closed in the 1960s and by the early '70s the community was abandoned except as a summer "camping" and gathering place. Elders remember it as a good place to live. The Old Fort is now mostly a ruin of log cabins, but the church still stands. On the August long weekend there is still an annual gathering of the Fort Nelson First Nation at Old Fort Nelson.

So, technically, the fifth Fort Nelson is located on the Alaska Highway, not the river, though the airport is close. The Fort Nelson airport was originally built as part of the North West Staging Route for flying warplanes to Alaska in the mid-thirties. The route was originally developed by the Canadian government as part of the supply line for a project undertaken to lease aircraft to Russia. The route was further developed by the United States with the idea of supplying their far-off state with defence materials without having to jeopardize them on the Pacific. The need for heavy machinery to build the airstrip was a problem. At this time there was only a winter road from Fort St. John to Fort Nelson, based on the old Fort Nelson Trail – a footpath in prehistory and then a packing trail, eventually used by the Klondikers in 1898, and then a winter road in the 1930s. See www.calverley.ca/Part03-Transportation/3-030.html for more on this history.

Mary Gibson Henry (1884–1967) was probably the first European woman to lead an expedition in northern BC. On her 1935 expedition, she collected plants in the Tuchodi River Valley, camping on the Tuchodi in order to visit the mountain named after her, Mount Mary Henry, located north of the Tuchodi Lakes. She carried on overland to Telegraph Creek and then to Alaska via the Lower Stikine. Henry was from Philadelphia and eventually served as president of the American Horticultural Society. She went on her first adventure in northern British Columbia with her husband and children, visiting the Liard Hot Springs, and was accompanied by her daughter, Josephine, on subsequent expeditions. Henry collected plants in remote areas of the American coastal plain, the Appalachian Mountains, the Ozarks and then the Rocky Mountains from New Mexico to northern BC.

Although few people in BC would recognize Mary Henry's name, she could be called the founder of the Alaska Highway. According to Dorthea Calverley's website on the history of the Peace River district, Henry's exploratory plant-collecting expeditions gave Knox Freeman McCusker, the land surveyor who mapped the route the highway would take, the chance to compile the information he needed to come up with his proposal. Henry hired him to guide her northern BC expeditions and through that employment McCusker was able to collect vital information about routes through mountain passes and the lands and waterways between the Peace River and the Pacific Coast. For more information on Henry and McCusker's expeditions, see entries 013, 042 and 043 at www.calverley.ca/Part3-Contents.html, the table of contents to Part 3 of Dorthea Calverley's *History Is Where You Stand*. This website is an excellent online resource on the prehistory and history of northeastern BC.

Though McCusker had travelled at least some portion of the most ancient and well-used First Nations trails paths of northern BC while guiding for Mary Henry, the route he mapped for the Alaska Highway did not follow the High, Davie, Moodie or Police trails nor the Trail to the Interior nor the Telegraph, Teslin or Taku trails in the main. It did take in the Fort Nelson Trail and parts of the trail network associated with the Liard River Valley and likely other lesser-known trails in northern BC as well.

The project was a colossal undertaking. It took 11,000 US soldiers and 16,000 civilians only 8 months and 12 days to construct over 2400 km (1,500 miles) of road and 133 bridges through eight mountain ranges. Now, Fort Nelson sits at mile 300, and the highway is its main street. For further reading on the construction and history of the Alaska Highway, try *Crooked Road: The Story of the Alaska Highway*, by David Remley.

The highway changed life in northern BC forever. The great influx of people and modern goods and the ease with which one could travel between communities made for major cultural changes for the First Nations. Traditional subsistence and fur-trade-based economies were greatly impacted.

The Tuchodi area was not of any importance to the HBC in its fur-trade activities, but the Dunne-za and Sekani people of northeastern BC became increasingly involved with the fur trade as more posts were established along the major waterways. The people began to include the fur-trading posts in their annual rounds even if they weren't located in traditional gathering places. The bands came together in summer and fall when the hunting was good to socialize and do business, then split up into small groups for the winter to hunt and trap. This did not much alter their basic subsistence economies. Hunting was their mainstay, including bison, woodland caribou and most importantly, moose. Beaver was also an important food source in addition to its value in the fur trade. There was once a trapper's community on the Muskwa River near the Kledo Creek confluence, called Weasel City.

The Dunne-za people in the Prophet River area signed on to Treaty 8 in 1910 and several small reserves were eventually established in northern BC: Prophet River, Halfway River, Doig River and Blueberry River. The Fort Nelson First Nation also signed an addition to Treaty 8 in 1910, but it wasn't until the construction of the Alaska Highway and the collapse of the fur trade that the First Nations' lifestyles changed radically again. The government was far away and communications were sparse, given the available technology and great distance. Once the highway was built this was no longer the case. By the 1960s, the price of fur dropped to the point where it was no longer an option as a livelihood and most communities had lost their traditional economies for good. With government monetary assistance and compulsory education, many of the First Nations people in the area became more sedentary and more reliant on the purchase of food from stores.

For more information on the prehistory, the fur-trade era and the modern history of the northern Rockies and Fort Nelson areas, see the Toad/Liard chapter of this book and also *The Fort Nelson Story*, by Gerri Young. Another good historical read on the fur trade in the area is Daniel Harmon's *Sixteen Years in the Indian Country*. Further materials on the Peace River country's connection to the Muskwa/Fort Nelson drainage can be found in the Calverley collection, at www.calverley.ca/table2004.html, as well as a huge list of links to articles about the First Nations in these areas, at www.calverley.ca/part1contents.html.

Some more minor events of interest to the traveller along the Tuchodi/Muskwa rivers route include a plane crash. In February of 1943, a Douglas C-49 took off from Fort Nelson on a flight to Fort Simpson. It reportedly carried 11 passengers and crew and an army payroll of $200,000 in United States currency and 400 pounds of gold bullion. On September 22, 1948, the wreckage was found high above the Tuchodi Lakes where the aircraft had hit the mountainside with great force, disintegrated, scattered and burned for over a mile. Much of the debris was buried four to six feet under rockslides and although 11 bodies were recovered, there was no record of anyone locating the missing cargo. The site can be visited on a horse trek from Tuchodi River Outfitters' home base. Maybe you will come back with more than a sore behind!

Another historical tidbit is in regard to Lack-a-Nookie Lodge. This is the name of Tuchodi River Outfitter's cabin on the north shore at the east end of the narrows between West and East Tuchodi lakes. The original cabin was constructed in the 1940s by the US army for officers on leave from building the Alaska Highway. They headed out to fish and enjoy the natural surroundings of northern BC, but they were obviously missing their wives or girlfriends and thus bestowed on the cabin its name. The creek nearby also is known locally as Lack-a-Nookie Creek.

A possible close encounter with a Big Foot (sasquatch) occurred about 3 km downstream of the Muskwa River Bridge near Fort Nelson in September 2000. A resident rockhound discovered fresh tracks he could not identify crossing his path. He photographed and began to follow the footprints. He claims he was right behind the creature until he became surrounded by spooked horses. His photographs of the footprints are intriguing. A report can be found at the Bigfoot Field Researchers Organization site, at www.bfro.net/GDB/show_report.asp?id=9778.

A recent mystery in the area is that of the hiker gone missing in the summer of 2008. According to an article by reporter Larry Pynn of the *Vancouver Sun*, a 43-year-old German hiker attempted a 40-day solo trek from the Tuchodi Lakes to Frog Lake, 150 km to the west. He was not carrying a communications device and when he didn't make his rendezvous with his floatplane, searchers were sent out. His last camp was found at the confluence of the South Gataga River with the Gataga River. A small dry bag with his wallet, maps and passport was found on the Gataga and his backpack was found 90 km downstream near the lodge at Terminus Mountain on the Kechika River. It is likely the hiker drowned crossing the Gataga River, but no one will know for sure. He disappeared in the heart of the 6.4-million-hectare Muskwa–Kechika Management Area (MKMA), the largest inaccessible wild space in northern BC.

The Tuchodi Lakes lie in Northern Rocky Mountains Provincial Park, where the hiker began his journey on foot. Established in 1999, this provincial park is the largest in the MKMA and the third largest in BC. The park was created because the area is representative of the eastern Muskwa Ranges, Northern Rocky Mountain Foothills and the Muskwa Plateau and of the associated visual and recreation features and opportunities for backcountry adventure.

The rivers and lakes, and in no small part the Tuchodi lakes and river, were part of the reason this area was given the highest level of protected status. The confluence of the Tuchodi and the Muskwa lies on the very eastern border of the park. The park only protects the upper reaches of the Muskwa River. A section of the Lower Muskwa, though not all of it, is in the MKMA. Though no mining and development can take place in the Northern Rocky Mountains Provincial Park, large tracts of the MKMA are open to development. See the Turnagain/Kechika chapter for more information on the creation, structure and vision of the MKMA.

A new provincial park is in the works on the Lower Muskwa River. As of 2006 it was going through the legislative process. It is to be located around Kledo Creek, likely with access where the road goes down from the Alaska Highway to the Muskwa River Boat Launch. It is called Kledo Creek Provincial Park, but no other information is currently available on the BC Parks website.

Oil and gas exploration and development is a high priority in northeastern BC, from the foothills to the boundary between the Yukon and NWT. According to a BC government bulletin, in the summer of 2005, Arkex Ltd. and Jebco Seismic Canada began acquiring an airborne geophysical survey over the MKMA, covering 3000 square kilometres of the Rocky Mountain Foothills. The survey was completed in 2006 and provides previously unattainable detailed information about geological structures underlying the area. You can bet the whole Muskwa River Valley, except where it lies in the two provincial parks, is open for business. How that will affect the foothills ecosystem is of great concern.

To get a full introduction to the MKMA, in colour, start your trip by perusing *Muskwa–Kechika: The Wild Heart of Canada's Northern Rockies*, by Wayne Sawchuk. Don McKay's book of poetry called the *Muskwa Assemblage*, the product of an art camp in the MKMA organized by Donna Kane and Wayne Sawchuk, is a lovely on-the-river read. *Walking the Big Wild: From Yellowstone to the Yukon on the Grizzly Bears' Trail*, by Karsten Heuer, will also get you all fired up about travelling in the MKMA and participating in its conservation. Contact CPAWS BC at www.cpawsbc.org and visit these other conservation organizations' websites for more on the current resource extraction issues facing the Northern Rockies and the Muskwa–Kechika Management Area: www.y2y.net, www.spacesfornature.org/greatspaces/northrockies.html and www.roundriver.org (click on Where We Work, then Canada/Muskwa Kechika/Reports & Publications).

Level of Solitude: * * The Tuchodi/Muskwa route is not for those with a jet boat aversion. August and September are the busiest months on the river, with mostly resident hunters from the region going up and down the river. Expect to see at least 10 jet boats on the Lower Tuchodi and Muskwa if you go in mid-August. You will likely see more in September when the moose-hunting season picks up. Technically, motorized craft are not allowed on the Tuchodi Lakes, but they do go up there if the water is high enough.

Other than the jet boats and hunting activity, Tuchodi River Outfitters, a few cabins and the Muskwa River Boat Launch, the Tuchodi and Muskwa rivers are pretty quiet. There are no roads crossing the rivers and no settlements along them. That said, given the oil and gas exploration in the area, I doubt the Muskwa will be quiet for long.

The shortened route to the boat launch has been run by a BC company, Main Current Rafting Expeditions, in the past. I only know of a couple of other canoeing parties that have paddled the route, so it is not going to be crowded with paddlers.

Wildlife: * * The Tuchodi/Muskwa route has good wildlife-viewing potential. However, if you go in prime hunting season in August and September, which is likely, given those are also the prime months for lower water, you won't see much for large mammals along the river. Hiking or horse-trekking trips to the alpine and subalpine will be your best bet, especially around the lakes and in the Upper Tuchodi River Valley.

In the alpine near the lakes there are major mineral licks frequented by elk and moose. Species also found in the high elevations of the Rockies include Stone sheep, caribou and mountain goat. In the lower elevations and valleys of the Rockies, such as the Tuchodi valley, elk, moose, grizzly bear, black bear, wolf, lynx and wolverine are common. There is a major concentration of Rocky Mountain elk in the Tuchodi and Muskwa drainages and they are a native species to the east slope and foothills of the Rockies, unlike the Manitoba elk that were introduced into the Kechika drainage in 1984. White-tailed and mule deer are also found in the watershed. Fur-bearing animals include beaver, marten, fisher, muskrat, mink, otter and snowshoe hares. Squirrels infest the established camps on The Peninsula!

The Muskwa Plateau has good habitat for elk, black bear and wolves. The young deciduous forest, river bottoms and numerous wetlands are also home to moose, caribou, black bear, lynx and beaver as well as other small fur-bearing species. Wolverines, grizzly bear, coyote and cougar are also present, as well as a small resident population of transplanted bison. According to a government source, plains bison, a non-native species, were introduced to the Upper Muskwa area in the 1970s. They are known to roam long distances, so if you see something you can't quite make out as a bear or an elk, it might be a bison or even a Big Foot!

Ruffed and blue grouse, trumpeter swans, various passerines and waterfowl such as harlequin ducks and mergansers are found along the route. You will likely see dippers, kingfishers, grey jays, woodpeckers, ravens and various songbirds, including warblers and vireos.

Fishing: ✳ ✳ for the Tuchodi and ✳ for the Muskwa. The Tuchodi Lakes are known for their lake trout fishing, some 5-kg lunkers as a matter of fact. Fishing for lake trout from a canoe usually involves trolling with a shiny spoon or finding a spot to cast where there is a water depth differential, like a sharp drop off a reef or underwater gravel bar.

The Tuchodi's aqua waters host grayling and bull trout (known locally as Dolly Varden trout), but truthfully, I didn't have much luck fishing the river. Grayling bite on flies or tiny spinners in clear, fast water. Bull trout often can be found lurking in the pools near the fast water, striking at anything moving and shiny. If you do have success fishing, be conservative with your catch.

Fishing is not good in muddy waters of the Muskwa. You might catch a northern pike or bull trout if you try at spots where a creek's clearer water mixes with the murky river flow. Pike pretty much strike at anything moving and shiny. You can use the same tackle for both pike and bull trout. I've had lots of success on other rivers with mid-sized spoons.

Camping, Hiking and Other Activities: ✳ ✳ ✳ for the Tuchodi and ✳ ½ for the Muskwa. You can camp at the West Tuchodi Lake put-in at an established campsite used by hunting and horse-trekking parties. It's a nice spot, but bears may be interested. However, given the topography of the lake, there is not much for natural spots to camp. You could try the creek mouths along its shores. East Tuchodi has more options for camping, but again the majority are established and used by hunting parties.

Once on the river, most groups will choose to camp on gravel bars and there are many good ones to camp on. There are also lots of established camps on the Tuchodi and on the Muskwa. Camping is not good on the Lower Muskwa. Plan your last days of paddling with regard to the camping spots described in the Trip Notes.

Swimming in the Tuchodi Lakes is an option for those who really need refreshment. The Muskwa is not overly cold, but who wants to bathe in such murky water!

There are lots of day hikes and multi-day treks to be done at the Tuchodi Lakes. There is a day hike with some great views up the Tuchodi's floodplain toward its headwaters or up the alluvial fan separating the two Tuchodi lakes. Day hikes can also be made on the horse trails running along the north shore of the lakes and up into the alpine. For multi-day options you can follow the historic High Trail all the way to Summit Lake or take the horse trail to Tuchodi River Outfitters and then way beyond to the north and east. For more multi-day hiking ideas, try Walkin' Jim, at www.walkinjim.com, and Karsten Heuer's book *Walking the Big Wild: From Yellowstone to the Yukon on the Grizzly Bears' Trail*. If you go off trail in the subalpine and alpine, walk carefully and tread lightly. This is a fragile environment because of the severe conditions and short growing season.

If you don't feel like doing much hiking but want to travel some of the amazing alpine around this area of the Northern Rockies by land, you could book a trail ride with Tuchodi River Outfitters or Wayne Sawchuk. It would be well worth it to add a horse-trek adventure to your itinerary if you have the time and inclination. The Muskwa Ranges are amazing and you can check out the site of the plane crash or take the High Trail on horseback. Book your horse trek ahead of time; drop-ins to Tuchodi River Outfitters will likely be disappointed, as the staff will be busy with their booked guests.

You can also hike lower down on the Tuchodi. There are creekbeds to explore and a horse trail that crosses the river. It heads south to the headwaters of Dead Dog Creek and beyond and north to a cabin in the upper Chlotasecta Creek drainage. The trails are shown on both scales of topo maps. The southern slopes of the Tuchodi valley host grassy ridges you can walk for miles.

Even on the Muskwa there is some hiking to be done. Besides taking a stroll up the Chiska River and Tetsa Creek floodplains, there is a local guidebook to hiking in the northern Rockies, *Northern Rockies Hiking and Motorized Trail Guide: From Mild to Wild*, by Heather MacRae, which outlines and provides maps for a couple multi-day hikes accessible from the Muskwa River. The Dunedin Trail and Teetering Rock hikes may be of interest.

See the Directory of Services and Organizations for contact information to obtain the hiking guide from the Visitor Information Centre in Fort Nelson and for Tuchodi River Outfitters, Wayne Sawchuk and other outfits offering guided horse treks.

Special Equipment: You will need a proper whitewater/tripping canoe that you are comfortable running up to Class 2+ rapids in. The rapids on the Tuchodi are very shallow and rocky, so a plastic boat is highly recommended.

Mandatory rescue equipment that you should have for any trip, but particularly for a fast-running river with continuous rapids like the Tuchodi, is one throw bag per canoe. The bag should be set up to tow, with a quick-release system in place. The rapids are bumpy and a swim would not be pleasant nor rescue from another boat easy. But, as the river is relatively narrow, swimmers should be able to self-rescue by swimming to shore. It is getting canoes to safety that you will primarily want your throw bag for. The Tuchodi's current is always swift, and there are fairly continuous rapids, so you need to be prepared to chase and tow boats. If you get into trouble towing, you must be able to disengage immediately. If you are self-rescuing, having the long line will help you get to shore more quickly. You will definitely need to carry a wrap/pin kit with you and know how to use it. See the Special Equipment section in the Tatshenshini/Alsek chapter for what you should have in your kit.

Bring a compass for hiking and know how to use it. Any multi-day hiking should be carefully planned ahead of time. You will need to be properly equipped with good hiking gear and with 1:50 000- and 1:250 000-scale topos of the area you plan on covering.

A water filter is a good idea, as "beaver fever" is always a concern. The Muskwa is so silty you will also want to bring water containers for collecting fresh water from clear creeks to give your water filter a break.

The Taiga Plain is known for having an active bug population in the summer months, though it usually dies down later in August with the cooler nights. You will want to take a head net, bug jacket, repellent or some combination of the three. I never go anywhere up north without my bug jacket with a hood and face net and repellent with lots of DEET.

I would carry pepper spray and/or an air horn to deal with potential bear encounters. Given all the hunting activity, there are likely bears around that have been habituated to human presence.

Trip Notes:

MAP NO.	GRID REF.	FEATURE	DESCRIPTION
94 K/2	064490	Put-in; Campsite	There is a large established campsite in a bay at the southwest end of West Tuchodi Lake.
		Hiking	You can hike anywhere, including up to the alpine, right from the campsite via the horse trail found here. Or you can paddle over to hike the Upper Tuchodi's gravel floodplain at the west end of the lake.
94 K/1 west	135539	Cabin	Just after the hoodoos on the north shore and near the east end of West Tuchodi Lake is a cabin. This is the location of the historic "Lack-a-Nookie Lodge" built and frequented by US army engineers on leave from their work on the Alaska Highway.
		Hiking	The creek with the huge alluvial fan backing up the Tuchodi's flow is locally known as "Lack-a-Nookie Creek." It's worth a scramble up the creekbed for a good view of the marvellous twin lakes and the surrounding mountains.
	145537	Rapids	In the approximately 2-km-long stretch of river between the lakes there are 850 m or so of **Class 1+** rapids. The rapids are shallow riffles with tight corners. Swifts follow the riffles all the way to East Tuchodi Lake. Be on the lookout for wood hazards and jet boats.
	163547	Campsite	There is an established campsite on the grassy knoll on the north side of the western end of East Tuchodi Lake.

187547	Campsites	Known locally as "The Peninsula," this bulb of land hosts three established campsites. The most established one has "furniture" and is located on the north side of the peninsula, near its neck. The other two have fire pits but are more exposed and closer together. One fire ring is out on the grassy knoll with a nice beach landing in front. The other is up on the east side of the peninsula, back in the trees.
	Hiking	There is a horse trail heading west from the neck of the peninsula. We hiked up it a long ways and branched off through the open forest to the grasslands above. You can pretty much go where you want in this lovely country.
193539	Camping	On the south side of the lake a natural camp can be made. There is a beach with a treed bench in behind.
210552	Cabin	In the bay at the northeast end of East Tuchodi Lake there is a hunting cabin.
218548	Camping	You can camp at the very end of the lake, near the river mouth. There is a beach to land on and a grassy area up behind for tents.
220547	Campsite	On RR about 150 m downstream of the lake there is an established hunting campsite.
		You are now about to commence the very fast downhill run of the Tuchodi River. Be very vigilant for wood hazards, especially at tight corners. We met a jet boat coming the other direction on this stretch and both of us had difficulty getting out of each other's way. This is a very narrow and swift little river with few eddies big enough to stop in easily.
223547 229550	Rapids	Across the outwash of Joplin Creek run four sets of shallow and rocky rapids up to **Class 2**, the third being the most difficult. It is tricky because the deepwater channel is very narrow. Watch for wood.
231550 237550	Riffles	Riffles continue for another 600 m after the Joplin Creek mouth rapids. The riffles average **Class 1+**. Watch for wood.
		For the rest of map 94 K/1 west there are **Class 1** riffles and wood hazards.

94 K/1 east	269565	Hiking	There is a horse trail crossing here. You can hike south or north from the Tuchodi River. To the south takes you past the upper reaches of Dead Dog Creek. Heading north, you are on your way to the cabins of Tuchodi River Outfitters. According to the 1:250 000-scale topo, the trail goes all the way to a cabin at Chlotasecta Creek, a feeder stream of the Muskwa River.
94 K/8 east	277572	Camping	On RR there are gravel bars on both the upstream and downstream side of the little creek mouth. Both make for good camping.
	279575	Camping	On RL there is camping on the gravel bar.
	290610	Campsite; Hiking	There is an established camping site here on RL that is used by hunters on horseback. You can hike from here. The trail to Tuchodi River Outfitters and points east goes past the campsite.
	305619	Lodge access	The most efficient way (paddling downstream) to get to Tuchodi River Outfitters is to take the small RL channel here. It is not marked on the 1:50 000 topo. You can also easily paddle upstream at the next left to arrive at the same docking area if you miss your turn.
			A stop at the outfitters is worth it. The setting is great and so is the hospitality.
			After the outfitters' place you run some riffles on your approach to what I call "Hoodoo Gorge," where lies the first significant rapids of the Tuchodi. The rock face on RR followed by the hoodoos is your cue to stop and scout.
	324625 328625	Hoodoo Gorge	Starting at the Margison Creek outlet on RL there is a set of rapids with two parts. The first drop starts with riffles that take you into a set of **Class 2** waves that has a hole on RL, depending on water levels. The second drop, a **Class 2+** chute with standing waves, takes you out of Hoodoo Gorge.
	329628	Riffles	Riffles follow in the braided section. The RL channel was deepest in 2005, but watch for new wood hazards.
	335636	Campsite	On RL is an established campsite used by boaters/hunters.
	340640	Hazard	The RR channel was blocked by a logjam in 2005. Be cautious on your approach.
	341643	Campsite	On RL of the RL channel is another established campsite used by boaters/hunters.

Now you are heading out of the Northern Rocky Mountains and into the foothills.

	378644	Camping	In the RL channel you can make a camp on RL on grassy flats sheltered by poplar and alder.
	390643	Campsite	On RR is an established campsite in the spruce forest.
	391643	Riffle	A **Class 1+** riffle follows the campsite.
	407642	Campsite	Another established boater/hunter campsite sits on RR.
94 J/5 west	416643	Campsite	A very large established campsite is in the trees on RR at the bend 2.5 km upstream from the mouth of Dead Dog Creek.

The next section of river is pretty and lively. There are high, eroding cliffs along much of the RL bank.

	417641	Rapids	For the next 2.4 km there are nearly continuous sets of rapids averaging **Class 2−**. Most are shallow and rocky with a few big boulders to look out for. The most difficult set, **Class 2+**, comes at the sharp dogleg left turn at the end of the stretch at GR 429625 This is a headwall rapid with a recirculating eddy on RR and a logjam on RL. It is a tight line. To scout, stop on RL when you see the headwall up ahead. You will have to bushwhack on RL to carry this drop.
	434626	Rapid	There is a **Class 2−** rocky chute here.
	437623	Rapids	For 200 m there are rocks, steep waves and cross-currents. Two large boulders sit near the bottom of the drop. This is a **Class 2/2+** run.
	443620 475604	Rapids	For approximately 4.4 km you will encounter a string of rapids up to **Class 2** in difficulty. Nearly every corner will have a set. This is a fun read-and-run section and the last of the significant rapids on the Tuchodi.

You will encounter more **Class 1+/2−** rapids and riffles up to the confluence with the Muskwa, but wood hazards, as always, are the main concern from here on down.

	526594	Hoodoos	There are erosion formations again on RL.
	528594	Campsite	On RR is a nice established campsite with views and trees for shelter. It is at the head of the marked gravel bar.
	552605	Campsite	On the foot of the island is an established campsite.

Riffles continue on this map, as do the wood hazards. There is a logjam coming up.

573642	**Campsite**	On RL is an established campsite with furniture.
600675	**Hazard**	In 2005 there was a large logjam on the larger of the islands on RR. Approach this section of river with caution, staying tight to the inside of the bend. The line was very tight for us and we had to punch and paddle through the boily eddy on RL to keep away from the hazard. Consider getting out on RL and lining.
599678	**Camping**	Just down on RL after the logjam, you can make a natural camp in the old channel. It's flat, sandy and has willows in behind. There is an eddy to pull into and an easy landing at the opening.
599679	**Rapids**	There are **Class 2−** waves at the bend with the islands.
		There are **Class 1+/2−** riffles all throughout the midstream gravel bar islands to come and all the way down to the confluence with the Muskwa. Watch for wood!
623683	**Camping**	You can camp one more night on the Tuchodi if you stop here. A camp can be made on the marked gravel bar "island."
		You may want to stop and fill some water containers. The Muskwa is muddy!
637692	**Confluence**	The Muskwa's flow is nearly doubled by the Tuchodi. It doesn't get any clearer, though. The pretty-coloured water of the Tuchodi quickly disappears into the brown Muskwa.
637693	**Camping**	You can make a natural camp on the marked gravel bar on RL just down from the confluence.
637695	**Campsite**	Just around the corner at the end of the marked gravel bar on RL is an established campsite. It has a view of the high cliff on RR.
625755	**Camping**	A natural camp can be made on the RL gravel bar marked on the map.
623763	**Rapids**	These minor rapids are made up of a rocky ledge on RR at the corner and some minor waves.
		Standing waves are common on the Muskwa, but they're easily run and often cheatable.
607780	**Camping**	A camp can be made near the foot of the gravel bar "island."
600787	**Camping**	You can camp near the head of the marked gravel bar on RL.

About 2.5 km downstream you will begin to see some lovely black sand cliffs. They are the highlight of this most scenic stretch of the Muskwa.

	577812	Rapids	Class 1+ waves go all around the bend.
	577817	Rapids	More Class 1+ waves are found on the next bend.
	564830	Rapids	There is a fun 800 m stretch of Class 1+/2− waves.
94 J/5 west	555842	Rapids	There are more Class 1+ waves under the pretty cliffs.
94 J/12	555846	Rapids	Class 2− waves before and around the bend here.
	554852	Camping	There is a nice camp spot on RL. There is a beach to land on and trees for shelter.
	548891	Rapids	There are Class 1+ waves on the bend.
	541897	Camping	You can camp on the gravel bar upstream of the mouth of Chlotapecta Creek on RL. There are trees in behind for shelter.
	544904	Rapids	There are some Class 2−/2 waves here. Fun!
	549905	Camping	The marked gravel bar on RR makes a good camping spot with pretty views.
	553905	Rapids	There are Class 1+ waves on the straightaway.
	557912	Rapids	There are Class 1+ waves in the narrows.
	563916	Rapids	There are Class 1+ waves before the bend.
	563925	Rapids	There are Class 1+ waves in the narrows between the braided sections.
	566939	Rapids	There are Class 1+ waves at the end of the RR channel.
	565945	Campsite	On RL there is an established camp just upstream of the Chiska River confluence. The kitchen is up on the bank in the poplars and you can land and put tents up on the sand/gravel floodplain. A walk up the river after supper is pleasant. You can also get clear water here.
	564959	Rapids	There are Class 2− waves here.
	563964	Rapids	More Class 2− waves go around the bend.

Look for waterfalls up on RR on the bend just before where Tetsa Creek comes in on RL.

	590985	Hiking	You can hike up the Tetsa Creek floodplain for a long distance. Check out the hiking guidebook listed in the Activities section of this chapter for multi-day hiking options in this area.

The next stretch of river is a braided graveyard of wood hazards. The current is a very fast 10–16 km/h. Be on your knees!

Camping is not good in this stretch.

	606983	**Rapids**	There are **Class 2–/2** waves here.
	617987	**Rapids**	There are **Class 2–/2** waves in the narrow section.
	623995	**Rapids**	In the RL (main) channel there are **Class 2–/2** waves.
	628997	**Hazards**	The RL bank slumped here in 2005 creating a mess of **sweepers** and adding to the **logjam**. The RR channel converging also makes for some tricky water with **boils and cross-currents**.
	703036	**Camping**	It is possible to camp on RL on the large marked gravel bar.
94 J/11			The Muskwa heads straight north from here through the Fort Nelson Lowland.
94 J/13	703163	**Boat Launch; Road access; Take-out option #1**	The Muskwa River Boat Launch sits on RL at the marked gravel bar. Besides the boat launch, there is a huge parking area with outhouses and cooking shelters.
			You could camp here if you needed to. There is no good camping for about 12 km downstream.
94 J/14	769220	**Camping**	It is possible to camp at the mouth of an old channel on RL. The landing and first part of the carry from the bank is mucky, but the terrain firms up near a high bank that you can tuck under to camp.
	777217	**Camping**	On RR is a small gravel/sandbar in an old channel opening that will do for a camping spot.
	808213	**Camping**	You can camp on a gravel bar up back in the far RL channel. The river is not well represented by the map here.
	891155	**Camping**	A camp can be made on RR at the gravel bar at the mouth of the unnamed creek.
	904152	**Camping**	There is a decent spot to camp here on the split-level gravel bar on RL.
	964140	**Campsite**	There is an established campsite on RR. You will see a trail up the bank to it.
94 J/11			There is only a tiny spot of river on this map and it is not necessary for your trip.
94 J/10	027116	**Camping**	On the RR marked gravel bar there is a sandy area to camp.

	039110	Campsite	Up on the RR bank is an established campsite with stairs and a trail up to it. There is no good landing spot, but at least there are no sweepers. Try the old channel mouth just downstream for a better landing.
			Note: there are two good natural camping spots coming up.
94 J/15	085126	Camping	On RR there is an elevated sand/gravel bar with trees for shelter in behind.
	087130	Camping	On RR, on the larger marked gravel bar, there is also a sandy spot to camp, with trees for shelter. This is the last good spot to camp on the Muskwa before the Fort Nelson River Bridge.
	152135	Confluence	The Prophet's waters join the Muskwa on RR. You can't tell the difference in the flows. Both are brown.
			The bridge up ahead at GR 158134 welcomes you to the outskirts of the beehive of oil and gas industry in northern BC, Fort Nelson.
	197163	Muskwa R. Bridge; Road access; Take-out option #2	This bridge is part of the Alaska Highway. You can get up to the highway on RR via a track from the gravel bar.
	265213	Confluence	Once again, you can't tell the difference between the Fort Nelson's flow and the Muskwa's.
	265204	Old Fort Nelson	To explore this old HBC post and abandoned village, ferry over to the Fort Nelson River's right bank and walk back up to the remains of the community.
	269218	Take-out option #3	You can take out here at the end of the gravel road and walk back up to the airport to get your vehicle(s). Or, you can drop off a couple drivers and have the rest of the party carry on down to the bridge. The walk to the airport is shorter and more pleasant from here. The 1:50 000 topo depicts the area quite well and you should find your way easily.
	280233	Fort Nelson R. Bridge; Take-out option #4	This is a "new" bridge on a logging road heading out from the airport. There is a huge gravel bar on RL with a track down to it from the logging road. Be careful if you are walking back to the airport for your vehicle(s), as the truck drivers will not be expecting pedestrians. You can walk up the ditch to be safe and it should take you about 45 minutes to an hour to get to the airport.

DIRECTORY OF

SERVICES AND ORGANIZATIONS

GENERAL

Federal Government

Canadian Heritage River System:
   www.chrs.ca
Environment Canada Hydrometric Data:
   www.wsc.ec.gc.ca/products/main_e.cfm?cname=products_e.cfm
Natural Resources Canada GeoGratis Home Page (Free Digital Maps Online):
   www.geogratis.ca/geogratis/en/index.html

Provincial Government

BC Ferries:
   www.bcferries.com
BC Geographical Names Information System (BCGNIS):
   http://ilmbwww.gov.bc.ca/bcnames

BC Heritage River Program:
   www.env.gov.bc.ca/bcparks/heritage_rivers_program/home.html
BC Ministry of Environment, Conservation Offices Contact Information:
   www.env.gov.bc.ca/cos/contacts.html
BC Ministry of Environment, Fish & Wildlife Branch:
   www.env.gov.bc.ca/fw/fish/regulations
BC Ministry of Environment, River Forecast and Snow Surveys:
   www.agf.gov.bc.ca/rfc
BC Ministry of Forests & Range, Wildfire Management Branch:
   www.bcwildfire.ca
BC Ministry of Transportation, Highways:
   www.drivebc.ca
BC Parks Index (alphabetical listing):
   www.env.gov.bc.ca/bcparks/explore/parks/index.html
BC Parks Tatshenshini–Alsek Provincial Park,
   Postal Bag 5000, Smithers, BC V0J 2N0.
   Phone (250) 847-7320; fax (250) 847-7659.
BC Parks Tatshenshini–Alsek Provincial Park Campsite Bear-Risk Assessment:
   www.env.gov.bc.ca/bcparks/explore/parkpgs/tatshens/tat_report.pdf
BC Parks Tatshenshini–Alsek Rivers Trip Fee Payment:
   www.env.gov.bc.ca/bcparks/explore/parkpgs/tatshens/parkinfo.html#river_fee

First Nations Governments

Acho Dene Koe Band
General Delivery, Fort Liard, NWT X0E 0A0
(867) 770-4141
Carrier Sekani Tribal Council:
www.cstc.bc.ca/cstc
Champagne and Aishihik First Nations:
www.cafn.ca
Central Council of the Tlingit and Haida Indian Tribes of Alaska:
www.ccthita.org
Dehcho First Nations:
www.dehcho.org/home.htm
Fort Nelson First Nation:
Mile 295 Alaska Hwy
RR 1 Fort Nelson, BC V0C 1R0
(250) 774-7257
www.fnnation.org
Gitxsan Chief's Office:
www.gitxsan.com/index.htm
Iskut First Nation:
Box 30 Iskut, BC V0J 1K0
(250) 234-3331
iskutnation@kermode.net
Kaska Dena Council:
www.kaskadenacouncil.com
Métis National Council:
www.metisnation.ca
Métis Nation of British Columbia:
www.mpcbc.bc.ca
Tahltan Indian Band:
Box 46 Telegraph Creek, BC V0J 2W0
(250) 235-3241
Tahltan Tribal Council:
Box 69 Dease Lake, BC V0C 1L0
(250) 771-3276
Taku River Tlingit First Nation:
www.trtfn.com
Treaty 8 Tribal Association
www.treaty8.bc.ca/welcome.php

US and Alaska Governments

Alaska Marine Highway System:
www.dot.state.ak.us/amhs/index.html
Glacier Bay National Park & Preserve, Park Headquarters,
Box 140, Gustavus, AK 99826
Phone (907) 697-2230; fax (907) 697-2654
Glacier Bay National Park & Preserve:
Box 137, Yakutat, AK 99689
Phone (907) 784-3295; fax (907) 784-3535
Special line for river information: (907) 784-3370

Glacier Bay National Park & Preserve, Outfitters and Air Services contact info:
   www.nps.gov/glba/planyourvisit/upload/Services.pdf
Glacier Bay National Park & Preserve, Permits for Tatshenshini/Alsek River Trip:
   National Park Service, Yakutat Ranger Station, River Permits,
   Box 137, Yakutat, AK 99869
National Ocean Service Tide Prediction Tables:
   www.tidesandcurrents.noaa.gov/tides06/tpred2.html#AK
Tongass National Forest Cabins:
   www.fs.fed.us/r10/tongass/cabins/cabin_info.shtml
Tongass National Forest Home Page:
   www.fs.fed.us/r10/tongass
United States Customs Ports of Entry:
   www.cbp.gov/xp/cgov/toolbox/contacts/ports/ak
United States Geological Survey National Water Information System:
   http://waterdata.usgs.gov/nwis/rt

Canoeing Organizations

Canadian Canoe Routes:
   www.myccr.com
Paddle Canada:
   www.paddlingcanada.com
Recreational Canoe Association of BC:
   www.bccanoe.com
Wilderness Canoe Association:
   www.wildernesscanoe.ca

Conservation Organizations and Information Sources

Canadian Parks & Wilderness Society BC Chapter:
   www.cpawsbc.org
Canadian Parks & Wilderness Society National Office:
   www.cpaws.org
Cassiar Watch:
   Box 5, Iskut, BC V0J 1K0
   james.bourquin@gmail.com
Citizens Concerned about Coalbed Methane:
   www.ekcbm.org
Dogwood Initiative:
   www.dogwoodinitiative.org
Ecojustice:
   www.ecojustice.ca
First Nations Land Rights & Environmentalism in BC:
   www.firstnations.de/index.html
Friends of the Stikine:
   www.panorama-map.com/STIKINE/stikine.html
Klabona Keepers/Sacred Headwaters:
   www.sacredheadwaters.com/home
Mining Watch Canada:
   www.miningwatch.ca

Muskwa–Kechika Management Area:
www.muskwa-kechika.com
Outdoor Recreation Council of BC:
www.orcbc.ca
Pembina Institute, Mining & Energy Issues in Northwest BC:
www.afterthegoldrush.ca
Rivers without Borders:
www.riverswithoutborders.org
Round River Conservation Studies:
www.roundriver.org
Save Our Rivers Society:
www.ourrivers.ca
Skeena Watershed Conservation Coalition:
www.skeenawatershed.com
Spaces For Nature:
www.spacesfornature.org
Wilderness Committee of Canada:
www.wildernesscommittee.org
Yellowstone to Yukon Conservation:
www.y2y.net

Emergency Services

Canadian Coast Guard, Pacific Region:
www.ccg-gcc.gc.ca/eng/CCG/Pacific and
VHF-FM radio channel 16 (156,8 MHz)
Emergency Response Centre:
1-800-567-5111 or 1-250-363-2333
RCMP BC Detachments Index:
http://bc.rcmp.ca/ViewPage.action?siteNodeId=27&languageId=1
Search and Rescue BC Index:
www.islandnet.com/sarbc/sarbc/sar-sarcan.html

Highway Services Information

Alaska Highway:
www.bellsalaska.com/myalaska/alaska_highway.html
Haines Highway:
www.bellsalaska.com/myalaska/ykhwy3.html
John Hart Highway:
www.bellsalaska.com/myalaska/hart_highway.html
Liard Highway:
www.spectacularnwt.com/wheretoexplore/dehcho/fortliard
Stewart–Cassiar Highway:
www.bellsalaska.com/myalaska/cassiar_highway.html

Maps, Charts and Indexes:

BC Parks Spatsizi Plateau Wilderness Provincial Park Map:
www.env.gov.bc.ca/bcparks/explore/parkpgs/spatsizi/spatsizi.pdf
BC Trail and Park Maps, Vancouver Public Library Online:
www.vpl.ca/research_guides/cat/C529

ITMB Publishing Ltd.:
  www.itmb.com
Map Town Ltd.:
  www.maptown.com
Muskwa–Kechika Management Area maps:
  (250) 787-0356, (250) 787-3534
Natural Resources Canada digital topo map download site:
  www.geogratis.ca/geogratis/en/download/scanned.html
NOAA charts:
  www.waypoints.com/tradcharts/singlecharts.html
Tatshenshini–Alsek rivers map by Cloudburst Productions:
  www.CloudburstProductions.net
Tongass National Forest Service:
  www.fs.fed.us/r10/tongass/maps/maps.shtml
NTS index to topographic maps for BC:
  www.maptown.com/canadiantopographical/bcntsindex.html
USGS topo maps:
  www.usgs.gov/pubprod

COMMUNITY AND COMMERCIAL SERVICES

Air, Floatplane and Helicopter Charter Services

Air North, Whitehorse, YT: air charters
  www.flyairnorth.com
Alpine Aviation, Whitehorse, YT: air and floatplane charters
  www.alpineaviationyukon.com
Alpine Lakes Air, Smithers, BC: floatplane charters
  www.alpinelakesair.com
Alsek Air Service, Yakutat, AK: air charters
  www.alsekair.com
BC Yukon Air, Dease Lake, BC: floatplane charters
  Box 99, Dease Lake, BC V0C 1L0 (250) 771-3232
  bcyukonair@xplornet.com
Canadian Helicopters, Edmonton, AB: helicopter charters
  (780) 429-6900 edmonton.office@canadianhelicopters.com
  Fort Nelson, BC: (250) 774-6171 tsmigorosky@canadianhelicopters.com
  Smithers, BC: (250) 847-9444 tbrooks@canadianhelicopters.com
  Terrace, BC: (250) 635-2430 csmith@canadianhelicopters.com
Deh Cho Air, Fort Liard, NWT: air charters
  (867) 770-4103
Deh Cho Helicopters/Great Slave Helicopters, Fort Liard, NWT: helicopter charters
  (867) 770-3116
Fjord Air, Haines, AK: air charters
  www.flydrake.com
Liard Air, Muncho Lake, BC: floatplane charters
  www.northern-rockies-lodge.com

North Caribou Air, Fort Liard, NWT: air charters
www.flynca.com
Northern Thunderbird Air, Prince George, BC: air and floatplane charters
(Smithers and Dease Lake)
www.ntair.ca
North Pacific Seaplanes, Prince Rupert, BC: floatplane charters (Tatogga Lake)
www.northpacificseaplanes.com
Pacific Western Helicopters, Dease Lake, BC: helicopter charters
www.pwh.ca/bases_dease_lake.html
Sunrise Aviation, Wrangell, AK: air charters
www.sunriseflights.com
Trans North Helicopter, Whitehorse, YT: helicopter charters
www.tntaheli.com
Tsayta Aviation/TAL, Fort St. James, Dease Lake and Telegraph Creek, BC:
air and floatplane charters
www.flightsnorth.com
Villers Air Service, Fort Nelson, BC: air charters
www.villersair.com
Yakutat Coastal Airlines, Yakutat, AK: air and floatplane charters
www.flyyca.com

Airlines (with scheduled flights serving northern BC, Whitehorse and Alaska)

Air Canada:
www.aircanada.com/en/home.html
Air North:
www.flyairnorth.com
Alaska Airlines/Horizon Air:
www.alaskaair.com
Central Mountain Air:
www.flycma.com
Hawkair:
www.hawkair.ca
Northern Thunderbird Air:
www.ntair.ca

Bus, Long Distance Taxi and Boat Transportation Services

Greyhound Canada: bus service
www.greyhound.ca/en
Liard Taxi (Ernie McLeod), Fort Liard, NWT: shuttle and long-distance taxi service
(867) 770-3025 or cell (250) 775-1518
Links to outfitters offering water taxi charters in the Wrangell/Stikine region:
www.discoverourtown.com/AK/Wrangell/Recreation-5593.html
Riverjet Adventures, Sooke, BC: water taxi charters in northeastern BC
www.riverjetadventures.com
River Jet Boat Safaris, Prince George, BC: water taxi charters
www.riverjetboatsafaris.com
Stikine RiverSong, Telegraph Creek, BC: water taxi service, shuttles, canoe rentals,
guided tours, lodging, store, café and camping
www.stikineriversong.com

Canoe Outfitters, Guided River Trips and Rafting Support Services

Alaska Charters and Adventures: Wrangell, AK: canoe and kayak rentals, water taxi
service, guided river, fishing and photography trips, lodging
www.alaskaupclose.com

Alaska River Outfitters, Haines, AK: raft support services
PO Box 444, Haines, AK 99827
(907) 766-3307, (801) 733-4669 or (801) 571-5980

Alaska Vistas: Wrangell, AK: canoe and kayak rentals, water taxi service,
guided trips, book store
http://alaskavistas.com/Vistas

Aquabatics, Smithers, BC: shuttles, canoe rentals, equipment sales, lessons, guiding
www.aquabatics.com

Back 40 Canoe, Houston, BC: shuttles, equipment rentals and sales
www.back40canoe.com

Backwater Paddling, Prince George, BC: shuttles, canoe lessons, equipment sales
www.members.shaw.ca/backwater

Black Feather, Parry Sound, ON: guided canoe trips
www.blackfeather.com

Brabazon Expeditions, Yakutat (Dry Bay), AK: transportation, gear and equipment
shuttles, camping, showers, meals, tours, communications
www.brabazonexp.com

Breakaway Adventures, Wrangell, AK: water taxi service, canoe and kayak rentals,
guided canoe trips and other tours, lodging
www.breakawayadventures.com

Dease River Crossing Campground and Cabins, Dease River, BC: shuttles, canoe
rentals, fishing, canoeing and hiking trips, lodging and camping
http://deaseriver.dinoscience.org

Earth Centre Adventures, Haines, AK: raft support services
www.flydrake.com

Equinox Wilderness Expeditions, Anchorage, AK: guided canoe, kayak, raft and
hiking trips
www.equinoxexpeditions.com

James Henry River Journeys, Bolinas, CA: raft support services
www.riverjourneys.com

Kanoe People, Whitehorse, YT: shuttles, canoe rentals and guided trips
www.kanoepeople.com

Main Current Rafting Expeditions, Smithers/Fort Nelson, BC: shuttles, guided
rafting and inflatable canoe expeditions
www.maincurrent.com

Nahanni River Adventures and Canadian River Expeditions, Whitehorse, YT:
guided canoe and raft trips, books on rivers
www.nahanni.com

Nature Tours, Whitehorse, YT: shuttles, canoe rentals and guided trips
www.naturetoursyukon.com

Northern Rockies Lodge/Liard Air, Muncho Lake, BC: shuttles, canoe rentals, air
charters, lodging, dining room, gas
www.northern-rockies-lodge.com

Northern Sun Tours, Smithers, BC: guided canoe trips, lessons
www.northernsun.bc.ca
Rainbow Glacier Adventures, Haines, AK: naturalist and custom tours
www.joeordonez.com
Red Goat Lodge, Iskut, BC: shuttles, canoe rentals, tours, lodging, camping
www.karo-ent.com/redgoat.htm
Shadow Lake Expeditions, Whitehorse, YT: shuttles; canoe, raft and gear rentals;
custom and guided paddling and hiking trips; other tours too
www.shadowlake.ca
Sila Sojourns, Whitehorse, YT: custom canoe, kayak, raft and hiking trips, outdoors
retreats and workshops
http://silasojourns.com
Spatsizi Wilderness Vacations, Smithers, BC: canoe, fishing and horse-trekking tours
www.spatsizi.com
Stikine RiverSong, Telegraph Creek, BC: water taxi, shuttles, canoe rentals, lodging,
store, café and camping
www.stikineriversong.com
Tatogga Lake Resort, Tatogga Lake, BC: shuttles, canoe rentals, parking, café, gas,
camping and lodging
www.tatogga.ca
Tatshenshini Expediting, Whitehorse, YT: shuttles, canoe rentals, guided canoe and
rafting trips and raft-support services
www.tatshenshiniyukon.com
The Bike, Hike and Paddle Touring Company, Iskut, BC: shuttles, guided paddling,
hiking and biking trips
http://bikehikepaddle.com
Turnagain Lake Lodge (BC Safaris), Prince George, BC: guided canoe, horse trekking,
fishing and hiking trips, lodging
www.bcsafaris.com
Up North Adventures, Whitehorse, YT: shuttles, canoe rentals, guided trips and
canoeing courses
www.upnorthadventures.com
Western Canada Outdoor Experience, Smithers, BC: shuttles, canoe rentals,
outfitting and a variety of guided tours, guest house, cottages and meals
www.fishtourcanada.bc.ca/html/hosts.shtml

Community Information, Tourism and Business Services

Acho Dene Crafts and Visitor Information Centre, Fort Liard, NWT:
(867) 770-4161
Bushbuddy Stoves, Iskut, BC:
www.bushbuddy.ca
Dease Lake, BC:
www.stikine.net
Fort Liard, NWT:
www.fortliard.com
Fort Nelson, BC:
www.northernrockies.org and www.tourismnorthernrockies.ca
Fort Nelson Visitor Information Centre:
Summer (250) 774-6400 Off-season (250) 774-2541 ext. 240

Juneau, AK:
   www.juneau.com
Haines, AK:
   www.haines.ak.us
Northern British Columbia Tourism Association:
   www.northernbctourism.com
Skagway, AK:
   www.skagway.com
Smithers, BC:
   www.tourismsmithers.com
Stewart-Cassiar Tourism Links:
   www.stewartcassiar.com/tourism
Tatogga Lake, BC, and Iskut, BC, Tourist Services:
   www.stewartcassiar.com/destinations/iskut
Terrace, BC:
   www.city.terrace.bc.ca
Tourism Northern Rockies (services and activities from Prophet River to Fireside):
   www.tourismnorthernrockies.ca
Watson Lake, YT:
   www.yukoninfo.com/watson/watsonlakeinfo.htm
Whitehorse, YT:
   www.visitwhitehorse.com
Wrangell, AK:
   www.wrangellalaska.org
Yakutat, AK:
   www.yakutat.net

Horse Trekking, Hunting, Hiking & Fishing Outfitters and Lodges

For general contact listings for hunting & fishing lodges in northern BC go to www.nbctourism.com/categories and on the right-hand side of page, in the "Interact" slot, enter the word Hunting and click Go; do the same for Outfitting.

Alaska Waters, Wrangell, AK: campground and RV park, guided river boat tours, water taxi service, lodging
   www.alaskawaters.com
Alsek River Lodge, Yakutat, AK: lodging and tours
   (907) 784-3451
Coal River Lodge & RV Park, Coal River, BC: shuttles, parking, lodging and café
   (250) 776-7306
Dease River Crossing Campground and Cabins, Dease River, BC: shuttles, canoe rentals, guided canoe, fishing and hiking trips, store, lodging and camping
   http://deaseriver.dinoscience.org
Folding Mountain Outfitters, Toad River, BC: guided horse treks and wildlife viewing, jet boat, fishing, photo safari trips
   (250) 232-5451
Main Current Rafting Expeditions, Smithers/Fort Nelson, BC: shuttles, guided rafting and inflatable canoe expeditions
   www.maincurrent.com

Rainwalker Expeditions, Wrangell, AK: bike and kayak rentals, guided tours, floating lodge
   www.rainwalkerexpeditions.com
Spatsizi Wilderness Vacations, Smithers, BC (Laslui Lake Lodge and Hyland Post): canoe, fishing and horse-trekking tours
   www.spatsizi.com
Stikine Trail Rides, Stikine River, BC: horse treks and lodging
   (250) 771-4301
Stone Mountain Safaris, Toad River, BC: horse treks, fishing and wildlife viewing, lodging and meals
   www.stonemountainsafaris.com
Tatogga Lake Resort, Tatogga Lake, BC: shuttles, canoe and boat rentals, camping, café, lodging and gas
   www.tatogga.ca
The Bike, Hike & Paddle Touring Company, Iskut, BC: shuttles, guided biking, hiking and paddling trips
   http://bikehikepaddle.com
Toad River Lodge, Toad River, BC: lodging, camping, gas, towing, café and laundry
   www.karo-ent.com/toadriv.htm or www.toadriverlodge.com
Tuchodi River Outfitters, Hudson's Hope, BC: jet boat shuttles, guided horse-trekking, hunting and fishing trips
   www.tuchodiriveroutfitters.com
Turnagain Lake Lodge and Turnagain River Lodge (BC Safaris), Prince George, BC: guided canoe, horse-trekking, fishing and hiking trips, lodging
   www.bcsafaris.com
Turnagain River Adventures, Turnagain River, BC: guided hunting trips
   www.turnagainadventure.com
Upper Stikine River Adventures, Telkwa, BC: lodging, guided horse treks
   (250) 846-5001 upperstikineriveradventures@hotmail.com
Wayne Sawchuk, Rolla, BC: guided horse treks and artist and naturalist camps
   www.muskwakechika.com

Vehicle Rentals

For Smithers, Fort Nelson, Terrace, Prince Rupert and Prince George, BC, go to www.nbctourism.com/categories, and on right-hand side of the page, in the "Interact" slot, enter the words Car Rentals and click Go

Whitehorse, YT:
   www.airport-carrentals.com/cities/whitehorse_yu_ca_yxy

REFERENCES

Books and Articles:

Akrigg, G.P.V., and Helen B. Akrigg. *British Columbia Place Names.* 3rd ed. Vancouver: UBC Press, 1997.

Archer, Laurel. *Northern Saskatchewan Canoe Trips: A Guide to Fifteen Wilderness Rivers.* Erin, Ont.: Boston Mills Press, 2003.

Asch, Michael I. "Slavey." In *Subarctic,* edited by June Helm, 338–49. Vol. 6 of *Handbook of North American Indians,* William C. Sturtevant, general editor. Washington, DC: Smithsonian Institution, 1981.

Austen, Peter. *Wild, Wild Wets: An Aquaphiliac at the End of His Paddle.* Surrey, BC: Heritage House, 2002.

Barman, Jean. *The West Beyond the West: A History of British Columbia.* 3rd ed. Toronto: University of Toronto Press, 2007.

Berton, Pierre. *Klondike: The Last Great Gold Rush, 1896-1899.* Toronto: McClelland & Stewart, 1993.

Bilsland, W.W, and W.E. Ireland. *Atlin, 1889–1910: The Story of a Gold Boom.* Atlin, BC: Atlin Centennial Committee, 1971.

Black, Samuel. *A Journal of a Voyage from Rocky Mountain Portage in Peace River to the Sources of Finlays Branch and North West Ward in Summer 1824.* Edited by E.E. Rich, assisted by A.M. Johnson, with an introduction by R.M. Patterson. London: Hudson's Bay Record Society, 1955.

Blake, Don. *BC Trivia.* Edmonton: Lone Pine Publishing, 1992.

Boudreau, Jack. *Mountains, Campfires and Memories.* Prince George, BC: Caitlin Press, 2002.

Boudreau, Jack, and Frank Cooke. *Wild & Free: The Story of Frank Cooke and Skook Davidson.* Prince George, BC: Caitlin Press, 2004.

Bowes, Gordon, ed. *Peace River Chronicles,* Vancouver: Prescott Publishing, 1963.

Budd, Ken, Ric Careless, Johnny Mikes and various authors and photographers. *Tatshenshini: River Wild.* Vancouver: Raincoast Books, 1993.

Butler, William Francis. *The Wild North Land: A Winter Journey by Dogsled across Canada to BC, Oregon and the Pacific.* Edmonton: Hurtig, 1968.

Caldwell, Francis E. *Cassiar's Elusive Gold.* Victoria, BC: Trafford Publishing, 2000.

Calverley, Dorthea, et al. *History Is Where You Stand.* Calverley Collection archive. Dawson Creek, BC: Dawson Creek Public Library, 1999, accessed 20091215 at www.calverley.ca/table2004.html.

Camsell, Charles. *Son of the North.* Toronto: Ryerson Press, 1954.

Cannings, Richard, and Sydney Cannings. *British Columbia: A Natural History.* Vancouver: Greystone Books, 2002.

Careless, Ric. *To Save the Wild Earth: Field Notes from the Environmental Frontline.* Vancouver: Raincoast Books, 1997.

Champagne and Aishihik First Nations. *From Trail to Highway.* Whitehorse: author, n.d.

Clarke, J.M. *The Life and Adventures of John Muir.* San Francisco: Sierra Club Books, 1979.

Coutts, R.C. *Yukon Places and Names.* 2nd ed. Whitehorse: Moose Creek Publishing, 1980.

Cruikshank, Julie. *Do Glaciers Listen? Local Knowledge, Colonial Encounters and Social Imagination*. Vancouver: UBC Press, 2006.

———. *Life Lived like a Story: Life Stories of Three Yukon Native Elders*. Lincoln: University of Nebraska Press, 1992.

Curtis, Rick. *The Backpacker's Field Manual: A Comprehensive Guide to Mastering Backcountry Skills*. New York: Three Rivers Press, 1998.

Dawson, George M. *Report on an Exploration in the Yukon District, NWT and Adjacent Northern Portion of British Columbia, 1887*. Montreal: Dawson Brothers, 1888.

Dease, Peter Warren. *From Barrow to Boothia: The Arctic Journal of Chief Factor Peter Warren Dease, 1836–1839*. Edited by William Barr. Montreal: McGill–Queen's University Press, 2002.

Demerjian, Bonnie. *Roll On! Discovering the Wild Stikine River*. Wrangell: Stikine River Books, 2006.

Denniston, Glenda. "Sekani." In *Subarctic*, edited by June Helm, 433–41. Vol. 6 of *Handbook of North American Indians*, William C. Sturtevant, general editor. Washington, DC: Smithsonian Institution, 1981.

Dobrowolsky, Helene. *Law of the Yukon – A Pictorial History of the Mounted Police of the Yukon*. Whitehorse: Lost Moose Publishing, 1995.

Fiegehen, Gary. *Stikine: The Great River*. Vancouver: Douglas & McIntyre, 1991.

Fiennes, Sir Ranulph. *The Headless Valley*. London: Hodder & Stoughton, 1973.

Finch, David. *R.M. Patterson: A Life of Great Adventure*. Calgary: Rocky Mountain Books, 2000.

Fisher, Chris. *Birds of the Rocky Mountains*. Edmonton: Lone Pine Publishing, 1997.

Fisher, Chris, Don Pattie and Tamara Hartson. *Mammals of the Rocky Mountains*. Edmonton: Lone Pine Publishing, 2000.

Fisher, Robin. *Contact and Conflict: Indian–European Relations in British Columbia 1774–1890*. Vancouver: UBC Press, 1992.

Fladmark, Knut R. *British Columbia Prehistory*. Ottawa: National Museums of Canada, 1986.

Francis, Daniel, ed. *Encyclopedia of British Columbia*. Madeira Park, BC: Harbour Publishing, 2000.

Frolick, Vernon. *Descent into Madness: The Diary of a Killer*. Surrey, BC: Hancock House, 1993.

Fumoleau, René. *As Long As This Land Shall Last: A History of Treaty 8 and Treaty 11, 1870–1939*. Toronto: McClelland & Stewart, 1973.

Gadd, Ben. *Handbook of the Canadian Rockies*. 2nd ed. Jasper, Alta.: Corax Press, 1995.

Giscombe, G.S. *Into and out of Dislocation*. New York: North Point, 2000.

Gordon, Katherine. *Made to Measure: A History of Land Surveying in British Columbia*. Winlaw, BC: Sono Nis Press, 2006.

Guinard, Joseph E. *Les noms indiens de mon pays: leur signification, leur histoire*. Montréal: Rayonnement, 1960.

Hacking, Norman. *Captain William Moore: BC's Amazing Frontiersman*. Surrey, BC: Heritage House, 2000.

Hall, Ralph. *Pioneer Goldseekers of the Omineca*. Kearney, Neb.: Morris Publishing, 1994.

Harmon, Daniel. *Sixteen Years in the Indian Country: The Journal of Daniel Williams Harmon, 1800–1816*. Toronto: Macmillan, 1957.

Hartling, Neil, with photographs by Terry Parker. *Alaska to Nunavut: The Great Rivers*. Toronto: Key Porter, 2003.

Harvey, R.G. *Carving the Western Path: By River, Rail and Road Through Central· and Northern B.C.* Surrey, BC: Heritage House, 2006.

Henderson, Bob. *In the Land of the Red Goat*. Smithers, BC: Creekstone Press, 2006.

Herrero, Stephen. *Bear Attacks: Their Causes and Avoidance.* Toronto: Hurtig Publishers, 1985.

Heuer, Karsten. *Walking the Big Wild: From Yellowstone to Yukon on the Grizzly Bears' Trail.* Seattle: Mountaineers Books, 2004.

Hoagland, Edward. *Notes from the Century Before: A Journal from British Columbia.* New York: Random House, 1969.

Hodgins, Bruce W., and Gwyneth Hoyle. *Canoeing North into the Unknown: A Record of River Travel/Natural History: 1874 to 1974.* Toronto: Natural Heritage/Natural History, 1994.

Holroyd, Geoffrey L., and Howard Coneybeare. *The Compact Guide to the Birds of the Rockies.* Edmonton: Lone Pine Publishing, 1989.

Honigan, John J. "Kaska." In *Subarctic*, edited by June Helm, 442–50. Vol. 6 of *Handbook of North American Indians*, William C. Sturtevant, general editor. Washington, DC: Smithsonian Institution, 1981.

Hoy, T.H. "Ringing the Changes in the Middle Liard Valley." ARCH 3000: Predicting the Past. N.p.: n.p., n.d.

Hume, Mark. *The Run of the River – Portraits of Eleven British Columbia Rivers.* Vancouver: New Star Books, 1992.

Jenness, Diamond. *The Sekani Indians of British Columbia.* Ottawa: Department of Mines & Natural Resources, Bulletin No. 84, Anthropological Series No. 20, 1937.

Johnson, Derek et al. with Trevor Goward & Dale Vitt. *Plants of the Western Boreal Forest & Aspen Parkland.* Edmonton: Lone Pine Publishing, 1995.

Karamanski, Theodore J. *Fur Trade and Exploration: Opening the Far Northwest 1821–1852.* Norman: University of Oklahoma Press, 1983.

Krause, Aurel. *The Tlingit Indians: Results of a Trip to the Northwest Coast of America and the Bering Strait.* Seattle: University of Washington Press, 1956. First published as *Die Tlinkit Indianer: Ergebnisse einer Reise nach der Nordwestküste von Amerika und der Beringstraße,* Jena: Hermann Costenoble, 1885.

de Laguna, Frederica. "Tlingit." In *Northwest Coast*, edited by W. Suttles, 203–228. Vol. 7 of *Handbook of North American Indians*, William C. Sturtevant, general editor. Washington, DC: Smithsonian Institution, 1981.

———. *Under Mount Saint Elias: The History and Culture of the Yakutat Tlingit.* Vol. 7, no. 1 of Smithsonian Contributions to Anthropology. Washington, DC: Smithsonian Institution Press, 1972 [29-MB PDF downloadable from www.sil.si.edu/eresources/silpurl.cfm?purl=697361.1].

Lawrence, Guy. *Forty Years on the Yukon Telegraph.* Vancouver: Mitchell Press, 1965.

LeBlanc, Suzanne. *Cassiar: A Jewel in the Wilderness.* Prince George, BC: Caitlin Press, 2003.

Leaming, Stan, with Rick Hudson. *Jade Fever: Hunting the Stone of Heaven.* Surrey, BC: Heritage House, 2005.

Lyman, Russ, Joe Ordóñez and Mike Speaks. *The Complete Guide to the Tatshenshini River, Including the Upper Alsek River.* Haines, Alaska: Cloudburst Productions, 2004.

MacKinnon, Andrew, Jim Pojar and Ray Coupé, eds. *Plants of Northern British Columbia.* 2nd ed. Vancouver: Lone Pine Publishing, 1999.

MacLachlan, Bruce B. "Tahltan." In *Subarctic*, edited by June Helm, 458–68. Vol. 6 of *Handbook of North American Native Indians*, William C. Sturtevant, general editor. Washington, DC: Smithsonian Institution, 1981.

MacRae, Heather. *Northern Rockies Hiking and Motorized Trail Guide: From Mild to Wild.* Fort Nelson: Tourism Northern Rockies, n.d.

Madsen, Ken. *Tatshenshini Wilderness Quest and Other River Adventures* [Vancouver]: Western Canada Wilderness Committee, 1991.

———. *Wild Rivers, Wild Lands.* Whitehorse: Lost Moose Publishing, 1996.

Madsen, Ken, and Peter Mather. *Paddling in the Yukon: A Guide to Rivers, Lakes and the Arctic Ocean.* Whitehorse: Primrose Publishing, 2004.

Mahaffey, Patrick. "Spatsizi and Stikine Rivers." In *Paddle Quest: Canada's Best Canoe Routes,* edited by Alister Thomas. Erin, Ont.: Boston Mills Press, 2000.

McClellan, Catharine. "Inland Tlingit." In *Subarctic,* edited by June Helm, 469–80. Vol. 6 of *Handbook of North American Indians,* William C. Sturtevant, general editor. Washington, DC: Smithsonian Institution, 1981.

McClellan, Catharine, with Lucie Birckel et al. *Part of the Land, Part of the Water: A History of the Yukon Indians.* Vancouver: Douglas & McIntyre, 1987.

McIlwraith, Thomas, ed. "'*Kuji K'at Dahdahwhesdetch' (Now I Told All of You): Stories Told at Iskut, British Columbia, by Iskut Tahltan Elders.*" Self-published booklet funded by the Endangered Languages Fund, 2003.

McKay, Bernard. *Wild Trails and Wild Tales.* Surrey, BC: Hancock House, 1996.

McKay, Don. *The Muskwa Assemblage.* Kentville, NS: Gaspereau Press, 2008.

Miller, Bill. *Wires in the Wilderness: The Story of the Yukon Telegraph.* Surrey, BC: Heritage House, 2004.

Mitchan, Allison. *Taku – The Heart of North America's Last Great Wilderness.* Falmouth, NS: Lancelot Press, 1993.

Muir, John. *Stickeen, the Story of a Dog.* Berkeley, Calif.: Heyday Books, 1990.

———. *Travels in Alaska.* New York: Modern Library, 2002, first published Boston: Houghton Mifflin Co., 1915.

Murray, E.H. *The Adventures of Yukon Joe.* Vernon, BC: E.H. Murray, 2000.

Nash, G. Stewart. *The Last Three Hundred Miles.* Prince George, BC: Caitlin Press, 2001.

North, Dick. *The Mad Trapper of Rat River: A True Story of Canada's Biggest Manhunt.* Guilford, Conn.: Lyons Press, 2003.

Northwest Brigade Paddling Club. *Canoeing and Kayaking BC's Interior: A Guidebook.* 6th ed. Prince George, BC: Northwest Brigade Paddling Club, 2002.

Olson, Wallace. *The Tlingit: An Introduction to Their Culture and History.* Auke Bay, Alaska: Heritage Research, 2004.

Parfitt, Ben. "Crossroads on the Taku Trail." *Beautiful British Columbia* 43, no. 4 (Winter 2001), 12–19.

Patterson, R.M. *Dangerous River: Adventure on the Nahanni.* New York: W. Sloane Assoc., 1954. Reprinted Erin, Ont.: Boston Mills Press, 1999.

———. *Far Pastures.* 3rd ed. Victoria: Horsdal & Schubart Publishers, 1993. First published 1963 by Gray's Publishing, Sidney, BC.

———. *Finlay's River.* Victoria: Horsdal & Schubart Publishers, 1994. First published 1968 by Macmillan Canada, Toronto, and William Morrow, New York.

———. *Those Earlier Hills: Reminiscences 1928–1961.* Victoria, BC: TouchWood Editions, 2008.

———. *Trail to the Interior.* 3rd ed. Victoria: Horsdal & Schubart Publishers, 1993. First published 1966 by Macmillan Canada, Toronto.

———. "With Butler on the Omineca." *The Beaver* 32, no. 3 (December 1952): 32–36.

Pielou, E.C. *After the Ice Age – The Return of Life to Glaciated North America.* Chicago: University of Chicago Press, 1991.

Pike, Warburton. *The Barren Ground of Northern Canada.* New York: Macmillan, 1892. (Readable at Onlinebooks, accessed 20100112 at http://is.gd/6924S)

———. *Through the Subarctic Forest.* New York: Arno Press, 1967.

Pojar, Jim, and Andrew MacKinnon, eds. *Plants of Coastal British Columbia.* Vancouver: Lone Pine Publishing, 1994.

Pollon, Earl K., and Shirlee Smith Matheson. *This Was Our Valley: The True Story of the W.A.C. Bennett Dam.* Calgary: Detselig, 1989.

PTC Phototype Composing Ltd. *British Columbia Recreational Atlas.* 4th ed. Surrey, BC: Heritage House, 1997.

Pynn, Larry. *The Forgotten Trail: One Man's Adventure on the Canadian Route to the Klondike.* Toronto: Doubleday Canada, 1996.

———. "Hardy Boys." *BCBusiness* 31, no. 7 (July 2003), 161–69.

———. "Lost on the High Trail: A Grand Adventure Turns Perilous in the Uncharted Northern Rockies Wilderness." *Beautiful British Columbia* 44, no. 2 (Summer 2002), 6–14.

———. "The Last Mountain People: In the harsh and majestic northern Rockies, six members of the Kaska Dena hold their ground against urban living and the threat of cultural extinction." *Beautiful British Columbia* 44, no. 1 (Spring 2002), 15–20

———. "Wrangling the Gataga." *Beautiful British Columbia* 43, no. 3 (Fall 2001), 6.

Raffan, James, ed. *Rendezvous with the Wild: The Boreal Forest.* Erin, Ont.; Boston Mills Press, 2004.

Ramsey, Bruce. *Ghost Towns of British Columbia.* Vancouver: Mitchell Press, 1963.

Remley, David. *Crooked Road: The Story of the Alaska Highway.* New York: McGraw Hill, 1976.

Ridington, Robin. "Beaver." In *Subarctic*, edited by June Helm, 350–60. Vol. 6 of *Handbook of North American Indians*, William C. Sturtevant, general editor. Washington, DC: Smithsonian Institution, 1981.

Ritter, Harry. *Alaska's History: The People, Land, and Events of the North Country.* Anchorage: Alaska Northwest Books, 1993.

Robbins, Chandler S., Bertel Bruun and Hebert S. Zim. *Birds of North America.* Rev. ed New York: Golden Press, 1983.

Sawchuk, Wayne. *Muskwa–Kechika: The Wild Heart of Canada's Northern Rockies.* Chetwynd, BC: Northern Images, 2004

Shaw, Anthony "The Magic of an Old Friend." *Kanawa,* Summer 2002, 46–51.

———. "Doing the Turnagain: Samuel Black's Enigma." *Kanawa,* Winter 2000, 4–11.

Sherwood, Jay. *Surveying Northern British Columbia: A Photojournal of Frank Swannell.* Prince George, BC: Caitlin Press, 2004.

Sibley, David Allen. *The Sibley Field Guide to Birds of Western North America.* New York: Alfred A. Knopf, 2003.

Slobodin, Richard "Subarctic Métis." In *Subarctic*, edited by June Helm, 361–71. Vol. 6 of *Handbook of North American Indians*, William C. Sturtevant, general editor. Washington, DC: Smithsonian Institution, 1981.

Steele, Peter. *Atlin's Gold.* Prince George, BC: Caitlin Press, 1995.

Thomas, Alister, ed. *Paddle Quest: Canada's Best Canoe Routes.* Erin, Ont.: Boston Mills Press, 2000.

Thompson, Judy. *Recording Their Story: James Teit and the Tahltan.* Seattle: University of Washington Press, 2007.

Thornton, Thomas F. *Being and Place among the Tlingit.* Seattle: University of Washington Press, 2007.

Turton, M.C. *Cassiar.* Toronto: Macmillan, 1934.

Twigg, Alan. *Thompson's Highway: British Columbia's Fur Trade, 1800–1850.* Vancouver: Ronsdale Press, 2006.

von Finster, A. Possible effects of climate change on the physical characteristics of fish habitats in the Yukon River basin in Canada. Water Resources Papers unpublished report. Ottawa: Environment Canada, 1999.

Voss, Jennifer. *Stikine River: A Guide to Paddling the Great River.* Calgary: Rocky Mountain Books, 1998.

Wainwright, Jack. *Canoe Trips British Columbia*. Abbotsford, BC: Wainbay Enterprises, 1994.

Walker, T.A. *Spatsizi*. Surrey, BC.: Antonson Publishing, 1976. Reprinted Smithers, BC: Interior Stationery, 1990.

Wenger, Ferdi. *Wild Liard Waters: Canoeing Canada's Historic Liard River*. Prince George, BC: Caitlin Press, 1998.

Wilson, Clifford. *Campbell of the Yukon*. Toronto: Macmillan, 1970.

Wright, Richard, and Rochelle Wright. *Canoe Routes British Columbia*. Vancouver: Douglas & McIntyre, 1980.

Young, Gerri. *The Fort Nelson Story: The Story of How a Town Grew out of the Wilderness*. Fort Nelson, BC: Self-publication, 1980.

Zuehlke, Mark. *The BC Fact Book*. Vancouver: Whitecap Books, 1995.

Web Resources:

Aboriginal Canada Portal (search for First Nations online):
www.aboriginalcanada.gc.ca/acp/site.nsf/en/index.html

Alaska Highway Information: www.bellsalaska.com/myalaska/alaska_highway.html

Alaska Marine Highway System: http://dot.alaska.gov/amhs/index.html

Alaska Tide Tables: www.tidesandcurrents.noaa.gov/tides06/tpred2.html#AK

Arctic Basin Archived Hydrometric Data: www.r-arcticnet.sr.unh.edu

BC Ferries: www.bcferries.ca

BC Aboriginal Education List of First Nations Names:
www.bced.gov.bc.ca/abed/map.htm

BC Geographical Names Informational System: http://archive.ilmb.gov.bc.ca/bcnames

BC Government Strategic Land & Resource Management Plans:
http://archive.ilmb.gov.bc.ca/slrp/lrmp/index.html

BC Heritage Rivers Program:
www.env.gov.bc.ca/bcparks/heritage_rivers_program/home.html

BC Parks Campfire Information:
www.env.gov.bc.ca/bcparks/explore/whatyou.html#campfires

BC Parks General Wildlife, Marine and Outdoor Ethics Information:
ww.env.gov.bc.ca/bcparks/explore/gen_info/wild_gen.html

BC Parks Home Page: www.env.gov.bc.ca/bcparks

BC Parks Index (Find a Park) Page: www.env.gov.bc.ca/bcparks/explore/parks/index.html

BC Population Statistics: www.bcstats.gov.bc.ca/data/pop/popstart.asp

BC Ministry of Environment River Forecast & Snow Surveys: www.env.gov.bc.ca/rfc

Bedaux Expedition Information: http://explorenorth.com/library/bios/bl-bedaux.htm

Big Foot Field Researchers Organization: www.bfro.net

British Columbian Treaties in Historical Perspective:
www.ainc-inac.gc.ca/al/hts/tgu/pubs/C-B/treC-B-eng.asp

Canadian Heritage River System: www.chrs.ca

Canadian Parks & Wilderness Society: www.cpaws.org

Canadian Parks & Wilderness Society, BC Chapter: www.cpawsbc.org

Canoeing the Spatsizi River:
www.env.gov.bc.ca/bcparks/explore/parkpgs/spatsizi/canoeing.html

Canoeing the Upper Stikine River (scroll down from Spatsizi section):
www.env.gov.bc.ca/bcparks/explore/parkpgs/spatsizi/canoeing.html

Cassiar Highway Information: www.bellsalaska.com/myalaska/cassiar_highway.html

Central Council of the Tlingit and Haida Indian Tribes of Alaska: www.ccthita.org

Choquette Hot Springs Provincial Park:
    www.env.gov.bc.ca/bcparks/explore/parkpgs/choquette_hs
Dease Lake and Stikine Region Community website: www.stikine.net
Dehcho First Nation Home Page: www.dehchofirstnations.com/home.htm
Denetiah Provincial Park: www.env.gov.bc.ca/bcparks/explore/parkpgs/denetiah
Dune Za Keyih Provincial Park and Protected Area:
    www.env.gov.bc.ca/bcparks/explore/parkpgs/dune_za
Dune Za Keyih Provincial Park and Protected Area Background Information:
    www.spacesfornature.org/greatspaces/duneza.html
Ecojustice: www.ecojustice.ca
Ecoregions of British Columbia: www.env.gov.bc.ca/ecology/ecoregions/province.html
Environment Canada Real Time Hydrometric Data:
    http://scitech.pyr.ec.gc.ca/waterweb/formnav.asp?lang=0
Environment Canada's Ecological Framework:
    http://atlas.nrcan.gc.ca/site/english/maps/environment/ecology/framework/1
First Nations Land Rights and Environmentalism in BC:
    www.firstnations.de/index.html
Fort Liard Community Website: www.fortliard.com
Fort Nelson First Nation: www.fnnation.org
Fort Nelson Trail: www.calverley.ca/Part03-Transportation/3-030.html
Friends of the Stikine: www.panorama-map.com/STIKINE/stikine.html
Glacier Bay National Park & Preserve Nature and Science webpages:
    www.nps.gov/glba/naturescience/index.htm
Glacier Surges: www.taiga.net/yourYukon/col130.html
Great Glacier Provincial Park: www.env.gov.bc.ca/bcparks/explore/parkpgs/great_gl
Hiking Trails on the Spatsizi Plateau:
    www.env.gov.bc.ca/bcparks/explore/parkpgs/spatsizi/hiking.html
History and First Nations of Northeastern BC: www.calverley.ca/table2004.html
History of Glacier Bay National Park & Preserve:
    www.nps.gov/glba/historyculture/index.htm
History of Glave and Dalton Expedition and Dalton Trail:
    www.north-land.com/ypa/JimmyKane.html
History of Stikine River Provincial Park:
    www.spacesfornature.org/greatspaces/stikine.html#history
History of the Acho Dene Koe: www.dehchofirstnations.com/members/fort_liard.htm
History of the Champagne and Aishihik First Nations (CAFN):
    www.cafn.ca/history.html
History of the Métis Nation: www.telusplanet.net/public/dgarneau/Métis.htm
History of Tongass National Forest, Alaska:
    www.fs.fed.us/r10/tongass/forest_facts/resources/heritage/heritage.shtml
History of Treaty Making in BC:
    www.ainc-inac.gc.ca/al/hts/tgu/pubs/C-B/treC-B-eng.asp
Iskut–Stikine Rivers Region Conservation Issues:
    http://riverswithoutborders.org/about-the-region/iskut-stikine
Kaska Dena Council: www.kaskadenacouncil.com
Kispiox Community History and Activities:
    www.kispioxadventures.com/english/pp/main.htm
Klabona Keeper's Society Home Page: http://sacredheadwaters.com/home
Kledo Creek Provincial Park: www.env.gov.bc.ca/bcparks/explore/parkpgs/kledo_crk
Laurel Archer's website: www.laurelarcher.com

Liard River Corridor Provincial Park and Protected Area:
www.env.gov.bc.ca/bcparks/explore/parkpgs/liard_rv_corr
Map of First Nations Territories in BC: www.bced.gov.bc.ca/abed/map.htm
Map of Tlingit Territories:
www.ankn.uaf.edu/ANCR/Southeast/TlingitMap/TlingitMap.pdf
Métis History of the Dehcho Region:
www.dehchofirstnations.com/members/fort_simpson_Métis.htm
Mining Watch: www.miningwatch.ca
Muskwa–Kechika Management Area official site: www.Muskwa–Kechika.com
Muskwa–Kechika Management Area background information:
www.spacesfornature.org/greatspaces/muskwa.html and
www.roundriver.org (click on Where We Work, then Canada/Muskwa Kechika/
Reports & Publications)
Northern Rocky Mountains Provincial Park:
www.env.gov.bc.ca/bcparks/explore/parkpgs/n_rocky
NTS Digital Maps Source: www.geogratis.ca/geogratis/en/download/scanned.html
NTS Index for BC: www.maptown.com/canadiantopographical/bcntsindex.html
Omineca Gold Rush, Trading Posts and River and Trail Travel:
www.settlerseffects.ca/pls/cats_web/WEB_EXHIBITIONS.show_exhibition?
WEID=51&LANG=EN
Outdoor Recreation Council of BC: www.orcbc.ca
Pembina Institute's site on Energy Issues Facing Northwestern BC:
www.afterthegoldrush.ca
Recreational Canoeing Association of BC: www.bccanoe.com/index.cfm
Rivers without Borders Homepage: www.riverswithoutborders.org
Round River Conservation Studies: www.roundriver.org
Sacred Headwaters Conservation Campaign: www.sacredheadwaters.com
Scatter River Old Growth Provincial Park:
www.env.gov.bc.ca/bcparks/explore/parkpgs/scatter
Sea Kayak Guides Alliance of BC Low Impact Guidelines:
www.skgabc.com/low-impact.php
Sekani First Nations Links and Culture: www.fourdir.com/sekani.htm
Skeena Watershed Conservation Coalition: www.skeenawatershed.com
Spaces for Nature: www.spacesfornature.org
Spatsizi Headwaters Provincial Park:
www.env.gov.bc.ca/bcparks/explore/parkpgs/spatsizi_head
Spatsizi River Background Information:
www.spacesfornature.org/greatspaces/spatsizi.html
Stikine River Background Information:
www.spacesfornature.org/greatspaces/stikine.html
Tahltan Bear Dogs: www.everythinghusky.com/features/beardog.html
Tahltan History: http://www.stikine.net/Tahltan/tahltan.html
Tahltan and Mining Concerns: www.firstnations.de/mining.htm?05-3-tahltan.htm
Tatshenshini–Alsek Provincial Park Information:
www.env.gov.bc.ca/bcparks/explore/parkpgs/tatshens/parkinfo.html
Tatshenshini/Alsek Rivers Campsite and Bear Activity Report:
www.env.gov.bc.ca/bcparks/explore/parkpgs/tatshens/tat_report.pdf
Tatshenshini/Alsek Rivers Campsite Maps (scroll down page):
www.env.gov.bc.ca/bcparks/explore/parkpgs/tatshens
Telegraph Trail History: www.telegraphtrail.org

Tlingit Culture: www.everyculture.com/multi/Sr-Z/Tlingit.html
Toad River Hot Springs Provincial Park:
    www.env.gov.bc.ca/bcparks/explore/parkpgs/toad_rv
Tongass National Forest Cabins: www.fs.fed.us/r10/tongass/cabins/cabin_info.shtml
Tongass National Forest Facts on Flora and Fauna:
    www.fs.fed.us/r10/tongass/forest_facts/resources/fauna_flora/life.shtml
Tongass National Forest Facts on Glaciers and Icefields:
    www.fs.fed.us/r10/tongass/forest_facts/resources/geology/icefields.htm
Treaty 8: www.ainc-inac.gc.ca/al/hts/tgu/tr8-eng.asp
Treaty 11: www.ainc-inac.gc.ca/al/hts/tgu/tr11-eng.asp
UBC Library Links to First Nations Resources:
    www.library.ubc.ca/xwi7xwa/nations.htm
Union of BC Indian Chiefs Historical Timeline:
    www.ubcic.bc.ca/Resources/timeline.htm
USGS Hydrometric Data: http://waterdata.usgs.gov/nwis
Walkin Jim's website: www.walkinjim.com
Wayne Sawchuk's Muskwa–Kechika website: www.muskwakechika.com
Wilderness Committee of Canada: www.wildernesscommittee.org
Yellowstone to Yukon Conservation: www.y2y.net
Yukon's 14 First Nations: www.yfnta.org
Yukon Prospectors' Association (articles on northern BC surveyors and prospectors):
    www.north-land.com/ypa

APPENDIX A

SCALE OF RAPID CLASSIFICATION

(Based on the International River Classification Scale endorsed by the RCABC and Paddle Canada)

Class 1: Fast-moving water with riffles and small regular-shaped waves. Channels are wide and easy to see. Any of the few obstructions are obvious and easily missed by novice moving-water paddlers. Scouting is not necessary and all paddlers will read and run. Risk to swimmers is slight and self-rescue is easy.

Class 2: Straightforward rapids with wide, clear lines which are evident without scouting. Channels may have obstructions such as rocks, boulders, small ledges, wood hazards or artificial features like bridge pilings. Medium-sized waves may be present. All of these features are easily avoided by paddlers with Intermediate moving-water skills, and they will read and run this level of rapids. Novice paddlers will likely scout. The risk to swimmers is low, and they are seldom injured. Group assistance, while helpful, is not usually required.

Class 3: Rapids with moderate-sized, regular- and/or irregular-shaped waves, which may be difficult to avoid and could swamp an open canoe. Large waves and strong hydraulics, including holes, may be present in the channels, as well as obstructions such as rocks, boulders and ledges. Complex and/or precise manoeuvres and a high level of boat control are required. Lines may have narrow passages. Wood or other dangerous hazards may be present, but can be safely avoided by advanced and exceptional moving-water paddlers. Scouting from shore is advisable for all skill levels, but is required for intermediate moving-water paddlers. Novice paddlers will only paddle these rapids in tandem with very skilled moving-water paddlers. Injuries while swimming are rare but possible. Self-rescue is not easy, and group assistance may be required to avoid long swims. Rescuers must be experienced in order to help.

Class 4: Intense, powerful but relatively predictable rapids with complex lines requiring precise manoeuvring in tight passages. Features include large and irregular waves, which will swamp an open canoe; turbulent water with boiling eddies with major eddy lines or fences; steep ledges; and blind corners. Rapids may require must-make moves to avoid dangerous hazards. Scouting is necessary for all paddlers. Risk to swimmers is moderate to high, and water conditions may make self-rescue difficult. Group assistance for rescue is often essential and requires practised skills. This class is only for advanced and exceptional canoeists paddling tandem whitewater canoes outfitted with thigh straps and flotation/spray decks or paddling solo boats outfitted for heavy whitewater. A strong roll is highly recommended. These are not the kind of rapids canoeists can afford to run on a remote river trip such as the ones described in this book.

Class 5: Rapids with irregular, unpredictable and violent features that may be extremely long and obstructed. Drops may contain large, unavoidable waves and holes or steep, congested chutes with complex, demanding lines. What eddies exist may be small. Dangerous hazards are not easily avoidable, even for the most-skilled paddlers. Swims are dangerous; life and limb are at risk. Rescues of any kind are difficult, even for exceptional paddlers. Scouting is mandatory, but may be difficult. No canoeist is going to run these kinds of rapids on the trips outlined in this guidebook.

Class 6: These extreme runs have almost never been attempted or are first descents of rapids that exemplify the extremes of difficulty, unpredictability and danger. The consequences of error are very severe. Rescue is likely not possible. Open canoes are not the kind of craft you want to be paddling this kind of water in. Enough said.

Note: All rapid classifications can be bumped up to indicate that a particular rapid is slightly more difficult than the class it belongs to, but not so difficult that it should be in the class above. For example, a tough Class 2 rapid listed in the guidebook will be called a Class 2+. Conversely, a minus sign indicates the rapid is not quite as difficult as the class above it, but shares more characteristics with it than with the one below. Thus, an easy Class 2 would be called a Class 2-. Some rapid classification systems make the distinction between technical and non-technical rapids. I have chosen to describe each significant rapid on the routes in the Trip Notes in such a way that the paddler will know whether it is technical or not, rather than use a more elaborate system of classification than I already do.

APPENDIX B

LOW-IMPACT CAMPING AND TRAVEL: PRACTICES AND ETHICS

Low-impact or minimal-impact camping and travel practices and ethics include the following general principles that apply to trips in any ecosystem. These principles are based on the Recreational Canoe Association of BC's Environmental Practices, the Sea Kayak Guides Alliance of BC's Low Impact Best Practices, and the Leave-No-Trace guidelines in Rick Curtis's *The Backpacker's Field Manual.* These sources are listed in the References section.

BC Parks' Provincial Parks Camping Ethics and Regulations can be found on their website, at www.elp.gov.bc.ca/bcparks/explore/whatyou.html. The site also gives specifics on camping and travelling in the parks your chosen river trip runs through, particularly with regard to campsites, campfires and dogs. Also available are links to general wildlife-viewing principles in boreal and marine environments, and hunting and fishing regulations. To check on fire danger ratings and open-fire bans in the area you are paddling in, go to bcwildfire.ca.

1. Plan ahead and be prepared.
Know what you need and bring what you need with you so your impact is as slight as possible. Do not rely on the environment to supply you. Do not use natural materials for shelters except in emergencies.

2. Research any camping regulations or unusual conditions.
Know and abide by the specific camping regulations of the area. Ecological reserves and provincial parks have use restrictions. Check with the BC Parks office in the region about local fire (and water) conditions. There may be a fire ban. You can check online for all areas of the province (not just the parks) on the BC Ministry of Forests & Range's Wildfire Management Branch website, http://bcwildfire.ca.

3. Use fire responsibly.
Campfires can start forest fires, and even small campfires scar the land. Carefully evaluate both the need for a fire and your ability to create one that leaves no impact. Use an "environmental" stove for campfire cooking. Using a gas stove may be mandatory in some areas and when areas are under fire ban, but it also a good idea in fragile ecosystems.

If you do have a fire in an established campfire ring, let it burn to ash and make sure it is completely out by dousing it with water. Clean out any bits of unburned garbage from the ash and pack them out. If you are at a site without a fire pit or cooking ring, make sure you put your fire on a surface that will not be scarred and where you can no-trace the fire. Do not put rocks around your fire pit; they will be scarred and picking them up will disturb the environment. The best-case scenario is to dig a fire pit in gravel or sand. No-trace the campfire by letting all wood burn to ash, then grind the ash to dust, dig it out and spread it evenly around your camping area. Alternatively, you can dump the finely ground ash in fast-moving water.

4. Concentrate your impact in high-use areas or areas not easily impacted.
You will have the least impact on the environment if you continue to use a highly impacted campsite or trail, or camp on a gravel bar or on a bedrock outcrop where there is little vegetation to impact.

5. Spread your use and impact in "pristine" areas.
You should avoid going into areas that are rarely travelled unless you are committed to low-impact practices. If the area is pristine, showing little or no impact, then spread out your use of the area, so that you don't create new bald-spot campsites, worn trails and so on that would encourage other people to also use the site and increase the impact to damaging levels. If you have to create a portage trail, study the implications on the environment before doing so. When hiking off trail in the subalpine or alpine where walking on vegetation is unavoidable, walk carefully and tread lightly.

6. Avoid places where impact is just beginning.
If a site is showing the beginning signs of impact, leave it alone and let it recover to its natural state.

7. Limit group size.
A large group of people in one camping spot can have a significant impact. Keep your group as small as possible. If you are a large group, pick high-use campsites that are already impacted, and do not choose a route infrequently travelled.

8. Pack it in, pack it out.
Whatever you bring in with you, you need to bring out. This means garbage, tampons etc. that cannot be burned with a small, hot fire that leaves little impact on a campsite. If you can't have a fire, take all garbage out with you. Pick up any litter you find and dispose of it properly. Do not sink cans or bottles in the water. Clean them and take them back home with you to recycle.

9. Properly dispose of what you can't pack out.
If you can't pack it out (waste water from washing or cooking, human waste – except in the case of the Tatshenshini/Alsek route, where you will pack your poop out), dispose

of it properly for the ecosystem you are in. In the case of northern BC, the rivers are cold and they do not have a lot of bacteria to break down soap or food waste, so if you are going to wash dishes or yourself, do it away from the water and use biodegradable soap and shampoo. Cooking water can be dumped in a sump hole. Burn left over food in a small hot fire. If you plan carefully, you should have little wasted food. Use your leftovers for lunches or snacks the next day.

Fish guts and carcasses can go into the river where the water is moving. They will get eaten by fish. Human waste should be buried carefully in cat holes in the moss or inorganic ground cover and far away from all sources of water. If you use toilet paper, burn it all in your campfire after cooking. Otherwise, use single-ply, unbleached toilet paper and bury it completely in organic matter away from the camping area and away from all water sources. If there are outhouses, use them.

10. Know your ecosystem and season.
Learn all you can about the northern BC ecosystem(s) and the season you'll be travelling in to determine how best to deal with waste.

11. Don't change the environment.
Don't alter the environment to suit youself. Don't cut trenches around tents or tarps or build fire rings, shelters or tables. Avoid damaging live trees and plants, especially the moss ground cover often found in the North; it took years and years to grow there. Don't hammer nails in trees for hangers, cut wood from live trees or damage branches when tying up tarps. Finally, leaving rock cairns by the portage trail may seem like a grand and even helpful idea, but maybe the person behind you wants to find their own way just as you did.

12. Leave what you find.
It is illegal in BC to disturb or remove prehistoric or historic artifacts. In terms of caribou antlers and other natural objects, why not leave them there for the next person to be able to experience the excitement of finding them, and the next person and the next.

13. Respect wildlife.
Do not feed wildlife and do not approach or disturb them in other ways. Research safety issues and how to avoid impacting the species you may encounter.

14. Respect others.
Be respectful of local inhabitants and other people you meet on your travels. Remember you are likely in someone's backyard. Conserve your use of the natural resources that they may rely on. Respect that the people you meet may be looking for quiet and solitude. Keep noise to a minimum if you have to camp near another party.

PLACE INDEX